NATIONAL SERVICE WIFE

By

Helen Wingate

RB
Rossendale Books

Published by Lulu Enterprises Inc.

3101 Hillsborough Street

Suite 210

Raleigh, NC 27607-5436

United States of America

Published in paperback 2013

Category: Life Story & Memoirs

Copyright Helen Wingate © 2013

ISBN : 978-1-291-50772-0

All rights reserved, Copyright under Berne Copyright Convention and Pan American Convention. No part of this book may be reproduced, stored in a retrieval system, or transmitted in any form or by any means, electronic, mechanical, photocopying, recording or otherwise, without prior permission of the author. The author's moral rights have been asserted.

Contents

DEDICATION 6
INTRODUCTION 7
FOREWORD 9
Chapter 1   Tradition! 23
Chapter 2   Reality 32
Chapter 3   Routines 44
Chapter 4   Baby Talk 54
Chapter 5   On The Home Straight 60
Chapter 6   Into Summer 79
Chapter 7   Letter to the Ministry 84
Chapter 8   Result 88
Chapter 9   Hard Times 101
Chapter 10 Recovery 113
Chapter 11 Disaster And After 117
Chapter 12 Zoo! 130
Chapter 13 Packing 136
Chapter 14 Home! 142
Appendix I   -   RAF Yatesbury 145
Appendix II -   The History of RAF Shawbury 148

DEDICATION

To my husband *Ever Present*

To my family *Present and Absent*

INTRODUCTION

When couples marry, and even these days when they decide to be together as a couple, they assume that they are with each other for good, with no separations. Apart from military personnel in wartime, couples live together.

Imagine an expectation of married life together, but instead of going forth with all the aims, and future plans in your jobs and promotions and finding your own home, being completely stymied by a Government saying you have to leave your job for two years and be transplanted, into a completely different regime, training for something you will never use. Salary completely stopped, and only given pocket money. The wife is pregnant, and being informed that on the birth of your child, you will receive no allowance, for the feeding, clothing and upkeep of the child, for the remainder of the two years, by the end of which the child will be 18 months old, eating food, wearing clothes.

Having to, albeit successfully, beg the Government for funds, otherwise there would be no income. Sounds incredible? Read on...

FOREWORD

The main theme of this book is the uprooting of Helen and Robert from their lives right at the beginning of their marriage, when all their friends and acquaintances were walking from their own weddings and honeymoons, straight into their new homes and starting the rest of their lives.

Realising then, and now, that they were not the only ones in this position, their complaint was, and still is, that their situation was almost unique in that married men were conscripted for two full years, and in their case the added dimension of pregnancy and birth loss. In the whole of the two years they did not meet any other couple in the same position.

They had known people who had completed their two years' National Service as single men, even as married men, but not with the above mentioned extra complications, and as mentioned elsewhere in the book, it was only a matter of time before the service of married men was reduced to a period of eighteen months, then soon after, cancelled completely.

Their story stems from Robert, having, as an unattached man, decided to finish his degree studies while working as Laboratory Assistant in the Research Station of the DCL. This took him up to the age of 21, when he and Helen met, fell in love and decided to get married, and hopefully live happily ever after.

To endeavour to keep their lives as near that of others, they delighted in making their wedding in the same traditional pattern, hoping that everything else would fall into place, whereas they might otherwise have had a few different aspects to their big day, trying to be a a little out of the ordinary

As they walked out of the church, then the hotel, then enjoyed their week's honeymoon, they still naively believed that all else could remain the same. They first decided to live together instead of hundreds of miles apart, during the first year when Robert was about to start training at a camp called Yatesbury, near Calne, Wiltshire. Helen's mother had recollected that during the war there was a 'Living Out' system whereby forces personnel could live out with their families while they were still based in UK.

The realisation that Robert was going to be serving for two years, the first on an RAF Radar Training Course, and the second using these skills. They both decided that this was because the Government did not know what to do with graduates, so placed them on these expensive Courses. The cost was £1,000 for each man, there being 20 on this particular Course, so a total of £20,000 for this one year, which the couple reasoned that a regular serviceman could easily have been placed on, thus saving time and money.

At the same time as this large amount was being spent, Helen, now pregnant, had been given as a Marriage allowance, a very small amount per week, but had been informed by the

Government that she should let them know as soon as the baby was born, so that they could adjust and increase the allowance.

To return to the beginning, for a moment, they discovered that they could find digs via the Billeting Office in Swindon, where they indeed found a place with a landlady, who gave them a bedroom, bathroom, use of the kitchen and living room for the substantial rent which the Government provided for 'Living Out' couples. These were mainly regulars as it happens.

The landlady was somewhat greedy, making sure she got the maximum rent from this vulnerable young couple, and went to the trouble of getting the Inspector to call and increase the rent as far as possible, even to the extent of declaring that they had the use of the front parlour solely for themselves, whereas of course this musty smelling cold room was totally unsuitable for the purpose. However, the couple were oblivious to her wiles, and let it all blow over their heads. It was between her and the Ministry.

Throughout their stay in Swindon, they never met people of their own age, and Helen especially spent her days, although enjoyably, never having the opportunity of conversing on her own level. This never bothered her, as she and Robert were living as they wished under the circumstances, living for each other, and just looking towards their future at home. She was preoccupied with the imminent birth of their baby, so other outside interests took a back seat in their thoughts and plans.

They settled happily, with Robert catching the camp bus each morning at the end of the road, returning at 5pm for their meal together, then off to the cinema or the pub or for walks. Some evenings they spent watching TV with the landlady and her husband, while Robert did his homework, and Helen knitted little baby items.

Helen spent her days walking into town, sometimes via the local Baths for a bath and shower. Visits to the doctor, or dentist, or ante natal clinics attended regularly by her, also culminated in the same lunch every day in the shape of a plate of tomato soup in Woolworth's Self Service Restaurant, then home for a nap, and ante natal exercises of her own. She was by now a natural birth fan, and full of enthusiasm obtained from a book written by a so called expert, but later learned painfully, that these were not as useful as promised in the book.

The months passed happily, and they even managed to fit in a New Year's holiday to Scotland, which they would not have attempted, had it not been for the landlady requiring their room for some visiting family members over the same holiday. On their return, an argument took place between Robert and the landlady over her insistence on them paying the rent for that period. Robert stood his ground and won, so gaining experience of life's trials to come.

The time came for Helen to travel back home to Scotland by Sleeper from London to Edinburgh, then by local train to her parents' home, where she spent the last waiting time, which turned out to be more than the expected month, running into a 6 weeks period.

The birth took place in the fashion of the 50s, with no husbands allowed, no pain killers, and no sympathy for a scared 21 year old left alone with her labour pains and told to keep quiet. The whole procedure, from beginning to end, lasted from 2am until 6.15pm, which could have been worse, but the young frightened woman was alone most of the time, and the experience was traumatic to say the least.

The wonderful letters sent by Robert are still kept, and his sheer joy is well recorded therein. In fact such words would not be necessary nowadays, as fathers are of course right there in the labour room sharing everything with the mother. He couldn't say enough to impart his joy, but with the excellent postal service, there was always a wonderfully expressed missive for Helen to relax with, adding to her contentment. Helen's Dad had sent the news to Robert via a telegram to him at the camp, using the local phone box, another service which is not available today.

Returning now to the large amounts that were being spent on training National Service graduates, Helen had been given as a Marriage allowance, a very small amount per week, but had been informed by the Government that she should let them know as soon as the baby was born, so that they could increase the allowance.

When Helen obediently informed them that the baby had been born on 24th February 1957, she received a curt reply to the effect that they had decided against paying her anything at all!

This is where Helen's skills had to take over, and she set out her appeal in a letter, explaining that she had no other income than what they chose to pay her, which at present as a marriage allowance, was meagre to say the least. Explaining that the child would be 18 months old by the time Robert's discharge came, growing into a toddler, with all that goes with that in the way of food and clothing. Her appeal to them to reconsider their decision, brought a response, in the form, not only of a substantial raise in the weekly allowance, but all the money back dated to24th March. This paid for her fare to Robert's next Posting in Shropshire, where he worked for a year on Radar Systems on Vampires, entailing at least once a week, cleaning two 12 inch aerials on the weekly flights, which took all of 30 minutes to carry out, the rest of the time doing almost nothing except play football in the camp teams.

In the space of the two years, their experiences were, among other things, the birth of their first child, the loss of their second and a couple of emergency operations, leading eventually to the birth a couple of years later, of their lovely little Caroline, who completed their family for the rest of all their lives. Constantly haunting them was and still is, the fact that the second child was probably a boy, so the son they never knew, and the brother the girls never had.

With the arrival of this their first child, all that awaited them now was the second Posting, where Helen could join Robert with the baby, and live it out till 11ᵗʰ September, then return home for good.

Travelling to Childs Ercall by rail was not easy, with a baby and a large pram, and even arranging that the local Police help them with the delivery of the pram by taxi after a very tiring journey by Helen in her state, still as yet unsubstantiated, of a second pregnancy.

Realising that she will in future be looking after two babies instead of one, this became a proposition to be fulfilled. However, it was not to be, and was realised in the loss of the baby at 20 weeks, after which an operation and a full recovery. Her time in hospital was again not to be relished, with the birth of a fully formed foetus, which now-a-days could have been saved, but the 1950s medical science had not yet developed.

Before fully recovering from giving birth only 6 months previously, another pregnancy must have been just too much for Helen's state of health, so she had yet another recovery to make, which included emotional upset, as we as physical trauma, and a sense of guilt hovering in the background.

Helen's mother came to look after them for a couple of weeks allowing Helen to gradually get fitter by gentle exercise and good food.

From now on it would be pure plodding onwards throughout the remainder of the winter, including another New Year holiday in Scotland, with the baby this time, so the three were going through their lives as well as could be expected, with the odd thrill now and again.

The couple decided to study together for an A level English Literature exam to help them break the monotony, and this kept them going for the months ahead, with no TV to distract them. The course was actually one available as an extra at the Camp, but they studied togerther at home, and Robert took their homework in to the class.

Several events had earlier taken place, on a National level, one of them being the Munich Air Disaster in February 1957, about a month after which Robert was in line to play against Bobby Charlton in his position in the team, RAF against Army, but Bobby did not play in that particular game, possibly due to having to recover from his traumatically tragic experience he'd just been through. As the ensuing summer progressed, visitors in the form of Robert's parents on holiday and later, Helen's mother again, all added to the quality of the time left in this place.

Apart from giving birth to their first child, then losing their second, then having emergency surgery, the remainder of the time was somewhat mundane and even boring. Helped by the A level English Literature Exam, they grew together, enjoying the richness of the language, and a love of Shakespeare for the rest of their lives, together with the joy of study generally.

The other tenants in The Hall, all officers and their wives and families, tried to persuade them to become regulars, with Robert easily in line as officer material, and with all the so called wonderful lives they could live, foreign cars, good accommodation, seeing the world etc., to which Helen and Robert merely poured scorn, saying the only thing they want is to return to their little room and kitchen in Scotland and live there forever. This must have puzzled the Officers, but it was a case of two different worlds and ways of living.

It is only now in 2013 that Helen has turned to the internet to find out about that lovely little village of Childs Ercall to find out exactly where they were living, and how interesting it could have been at the time, if they had had some choice in the matter.

Helen has taken the opportunity of looking back with interest at the places they lived and spent their time all those years ago, and has inserted descriptions of them now, including Yatesbury, Shawbury, Swindon, Childs Ercall, and Shrewsbury, all with interesting histories. It is a pity she was so intent on looking towards home in 1956/58, with no means of discovery or internet to stimulate her attention.

She would now agree that it is better late than never...

Their ambitions at last came to fruition, when on 11th September, 1958, they travelled home for the last time, to their little paradise, and to where they should have settled the day after their return from honeymoon two years earlier.

Jennifer Lawson

Poet & Colleague

Chapter 1

Tradition!

We emerged from the church, glowing in the supreme happiness which every young couple relishes, joined together forever, and followed by our loving families, bridesmaid, groomsman and friends, posing for the vital photographs which would be distributed among the older members of the family and proudly displayed on sideboards for years to come. I as the bride had, with the help of mother and aunty, easily arranged the whole occasion, with no trouble whatsoever.

Everything was to take place at the Station Hotel, and the cake was especially baked and iced by the local Co-op, just around the corner.

This was delivered by them to the Hotel, on the morning of the wedding, just as they had done on hundreds of similar occasions in the past. The taxis, the minister, church organist, music, were all easily ordered as had been by hundreds of brides and mothers in the generations of family weddings, and all doing the same, and wanting the same result - a perfect day from beginning to end.

My dress and that of the bridesmaid were carefully chosen and bought in one of the Glasgow bridal shops, and my sweet bridesmaid was overjoyed at the generous gift from me of her lovely pale pink gown which could easily be converted, or in fact was already an evening dress, for attending many a big dance or ball in the future.

Everything was undertaken so easily, being the same as everyone else's wedding arrangements that everyone from the hotel onwards knew the drill, having performed it all on countless occasions. The act of being the same brought a sense of security, hopefully a guarantee of our future, simple lifestyle. All expected and taken for granted in this world of dreams coming true, in the form of steady jobs, engagement rings, and life plans.

In the 1950s, these were the dreams of young men and women going through the rituals of tradition. The cost, although considerable, was as nothing compared to the elevated wedding costs in this 21st century, probably around £50 to £70, with no headaches, big deals, just pure satisfaction. The local well established family run Taxi

Company were able to undertake with no problems whatsoever, the running of the whole thing if necessary, and I just had to hand them the list of wedding guests and their addresses, to feel confident that each would be picked up at exactly at the time specified. On this occasion, because of the numbers, the Taxi firm suggested that the main body of guests be transported directly from the church to the hotel en masse, by coach, after the bride and groom and attendants were transported by the huge black shiny limousine style cars. All of this taking only a few minutes, the hotel being beside the railway station, a couple of streets away.

The wise old parish minister had pronounced us husband and wife together; we had signed the register with our parents and attendants, and had eagerly marched back up the aisle beaming triumphantly and onward to the reception.

After the usual speeches, witticisms by the Minister, and the best man who didn't forget to mention the beauty of the bride and the bridesmaid, the father of the bride and finally the bridegroom himself, came the party, dancing and singing, right up to the final departure, and beyond, of the happy pair.

Some guests had brought their sheet music with them and they were the ones expected to perform the same songs or pieces which they had always done, to the sheer delight, and even relief, of the bride, groom and the rest of the guests. The musician chosen to accompany them was the main performer though, with knowledge of every song, piece of music, old or modern, and on this occasion was booked by my brother, a musician himself, a trumpet player in the local brass band, as well as a leading light of the fantastic dance band which played in our Town Hall every Friday, Saturday and Wednesday nights. In fact that is where most of the couples meet up and then end up walking up the aisle so happily.

I had changed from the fabulous wedding dress into my going away suit, aided by my bridesmaid. We were off on a very special honeymoon. Flying! To the Isle of Man! Us! In an aeroplane! As we stood at the main entrance to the Station Hotel, waiting for an uncle to drive us to the Stirling Rail Station, where we would catch the next train to Glasgow, we were showered with confetti, well wishers everywhere, and given a good send off. I forgot to ask my Dad for my purse, which he had been keeping to be replaced in my handbag for the week in Isle of Man. Never mind, it would be in the same pocket awaiting my return in a week ready for use.

It seemed very easy to catch the right train, which connected us with the coach taking the passengers to the Renfrew Airport, which was then a much smaller version of what later became Glasgow Airport. The plane itself turned out, to me, to be just a bus with wings, and I could see no difference at all in the seating arrangements. I was so pleased I was able to step off when we landed at Ronaldsway Airport, having just managed to hold down the rather large meal I had consumed at the Wedding earlier in the day.

Arriving in the Santa Rosa Hotel on the front in Douglas, we wasted no time after consuming the supper the hotel had laid aside for us; then took a long explorative walk along the front. For the next week we were able to live in this glow of holding on to what every couple took for granted, the beginning of life together, and to live happily ever after. We sunbathed on the beach after a hearty breakfast, danced to the rhythms of Ivy Benson all female band in the afternoons, as well as the Joe Loss band in the evenings, 'Don't You Step On My Blue Suede Shoes', everything as enjoyable as promised by the Travel Agent weeks ahead of the date.

The evening and night panoramic views from our window, with the view of sea and sky had the added bonus of a full moon, shining in full glow with no clouds on the horizon, and the morning light filled the room waking us up at just the right time for breakfast, so the idyllic week passed all too quickly, with our hopes that it could last longer.

The other day Robert told me how much our Honeymoon cost. In 1956, the flight, hotel for 2, including 3 meals per day for a week cost him his savings of £12!

We were 21 years old and very, very happy. The short week came to an end only too quickly, and soon we were back on the bus with wings, with not much air conditioning as I remember, adding to my feelings of nausea and heat, and so glad to alight into the fresh August air.

Chapter 2

Reality

Only when we arrived back at my parents' home, did we allow ourselves to wake up to the fact that we were not to be like our many friends, who had gone through their wedding and honeymoon, to return back to their own little place, return to work, and begin to take up the realities of life.

No, ours was to be different, since Robert had some time ago, while still an unattached man, opted to continue his studies into his 21st year, rather than interrupt them at 17 and a half. Having now completed, he was committed to the task of National Service, which we both had to accept as part of life in the 1950s.

Due to start National Service, and as a young married couple, we were reluctant to be apart during these precious first two years of our life together. Having just started off on married life, both working, Robert in the Research Lab of the DCL, while still studying, and I as a Secretary in a local Legal Firm, we were living temporarily with my parents. His call-up seemed to happen all too suddenly and before we had a chance to get down to finding our own place, the dreaded date was upon was. We could see no reason for his having to go away, especially as there was no war! Why take married men?

Having lived through World War II, with all its absences of fathers and male relatives, we thought everyone had had enough. Perhaps we were just a young naive couple going through the natural process of life, with post war politics being of no interest to us whatsoever.

It was hardly credible that married men were recruited, and for two whole years, something which was later, - but too late for us, after Robert's discharge, - altered to unmarried men only and then reduced to 18 months' service. We realised that we were not the only ones in this position, but never, during the whole two years, did we ever meet a couple in exactly the same circumstances.

We had witnessed many a younger lad going off into the National Service at the early age of 17, mainly pre apprentices, returning home at 19, just ready to take up their jobs where they'd left off. They seemed to have had in the main, experiences which rendered them quite happy and all the more determined to restart their lives and to settle down. Robert had been working while taking yearly exams leading to his degree, so had taken the opportunity of the extra time allotted. By the time we were married, the extra time had of course, been used up.

Leading up to the final date of departure, we tried to find a loophole, some way of avoiding this drastic step in our lives, filling in forms in the vain hope that some forgotten medical condition would emerge, to render the whole Registration null and void. We could only come up with an ear condition, which Robert had sustained in a childhood swimming incident. All was of course to no avail, as unfortunately, unlike his two best friends, who had each in the past, suffered minor lung problems and were exempt, he passed at Grade A. Being recruited into the RAF, he was thus prevented from continuing his career and studies, instead being sent off for eight weeks' initial training or 'square bashing' as it was laughingly called, at RAF Padgate, which we of course considered a complete waste of time.

During this time, my mother had been telling us of all the young married couples she had met during the war who had been able to take advantage of the 'living out' scheme when the wife could join the husband while he was still based in Britain, and were helped with the rents by the appropriate Government Dept. This was probably no more expensive than the cost of the serviceman living in camp, with payments to the wife living elsewhere. On my mother's advice and with her encouragement, we applied for the same, and were happy to learn this living out method was still in operation. We were only too pleased to obtain the forms and complete them as soon as possible, so that we could take advantage of moving together as soon as the initial training period was over, and start the first year of the posting from the first day.

An important factor in all this was, of course, Robert's earnings being suddenly reduced to nil, and replaced by a meagre sum of something like eighteen shillings per week, which was his personal pocket money, with something extra in the form of a marriage allowance, paid to me via an Allowance Book containing tear off dockets to be cashed at the Post Office each week.

The Air Radar Technical Course that Robert was to take, was at the Training Course at Yatesbury, the camp near Calne. Since he was a graduate, he was placed with other graduates, on the one year course, after the eight weeks of square bashing at RAF Padgate. I have added an appendix at the end of this narrative, describing more fully, Camp Yatesbury. The cost of the Course was £1,000 per man, which was a lot of money in the 1950s. There were 20 men on this particular Course, so £20,000 was the cost to the Government and therefore to the Tax Payer. I have always maintained that they could have had regulars taking this same course, and thus been of more benefit to the country since they would not have terminated. They would have continued through years of 'Cold War' situations with no wastage of money on men who were discharged back into civilian life. On the second year, after the Course concluded, his work would be carried out in another part of the country, which I will describe later.

This remained a sore point for a long time, and indeed the loss of 2 years' earnings as well as potential salary increments, took several years to make up for, making these years very difficult. In fact it was very probably these National Service years that made us both ambitious to achieve what we had missed, and much more besides.

The date for Robert's departure to start his eight weeks' training came around all too soon. Walking to the railway station on that lovely September evening in 1956 is a clear memory, as is the fairly cheerful farewell scene, each of us consoling the other with plans for the first

Leave, but I left the station in tears and utterly distraught. Taking the long way home in an attempt to calm myself, I lingered before having to show my parents how upset I was. I also tried to avoid bumping into friends in case they asked about Robert's departure, as I couldn't have faced anyone in my emotional state. The lovely western views on my walk home that beautiful September evening are still in my memory, and so are the tears...........

The first four weeks passed slowly, but soon the first Leave arrived. There appeared at our front door, in the middle of the night, a heavier, robust Robert, after the weeks of three square meals a day, consisting of a great deal of starch, which must have been necessary to supply the energy required for the strenuous exercises these young men performed daily.

Over the week of Robert's Leave, we discussed the possibility of my joining him when he got his next posting. Well, if OK in wartime, why not now? We were delighted that this was entirely possible, so our combined energies were concentrated on enquiries, applications, and information sheets.

As for me, well, I was pregnant, so all the more reason to be together. This was definitely not the time to be apart.

Towards the end of Robert's second Leave, marking the end of Square Bashing and the beginning of the main Radar training Course, we packed and took the train, and on our eventual arrival in the small town of Calne and with the innocent confidence of youth, we set about looking for digs. I seem to remember Calne as being the place where the famous

Harris Sausages were made, and there was a huge advert on a wall near the station showing these wonderful mouth watering food items. Many a time in the future months we would enjoy these deliciously nutritious and meaty sausages.

Finding a Bed and Breakfast in a Guest House, we had a good night's sleep in the most comfortable bed I had ever known, smothered in a huge eiderdown. This was in the days long before duvets, so really unheard of where we came from! The mattress was so soft; we sank into it and fell into deep slumber. When we woke up I felt we were like the Babes in the Woods! Over breakfast the owner advised us that the best place to find permanent digs was Swindon, so we immediately took the short journey there, and on applying at the Billeting Office, managed to find a suitable place to live.

Chapter 3

Routines

The tall landlady greeted us at the door of her neatly well-kept home. She seemed to be reluctant to accept us, claiming that she had never applied to be a landlady, but however, she would take us in, almost doing us a favour, and making sure the official forms were in order and that she would be paid the appropriate rent by us, which we would receive via the living out allowance.

We were only too pleased to be settled, and we had a bedroom and the use of the kitchen and bathroom as well as share the living room in the evenings for TV viewing. Later on, we discovered she was claiming rental for the front parlour which we were supposed to have for our evenings. She saved on the heating of this musty smelling unused parlour, which we never ever used, and only entered the day she had the Inspector round to show as this supposed part of our digs. We were oblivious to her deviousness, and didn't really care as long as we could afford the rent, and be settled in together.

We spent evenings in the living room, watching TV with the landlord and landlady, Robert doing his homework, and I knitting some little baby items. Sometimes we would go out for walks, and being rather shy, we were happy doing this. We sometimes went to a pub for a quiet soft drink and a pint for Robert, and many evenings to local cinemas.

Our bedroom was comfortable, and here we spent most of our time when indoors. Robert's daily routine was getting up at about 7am, breakfasting by himself, and catching the Camp Bus at the end of the road, returning at around 5pm, when I had his meal ready. The bus was for the use of all the living out personnel of the various camps, which I imagine consisted of regular servicemen and their families.

The landlady spent most of her time each day next door with her mother, doing the housework there as well as her own, so I did not see much of her.

My routine was being awakened by a pneumatic drill at about 8.30am, as the roads were being repaired, having breakfast, then going out every weekday morning, walking into town, never using a bus. I never met or spoke to people my own age during the days, but was perfectly happy spending my time day after day in this way. Being together in the evenings through to each new day, was all Robert and I wanted or needed.

Swindon is a large town, on the main railway line from Paddington to Bristol and lies midway between the major towns of Reading and Bristol. This had a particular appeal to us as we were within easy reach of London and Birmingham and so on to Scotland.

Swindon had been named an Expanded Town under the Town Development Act of 1952 and the population was growing rapidly, particularly due to the large railway works of the GWR.

Like most men in the area, our landlady's husband, worked for GWR (Great Western Railways) and after WW2 Britain decided to continue with steam locomotion, unlike the rest of Europe which opted for diesel. The railway system in Europe, during the war had been completely destroyed. In Britain, the Government decided to spend money on the Welfare State, prioritising housing and the Health Service to the detriment of rail travel.

Britain's railways had been nationalised on January 1, 1948, bringing to an end the GWR's 113-year story. Do you remember LMS, LNER and SR? With GWR they became one company on Nationalisation, namely "British Rail".

In 1956, when we sought accommodation in Swindon, the works were still covered by a huge 85 acres of roofing, but the decline of the works was as rapid as its expansion over a century earlier.

We sometimes look back and wonder what happened to our landlord? Did he lose his job? Almost certainly! Did he get a good redundancy settlement? Almost certainly!

Several years after we left Swindon, the town became a centre of the digital revolution and with a population, now, of over 200,000, it is a vibrant industrial and commercial centre.

Robert and I could look forward to social housing in the future, if we were lucky, and of course, I was well looked after during my pre-natal period. Sadly, on our arrival in Swindon, the GWR Works' greatest days were already behind it.

One day I discovered Yoghurt! At last it had arrived in this country, after years of reading about it in Gayelord Hauser's books on the five magic foods - Yeast, Molasses, Wheatgerm, Skimmed Powdered Milk, and Yoghurt. This I found in a small dairy shop in Swindon, plain and raspberry favoured, in small glass jars. I had been introduced to yoghurt while on holiday at my friend's home in Norway when I was 19, and where it was sold everywhere, even delivered daily to doorsteps like milk, whereas in Britain it was as yet unheard of.

Many days I went to town via the local Baths, where I had a lovely warm soak in one of their huge baths with the usual overhead shower, which was preferable to using the bathroom in the digs, being afraid I didn't clean the bath sufficiently well for the lady's taste. I now wonder what she thought. Perhaps she didn't realise I took these baths a couple of times a week; perhaps she thought I was 'dirty'. Some days I had dental appointments or antenatal clinic or a Dr's appointment, so the time was well used, and these stops were always handy, being on the way into town. The NHS was well and truly in force now, with everything free. As we had decided that I would return home to Scotland for the birth about a month prior to the due date, this was all in hand, and the transfer booked.

I must have been so very healthy, walking every day, eating quite well, keeping weight down, with good colour in my cheeks; no wonder my figure returned to slim immediately after the birth.

The road always led, by lunchtime, to Woolworth's Self Service Restaurant, where I had tomato soup every single day, a little rest, a final walk round the big beautiful shops, gazing at the lovely clothes in M & S, but without envy, knowing that one day in the future I would be able to buy some of their colourful blouse/smocks, but just not now. I would pick up some bakery items from one of the lovely home bakery shops and learned the names they give to e.g. pancakes, for the area, being different from Scottish food names. I got used to the local accents and the people were kind and friendly, but that was the extent of my daytime communications, as I never met anyone from my own generation with a view to socialising. Again, this did not worry either Robert or myself, as we were happy to see each other in the evenings, and just marking time until it was all over, the first event in the birth if our baby, being next on the agenda.

Chapter 4

Baby Talk

Sometimes I would bump into the wives of some American Forces, with their lovely black babies in their gorgeous large prams. They looked so sweet and beautiful with their curly hair and big brown eyes, all set against spotless pink, or blue or white satin pram coverlets. I was looking forward to my turn in a few months' time back in Scotland.

When our landlady found out I was pregnant she gave us a sort of third degree, asking if we were happy, stating that we were still babies ourselves making judgement we thought she had no right to make, but we were obedient kids and answered all her questions, the main one being where I was going to give birth. Well what would we reply to that? I quickly reassured her it would not be in her house, but back home in Scotland, so no need to worry.

I developed some high minded theories though, about childbirth, having discovered a book on natural childbirth, without the use of any drugs (not that there was much to choose from anyway) using breathing exercises as well as physical postures to help the natural forces. These exercises I faithfully carried out daily, being convinced that I could have a home birth, not bothering with hospitals. I was sure I would feel no pain whatsoever! Naive at 21, and full of fresh confidence and hope, being modern and different, I was far too clever.

The days passed into weeks and months, through the cold weather, even a trip to Scotland over Xmas and New Year, as the landlady needed our bedroom for some visiting family over the holiday.

We enjoyed our Xmas/New Year break, meeting up with some of our friends, but mainly family, then returning on a long haul train journey overnight. We came back with two lovely Scottish presents for our landlady, who remarked, not that we were generous, but 'extrrravagant!', added to which Robert had to have an argument with her as she charged us rent for the week we were away on holiday, she having asked us in the first place, to vacate, to make room for her visitors. This is where Robert came to have experience in arguing for our rights, and he won!

Every night Robert would massage my now extending tummy with olive oil, to prevent stretch marks, and this worked, with still never a mark in sight, after three pregnancies over the years. So, ladies, never mind the expensive lotions, olive oil is enough! By Robert administering this, it served the other purpose of him having contact with his unborn baby. I remember towards the end of our stay there, many months later, we went to the new Bill Haley and the Comets film 'Rock Around the Clock', a notorious presentation which had built the reputation of causing riots in the aisles; so very brave of me going as a 7 months pregnant woman, 'See You Later Alligator'. Luckily we experienced no riots, just noise.

From January into February, we enjoyed our evening routines, making the most of our time, before I was to return to our home town in Scotland to have the baby. We spent a wonderful month, ending in a fond farewell, sadly taken as Robert put me on the Sleeper to Edinburgh on 10th February 1957.

It was a Sunday evening when we caught the train to London, where we had booked my ticket on the Sleeper. Robert had his own luggage for returning to live at the camp where he would rejoin his friends on the Course, and await word of our baby's arrival in March.

The other passengers in that 4 berth sleeper took one look at me and, noting that I was about to climb up on to the upper berth, offered to let me have a lower one. They were probably afraid I would fall out during the night, or even start Labour on the long journey north. I, being me, said 'Oh it's ok. I'll be alright. I'll be strapped in' so up I climbed, possibly much to their concern, but I slept like a baby all the way.

Chapter 5

On The Home Straight

I awoke in the Caledonian Station in Edinburgh, to the welcome sound of cups of tea and toast, from the attendant. Dressing, I caught the train to my home town from the same station, arriving when many of my old friends were on their way to work. It was a pleasant coincidence meeting them just outside the large Station entrance, and they greeted me with 'hello Helen, great to see you back! On the last lap eh? You are wearing ankle socks!' Here I was, and the baby was going to be born here in Scotland, just as Robert and I had hoped. I got a bus to my parents' prefab and settled in with a nice breakfast with mum. We had bought the large black shiny Silver Cross pram with our only money, which was £45, and there it stood in the bedroom in all its glory. I think the same pram now-a-days costs about £500, but so well worth it, built like a car with all the suspension perfect, and lasting for years. During this month my parents moved to their new council flat, where I had the use of the bedroom, complete with pram, all until we were able to move into our own little place nearby.

I was on the last straight with high hopes that I'd only be waiting the one month, which in the end turned out to be 6 weeks, the first baby as usual, being a couple of weeks late. In fact on the actual due date, Robert turned up on a surprise Leave, in the hope that he would be around for the birth, only to have to return, nothing having happened, except a lovely weekend together, living in hope and expectation. During that break though, we obtained a small Room and Kitchen type house just along the road, where I was able to live for the next few months with our baby. Robert's father had managed to obtain it for us from his Employer, at a small affordable rent. The little house was like a paradise for me and the baby, and Robert when he got home for a break. I had a happy time, with friends visiting regularly, all adoring our baby.

Where were we going to live once we knew the ultimate destination of Robert's final Posting? Our plans were well in hand and always on the drawing board.

Just as I was thinking the baby was never going to appear, I went into Labour at 2am on a

Sunday morning, 24th March actually. My Dad had to do all the running around that Robert would have done, like the phoning for the ambulance at a local phone box, and my Mum had to go with me in the ambulance to the Nursing home at Airthrey Castle, where now stands Stirling University, at the foot of Wallace Monument overlooking the city of Stirling. I had been advised by my brother not to have a home delivery after all, as his wife, Isabel, had gone through her labour in hospital, which was no picnic, but had it been at home, would have been so much worse, with no equipment or extra nursing staff.

My waters broke, and then my mum and dad each held an elbow as they carefully helped me down the outside stairway, trying to avoid each icy step.

I was very glad to have agreed with my brother, and as my mum sat in the Ambulance with me on that very icy night, she simply said 'just do as they say'. That was the last I saw of her as they slammed the big outside door on her, after she kissed me goodnight.

They took charge of me, putting me in a big bath, just when I wanted to get into bed, painting my lower quarters with some sort of disinfectant fluid, so I was then allowed into a bed, all the while, with pains getting worse, and so much more painful than I had expected. There was nothing about this in the book I had been following for months! In those days no husbands were allowed anywhere near the Labour room, so even if Robert had been around, he would have been shown the door, just as my mum had been, and told to phone the next day.

When Dad phoned the hospital from the local phone box down the road, each call was met with him being told to ring much later on. Meanwhile I was a 21 year old, all alone in a Labour room, lying for hours, and being told to be quiet as it was a Sunday Visiting Day and the Visitors were not to be disturbed by my moans on such a lovely sunny afternoon. Nurses came and went, but only to take temperature, blood pressure etc and be told to take a breath of gas and air from a big hand held mask which I could hardly hold it was so heavy. One said to me 'God doesn't give pain we can't stand, so yes it is bearable, - you'll see!'

On and on it went, and by about 5.30, pm I was still lying there with no real help or advice, from one nurse on duty after another, telling me to be quiet and it would not be long. I thought it would never come to an end and that there was no baby after all. I also wondered what Robert would have thought of this, but he would not have been listened to anyway. They were in total command, so anything could have happened. My sweet little daughter was born at 6.15pm, and my Dad had just been on the phone as instructed, to be told to ring again at 6.30pm, which he did, my mum having told him not to come back till he had real news.

He then had to go to Robert's parents' house and tell them, but only after sending a telegram to Robert right from the telephone box, which was so easy in those days. This is impossibility in this modern age, but of course we have mobile phones, and internet, as well as the baby's father being right there holding the hands of the mother to be and taking an active part in the birth.

Poor Dad, with all that running around, but he would probably be so excited and invigorated for work the next day. .

Robert had a couple of breaks during the Spring and early summer, and in fact the first of these being when the baby was 3 weeks old, which was the first time Robert saw his child. I wonder how the young dads would take this now- a- days. Not only were dads not allowed into the Labour room, but National Servicemen were not considered for Compassionate Leave for any birth so they had to wait till the next due official Leave. What would be regarded as

'Compassionate'? Well maybe a family funeral, but not much less, something I resented for years to come. Everyone saw our baby, even strangers, except her own father, so by the time Robert did see her, she had changed

I was ecstatic; a little girl! What could be better! I knew Robert would feel the same. I have some of his letters telling me all about it in his 21 year old excited hand, with his friends teasing him in the background. In those days there were three deliveries of post per day, or perhaps by this time reducing to two, and always guaranteed to receive the post the next day, so sometimes I got as many as two letters in one go. I can see how a new father in these circumstances, with no outlet of physical contact and no immediate way of getting his feelings expressed simply, with the added burden of being in a place he doesn't want to be, would write at such length, with the great need to be saying it and still feeling it isn't quite enough. Here is the first one

My Darling,

I am just settling in for the night and at this moment am snuggling into my bed covers. I am so happy and have laughed all day. All the lads have been just wonderful to me and are starting to call me 'Dad' already. I feel so old, so mature, so virile and so proud beside all these youngsters (some of them are older than me). Do you know, honey, that I have hit the headlines, and becoming a papa has had a strange effect on most of the lads in the billet. Alan openly admitted that he wished his wife was expecting. Alex followed up with the same idea and a few of the single chaps are talking about getting engaged. They must think I am stealing a march on them. But darling I am claiming all the glory and forgetting the main actress already. Today has been so happy for me and I received the telegram, which I now have stuck to my locker, where it will stay to feed my excitement. I have been telling everyone here just how wonderful you are, and what a good job you did, even before I know the facts myself. I am just longing to hear all your news so that I can dream about you all day long. Oh darling I am so thankful for all you have done for me as my wife. I will do anything to please you when I come home, so you just snap your fingers. You will be very happy darling, with your little daughter. I can just see you dote over her just now. I bet you look at her all day long and can't sleep at night in case the little one starts to cry for something.

I would be just the same too if I were home. You don't know what an impact this has meant for me. I can still hardly believe the news. It is all too wonderful and miraculous. I did not think we had it in us. Oh, I love you my darling, I love you more each day and I would do anything for you, anything at all. Is there anything you want or need which you want me to know? Is there anything you want to tell me? I am so pleased with you my dear, so you must never worry about me. I have been thinking about middle names and at the moment I think perhaps Yvonne is a waste of a good name to be thrown into obscurity. Don't get me wrong, darling, nothing is good enough for little Roslyn, but it is only a question of getting the right effect. Roslyn ....Wingate. I think perhaps a name with three syllables would be nice. Can you think of any? You must let me know your views. I hope you are well my pet. Are you in hospital or at home? You don't know how eager I am to find out and I want to know so much about everything that happened. Oh darling I love you passionately, I love you tenderly. I could not live without you. I shall adore our little daughter too. Oh how I want to see you and dote over you. I have been singing, smiling and laughing all day long. You have made me so happy. Look after yourself, honey, now that it is all over and I will see you in all your glory at Easter. Give my love to everyone, especially my little girl, and remind her she does have a 'dadda'. I pray for you both and both and you are always in my thoughts. I can see pink covers draped over the pram now. The sun is shining and there you are slim and oh so beautiful the woman in my dreams, the girl I love so much, my very wonderful wife. God be with you both. I am so very happy and contented now. Bye bye darling, bye bye baby. I love you both. Robert xx

The next morning it was understood that newborns were not given to their mothers as were supposed to wait some hours before being fed. However an old school friend of mine was a nursing sister there and brought my baby in for me to hold. What a wonderful feeling it was! Also my mum came and visited that morning, in place of Robert, so when she arrived by my bedside, her face was glowing, with a huge grin from ear to ear, as she had just been to the nursery to see the babies. I asked her if she was sure she had seen the right one. 'See the right one? I could have picked her out myself!' she said. 'She is just like Robert!' Yes she was, and I only wish Robert had been able to see for himself, as she changed quite soon afterwards. With no Leave of Absence for 3 weeks, as mentioned before, having a baby being not important enough to be considered for Compassionate Leave. Something I resented for years, and in fact still do.

Since I had been given a place in the Maternity Home for the delivery only, having originally opted for a home delivery, then chickened out, I expected to be allowed home that day, but they decided to keep me for 4 days. This was probably a good idea, allowing me time to rest during the nights, and get some strength back. After 4 days my mum came in the ambulance and brought us home. Mum and Dad's small flat was large and roomy enough for us all, so I had the bedroom, and slept in the big bed. The baby slept in the large luxurious pram, mum and dad being comfortable on the bed settee in the living room. We had many family visitors, starting with Robert's parents, then my brother popped in from work, and of course my grandmother was a daily visitor, offering wonderful advice and singing to the baby, as happily as she rocked her on her knee. Good old fashioned advice was proffered all the time, and I listened and valued it with respect and deference. Aunts and cousins appeared, all with gifts and loving wishes and cards. Being a beautiful springtime, it was perfect for me going out in the sunshine, dressed in my neat clothes, pushing the pram so proudly.

Robert's RAF friends, all of whom, he maintained, envied him being a father, had sent me a large bouquet of flowers, which in the end did not arrive, as probably sent to the original address in our home town, forgetting that Mum and Dad had moved. They also sent a lovely card, which was to me, so very welcome. I received so many lovely cards from new friends and old.

The nicest of the cards of course came from Robert. The birth was so near Mother's Day that one day I got the beautiful Mother's Day card from him and the baby. He composed 2 verses on it himself, one from him and the other from the baby, each ending with a kiss. His letters at that time, were those of a new father, with all the excitement and love poured out on paper, whereas we would both of course have preferred the physical expression, but I have these letters still, and passing these on, with that Mother's Day card, to the now 56 year old daughter, who will treasure them I am sure.

Card from Robert on birth of Roslyn: - A Mother's Day Card –

A Message to Mother on Her Day (front page)

Then inside:

Nobody knows all the love that goes to you this happy day! (at top of double page)

Nobody dreams of the constant streams of thought that flow your way!

Inside continued:

Oh darling dear what can I do
To please my lady slim and fair
A flame inside me burns in lieu
Of silent words which I don't dare

Robert xx

This world around, so big and wide
I view through eyes not yet with sight
But on this day and at your side,
I feel so safe and free from night

Roslyn x

Then along the bottom of inside card:

We two, wish you all the happiness and success in your new vocation – a mother.

I was soon able to move into the little room and kitchen house with the baby, so giving my mum and dad their bedroom back...

Chapter 6

Into Summer

Robert had an Easter Break enjoying settling into the house, and this was the first time he had seen the baby so we were a little family for the week or ten days. After he went back, it was baby and me, going through our daily routines together instead of the three of us, but happily in continuous sunshine which seemed to go on throughout the summer, with no rain or clouds to be seen. I had such a suntan that people kept asking me where I had been on holiday - me! - Just walking every day to town with the pram. I lived on Robert's letters, and he on mine, with the still two or three deliveries per day, so there was always one on the door mat. Robert's Course still had some weeks to complete before his second year's posting, when Roslyn and I were due to join him so I was quite patient waiting and meantime enjoying being with my baby and the routine we had established.

I had a couple of friends who visited together on a Thursday evening, one of them being Robert's cousin, whose boyfriend was himself serving his National Service abroad, the other of them on a Saturday night straight off the bus from the Dancing when, over some supper, she would tell me all about how it went. She always stayed the night and left next day, then we would all meet up again on the Thursday, full of fun and laughs. That Saturday night friend now suffers from Alzheimer's and dear Alison still remembers everything from our childhood at school, but nothing of 5 minutes ago......Please! Somebody! Anyone! Find a cure for this! I recently visited Alison in the lovely Home she is in, and imagine my almost blood curdling and certainly touching experience when my old friend asked me how my mum is, and when I told her she had passed away, she said 'Oh I really liked your mum Helen!' To think she could remember and have feelings for my mother from 60 years ago, yet she couldn't remember what I'd said 5 minutes ago! This had such a heartrending effect on me that I would do anything to help any progress in finding the causes and a cure.

On Robert's Breaks, we tended to pretend we lived here all the time. Wishing that there was no National Service far away, made us impatient to get the second and final year started. This happened in due time, and when Robert discovered it was to be in a Camp called Shawbury, near Shrewsbury, Shropshire, he immediately set about finding digs for us, succeeding in finding a small flat in The Hall, Childs Ercall, near Market Drayton. Ours was the smallest and most modest of a group of 5 or 6 flats rented out to RAF personnel, mainly officers and wives, and their children. He wrote and asked me to send his bike by rail, as he intended to cycle every day to the Camp to what was now his job. This I immediately did, it being so easy in those days to simply put a label on anything, and send it by rail. Very easy and very cheap! Trains ran on time, fares were cheap. There was always a Guards' Van with Guard/Porter for all sorts of items, like luggage, bikes, prams, even livestock like pets I suppose, trunks, chests, crates, and always porters available, so all I had to do was drop the bike off at the ticket office, pay the fee and leave it. It was duly delivered the next day.

I set about preparing for our departure, now quite experienced in planning, packing, and noting train times, which were all so very easy, no shortage of trains and connections in the 1950s, all cheap, all running on time, all bookable, plenty of connections, with porters at the ready on every station.

Chapter 7

Letter to the Ministry

When I had become pregnant and originally told the RAF Ministry Pay Office, they replied that I should tell them when the baby was born, so that they could adjust my allowance.

This I now did, only to receive a reply saying they were not going to increase the allowance. At this time I did not know how much the Courses were costing the Government, and how little the country was benefiting from National Service wastage

Now came the beginnings of my experience of life, having to re-apply, complain and hopefully succeed. My letter to the Ministry went something like this -

Dear Sir,

I have received your letter informing me that I will not be receiving extra allowance on the birth of my baby on 24th March 1957.

May I point out that as a newly born baby she is living on milk alone, but in a few months she will be weaned on to baby foods, which I will have to buy and the prices for which I do not yet know. By the time my husband is discharged from National Service, she will be one and a half years old, and eating proper food, which again costs money, which at present I do not have.

My husband was taken into National Service after we were married and I was pregnant, so we were both reluctant to be in this position. His salary was curtailed, and he could have been earning at that time £12 - £13 per week, and now with increments, a bit more for the support of his wife and child. He receives 18 shillings per week, as pocket money from you, and I, £1.10 shillings, with which I pay rent of 8 shillings, and buy my own basic food with the rest, with nothing at all left over for clothes or extras during this temporary, but long, setback in our lives. Needless to say, my husband's call up is disrupting our lives and we are very unhappy and only looking forward to his discharge, which can't come a day too soon.

We have had to buy a pram, and all the baby clothes. Items which before we are finished we will have to buy, i.e. a push chair as the baby grows and begins to walk, as well as toddler's clothing. We have neither money nor income other than what you decide we should have, and I now request that you reconsider your decision and let me know as soon as possible.

Yours faithfully,

Mrs Robert Wingate

P S - by the way please excuse the letter written in pencil, as my ink has run out and I am unable to spend money on replacement of such a luxury.

Chapter 8

Result

This letter brought a good response, not only of an increase in the allowance, but in the whole back pay, dated right back to the baby's birth date. My mum always said the letter would have been stained with the recipient's tears as he laid it on the Paymaster's desk.

The back money received paid for our fares; mine, together with the cost of transporting the large pram containing the baby bath and other items carefully packed by myself and my sister in law Isabel in the pram, covered with ribbed cardboard from the co-op where she had worked.

How to get the pram to our destination? Well once again my mum had known a few cases during the war, so her input again came to our rescue. She advised us to contact the Police in the place where we were due to arrive by train, and get them to help transport the pram to the address, which happened to be a few miles out in the countryside. So we were to get from Shrewsbury Station to Childs Ercall, the nearest small town to that village being Market Drayton, but no transport other than bus or taxi.

In fact by that time, Robert had done his own homework, but luckily my mum's advice worked best of all, and as I arrived with the baby and the porter pushing the pram, two tall Policemen were waiting at the entrance to Station, with a Taxi Driver by their side, and they got him to lift the pram on to the back of his vehicle, along with instructions as to the fare to be the lowest possible for us. Robert took charge of carrying the baby, so for the first time for hours, I was free to walk empty handed, and our good little baby, had not cried during the whole journey, which must have started out at about 8.30am and it was now about 6pm or later. I am not really sure of the times.

The journey had started for me by my Dad coming along, and picking the baby and me up, walking with us and the pram to the local station, going with us to Glasgow, walking with us from Queen Street Station to Central, and standing in the queue for the express train to Shrewsbury via New Street, Birmingham, although I am now doubting that, and wondering whether it could have been via

Crewe, as would be the case now-a-days. Anyway, I know that when we reached that connection, it was only a short trip from the platform across to the parallel one, the Porter pushing the pram while I hurriedly followed with the baby in my arms, and dragging a holdall behind me along the ground.

When I sat on the train with the six months old Roslyn in my arms, the pram in the Guard's Van, it was peaceful as she was a good baby, making no sound whatsoever, content and cosy on my lap. I was the one who became tired, not having realised how long the journey would be. The other passengers were kind and friendly, adoringly looking at the sweet baby, and at one point I reluctantly asked one of the older ladies if she would be kind enough to hold her while I went to the nearby toilet. Of course she would, and then I changed the nappy and packed it away. No disposables in those days, so had to take everything home to be washed of course.

As we got nearer the destination, I must have looked so pale and tired, and got to the stage where I was asking the others where we were and how long would it take and were we nearly there, like a child. They assured me it would not be very long before we reached Shrewsbury. I was nearly sick with fatigue and exhaustion and virtually unknown really to me at the time, pregnant again. Living on Leaves is not exactly the normal way to live, so here we would go again and in fact although I had suspected it, I couldn't really believe it, and was never quite sure, so just put it to the back of my mind and Robert's too. The Contraceptive Pill was not only unheard of, but so far out of sight that it did not even appear on the horizon of medical science at that time.

Being together was the answer to everything, and the alternative was unthinkable. So a young, pale couple with a gorgeous little baby arrived at the Hall by taxi that Saturday afternoon, to be greeted by a kind landlady, Mrs. Herrick, the owner of this lovely Hall. She adored Roslyn from the start and was always kind and tender to us.

The flat, being towards the back of The Hall, consisted of a living room with kitchen so with sink, cooker, and fireplace, and a bedroom, with a large communal bathroom along the hall, shared by some tenants, and always available, where I ended up bathing Roslyn, after the initial fireside living room bath times for the next few months. At first Robert was to report to his Course base, so for the first week I was alone with the baby, but at the end of that week, the three of us were well settled, with Robert cycling every day to the Course, starting out at about 6am, the journey being 10 miles in each direction, having to stop and cut through a field about halfway through. This Robert did in all weathers, snow, ice, rain, and sun, sometimes having to chase sheep across a field, so very eventful in both directions.

The work which Robert now did, after taking the £1,000 Course, consisted of once a week, being part of a team which serviced Rebecca Mk III Radar equipment on Vampire Jets. His part was to clean down two twelve inch long aerials using emery paper, and re varnish them, this taking all of say, half an hour. He also checked the cabling from these aerials to a small box in front of the pilot's console, to make sure it did not come loose during a flight. I again maintain that a regular RAF man could have taken the Course and been trained to do these tasks, thus saving the Tax Payers' money. This was the main part of his work, although he had originally learned the full extent of the Course at Yatesbury, which in itself was a high quality one. However, the application of what had been learned, was less than useful, once the work commenced at Shawbury. For the rest of the time, day after day, week after week, he did very little, except join the football team which played the other camps regularly during weekdays. In September 1957 he and I took an A level English Literature course together, but I will relate more of this later.

Now in 2013, I feel the village of Childs Ercall deserves a write up, since we lived there for a year in 1957/58, albeit with the desperate desire to leave as quickly as possible, but here is the history -

Child's Ercall, located in the rural countryside of Shropshire, close to Market Drayton and Shrewsbury is a small village of some 600 residents.

"Ercal", its rather unusual name is thought to be derived from the Celtic or Welsh for "Holly Thicket" which is "Ar-celen" with "Child" simply referring to "Little". Ercall Magna, close by, became known as High Ercall to distinguish between the two villages.

At the centre of the village is the village green with the old sandstone Church of St Michael, with its 12th century doorway, a 13th century arcade and 14th century aisle, the church being situated at one end of the green.

The impressive stained glass is by Charles Eamer Kempe.

The first stone Church was built in the 9th century replacing the timber structure thought to have been destroyed by the Danes, who laid waste the land, due to its flatness and poor defence possibilities.

The dedication of the Church to St Michael is an indication that the Church was originally founded by the Celtic Church. It is possible that a Mercian settlement of Celtic monks reached Ercall between 788 and 803.

The first stone Church was a simple rectangular building. One semicircular window still remains in the east end of the north aisle. Later at the beginning of the 13th century aisles were added.

Records show that the village, which was mentioned in the Domesday Book of 1086, was described as a small settlement of twenty three farm workers, their families, a "Frenchman" and a priest.

However, Pre-historic stone implements found in Ercall Wood indicate that the settlement is much older and has been in existence from before the Bronze Age.

At the dissolution of the monasteries in 1539, King Henry VIII confiscated all monastic properties and sold or exchanged them.

By the end of the eighteenth Century, the estate with the residence called "The Old Hall" had passed into the ownership of the Corbet Family. The Corbets had been major land owners since the Conquest. The Corbets would appear to have lived at Ercall throughout the seventeenth and eighteenth centuries.

1835 maps show that the land was reclaimed by small tenant cottagers and farmers. A thousand acres in the Manors of Childs Ercall and Howle were privately enclosed in 1801. After enclosure, the Corbet Family began a programme of improvements following the pattern of the revolution in farming taking place during the mid to late nineteenth century. New cottages were built for tenants and farm workers, together with a village hall and Church School.

The farming revolution saw the birth of farmstead buildings throughout the County. Building work continued after the Second World War with the construction of Council houses to accommodate the rural workforce.

More recently the character of the village began to change with people now working in the surrounding County Towns.

Close to the Church and School, there is a long drive, leading to an impressive residence, locally called the "The Old Hall", which is mentioned above.

Chapter 9

Hard Times

Cycling 20 miles a day during the week, brought about a fatigue, which could be made up for at weekends, so we had restful days, with me going sometimes to Shrewsbury by bus, or to the nearby town of Market Drayton by bus, taking the baby in the new pushchair. My routine became almost boring but meeting the local people was nice, and the shop owners, one of whom was Scottish, so with an accent I could recognise.

The other tenants were all Officers and their families, mainly RAF, and all temporarily in this billet, whereas we were definitely temporary, and gladly making no bones of it, with our aim to be back home in our little room and kitchen. This seemed to horrify them, saying how well 'Bob' would do as an officer, and how we would have all that the RAF could offer to officers, like a foreign car, luxury digs and best schools for the children wherever we went. I could think of nothing worse and they must have thought we were mad, just wanting to be home in our little house in Scotland, never to move again.

At one stage I noticed a second hand radio in a junk shop, and bought it, so we could listen at least to the radio. Robert managed to fix it up on the mantelpiece, with a connection to the centre light. This was fine, but every time I reached up to switch it on, an electric shock shot up my arm, but this never deterred me, so desperate was I to hear the lovely dramas and music.

At the back of our minds though, at this time, was the fact that I was pregnant again. Leaves/breaks being so different from the normal way of living, and of course no birth control pill, as mentioned earlier, anywhere in sight.

The criticism of our 2 pairs of parents had been also a threat to us, and they seemed to be able to tell us off for being so stupid as to become pregnant so soon after the first 'mistake'. We took it on the chin like the well behaved children we were, so it was better to be away from the home town scene, where we could now try to put it out of our minds, as after all maybe I was wrong, maybe it was just a mistake and I was not pregnant.

The idea took ages to settle into my mind, and as I bathed Roslyn each evening and cuddled her and tucked her into bed, I began to think, of putting two little ones to bed at night, just as I was doing with this beautiful one. What if it were a little boy. Robert would really love to have a son. I still could not imagine loving any other child as much as I did Roslyn. How can you love any more than you do or divide your love up? Still I felt content that there would be another little one in our happy family, so four of us instead of three.

As if by some sort of punishment, just as I was getting used to the idea, my waters broke on a 20 week pregnancy or five months as the doctors calculated.

I was taken in to the Shrewsbury Infirmary wearing RAF pyjamas, not in so much great pain but shivering and shaking, with the visiting GP telling me that Robert would have to take Leave to look after the baby.

I was distraught, saying 'but he hasn't changed a nappy in his life!' The GP said 'well he'll just have to get used to being tangled up with safety pins!' To say this worried me is putting it mildly, so my mum was summoned by the wonderful mail that existed then, and she arrived a couple of days later. After Mrs. Herrick had taken one look at the RAF pyjamas and asked me if I had any nighties, my reply was only the see-through glamorous ones, and definitely not suitable for a hospital. She decided to lend me one of hers, which I eventually wore, but that was the least of my worries at the time. Arriving at the ward starving, I was only too ready to devour the wonderful meat balls they laid out in front of me. 'Well, she's got an appetite' said one of the nurses. Yes I surely had, and tried to settle down that evening.

Far from home, and weak, my strength not yet back after giving birth only just over six months earlier, and travelling far away from home, I had not yet got over the journey and the trauma of it all. I told them we had not expected to become pregnant, and worried about having another baby so soon, but I now realised I could just as easily look after two as one. They said they could not promise anything, and that it was most likely going to come away and be lost as they could not save a five months or 20 weeks miscarriage. I just had to relax and wait, so I went to sleep, worrying about everything, especially about how Robert was getting on with putting Roslyn to bed and waiting for my mum to arrive.

The next morning very early, the early shift of nurses arrived, with bedpans and other items for the whole ward, and I was able to use one urgently in the grey morning light. Easily and without realising what was happening, the miscarried baby slipped out into the bedpan, and when the nurse came to collect it we both looked and saw the well formed child floating in the fluid. I tried to avert my eyes as I did not want to see the sex of it, dreading the fact that it could have been a boy, and just what we had wanted, so I said to the nurse, 'please don't tell me the sex' 'Ok' she said, and went away to the other nurse, who then came and took it all away. The second nurse said 'oh it's a little boy' 'oh no' I said. 'Oh, well no...... 'maybe I got it wrong'. She then added, having perhaps realised my thinking. I don't know......how they can decipher our emotions at such times. They are only doing their jobs. The whole thing was taken away, and I never saw it again, and probably disposed of in some hospital incinerator, with no more to be said.

I really think it was a boy, and soon the guilt set in, of how we had felt so stupid becoming pregnant so soon after the first, and what would our parents say etc. Everyone would think we were stupid. What a way to live, and how abnormal even for those days. We had lost our child, boy or girl, so were filled with guilt for a very long time after that. We never did have a son, and felt the loss of this one for many a year. My pain was not at an end though, and straight away a couple of strong nursing sisters came and started pressing down on my abdomen, trying to get the afterbirth away before the uterus contracted too much. This was very painful, and my cries could be heard all over the ward. They were only partially successful, and the next day I was wheeled into the operating theatre to have the afterbirth removed. It was only then that my pains disappeared, and I felt some sort of normalcy.

In the ward just across from my bed, was a woman who had just given birth to a baby boy, and as she tried to breast feed the baby, behind the drawn curtains, she started shouting at the infant, scolding it severely and swearing at it for not taking hold of the breast.

This upset me so much that I looked around and saw that nobody else, including the nursing staff, seemed to be bothering. Even Doctors were passing through the ward, with no response from them, so I started saying in a loud voice 'what is that all about? Isn't anyone going to say something to that woman? Here am I having just lost a child, just dying to feed a baby, and there she is shouting and screaming at a newly born infant. Give the child to me and I will feed it!' They all got worried as she kept on shouting at the baby. Eventually a doctor went behind the curtains and started to reason with the woman. 'You must be nice to this baby, and not shout at it. It is not the baby's fault that he cannot feed the way you want him to at the moment. You are upsetting other patients the way you are shouting. We will be keeping our eye on you while you are here in this ward. You must be nice to this baby. You are upsetting that Scottish woman with your shouting'.

My mum had arrived and Mrs. Herrick drove her to visit me, and the following evening one of the Officer's wives did the same for her. The distance was quite far, so we thanked them and said not to bother taking it in turns after this, as I would be home the next day. It was very touching that they were all very kind to us. Robert was back at the Camp and work, and my mum was delighted to be looking after her darling little granddaughter.

Much later on, after a couple of years, we had our second little daughter, Caroline, a sweet beautiful baby who filled our lives with a second joy, not only as a sister to Roslyn, but as our youngest, forever full of innocence and delightful calm throughout her whole childhood. Later in this narrative, I will describe her birth which took place in 1959, and although not within the time scope of this book, I feel it is only fair to her to give a full description of her arrival into this world.

Chapter 10

Recovery

On arriving back from hospital, and after spending some good quality time with my mum and Roslyn together, it was time for mum to return home. I took over the reins again, while trying to truly recuperate and get my strength back, by resting, eating well, and generally getting into a quiet routine while pacing myself regarding healthy exercise.

Going through autumn into winter, Robert managed to keep from absolute boredom at his 'work' by playing football for his camp team, every Wednesday afternoon, when they played other camp teams. This helped him to keep fit, while I walked for miles with the pram, although always along the same country lanes.

We decided to take a trip home to Scotland for 10 days, so managed to fit in a New Year celebration with friends and family. The long train journey was not difficult on the outward journey, with the push chair and some luggage, but on the way back we found we had to walk for many miles from the station, having miscalculated our timings. We trudged over fields and shortcuts in the dark, which took a couple of extra hours, and yet it was not really such a 'drag' as the modern saying would state it, as we were now plodders in every sense of the word. Baby Roslyn was as usual, as good as gold, sometimes asleep, and sometimes awake, but content and secure as always.

Once back in our flat, and after a good rest, our new year truly started, and being the second and final stage/year, we were rarin' to go, looking ahead to 11th September, the day of Robert's discharge. Again, now in 2013, I feel Shawbury deserves a description so I have added an appendix at the end of this narrative.

Using our time as best we could, to make the time pass as quickly as possible, we had decided the previous September to study and take an A level English Literature exam, just for the heck of it, thus taking us through to June 1958, when the exam date occurred. Not having a TV, nor even desiring one, we had plenty of time to study together. The plays were Henry V and Romeo and Juliet and the book was George Bernard Shaw's Pygmalion, all of which kept us going although of course because the exam was being run through Robert's camp class, I could only do the work at home, but he took my work with him to the class. We were well into Shakespeare's history plays, then the romantic, keeping a good balance, with comedy/drama in the form of GBS. We have kept this sort of pattern in our retirement years and now well into our 'twilight years', but without the added excitement of exams!

Chapter 11

Disaster And After

On 6th February 1958, on our little worn out second hand radio, there came a blood curdling announcement in the form of news of the Manchester United Air disaster in Munich, during the European Cup competition. The event was indeed a National tragedy and the whole country tuned in and listened with bated breath to every announcement. The Busby Babes were the cream of their crop, and eight of these young players lost their lives. There were 23 fatalities, eight of whom were Journalists as well as the eight young players. The whole tragic incident went down in history as one of the most famous air crashes of our times.

It was around this time that Robert, playing for his camp side against other camps, was picked to play for the RAF team, still on Wednesday afternoons, and his position was right half. It was about a month after the Munich Air Disaster that the next match was due to be played, the RAF against the Army. When they turned up, Robert noticed that his position was to be against inside left, Bobby Charlton, who had a month earlier been in the crash.

So although Bobby had been in that tragic crash, nearly losing his life, he was still expected to do his duty as a National Serviceman, at least on the football field. Robert braced himself, although he had become used to playing against some really good players who in civilian life were professionals. He was somewhat relieved on this occasion though, to see Bobby on the sidelines, just walking up and down, with a heavy coat over his shoulders, having decided not to play, or perhaps it was through doctor's orders. But Bobby was there just the same, with the team. Robert's opponent that day was a substitute.

Some of Robert's friends visited us, one of whom became Uncle Mike to our two daughters, Roslyn and Caroline, as children over the years, when he visited us in Scotland and later on in Bracknell, always bringing toys from the large Regent Street Toy Shop Hamlyn's.

The first time Mike came to Childs Ercall, he looked after Roslyn to let us go to a concert by the Halle Orchestra in Manchester. Since he was inexperienced in babysitting, I spent the day preparing the baby, so that she would be very tired and sleep during his visit. I must have done something wrong though, in that I had put her to bed too early, so she was wide awake for most of the time poor Mike was on duty. We enjoyed the Halle very much, but when we arrived home at about 9.30pm, Mike was pacing the floor with her, and I suspect even singing to her. As soon as I took over, she dropped off into a deep sleep, much to Mike's surprise. 'Why did she do that for you and not for me?' he asked in astonishment. My reply was 'Never mind, let's just have supper and relax while we discuss the Halle'.

Another sweet thing that involved our studies was a Birthday Card from Robert where he quoted a speech from Henry V, which has been so valued by me among the several others over the years as well as the wonderful speeches from Romeo and Juliet. I always seem to turn to the moon and have written such a lot of my own poems around the moon, but here is what Robert quoted to me on that 23rd birthday –

'But a good heart,(Kate) Helen, is the sun and the moon; - or rather the sun and not the moon, for it shines bright and never changes, but keeps his course truly. If thou would have such a one, take me; and take me; take a soldier; take a soldier take a king; and what say'st thou, then to my love? Speak my fair and fairly, I pray thee.'

In the springtime my mum visited again, having found her way more easily now that she became used to the Rail journeys. It seemed to coincide with Roslyn reaching 15 months old, and she began walking quite suddenly, feeling her way along the wall with her hands. Mum was sitting on the couch, when she nodded towards the little one, and there she was, standing at the wall. We both turned her round to face the centre of the room, and off she went! I'm glad mum was there to see at least some of the happy family highlights.

During a week of lovely spring weather mum and I took little trips by bus to the shops in Shrewsbury; and also to Market Drayton where Robert and the baby and I sometimes shopped on Saturdays.

We liked the half timbered and red brick buildings in the town centre and the beautiful 14th century church, with the tomb of Thomas and Elizabeth Bulkeley, who turned out to be distant relatives of 3 presidents of the United States; Calvin Coolidge, George Bush and George W Bush.

However, the town's most famous son was the brilliant administer and soldier, Clive of India. With a force of 1000 English troops and 2000 sepoys he defeated a 50,000 strong enemy at Plassey and India fell to the British.

He was elected Member of Parliament for Shrewsbury and received an Irish Peerage.

Mum had a lovely holiday with us, before she left for home. The knowledge that we would be following her in early September was a prospect she looked forward to with great relish. She was sub- letting our house out to a career woman, which helped us with some furniture expenses, until our return.

One morning very early, I opened my eyes in the grey of dawn, half awake, and I saw a figure opening our bedroom door, and peeping in momentarily. She was dressed in a neat grey dress of Victorian style, like something of the style of Jane Eyre, and her dark hair was set in a neat 'earphone' shaped style. She could have been a housekeeper inspecting the store rooms, of which I believe, our flat had been one, having meat hooks in the bedroom ceiling. She closed the door as quickly as she had opened it, and disappeared. Was this a ghost? If so, I was not afraid, and not even surprised, as this was an old house, and probably been well run in the old days, by such staff. There would have been a housekeeper.

Now in 2013 I find myself pondering on this experience, and surprised that I did not make more of it at the time. Perhaps I was so involved in the everyday happenings of life that I quickly forgot what had taken only a few seconds of a half awake/half asleep state of consciousness. The explanation when it happened, was, to me, quite simple; and now equally simple, I see it as a mere time lapse from a different dimension which I was somehow able to accidentally tune into through no talent of mine.

On one occasion Robert had to fly with the crew to Gibraltar on a navigational test flight, which was the norm, and all the crews had to take their turn. It was quite interesting for him, seeing the sights including the famous apes, and he came home laden with presents for us, especially for Roslyn, consisting of a toy dog, and a full rig out of pink satin pyjamas in mandarin style, with everything that went with them like slippers. She looked so cute in them, and he brought a lovely Spanish style basket for me, which held a lot, and was very handy as well as attractive.

During the summer, Robert's parents came to visit, as they were holidaying quite nearby, so we had a lovely time shopping in Shrewsbury. They had driven all the way from Scotland, which they liked doing at that time in their lives. We enjoyed going for drives to various parts of Shropshire during their week's holiday, which cheered me up. They returned home to Scotland, having enjoyed a very pleasant stay with us.

We always looked forward to paying regular visits to the town of Shrewsbury. It lay south of where we lived in Childs Ercall and nearer the Welsh border, and because of this position it gained great historical significance. Although our visits were mainly shopping trips by bus, I feel the town now deserves a write-up in 2013, as follows -

The town was recorded in the Domesday Book and it was after the Norman Conquest that Roger de Montgomery, a Norman Earl and powerful Kinsman to William the Conqueror was given Shrewsbury as his headquarters and he founded the Castle (1074) and the Abbey (1083). At that time the name of the town was 'Salopsbury' from which the name 'Salop' is thought to derive, and now 'Salop' is the shortened version of 'Shropshire'.

For the next two hundred years Shrewsbury was involved in wars with the Welsh, who made repeated, unsuccessful attempts to capture the town.

In 1403 the Battle of Shrewsbury was fought. Six thousand soldiers were killed in only three hours, making this one of the bloodiest battles in English history.

During the Tudor and Elizabethan periods there was significant trade in Welsh Wool and Flax. The powerful wool traders or Drapers built many of the magpie black and white mansions that still line the elegant streets of Shrewsbury to this day.

At the time of the Civil War, Shrewsbury supported the King. However the town fell to Parliament troops in 1645.

Despite the closeness of Ironbridge, the birthplace of the industrial revolution, Shrewsbury changed remarkably little until the Victorian era, when steam transformed Shrewsbury into a railway town. It was during this period that Charles Darwin was born and educated in Shrewsbury. The religious establishments of the day in Shrewsbury and the wider world, strongly objected to his "Theory of Evolution", but he is now considered to be one of Shrewsbury's favourite sons.

Chapter 12

Zoo!

During the summer, we managed to take a couple of coach trips to Manchester, one being to Belle Vue Zoo. A lot of the village children were on the coach with their parents, which was a pleasure for us to see them, and Roslyn took quite an interest in two of them who were sitting in their seats in front of us. They kept turning round and playing with their hands along the back of their seats, and Roslyn copied and touched their hands continuously, to which we took no notice as we were so pleased to see them being so friendly.

The journey to the Zoo was a pleasant one, and the children all seemed to love the animals. Unfortunately, a couple of days later, I noticed a mark below Roslyn's eye where she always used to rub with her finger. This was a habit she had developed, but because of this, the mark became a worry, the unsightly mark showing the skin was peeling away and getting dangerously close to the eye itself.

I took her to the cottage Hospital in Market Drayton, the dept now-a-days would probably be called the A and E, as I had been attending there a couple of months earlier with a broken rib which had been strapped up. I therefore felt comfortably familiar with the nursing staff there, and felt they could help me work out what was affecting the skin under her eye. They were not qualified, they said, to diagnose anything, so told me to go to the GP, which I did that day. The GP took one look at it and pronounced that it was nothing to worry about. I therefore went home but still worried about this mysterious affliction. How could it be 'nothing'? especially as it was travelling closer and close to her eye. I couldn't sleep for thinking about it. Where was it going to end? What would happen when it reached into her eye? Did this have a name? Yes, as it later turned out - Impetigo!!!

I took myself back to the A and E, and was treated quite badly when I tried to get them to take some action. I told them the Dr had said it was 'nothing' to which they replied 'well if he said it was nothing, it'll be nothing'. I said emphatically 'this is NOT NOTHING!' They could only tell me to go back to the GP.

I said the GP didn't open until 5pm, but the bus left Market Drayton for Childs Ercall at 5pm, and the Chemist would not be able to fill any prescription before that time and I would be stranded and not be able to get back home. Their reply to this was - 'Well if you love your daughter so much, why don't you get a taxi?' to which I replied 'I am the wife of a National Serviceman and can't afford £2 for a taxi!'

They did not seem to realise that a taxi would cost such a lot, and queried my reply, so I had to prove to them that my mother had had to pay over £2 for a taxi from Market Drayton to Childs Ercall a couple of weeks earlier. After all this arguing, late in the afternoon, someone scampered off to the phone. I was then instructed to go back to the GP who would see me a little earlier than 5pm, allowing me time to get to the Chemist for a prescription, and I hoped, to the bus which luckily stood outside the chemist shop, although I had no way of knowing that it would not leave on time at 5pm.

Hurrying along the road to the GP' s surgery, the Dr came into the office with only just enough time to fill out a prescription. I then had to hurry along the road to the Chemist's which was a reasonable distance away, pick up the prescription, and dash to the bus, fold up the pushchair, and settle us both into a seat.

The treatment was for Impetigo, although luckily, not the violet colour but a clear lotion. Why was life so difficult? Why so awkward? Why were people so unhelpful initially, only to reverse their attitude when all is revealed and proved to them? Why had it have to be proved anyway? And lastly, why was nobody prepared to apologise, or even to explain anything to me.

I was simply handed a prescription with no explanation whatsoever, except printed thereon was how many times a day to apply. I now feel that the other children of the village had already been treated for this highly infectious condition and it became very clear that Roslyn's condition was now easily diagnosed. All I wanted was to keep it away from her eye, so by relating this, I am not intent on describing skin conditions, but really talking about attitudes of 'officials' and 'professionals'. Whew! The condition cleared within days.......

Chapter 13

Packing

I started packing about six weeks prior to our leaving date, as I couldn't contain myself and having lots of unusable clothes now that it was summer, I found I could pack the winter's; in fact all the clothes of myself, Roslyn and Robert which would be too warm for summer use. These were sent off by Rail once I had the appropriate cases packed.

I later turned to the big pram, and packed it with contents which were now not in use, like the baby bath and other similar items. These were picked up by the British Rail transport, which in turn would go by train and initially be delivered to my parents' home, much to my mother's now growing excitement.

Next came the Baby Burco Boiler which had been a wonderful item for turning out spotlessly white nappies and towels. The toddling Roslyn soon got the message, and started helping me pack extra items into the boiler, whereas I kept my eye on each item she added. They were easily retrieved, except for one which I obviously missed. I just could not locate the small poker for the fire, and of course my mum found it with the other items back home in Scotland on receipt of the Burco.

Some world events that took place during our National Service in the two years 1956/58 were notable. Grace Kelly married Prince Ranier; Velcro was introduced; Elvis Presley became an actor in the film 'Love Me Tender', so his fame increased; Sputnik 1 launched by the Russians so Space Age truly started; Premium Bonds introduced; Stereo LP Records first sold; Average house prices were £2,170; Channel Tunnel first proposed; Christian Dior died.

As mentioned earlier in this narrative - here are the details of Caroline's birth -

Roslyn was two and a half years old. It was August 1959 and I was pregnant, with the baby due in October, but one morning, just before I was due to attend the ante natal clinic, my waters broke. This proved convenient, as the clinic would sort it out.......Well yes they did, by sending me by ambulance back home, to pick up my case which was meant to be ready packed for confinements as per the instructions in those days. Being August, Robert was on holiday and looking after Roslyn, so we quickly distracted her attention of my leaving by sitting her in the middle of my wedding dress which we had just unpacked from the 'confinement' case. This amazed her, being surrounded by white, so I kissed them both and off I went in the waiting ambulance to the lovely Airthrey Castle Maternity Hospital, situated in beautiful grounds at the foot of the Wallace Monument, overlooking the city of Stirling, and later part of the campus of Stirling University.

On arrival, I received the usual treatment, an examination, a bath and full preparation for imminent birth, not realising that it would take at least a further week. To my surprise, I found out they were giving me medication to prevent the birth from occurring, although it was sensibly stated by a Nursing Sister that if this baby is due to be born, nothing in this world would prevent it.

After what seemed a long week in the heat of this summertime, I went into labour in the early hours of the morning of 30th August, and showing the baby to be in the breech position, the nurses seemed to think they could deal with it themselves, without calling the resident gynaecologist on site. After much effort, they had to give in and send for the young doctor from upstairs, who took over with relish and aplomb. After successfully thrusting his hand into my uterus to secure first one leg, then the other, out, then the full body, at which point I blacked out, almost consciously during that moment, saying goodbye to Robert. However, this must have lasted only a few seconds, as when I came to, there was my lovely little baby, weighing only 3lbs 6ozs. At this stage she was taken straight away to the baby care unit along the corridor, where after six weeks of care, and weekly visits from us, she was ready to be taken home and join the family.

Chapter 14

Home!

We said our found farewells to Mrs. Herrick, our lovely landlady, early that morning, and off we went to the railway station, in Shrewsbury, via the bus.

We had the pleasure of not having to carry luggage, having sent it all off by separate Rail, so we just had the push chair, and a couple of small bags to deal with, making the journey so easy on our way home on this now familiar journey for the last time. It was a pleasant day, making the whole journey easy and smooth, ending up at Stirling Station where Robert's father picked us up in his van and drove us to our little house, where both pairs of grandparents had been preparing for our arrival, with good food and comfort as well as lots of happy banter and plans for Robert going back to work.

All attention on wee Roslyn as she for example, made her way towards the bedroom door. They were amazed that she knew it was bed time. They were also amazed that she didn't know what to do with sweeties, as she thought the Smarties they gave her were little buttons. All she had ever had was the 1p chocolate bar per day, after lunch. This soon changed with the meeting up with grandparents on a regular basis!

We were so very happy to be home, and it really was our idea of paradise. At last settled exactly where we had wished to be on arrival back from our honeymoon two years ago................

The End

Appendix I - RAF Yatesbury

In November of 1956, Robert was required to report to RAF Yatesbury, in Wiltshire. Looking up a map I established that it was some 16 miles south of Swindon on the A4 road, lying between Calne and Marlborough. Calne, I realised was a mere 4 miles west of the camp and the nearest town to the camp, for living-out purposes.

The airfield was first established in the First World War, when a small fleet of Avro 504s were used by the Royal Flying Corps and this was developed into a permanent camp in the interwar years, especially from 1936 onwards. RAF Yatesbury was then established and became well known to many airmen who served in the Second World War.

In WW2 it became the RAFs major centre for training airborne radio and radar operators and the base became No2 Radio School, which operated alongside the rather grand buildings of the flying school.

Before closure the camp was home to the Radar and Wireless training school and after closure in the 1960s the Radar and Wireless training school was transferred to RAF Locking.

The aircraft hangars and air strip, although now farmland can still be seen from the A4 and planning has been granted to convert the air base into residential flats. Due to the current economic climate, work has stopped on the conversion until the economy has improved.

When living out of camp in Swindon, on every working day, Robert was transported from Swindon to Yatesbury by camp bus, which wound its way south through the villages of Wroughton, Broad Hinton before turning westward at the Avebury Rings to proceed along the A4.

Appendix II - The History of RAF Shawbury

The station's association with flying goes back to June 1917, when Flying Training and the Aeroplane Repair Section of the Royal Flying Corps were established on the site of today's airfield. This closed in 1920 and the site was returned to its original agricultural use.

Shawbury, as a Flying Training School, was again activated in 1938 and by mid-1940 the Flying Training School was consolidating the training given by civilian instructors to prepare pilots for operational squadrons.

In 1942, now renamed as No 11 (Pilot) Advanced Flying Unit, the unit received its pilots for training from overseas bases - mainly in the USA.

In January 1944, Shawbury saw a major change of role and became the Central Navigation School (CNS), with the remit to improve the standard of practical air navigation and bombing accuracy. This role was extended to consider navigation as a science and to carry out research into world-wide navigation.

In February 1950, Shawbury became the School of Air Traffic Control. It retained its function as Central Navigation School and was renamed the Central Navigation and Control School.

When Robert was posted to RAF Shawbury in 1057, as an Air Radar Fitter, it was to service radar equipment and support the training given to Navigators and Traffic Controllers, Lincolns, Ansons, Vampires and Provosts were used for this training.

On 1 April 1997, RAF Shawbury changed its function, once again and is currently the Tri-Service Defence Helicopter Flying School.

AMERICANADIAN DIARIES

AMERICANADIAN DIARIES

Greenhorns Over the Pond

John Trueman

Also by John Trueman

Grass Roots

A season in the life and games of a Sunday League football team

Available as an e-book from Amazon

Grammar School Boys

The ups and (mainly) downs as life as a schoolboy in the 1960's

Available as a paperback and e-book from Amazon

Brains at the Airport

Highs and lows of moving to a remote Spanish village

Available as a paperback and e-book from Amazon

AMERICANADIAN DIARIES

First published by Amazon Kindle Direct Publishing at amazon.co.uk in January 2026

Copyright © J G Trueman 2026

All rights reserved. No part of this publication may be reproduced, stored in a retrieval system, or transmitted in any form or by any means, electronic, mechanical, photocopying, recording or otherwise without the prior permission of the author.

The events in this book are based on many hours of video, hundreds of still photographs and my ancient memory supported by my wife's excellent memory.

All events described are, therefore, probably a true and accurate record, more or less.

Some names have been changed to avoid embarrassment (the author's).

johnnytrueman@yahoo.com

AMERICANADIAN DIARIES

For those who helped nurture and share my love of all things American, especially;

- Rick Bowling who shared my passion and whose tales of the wild west encouraged my adventures.
- Roger Hughes and Mike Slater whose company made the visits to the great city of Dallas, Texas the highlight of my career at WH Smith.
- All the wonderful American and Canadian folk whose friendship and hospitality made each trip across the pond so special.
- Extra especially, my wife Sue, with whom I shared my adventures and was the best pardner a rootin' tootin' sun-of-a-gun cowboy could ever wish for.

AMERICANADIAN DIARIES

Chapter 1	The Pinehurst Kid
Chapter 2	Disney's Florida
Chapter 3	Dallas Texas
Chapter 4	New England
Chapter 5	The Appalachians
Chapter 6	The Rockies
Chapter 7	Colorado
Chapter 8	The South East
Chapter 9	The North West
Chapter 10	The Great Lakes
Chapter 11	New York New York
Chapter 12	Dixie

CHAPTER 1 – THE PINEHURST KID

In 1954, just nine years after the end of the Second World War, I was six years old and had never seen a cowboy, a cowgirl or a native American Indian. Although all the boys in our street in Pinehurst, a post-war council estate in Swindon, had played cowboys and Indians using sticks for guns and galloping around on make-believe horses, I had no real idea what a cowboy was, what they looked like, what they wore or what they did for a living except gallop and shoot ill-fated redskins, just because they had red skin. Sometimes I was one of the unfortunate Indians, copying the older boys by whooping loudly and dancing round in a circle before falling over dead, having been fatally shot with a stick. The good thing about being dead was that we could be immediately reincarnated as cowboys and were soon back in the saddle again. We learnt how to play the game mainly from Bob

AMERICANADIAN DIARIES

Mason, an older boy living in a house opposite to ours, who had seen cowboys and Indians at the Savoy cinema on Saturday mornings and became our coach in the rules of the game. This ensured that he was always the sheriff and, therefore, the last man standing, although the rest of us cowboys and Indians had little idea what a sheriff was.

At that time, I had never seen a television. I did not even know of its existence until my friend and neighbour Michael Millmore's family bought a tele and my sister Rae and I were invited to their house a few times to watch *The Cabin in the Clearing*. Michael, his elder brother David and I would sit together on their settee, enthralled by thirty minutes of high adventure on the American frontier, with a brave and compassionate cowboy family protecting their homestead from attacks by frightening, savage Injuns. Rae spent much of the time hiding behind the settee, particularly when the Indians attacked.

It was years later that I discovered that *The Cabin in the Clearing* was a British television series created by the BBC (there was only one channel in those days) and there were only five episodes made. The series was transmitted live, so unfortunately no episodes survive. I now wonder how stories of the American West created in a studio in Shepherds Bush, using British actors, half a century before convincing computer animation was even conceived, could convince us that we were in Ohio in nineteenth century America. Even the friendly Indian, Mul-Keep-Mo, was played by Ewen Solon, a New Zealand actor better known for his role as Sergeant Lucas, Maigret's right-hand man in another early TV series. But convinced I certainly was, such that American cowboys became a lifelong obsession.

The Christmas following our introduction to the Wild West, I made it clear that nothing but a cowboy outfit would do as my present from Father Christmas, although by this time Bob Mason and his brother Mick had convinced all the lads in the street that Santa did not exist. My older sister Rae had also seen through the subterfuge but we agreed that we should go along with the pretence anyway so that our parents would not be upset and we would still get presents. My demand was met and, on Christmas Day, I opened my packages at five o'clock in the morning and became the proud owner of a cowboy hat, a cowboy waistcoat, cowboy trousers and a cowboy gun with a cowboy holster and cowboy belt. Perhaps the Mason boys were wrong about Father Christmas after all. I could barely wait for daylight when I could go out to play and show off my new outfit to the boys in the street. With my hat tilted at a rakish angle and six-gun at the ready, I stepped out to shoot as many Indians as possible, safe in the knowledge that I would be the clean-cut, brave and handsome lawman, hired to clean up the mean streets of Pinehurst. I had privately labelled myself The Pinehurst Kid and thought that perhaps I could even take over as sheriff. I was somewhat surprised and disappointed when my friends Brian Mason, Mick and Johnny Paines and Michael Millmore produced large, coloured ray guns and announced that they were now spacemen who were out to kill as many Martians as possible before dinner, perhaps because the aliens had green skin. I refused to compromise and joined the game as the first ever space cowboy, fifteen years before the Steve Miller Band made the term famous, although I found killing invisible Martians much less satisfying than the ritual slaying of whooping Injuns.

My obsession continued throughout my childhood, although playing cowboys in the street gave way to football, cricket and tennis or hide-and-seek and knock-door-runaway. When my parents finally installed our own television, rented from Radio Rentals (which always confused me as it was not a radio,) I would watch each and every cowboy programme transmitted into our sitting room. There were plenty of them as, it seemed to me, by this time the whole country had followed my lead and was obsessed by Western culture. I watched *The Big Valley, Bonanza, Cheyenne, The Cisco Kid, Gunsmoke, The Lone Ranger, Rawhide, The Virginian,* and *Wagon Train,* transported away from dreary old England to the young and exciting frontier towns of the emerging United States of America. My limited pocket money was spent on cowboy comics romanticising the exhilarating adventures of baddies like Billy the Kid and Jesse James, or goodies like Kit Carson, Roy Rogers and Tom Mix. There were other publications with intriguing titles such as *Straight Arrow, Blazing Six-guns* and *Ghost Ride,* but the ones that fascinated me the most were the exploits of anyone called "Kid." I discovered Kid Cody, Kid Colt and Kid Cowboy alongside Rawhide Kid, Ringo Kid, Cheyenne Kid, Oklahoma Kid, Western Kid and Two Gun Kid. As a rough, tough, son-of-a-gun who took no lip from no-one, I briefly considered formally changing my name to the Pinehurst Kid, but thought that my mum would tell me off.

As I grew (slowly in my case), my obsession waned a little but I retained my interest in all things American. I still enjoyed Westerns, but had now included gangster programmes in my must-see list. The first and best to grab my attention was *The Untouchables*. The American-produced series which focused on the real-life squad of Prohibition agents employed by the United States Department of Justice and led by Eliot Ness, played by the incomparable Robert Stack, to bring down the bootleg empire of Al "Scarface" Capone. Capone appeared in only a few episodes but was played by the brilliant Neville Brand, who was also my favourite, and probably the best ever, western baddie. I watched every episode – the only programme guaranteed to make me stay home, even taking precedence over my new-found hobby of hanging around the local off-licence and smoking Bristol cigarettes.

It was here that one or two of my smoking *amigos* brought their transistor radios and we would listen to the latest pop music hits crackling on Radio Luxemburg as we puffed away. In our house, the wireless was non-stop Light Programme, which also played pop music, whilst other friends' houses were furnished with radiograms playing not only wireless programmes, but singles (45s), extended play (EPs) or long-playing (LPs) records. This was the time that British pop was taking over the world with the Beatles, the Rolling Stones and The Who, but I was always drawn to songs by American artists, not only those that everyone else listened to, Elvis Presley, the Beach Boys and the Everly brothers, but lesser-known, or at least, less popular singers: Connie Francis, Skeeter Davis, Marty Robins, Hank Williams and, best of all, Patsy Cline. I still get goosebumps when I hear Patsy sing *Crazy* or *I Fall to Pieces*. In addition to these artists and their songs, I was particularly struck by songs with American place names which made them sound exotic and glamorous. I longed to be twenty-four hours from Tulsa, catch the midnight train to Georgia or the last train to Clarksville. This did nothing to assist my assumed personality as a cool, streetwise mod, so my infatuation was kept well hidden. Whilst my mod compatriots were constantly listening to the British blues-rooted bands like the Yardbirds and the Small Faces, and experimenting with American Blues artists like Sonny Boy Williamson and Howling Wolf, I was secretly sneaking into Duck, Son and Pinker in Swindon on Saturday mornings, searching out LPs by country artists. I continued to expand my music knowledge by listening to Johnny Cash, Tammy Wynette, Loretta Lynn and George Jones. It was just a great pity that I had no-one to share my infatuation.

CHAPTER 2 – DISNEY'S FLORIDA

I was determined that one day I would go to the USA to visit cowboy towns, gangster cities and the many places mentioned in my country music playlist, but my plans were postponed by more important things, working long hours to support a very happy marriage and provide for my wife and two great sons. The first trip that I made *over the pond* did nothing to assuage my ambitions stateside, but did little to satisfy them either. When my two sons became teenagers, Sue and I booked the almost obligatory trip to Disney in Florida. Disney World Resort was, at that time, almost a rite of passage for families, replacing Butlins or the Spanish Costas as the *go-to* holiday destination. My memories of the package trip are vague, but Sue kept a daily diary of events, so I do know that we spent a week in Orlanda followed by a week in St Petersburg. Although the diary and accompanying photographs bring back some happy memories, I recall many minor incidents which were not recorded. I remember staying in the Orlando Marriott on International Drive, which reminded me of the many inexpensive hotels I had stayed in when travelling for work in Blighty. Quite what I expected in America, I do not know but it was not the ugly square box with noisy plumbing that we found when we arrived. We could just as easily been in a Holiday Inn on a ring road around Bristol or Birmingham. That said, it was clean and comfortable with surprisingly large beds, but just did not seem "American" enough to satisfy my expectations. That week we visited the Epcot Center, Wet'n'Wild, Magic Kingdom, Universal Studios and Typhoon Lagoon. We dined at the Country Kitchen, America, Carmente's Italian, Dunkin' Donuts, The Punjab Indian Restaurant, the Western Steer and the inevitable MacDonalds. All the theme parks and restaurants are now blurred into one confused memory of queues, rides, water slides, chicken and fries and being totally knackered.

I was relieved that we had booked the following week in the quieter resort of St Pete's (I had by now adapted to the American vernacular) in the Radisson Suites. Although still international, this hotel seemed somehow more American and was certainly more peaceful, promising a week of rest and recuperation. Although the journey took us from east to west across Florida, the agreeable drive on the Interstate Highway Interstate–4 took less than two hours. We drove through delightfully named places: Oak Ridge, Lake Buena Vista, Celebration, Championsgate and Plant City before reaching Tampa and crossing the Courtney Campbell Causeway over Old Tampa Bay and finally heading south to St. Pete's. Much of the time driving, I spent debating whether or not the road should be renamed Intrastate Highway, as Interstate suggested that it ran from one state to another, not within one state. My hypothesis was ignored by Sue and the boys who unsurprisingly deemed it unimportant, although I was not convinced. We also passed a couple of signs emblazoned with the word *Subway*, which caused some consternation as I explained to my family that an American subway equates to an English underground system, but I was unable to explain why a motorway exit near the small and remote settlement of Plant City would have an underground station. Sue and the boys were not interested anyway.

Having thoroughly enjoyed the drive and settled into the Radisson Suites Resort on Sand Key, I finally began to feel that I was in America. I accept that it was a holiday resort and not Dodge City or Chicago, so I would not get to see cowboys drinking shots of redeye in a saloon or gangsters blasting each other away with machine guns, but this felt somehow more real, at least as real as an American visitor to England would feel that a week in Weymouth opened up the real Britain. Despite one more visit to a theme park at Busch Gardens and thunderstorms at three o'clock every afternoon, the week went well. Busch Gardens was a disappointment, possibly because we were theme-parked-out and because number one son Billy was travel sick on the drive there, exacerbated by being thrown about on the first roller coaster ride, so I had to accompany number two son Daniel on all the future rides. This was not my idea of an enjoyable time but seeing Dan's face light up with pleasure was worth it, particularly as Sue was nursing Billy whose face was not particularly lit up as he vomited in the park gardens.

That apart, we lazed around the pool, strolled along the silver sands of Sand Key beach collecting large, unidentified shells, ambled along John Pass Boardwalk and shopped at the Countryside Mall. Each afternoon we sheltered from the inevitable storm. The boys went snorkelling despite a sign warning them to *Beware Stingrays,* as Sue and I watched and relaxed. We went birdwatching to see pelicans, storks, herons and other unidentified waterfowl. We also enjoyed mammal spotting, identifying armadillos, porcupines and raccoons, albeit they were all squashed flat on the highway. We included one more trip, to the Dali Museum in St Pete's to add just a little culture to our visit. This was a memorable and unforgettable experience, except that I can remember nothing about it. Our last day was, however, memorable because we were confined to barracks when *"Beryl, the second tropical storm of the season, raked Florida's coast with rain and winds up to 50 mph..."* according to the St. Petersburg Times (We kept a copy of the front page). We stayed in our room and, whilst Sue set about packing for our return home, the boys and I watched rubbish, particularly banal advertisements, on American television and discussed the week's highlights, which seemed to consist mainly of visits to the China Sea Chinese restaurant, Cha Cha Coconuts restaurant, Adam's Rib restaurant, JD's Steak restaurant and The Hungry Fisherman restaurant at Indian Rocks.

The trip introduced me to some of the strange habits and customs of our trans-Atlantic cousins. We were at breakfast one morning at the Country Kitchen and ordered a coffee for our eldest son. When the waitress delivered the drinks, she looked appalled that the coffee we ordered was for our tall, slim, fifteen-year-old and, although she never said anything, her expression of disgust was apparent. A family on the next table noticed the indiscretion and looked at us with a mixture of disgust and disbelief. The fact their own two fat lumps of children were washing down a mountain of pancakes and syrup by glugging pints of sugary, caffeinated cola seemed to pass them by. And why have the words "please" and "thankyou" been eliminated from the vocabulary of the great American public? In bars and restaurants, you hear, "Bring me a steak," or "Give me beer," without ever including the courtesy words so essential to the British. When the steak or beers arrive, no word is spoken. No thanks are offered, yet this is not considered rude. I wondered when this basic politeness was abandoned. And, talking of drinks, I was amazed to see everyone walking around with cardboard cups of coffee. If they fancy a beverage, I opined, why do they not stop and sit down and drink in a civilised manner? What is so important in their lives that have to drink on the go? I said to Sue, "Thank goodness that appalling habit will never happen in England." Little did I know.

The idea of queuing is another stranger to our hosts. As we queued patiently for the rides at the theme parks, sometimes for half an hour, we found that a family group would push its way past to join Auntie or Grandma who had been queuing on behalf of the whole family. In such instances, I showed my displeasure by giving Grandma a stern look.

Despite the odd natives, we were all enamoured by our first visit to America and vowed that we would take more trips there but, for reasons lost in the mists of time, we never took the boys again and it was another five years before Sue and I restarted our travels of discovery to the New World.

CHAPTER 3 – DALLAS TEXAS

In my work role as a Project Manager for WH Smith, I was responsible for the implementation of all new computer systems for the Logistics Division, and it was proposed that a new Warehouse Management Computer System was required. After a thorough and detailed research period, the management team decided that that the most beneficial and appropriate system was provided by a software company based in Dallas, Texas and rather unimaginatively called Dallas Systems Corporation or DSC. Having made the decision, the necessary legal agreements were signed and sealed and the project began in earnest. The Project Director was my boss at the time, Roger Hughes, who took overall control of the implementation, with our colleague Mike Slater managing the resulting changes within the Distribution Centre operation. We made a formidable team, with Roger a fine strategist, using his networking skills to recognise and propose forward thinking objectives and Mike was an admired and respected Industrial Engineer who brought a deep understanding of warehousing and logistics to the team. My responsibilities were the implementation and integration of the IT systems within the existing Logistics systems. It all sounds rather technical and boring, but I was in my element and treated the whole thing as a sort of challenging cryptic crossword, carefully examining the issues and problems as clues, until problems were uncovered, answers were found and the crossword completed. And using the clever IT technicians to resolve the more complicated issues.

Roger, Mike and I travelled to Dallas in the early days of the project, accompanied by Dave Grange representing the WH Smith IT division, where we spent tiring days at the software company's head office on a dull business park, attending continual meetings, presentations and informal discussions about the Distribution Centre Management and Control System. It was just about as thrilling as that sounds. I remember almost nothing of the plethora of meetings, but I do remember staying at the Bristol Suites, a large and impressive hotel in downtown Dallas, although quite what *downtown* meant, I never fully grasped. I remember that each huge suite contained huge bedroom with a huge bed, a huge bathroom and a kitchen, not that the latter was ever used. There was also a large television with fifty-seven channels and nothing on, nothing worthwhile that is until we discovered the pornographic movie channel. This was a pay-to-view channel which offered ten minutes free viewing before the film cut out and payment was requested. Roger, Mike, Dave and I soon realised that we could watch ten free minutes in one room before dashing to the next room for the following ten minutes and quickly moving on again to see another ten minutes in the last room. As the films seldom lasted more than 40 minutes, we therefore managed to see a full porno for nothing. The slight embarrassment was that all rooms were on balconies overlooking the hotel's impressive lobby and reception, such that the receptionists and arriving or departing guests could see the four giggling Englishman scurrying from one room to another. We gave up our little game after just one film to save further embarrassment.

The week also introduced me to some more American eccentricities, especially concerning the Texan appetite. Taking a well-earned lunch break from scrutinising goods-in, picking, stock-taking and despatch software, we strolled to small diner on the business park. The menu was displayed on a large board and left me somewhat confused with chicken fried steak (was this fowl or beef?), cornbread and pinto beans (I guessed that this was not Heinz beans on toast), enchiladas, buttermilk biscuits, brisket sandwich and other foods, the contents of which were a mystery to me. I guess that Mike and Roger were equally confused as we all plumped for something we recognised: a good, old-fashioned burger. I was first to order and the short, very stocky lady behind the counter asked, with a long, slow Texan drawl, "Dy'all want everthin' on it?"

As I had no idea what "everthin" consisted of, I simply nodded and quietly responded, "Yes please." The lady proceeded to fill the burger bun with a variety of "everthin," slaw, which I later found out was coleslaw, cheese that looked like sheets of plastic, and tasted like it, jalapenos, onions, pickle, tomato, lettuce, and other unidentified bits and pieces. As she handed me the creation over the counter, she was forced to hold the top half of the bun in place to stop the whole thing toppling over. I carefully carried my meal to the table, gently holding it together until joined by my English and American comrades. I was somewhat worried that the burger was so unstable and wondered what the Texan etiquette was in eating such a monster, particularly as no cutlery was available. In the end, I decided that I should compress the megalith by pressing both bun halves together and try to bite into it. All went well with the compression but the bite caused most of the fillings to shoot out across the table, leaving me holding two sorry-looking burger halves. As I reached forward and scraped the previous contents of my lunch across the table towards me, no-one said a word, our Texan host simply continuing his monologue on the virtues of automated warehouse put-away.

Our introductory week to Texas was challenging work with little time for play, but this was to change dramatically with for future visits. Each September DSC held a User Conference in the Bristol Suites, entertaining clients from across the USA and Europe. The European contingent included guests from a retailer in Belgium and from the United Kingdom representatives from Tesco, John Lewis and, surprisingly, the Royal Air Force. The conference began with a welcome reception on Sunday evening and finished at close of play on the flowing Thursday. After some constructive accounting, considering flight fares, hotel costs and benefits of the trip, Roger worked out that it was cheaper to travel from Saturday to Saturday, hence we had Saturday evening and Sunday to prepare for the next week's travails and the following Friday to review and consolidate what we had learnt at the conference. The fact that the preparation and consolidation took place on the golf course, in shopping malls, in local bars and relaxing restaurants was purely coincidental. Roger, Mike and I made up the team from WH Smith at the conferences for the next three years and my memory of the conferences blur into one, but I can clearly remember a number of incidents which took place during this period.

The opening reception was a boozy affair as old acquaintances were renewed and new relationships cemented over bottles of Budweiser, before a meal and retirement to the bar for more beers. In our first visit, the hotel had prepared a handsomely decorated table of various flowers and fruits, impressively and artistically displayed in the reception area. Although very slim and fit, Mike was known for his somewhat voracious appetite and, during the general milieu of introductions, hand-shaking and small talk, he was quietly nibbling fruit from the display to satisfy his hunger. No-one really noticed until an embarrassed waiter tapped him on the shoulder and said, none too quietly, "Excuse me, Sir, but you are eating the table decoration." It was decided that perhaps the introductory sessions had run its race and we should all head to the dining room and eat

As preparation on the Sunday after our arrival, Roger joined other delegates and DSC staff in a round of golf. Mike and I had no interest in the game, so we hired a car and drove out of Dallas with no particular place to go. We headed north out of the city, but exactly, or even approximately where we drove, I have no idea. I do remember that I felt incredibly relaxed and content, pottering through small-town Texas with good company and a feeling of excitement and gentle exhilaration that I had rarely experienced before. I also remember stopping at a street market somewhere along the drive and Mike and I were both fascinated to see second-hand guns openly on sale, but I resisted the opportunity to resurrect the Pinehurst Kid and purchase a Colt 45. Mike could not resist buying a pair of small round-lensed sunglasses which he proudly donned and strode amongst the stalls looking like John Lennon without the fringe.

Near Lake Ray Roberts, we stopped in a small town called Tioga, Texas and, unsurprisingly, Mike was hungry. Tioga in Grayson County is little more than a village, with a population of less than a thousand and has the feeling of an old and somewhat run-down cowboy town. I loved it. We stopped in Gene Autry

AMERICANADIAN DIARIES

Drive (I was thrilled to find out later that Tioga Texas was the birthplace of the Singing Cowboy) and called in to Clark's Outpost Restaurant and Club for lunch. It was like walking into a western saloon/diner after long cattle drive as we entered, shaking off the dust from the drive and selecting our table as the other customers looked away, obviously unnerved by the two tough desperados. We strode menacingly across the saloon and sat at a table, aware that the local sheriff was probably on his way to take our six-guns and throw us in the town lockup. The wooden floor was covered in sawdust, and large hams hung from the ceiling beams, complementing the rough western atmosphere. Our cover was blown as we sat at the gingham-covered table beneath a wall covered with photographs of cowboys, horses and cattle and were immediately baffled by the menu. We were too embarrassed to ask about brisket queso, loaded brisket tots and calf fries, so quietly and politely settled for smoked meat sandwiches. I avoided asking for *Everthin' on it*, but again the burger roll was stacked with different meats and a stood good six inches high. Even Mike struggled to finish the snack and we were starting to understand why there are so many fat Texans and wondered what they would make of a delicate British sandwich cut into triangular quarters with the crusts removed.

The following conferences passed in a fog of presentations, workshops and discussions followed by evenings of over-indulgence at the hotel bar or excursions arranged by our hosts. I am unsure on which of the conferences the following incidents took place, but remember each occurrence with great clarity. There was one free afternoon when all delegates decamped to a local gymnasium and indulged in what I thought to be pointless exercises. Mike was thrashing all-comers on the squash court, Roger was enthusiastically using all the gym equipment and I was mooching around talking to any like-minded souls who found rowing a machine on dry land somewhat pointless. Roger then called me over to a running machine and encouraged me to try the piece of equipment and, as he was the boss, I felt duty-bound to accept his invitation. The machine was supervised by an attractive young lady who smiled sweetly as I climbed on to the treadmill, holding on tightly to handles at the front. I smiled back and said, "I can really feel this doing me some good."

"Sir," she said, "You don't seem to understand. You haven't switched it on yet." I nodded politely, switched the machine on and remained still as the treadmill belt carried me backwards, where I stepped off at the rear. I grinned happily and said, "Now I see. Can I start again?"

The poor lass looked at Roger, then looked at me with an air of total bewilderment and said, "No sir, you still don't understand. It's a running machine. You have to run on the machine." I thanked her and was tempted to run on the belt without switching it on, but resisted and managed a minute or two of using the equipment correctly. She looked very relieved and quite proud that she had educated this simple Englishman in the use of a piece of gym equipment.

It was not the only situation where a native Texan failed to appreciate my attempts at humour. One evening, an outing had been arranged to the Million Dollar Saloon, a *Gentlemen's club* on Greenville Avenue, Dallas and something of a revelation to the innocents abroad. We entered the dimly lit hall and sat at a table before ordering beer. As our eyes adjusted to the gloom, it became apparent that the waitresses had forgotten to dress properly and were wearing just a bra and skimpy shorts, but with very high-heeled shoes. I remarked to Mike that they'll catch their death if they don't put their jumpers on. I then noticed that there were two or three ladies shining boots for customers. The men were seated, looking down as the very large-breasted shoe-shine girls polished and buffed so rigorously that it was a wonder that their big bouncing bosoms managed to stay within the confines of their tiny bras. Every minute or so there was an announcement over the PA system which said, "In ten minutes, it's showtime," "In Five minutes, it's showtime" "In two minutes, it's showtime," and finally, "It's showtime." The announcement was greeted with loud cheers from the clientele and, out of nowhere, attractive young ladies appeared and were called over by some customers to dance on their tables. They were naked except for a minuscule G-string. Every so often a customer signalled to the dancer on the table, who would bend and speak to the man. He would then tuck paper money in her G-string. I never understood why or heard what was said, but the most popular dancers, generally those with the biggest breasts, had a great amount of money tucked in to the belt which then looked like a mini skirt of dollar bills. After an hour or so, and a few more beers, I became bored. When the next "Showtime" was in full swing, I nudged Roger and Mike and said, "Watch this." I crossed the hall to where a small Latino cleaning lady, dressed in T-shirt, jeans and basketball boots was standing on a side table and polishing the mirrored wall. I caught her attention and said, "You're doing a great job," before flamboyantly tucking a five-dollar bill into her basketball boot. I turned to accept the applause of my colleagues but they were too busy watching the topless dancers to notice. Two large men in evening dress did notice however, and caught me by the arms before escorting me to the exit, where I was told that I was not welcome. I refrained from criticising their lack of a sense of humour and took a taxi which was waiting outside back to the hotel. I had a long chat with the driver, a pleasant black man, about racism and was surprised when told me that Texas was a very racist state. I had seen no racism during my visits there, but then, he was the first black man I had talked to. I was able to get back to the Bristol Suites and enjoy a quiet beer or several in the hotel bar, which was much more to my liking.

On 22 November 1963, President Kennedy arrived at Love Field airport in Dallas before his fatal motorcade drive and assassination. There is a famous piece of film of him *deboarding* the plane with his wife Jackie, which I had seen many times on television and I was excited when we were offered the chance to visit Love field. The drawback to the visit was that we were to be given a flying lesson in a small, single engine plane. I am not an adrenaline junkie and suffer badly from motion sickness, so prefer to keep my feet firmly on the ground, but was railroaded into taking the flight. As we sped along the runway and the instructor pulled back on his joystick, I wondered how the hell I had allowed myself to get in the hair-raising position, but once in the air I took over the controls and found it surprisingly pleasant as we soared and circled over the Texas countryside, with the skyscrapers of the city emerging in the distance. It fleetingly made me wonder why so many huge buildings were crammed into one small downtown area when there is so much free land around the city, but I was concentrating hard on keeping the plane steady so the thought quickly passed. On making a smooth touchdown, I felt very pleased with myself, but had an inkling that the pilot may have helped me a little with the landing.

Of the many memorable moments on the trips, one sticks in my mind. The Dallas College American football team was playing the college team from Oklahoma City, Oklahoma. This was apparently an annual fixture of fierce rivalry and, although the two towns were over 200 miles distant, considered a local derby, locally known as the Red River Shootout, the Red River

Rivalry, or the Red River Showdown. In English terms it is perhaps like Manchester United versus Liverpool (The M62 Shootout or the Ship Canal Showdown?) Roger, Mike and I had chosen a quiet evening in Benihana, a Japanese restaurant near the hotel. We were aware of the game and that there were some rowdy guests milling around the hotel, but having attended football matches between Swindon Town and Reading Football Clubs, we were not worried about a few college students from Oklahoma. In the early hours of the morning, I was awoken by the piercing scream of the fire alarm in my room, followed by the sound of people in the corridor outside and shouts that we must leave our rooms immediately. The electricity was not working so, in darkness, I dragged on a t-shirt and jeans, found my trainers under the bed and scurried out to join the throng of guests. We were directed to the fire escape and out into the car park via the back stairs. Roger and I found each other and he was similarly attired in the first clothes he managed to find in the darkness, as was everyone else. Mike was nowhere to be seen. The general hubbub of voices as guests were reunited and greeted each other whilst asking what was happening suddenly ceased and we looked at the fire escape door to see Mike immaculately dressed in pyjamas underneath a smart dressing gown, wearing tidy slippers and clutching a small leather toilet bag. The scruffy t-shirted assembly stared in amazement at Gentleman Mike until we explained, "He's English," when the crowd nodded in understanding and continued their excited chattering. After perhaps half an hour, we were allowed back into our rooms and told that it was a fire alarm set off by some excited Oklahoma supporters as a prank.

One particular visit to User Conference, we were accompanied by our senior manager, Geoff Skillen, who either wanted to check that our attendances were not simply *jollies* or perhaps because he fancied a jolly for himself. Geoff could best be described a rough diamond, a hard man who had climbed through the ranks in WH Smith to achieve his high status and, despite his well-deserved success, had never lost his tough persona. The Saturday evening that we arrived, we were invited out by the director of the British arm of the software company and settled in a pleasant restaurant downtown. We ordered our food and the waiter, a spotty but pleasant young man, took the order and told us that, "Your starters'll be cruisin' on in," which we found an amusing colloquialism. Along with food, we ordered a dozen bottles of beer which arrived first, and were left in an ice bucket by the side of the table. No glasses were delivered so, when the waiter cruised on in with our starters, he was asked for glasses. He looked surprised and explained that this was not usual as beer is usually consumed straight form the bottle. Geoff was less than impressed and told the waiter, "I've just been out the back and seen a dog pissing all over the beer crates, so get us some glasses." The glasses were duly delivered. I remained surprised that, even in the smartest of restaurants we visited, beer was often consumed straight from the bottle.

We were invited out for a meal with our Texan hosts one evening, and were entertained in a large, up-market steak house. Our American host ordered a large T-bone steak (with no "please.") On being politely asked how he would like the steak, he replied, "Just take off the horns, wipe its ass and bring it on in." I resisted the temptation to use this reply at our local Berni Inn in Swindon.

One of our regular visits made by Roger, Mike and me during our educational visits to Texas was to Fort Worth, the historic twin city of Dallas. It was the centre of the longhorn cattle trade and part of the famous Chisholm trail, a route taken by cattle drives which was the origin of the cowboy legend. Its old town is now a historic site trading on its western history. It is a cross between a theme park and a film set but I loved it. We soaked up the cowboy atmosphere, strolling along Main Street, Rodeo Plaza and Mule Alley and stopping for a beer in the White Elephant Saloon. On one occasion we visited Leddy's Boots and Saddles a famous store renowned for its cowboy accessories. While we were browsing the cowboy boots with no intention of buying, a very helpful assistant approached and recommended certain boots but, as they would have looked ridiculous on my portly five feet six frame, I politely rejected each suggestion. After several rejections, she grabbed a pair of boots and forced one into my hands, saying, "These are perfect for you, sir, they are made of kangaroo hide."

As I studied the boot, I started to gently to toss it into the air, catch it then toss it again. "I see," I said, "I can tell that they're kangaroo."

Her demeanour changed somewhat as grabbed the boot and said, "Sir, you are not a serious customer. Kindly leave my store." I left, hanging my head in shame, although by now getting accustomed to being thrown out of places in Texas.

The year of Geoff's visit coincided with the Fort Worth Pioneer Days celebration, described as *A festival commemorating Fort Worth's early pioneer and cattle rancher heritage with country music, rodeos, and Wild West shows.* On our day off, we took the short drive to Fort Worth to soak up some Western culture. Most of the attractions took place later in the day and throughout the following week, but we were able to wander round in the sparsely attended event and enjoy the cowboy atmosphere. My main memory of that visit was Geoff deciding that we needed a drink and approached one of the many beer stalls and ordered, "Four Togo beers, please."

The young man in the booth looked confused and said, "Beg pardon, sir."

Geoff repeated his order, "Four Togo beers," and pointed to the large sign advertising, "BEERS TO GO." The confused server poured four beers, but still failed to understand where the "Togo," request came from. Visits to the Pioneer Days celebration became an essential part of future visits to Dallas.

Another coincidental attraction taking place at the same time as the Dallas User Conference was the Texas State Fair, an event similar to an English country fair but, as it was American, particularly Texan, much larger and more brash. We decided to visit the event one year (I forget which) but again our visit coincided with the fair's quiet time, and nothing much was happening. I remember just two incidents. The first was wandering around the collection of longhorn cattle where one particularly impressive beast was accompanied in the pen by a man whom I assumed to be its owner. He was a huge fellow and it was a fair contest who weighed more, the bull or the owner. As he (the owner) proudly sat on a bale of hay, his huge frame squeezed into faded dungarees and topped by a red face the size and shape of a basketball, I estimated his weight to be at least thirty stone. I was amused to see that he was holding on to a can of Diet Coke. I was very tempted to take a photograph of the spectacle but thought it better not to annoy him. I now greatly regret that decision.

One stall at the fair was selling t-shirts emblazoned with the words *TEXAS STATE FAIR*, and I thought it an ideal present to take home for my boys. I approached the stall holder, a gawky teenager and one of the few black people I had seen there, and asked for two T-shirts. He asked, "Say, where are y'all from?"

I replied that I was from England and just visiting the great state of Texas. He smiled a broad grin and said, "I have a brother in the army and he's in Germany, England. His name's Dwayne, do you know him?"

I apologised and explained that I had never met Dwayne. The lad looked very disappointed.

The hosts' preoccupation with having a fitness programme during the conference moved on from a local gymnasium and another year took place at the Texas Stadium, then home to the Dallas Cowboys American Football team. All delegates and Dallas Systems employees were bussed to Irving, a suburb in west Dallas and we were shown into the changing rooms to prepare for our day's exercise. The American contingent was excited that they were using the same changing space as used by the Dallas Cowboys and were particularly in awe of the names above each changing space. They all seemed to be deliberately avoiding one space labelled *TROY AIKMAN*, which meant nothing to me, so I sat my arse on his seat and began to change. I was later told that Troy Aikman was the greatest football player that ever played for the Cowboys and I had invaded his hallowed shrine. I pointed out that I had once used the same changing room as Tony Hicks at Penhill Recreation Ground, and he had once played in goal for Swindon Town. The Americans nodded in confused acceptance of my boast. We then went on to the pitch and played silly games which I did my best to avoid and was pleased that Geoff was of like mind and we sat in the stand, enjoying the chance to relax while waiting for the boys to stop playing.

WH Smith had, at that time, opened a number of stores in the USA and the head office and distribution centre was situated in Philadelphia, Pennsylvania. Geoff had arranged a visit there when the conference was ended and the contingent, with the excuse that a new WHS attendee, John Burton, who had taken over from Mike as the Chief Industrial Engineer on Mike's promotion, could review their distribution process and, perhaps, offer his advice and share his experience on the operation. We flew from Dallas, hired a car and all made a visit to the Company Head Office. It was apparent to me that our visit was not received with any great enthusiasm and the American operators looked on us with some suspicion, not wanting any interference from the parent UK company. We left the strained meeting and drove to the pre-booked hotel, before meeting up again that evening and being taken for dinner at a typical American restaurant, the meal consisting of beer, steak and more beer. The following day, I volunteered to take Burton back to the Warehouse to complete his investigations, leaving Geoff, Roger, Mike and me free for the day. We drove into the centre of Philadelphia and made the obligatory visit to the Independence National Historical Park, including Independence Hall where the Declaration of Independence was drafted and signed. It was an interesting tour of the surprisingly small building, reminding me somewhat of Swindon's Town Hall. After the tour guide thanked his audience for our interest and explained that this was the first tour he had given and, as we filed out, waited with his hand out for a tip. I thought it odd as he was a middle-aged chap who seemed to have the presentation *off pat* and anything but a *rookie,* so I didn't tip him. On leaving the hall, we passed the small building which housed the famous Liberty Bell and intended to pay the entrance fee to see the iconic piece of American history, but there was a very long queue, so we went for a beer instead.

That evening, we met up in the hotel restaurant for a last supper before flying home the next day. We discussed the visit, what we had learnt (not much) and what advice Burton had offered to our hosts (not much) and ate a fine meal (much too much.) Geoff asked for the bill and paid with his credit card before we retired to the bar for a final beer. After two or three minutes, the hotel manager approached our table and explained that the waitress was in tears and was worried that she had done something wrong and asked why we had committed the cardinal sin of not leaving a tip. Geoff politely apologised and explained that he had simply signed the credit card slip and not noticed that there was space to be completed for the gratuity. He, of course, rectified the omission and gave a larger tip than was necessary and I learnt a valuable lesson for all future trips to the Americas - tipping is not discretionary.

Texas Stadium was not our only visit to a Sports arena. One year, we were invited to a ball game at Globe Life Field in Arlington Texas near Fort Worth. The game was between Texas Rangers and New York Yankees and I had little idea of what was happening, but was captivated by the atmosphere of the event. I never realised that a game of rounders could be so exciting. This fixture was apparently an old and fierce rivalry for reasons that escaped me, but we were seated near a group of rednecks who were very vociferous in their dislike of "Damn Yankees," and many stronger epithets. I was again reminded of the rivalry displayed between Manchester United and Liverpool supporters. One very civilised part of the proceedings was that in the aisles between seats there was a constant stream of beer sellers. When a supporter of either team wanted a beer, they would pass their money along the row to the seller who would give the beer to the closest person and the beer was passed along the line to the drinker, and not a drop was spilt. I couldn't see this happening on Liverpool's Kop or Manchester's Stretford End.

Another confusing interlude was that, between innings, large electronic screens around the stadium showed a pair of dice rolling, before stopping and displaying its two numbers. Whenever they stopped, sections of the crowd would erupt in loud cheers. I never understood why, but joined in the cheering, nonetheless. What with the beer, the dice and the general atmosphere, it was a memorable experience, except for the score which I do not remember or perhaps I never understood in the first place.

On another of our visits, Roger had persuaded the Logistics Divisional Director, Colin Warwick, to give the keynote speech at the conference. The DSC management were enthusiastic about the opportunity to have a distinguished speaker who was able to present a worldwide perspective on the future of logistics in the 21st century. Geoff was keen to attend another conference and thought it beneficial to invite the young Warehouse Manager, Charlie Jenkinson, along for the experience. Burton was again invited to attend bringing the total of WH Smith delegates to six. To satisfy Company regulations, the party had to be split when travelling, so that the whole management team would not be killed in the event of a plane crash. On this happy note, I was selected to travel with Colin while the other four travelled together. Colin's wife Freda had also been invited, so we three set off from Colin's home one morning with plans to meet the rest of the party in Dallas. I was very happy with this arrangement because, travelling with a director, we were booked into business class seats on the plane. Freda was a heavy smoker, so she and Colin assumed seats in the smoking section and I sat a few rows in front. As I sat luxuriating in the large comfortable seats, several DSC staff from the English office passed me in the aisle, heading for *cattle* class. I smiled smugly as they passed and perfected a royal-style wave in greeting. They glowered.

I was always in awe of Colin: tall, smart, intelligent, worldly-wise and well-spoken, all the things I was not, but on arrival at Dallas Fort Worth Airport I saw his more human side. After collecting our luggage, Colin asked, "What do we do now?"

I was a little surprised, but replied, "We just get a taxi to the hotel."

"Taxi. Right," Colin stated emphatically and strode off towards the door. The wrong door. As he left us, I said to Freda. "Er, he's going the wrong way. The taxi rank is over there," pointing in the opposite direction to Colin's target."

"That's OK," Freda replied, "He always does this sort of thing, he'll be back." We waited for a couple of minutes and a flustered Colin returned, saying, "I can't find a taxi."

I politely and somewhat sheepishly replied, "No Colin, they're over there, by the big sign that says *Taxis*."

"Right," he responded and marched off towards the correct door.

As we were in the taxi, the driver, quite understandably I thought, asked where we were going. "I've no idea," Colin stated seemingly surprised at the question. "John, where are going?" I gave the driver the name and address of the hotel and all was calm. Calm that is until we arrived at the Bristol Suites when the driver, again quite understandably, asked for some money. Colin looked a little shocked and said that he didn't have any American money, so I paid, giving the driver a good tip for his politeness and understanding.

After booking in at reception, "Colin again looked confused, "What do we do now?"

I checked my watch and said, "It's now five o'clock so we'll go to our rooms, get showered and changed and meet in the hotel bar at about six."

Freda's face lit up and the plan was agreed. I was in the bar having met our WHS colleagues and relating the airport and taxi sketches, when Colin and Freda made their entrance. "Well done, John," he said looking at the assembled group, "Hello Geoff, hello Roger, hello Mike, hello Charlie," he said, again looking somewhat bemused at the assembly, then added, "Who the Hell's running the bloody warehouse in Swindon?"

As the system was successfully implemented and had been running for a few years, the attendance at the User Conference became less of an attraction, except for Roger and me. Roger was the ultimate networker and I worked for him in supporting the IT systems in all WH Smith warehouses, so it was essential that we both attended, or so my boss insisted. On Roger's final appearance, Dallas Systems announced that a special programme of events was being arranged for delegates' wives. The events were free, the hotel was effectively free for partners as the Bristol Suites Hotel was booked by the room rather than the number of occupants, so all we needed to do was pay the air fares for our wives. Thus, Sue and Joanne accompanied us on another memorable week in Dallas.

On the Sunday, Roger was taking his usual walk around a golf course hacking away at a little ball and networking as he went, so I took the ladies to Fort Worth, again to attend the Pioneer Days celebration. It was an enjoyable day as we wandered amongst cowboys, Indians and pioneers, eating tater skins and listening to some good ol' country music. We spent the entire day there and, not encumbered by the need for Togo Beer, we saw much more of the fair than my previous visit. The locals paid particular attention to two attractive English roses and we took many photographs of them being seduced by rough, tough western hombres. I felt quite proud that I knew my way round the historic quarter and had a high old time absorbing the western culture, although I was a little dismayed that Sue and Joanne checked every single stall selling anything remotely to do with cowboys, with no intention of buying the goods. The highlight for me was attending a rodeo held in Dickies Arena (a name that made me snigger until Sue gave me one of her *Don't be childish* looks.) We found excellent seats in the arena and stood somewhat embarrassed with our hands on hearts whist the Star Bangled Banner was blasted out over the tannoy. We watched a series of exciting rodeo events, until the girls quietly suggested that they had seen enough Texan jockeys chasing cows and falling off horses, so it was time to leave. I was awakened from my cowboy dreamland and reluctantly had to agree to the ladies' wishes. I think that they were suffering withdrawal symptoms from a dearth of shopping, but I vowed to attend another rodeo and had the ideal opportunity the following year.

Roger and I didn't see much of our wives for the rest of the week as we again were preoccupied with various courses, lectures, presentations and discussions, whilst they went on arranged trips for shopping, sightseeing, shopping, dining, shopping and shopping. We did have one memorable evening together when all delegates and partners were invited out to the Trail Dust Steakhouse, a cowboy themed restaurant we had attended on previous visits, famous for its huge steaks, line dancing and, somewhat bizarrely, a slide from the upper to lower floor. In the entrance to the restaurant was a long bar where we waited for tables to be available. Here we ordered beers which the barman slid along the bar to be caught by the customer as it skidded to a halt, as seen in hundreds of cowboy films. On the way in to the actual restaurants there was a sign reading *No Neckties.* Apparently, if any customer ignored the sign and tried to enter wearing a tie, a member of staff would cut the tie off at the knot. There were many tie offcuts pinned to the wall to verify the warning.

The menu was steak, chicken or burgers and, as we were in cow country, we all went for a steak. The choice ranged from an eight ounce *Tenderfoot* through a fourteen ounce *Cowgirl* and a twenty ounce *Cowboy* to a twenty-eight ounce *Bullshipper,* all grilled on a huge indoor barbeque which spat and spluttered as large flames jumped from the pit. I wasn't surprised to learn that the restaurant burned down some years later.

After the meal, a country music band played great country music and tunes by my favourite artists of the day – Garth Brooks, Alan Jackson, Brad Paisley and George Strait were all covered. With an excess of steak, beer and good music, I was in cowboy Heaven. The spell was broken for me when the dancing started, I have never been a dancer and have so sense of rhythm or timing, so I simply cannot dance. A slow shuffle to *Lady in Red*, hanging on to Sue at the end of a drunken wedding reception is about all I can manage, so I stayed away from the dance floor. One of the Dallas hosts was a tall handsome man who wore western style clothing all the time, including to the office. This evening, he seemed even taller and more handsome than usual in his best cowboy clothes and boots. Even his name sounded like a cool cowboy, Hobert Brown. Hobert was playing the perfect gentleman and asking some of the delegates' wives to dance and, during an interlude, Sue whispered to Joanne, "I hope he doesn't ask me because I definitely will not dance with him."

Almost on cue, the music restarted and Hobert strode across to Sue, bent down slightly and asked in a deep Texan drawl, "Excuse me Ma'am, would you like to dance?" A starstruck Sue gazed at Hobert and, in a voice an octave or two higher than usual managed a squeaky, "Yes." As they smooched around the dance floor, Hobert looking down at Sue and talking deeply but gently, as she looked up at Hobert like a lovesick teenager, I repeated to Joanne, "She is definitely not dancing with him." The music stopped and couples left the floor, but Hobert and Sue stayed together, Sue hanging on to her new Western beau as he tried to escort her back to our table. He managed to almost carry her back and deposit her back in her seat, with a deep, "Thank you so much, Ma'am." Sue just sat down with a look of total enrapturement and watched her new hero cross the floor back to his table.

The evening finished with a session of line dancing and, bowing to peer pressure and a surfeit of Coors Light, I joined in. We formed three or four lines and began to dance as the band belted out *Cotton Eye Joe*. While everyone else was doing their brushes, scuffs, heel spreads and toe splits, I was stumbling about like a drunk on an escalator. And each time the lines of dancers turned, I turned the wrong way and spent half the time facing in the opposite direction to my line dancing *compadres*. As Sue pointed out, "It's strange how everyone else got it wrong except you."

On our last full day in Dallas, the conference had finished and we had a spare day so Sue and I accepted the offer of another flying lesson in a light aircraft. I was particularly keen following my success as a pilot in a previous year. We joined a few other delegates in a minibus to drive to Love Field but, by the time that we arrived, I was feeling the effects of motion sickness. I had recovered in minutes and, as Sue was a little apprehensive about flying in a two-seater single engines aircraft that looked as if it has assembled from an Airfix kit, I did my best to reassure her and insisted that I take the first flight to demonstrate just how safe It was. As we taxied along the runway, I started to sweat and felt that all was not well. We reached the height where the pilot hands over the controls and I stuttered to the trainer that I wasn't feeling too well and could he please pass me a bag. I vomited violently, filling the plastic bag before pleading to be taken down to feel solid ground under my feet. I clambered out of the plane once it had landed and made my way to the waiting area clutching my bag of orange sick, depositing the vile vomit in a bin on the way. I tried to look cool and relaxed as I encouraged Sue to take her turn as co-pilot before diving into the toilet to empty what remained in my stomach. To add salt into my vomitus wound, Sue flew the small aircraft with no problems and said how much she enjoyed the experience.

We still had the afternoon free and took a taxi to Dealy Plaza and the West End Historic district of downtown Dallas to visit the site of the 1963 assassination of President J F Kennedy. We visited the sixth floor of the Texas School Book Depository from where Lee Harvey Oswald fired the fatal shot, spent a long time in the sixth Floor Museum, walked on the grassy knoll and wandered around the John F Kennedy Memorial Plaza. It was a very moving experience, but the nagging doubt remained that there was something more to the assassination than we were told.

My last visit to Dallas and its famous, or infamous, User Conference followed the next year. At that time, I had been working on various projects with Rick Bowling, who functioned as the IT representative on the Logistics Division system developments, of which I had responsibility still reporting to Roger. Rick was a kindred spirit in the fascination with all things American and had visited the USA a few times and, in calmer periods at work, would enchant me with stories of his adventures travelling in the New World. For reasons that were never made clear, Roger decided that he would not attend the annual get-together, but insisted that a presence there was essential to maintain the Company's leading position in the retail logistics world. He further suggested that Rick should attend in order to strengthen the relationship between the Logistics and IT communities in WH Smith. It took all of Roger's guile to persuade the IT management that Rick's attendance would be an asset in future developments, so the visit was authorised. I was very happy with the decision as I would now have a colleague who shared my fascination with all things Western, with the added bonus that Rick had become a good mate by this time.

On our arrival at the Bristol Suites, we discovered that there was a rodeo that evening in Mesquite, *The Rodeo Capital of Texas,* an easy half hour drive from the hotel. This was not simply a local rodeo like the event I had seen the previous year, but was a *World Famous* rodeo with the top cowboys, including World Champion Ty Murray. We immediately hired a car and, after an impatient wait for it to be delivered, set of like two excited kids on a trip to Disneyland. We arrived early and, after paying the entry fee, had time to wander round the preparation area. I was surprised that we were allowed *backstage* where the cowboys were preparing for their sport and all the animals were penned. A further revelation was that the competitor cowboys were not the gnarled and wrinkled old cowhands depicted in films and television but were small, slim youngsters, most appearing to be no more than teenagers. We also met a barmy rodeo disciple. He was wrinkled, gnarled and old and stood by a pen which held an impressively large, long horned bull. We, as English gentlemen, wished him a good evening and he immediately started telling us far-fetched stories of his life as a rodeo star. He explained that the bull he was standing near was an old adversary who had almost killed him several times in the past, and he rambled on about other bulls he had encountered. We were not rodeo experts, but it soon became clear that not all the bullshit came from the penned animals. What the unofficial tour did enlighten me to was that the animals travel with the rodeo, so the participants are bucking on the same broncos and bulls at each event. That had never occurred to me before, perhaps as I was more of an aficionado of bull fighting when living in Spain, and their bulls never made a second appearance.

Again, the proceedings began with a loud and proud rendition of the *Star Spangled Banner* as Rick and I stood to attention trying not to look too conspicuous, then the action began. We watched tie-down roping, team roping, steer wrestling, breakaway roping, saddle bronc riding, bareback bronc riding, bull riding and barrel racing. Although we were sometimes confused as to who was doing what to whom and who won which event and why, it was an incredible evening, and Rick didn't want to cut it short to go shopping. We arrived back at the hotel in time for a few beers and found that a number of other delegates had now arrived, some of whom I had met before, many I had not. The introductions and talk of warehouse management systems was enthralling, but we had had enough excitement for one day, so Rick and I settled into a corner and discussed the finer points of rodeo before an early night.

AMERICANADIAN DIARIES

We still had another full day before the conference started, and the obvious way to spend it was at the Fort Worth Pioneer Days - Yeeha! But first breakfast called and Rick had decided that we couldn't stand the thrill of discussing more work stuff with other delegates so we took the car to Denny's, a diner famed for its breakfasts and just a short drive from the hotel. We both went for the full American breakfast, bacon, patties, sausage, two eggs (over easy), buttermilk pancakes and a side of Texas toast. We were pleased that the diner was offering a two-for-one deal that day, so our expenses claim would be more acceptable. On the next table was a huge black Texan lady who waddled in, sat down and ordered a full breakfast, claiming the two-for-one offer. Rick and I were stuffed with one breakfast, but our neighbour devoured two with no trouble. It was good to see that she took the healthy option by washing the meal down with a diet coke, before waddling out again.

Replete, we set off to Fort Worth for another day of cowboy culture. Although my third or fourth attendance at the event, I was seeing it through the excited eyes of someone else who was a western fanatic. We had a splendid time, meeting more cowboys in full regalia including holstered six-guns - big irons on their hips, pioneers in racoon Davy Crocket hats, civil war soldiers where those in Union blue were outnumbered by *Rebs* in Confederate grey. We watched a shootout in the street and were pleased, if unsurprised, that the sheriff won, and chatted with native Americans in their tepees. We dined on fried potato curls and Coors Light whilst listening to country music, photographed with Handsome Hank, The Lonesome Long horn, and rode a mechanical bull. We also tried on a few cowboy hats in Leddy's as they had obviously forgotten that I was banned.

As a break from the round of presentations, DSC had arranged a cultural visit to Southfork, the home of the Ewing family in the popular TV Series *Dallas*. The ranch was a little disappointing as the compact interior of the house bore no resemblance to that shown on television and we were informed that it was because the indoor scenes were shot in a studio. The swimming pool looked huge on TV but was, in fact, quite small and exaggerated in the series by clever camera angles. That said, it was a splendid day out and certainly beat trying to stay awake through more lectures on warehouse stocktaking.

There was also a spare day before flying home, so we drove downtown and I paid my second visit to the Kennedy memorial and the sixth floor. Rick was even more convinced than me that the assassination as portrayed left questions unanswered. We also called into a couple of shopping malls to look for gifts to take home to our loved ones. We found one shop selling Dallas and Texas souvenirs, the type of tourism rubbish found in all cities and resorts, including everything tacky from fridge magnets to t-shirts and plastic cowboy hats. We were chatting and bought a couple of items when the assistant, a pretty young lady, said, "Say, are y'all from New England. I have a friend in New England and she talks just like you."

I was stumped as to what to say, but Rick replied, "No. we are actually from old England."

She thought for a moment, looked confused and said, "Old England? I don't think I know that state." Rick was now also stumped so we simply smiled a sympathetic smile and left the shop with our fridge magnets.

There were to be no more visits to Dallas and no more User Conferences, as a major reorganisation of WHS head office staff meant that the old team was disbanded, most leaving the company for fresh challenges. Rick and I remained friends and chatted often, reminiscing about our jaunt. He also continued to fascinate me with his tales of other trips to America and my appetite was further whetted. As our boys were now grown up, and freedom approached, Sue and I began planning our American adventures in earnest.

CHAPTER 4 - NEW ENGLAND

At about this time, I discovered Bill Byson. Not that he needed discovering of course as he was already a very popular author, but I had never read any of his books until I bought a tatty copy of *Notes from a Small Island* at a WH Smith staff sale of damaged books. The main incentive for the purchase was that it was priced at just a few pence. The book tells the story of Bill's exploratory trip around Britain before returning to his native America. He uncovers many of the oddities and eccentricities of our country and, in particular, the curious and sometimes bizarre foibles of the British people from a foreigner's perspective. I loved the book, his easy flowing narrative and acute observations had me enthralled. I followed this literary awakening with the purchase of an earlier Bryson book *The Lost Continent* (disappointingly, I had to pay full price less WH Smith discount for this one) which followed a similar unearthing of the quirks of his own country and its people during a trip around the USA in search of the typical American town. He failed to find it. I was hooked, and my next purchase (with discount) was *A Walk in the Woods*, where Bill and a companion attempt to walk the long-distance path following the 2,200-mile Appellation National

AMERICANADIAN DIARIES

Scenic Trail from Georgia to Maine, passing through fourteen states. One of his ambitions during the walk was to see bears in the wild but never did. And he never finished the walk. Due to Rick's enthusiasm and Bill's descriptions of the USA, I was finally ready to take the plunge and go west, though not exactly as a young man. After her initiation to the big country in Dallas, Sue was also very keen, so we began planning our first road trip. It was, we agreed, to be the holiday of a lifetime. We also agreed that it would be wise to follow in the footsteps of the first settlers and begin our adventures with a trip to Boston and New England. We bought a large road atlas of the USA and began to plan our route, with regular insights and snippets of advice from Rick.

I was reading the Mail on Sunday during this period for the sole reason that my literary hero Bill Bryson had, by now, returned to live in the US and wrote a weekly column about his time back in his home country. Once again, I was captivated by his descriptions of life in New England and it confirmed that our initial idea of starting our visits in the northeast was correct. At work in WH Smith, *The Bookseller*, a trade journal for the book trade was widely circulated and I always read it with interest. This was not just for work related data, but because I loved books and discovering new authors and publications was of great interest. In one issue, I was happily surprised to see a letter from Bill Bryson published requesting booksellers not to stock one or two of his early works which he now deemed unworthy. This demonstrated what a genuine and honest man he was but, more importantly, it published his home address in Hanover, New Hampshire. I wrote to Mr. Bryson and included a caricature of him sitting in a pub with a pint, which is how he seemed to spend most of his time in *Notes from a Small Island*. In my letter, I said how much I enjoyed his books and articles about America and was planning a trip to New England in the near future. I naively suggested that I would love to visit him in Hanover during our journey. Bill wrote a very friendly letter back thanking me for the caricature and saying that he was getting it framed to display in his office. I wanted to frame the return letter, but Sue was less than enthusiastic, so it is now stored somewhere in my mementoes file. A few weeks after our communication, I was reading Bill's column in the Mail and he reported that it was a strange phenomenon how readers of regular columnists imagine that they know the writer personally and he reported that some readers actually thought it a good idea to visit him. He indicated that it was not a good idea and he didn't want any visitors. Whether he was referring to me, I know not, but I was miffed and Hanover, New Hampshire was crossed off the itinerary.

At that time, Virgin Atlantic were offering a fly-drive package which included a flight and a list of available accommodation. This seemed a practical and straightforward way of beginning our adventures, so the planning of our first trip was under way. As we were both working at the time and holidays were limited, Sue and I carefully studied our newly purchased American road atlas, to ensure that we made the most of the two-week vacation. We discussed whether or not to stay in Boston for a few days but, as neither of us are particularly fond of cities and far prefer exploring country areas, we decided that, from Boston, we would head north and visit Bar Harbour, Maine to explore Acadia National Park, before heading back south via the White Mountains, then moving on to Cape Cod and returning to Boston for the flight home. We would pass near Mr. Bryson's home in Hanover but thought it prudent not to call in to see him.

All was arranged and we waited impatiently for the holiday to begin. The eight-hour flight passed without incident and we landed at Logan International Airport stiff, tired but very excited. We found the Dollar Car Hire area and picked up the Dodge car as arranged by Virgin. So far, so good, but the things went slightly awry when I couldn't find my way out of the airport concourse. We took the wrong exit road somewhere and seemed to be heading straight for a runway, so I stopped, turned around and headed back to the car pick-up point, where I was somewhat embarrassed when asking the desk clerk the way out. I blamed the mishap on the fact that the car had the steering wheel on the wrong side and it was an automatic and I was used to changing gear. The desk clerk looked even more confused than I was.

The drive from the airport to Bar Harbour was another eight hours travelling so, quite sensibly, we had booked an overnight stop at Kennebunkport, Massachusetts. This broke the journey with an easy three and half trip, or it should have been. Our carefully planned and documented route took us from the airport on to US-1 North via the Sumner Tunnel, which led directly on to the I-95 North to Kennebunkport. This would have been an easy drive except that, when we got to the tunnel, the entrance was closed and all traffic was diverted. We had no choice but to follow the flow of traffic away from the tunnel.

We were driving on the wrong side of the road, in a car with no gears, around a busy city and had no idea where we should be going. Sue had the road map, which was so complicated that it was more hindrance than help, so we just followed any signs that indicated *North* and prayed. We followed a minor road as I tried to comfort a worried Sue by telling her that we would be OK as long as kept the sea on our right, but as we couldn't see the sea this did not help. We passed through Salem and were tempted to stop and ask any local witches for help by casting a spell, but none appeared. We passed through other small towns including Ipswich, Newbury and Salisbury. Again, I tried to sound confident by telling Sue that at least are back in Wiltshire, so could get home easily. This did not help. Eventually and more by luck than judgement, we found the US-1 again and, although we had missed its junction with I-95, we were finally on the map and we knew that we were going in the right direction. We never did find our way on to the I-95, but enjoyed our trip through North Hampton and Portsmouth before arriving in Kennebunkport some two hours late. We found our hotel, the Sundial Inn, in the late afternoon. It was on the sea front at Gooch's Beach and was a small but impressive colonial building, to our eyes very American which added to our enthusiasm. After settling into our spacious room with a splendid view over the bay, we were too excited to rest and immediately decided to go out to eat. We strolled up Beach Avenue and crossed the Matthew J Lanigan Bridge into the old town and harbour. It was everything we had dreamed of and more. A small seaside town with neatly painted clapboard houses perched on stilts in the harbour, reminding us of Amity Island and we half expected to see a large shark hanging in the harbour. Amongst the houses and shops there were quaint restaurants with names like The Clam Shack, The Boathouse and, perhaps a little worryingly, The Hurricane. We selected Allison's on Dock Square, and ordered our meals. I cannot remember what we ordered, but I do know that we couldn't eat much. Not that it wasn't good fare, but we simply could not eat. The waitress seemed upset until we explained that we had just arrived after travelling for most of the day and were very tired. Perhaps the fact that we overtipped helped ease her distress. It was then that we realised that it was about nine o'clock US time, which means that our body clocks were registering two AM. Little wonder then that we were not hungry.

The following morning, we were awake and strolling along the beach at six thirty, our internal clocks refusing to let us sleep any longer. It was a beautiful morning as we soaked up the early morning sun, the ocean air and the exciting atmosphere, spending half an hour watching little chipmunks, running over the rocks near the beach. We returned to the hotel for a fine breakfast and, with some trepidation, continued our journey north.

Surprisingly after the previous day's travails, we had a pleasant and carefree four-hour drive, finding the I-295, the I-95 and US-1, destination Bangor, Maine. I felt like king of the road with no driving problems, except ineffectively trying to change gear every now and again. From Bangor we headed south on the 1A, even having the courage to pull off the highway at Ellsworth on the way to take a break and enjoy a coffee and a snack at Sylvia's café. Driving in America was a piece of cake.

We crossed the Trenton Bridge to Mount Desert Island to reach Acadia National Park and our destination of Bar Harbor. We found our hotel, the Hampton Inn, after asking Sue several times, "How far is the Hampton Inn?" which appealed to my smutty sense of humour but which Sue didn't understand and patiently replied with the ETA each time. The hotel was, as ever, very impressive with large and spacious rooms, huge twin beds, a desk, a settee and, again, impressive views over the ocean. I was beginning to realise that my usual stays with work at a Travelodge in the M1 near Dunstable would never be the same again. We had made good time on the journey and had most of the afternoon left, so decided to make a quick visit to the visitor centre at Hulls Cove a few miles north of the hotel. Whilst Sue indulged in her keen interest in geology, studying the area's igneous rock, glacial erratics and striations, I concentrated on the many hiking trails before producing a detailed walking plan for the next three days.

AMERICANADIAN DIARIES

With my plans complete and Sue happily content that our hikes would uncover the effects of millions of years of erosion created by glaciers and volcanic action, we pottered into the town of Bar Harbour for a look around and to identify a restaurant for that evening. Again, the town was everything we had imagined. We wandered on to the jetty, watching boats come in and out and admired the town, nestling in a small bay overlooked by an impressive range of mountains. We found a small bar just off Main Street and it looked ideal, a cross between Cheers and Mo's Tavern, and selected a restaurant on the waterfront, before returning to the hotel. That evening we drove back into town and entered the selected bar. We took our place in the long bar with most stools taken by middle-aged men drinking and chatting amiably, although I didn't see Norm, Cliff or Homer. We ordered our drinks and were enjoying the atmosphere, when a scruffy and drunk young man, ungallantly sitting on a stool whilst his girlfriend stood next to him, began badly mimicking our accents. He was a typical skinny feral ferret, the type of young ne'er-do-well who is common enough in the rougher pubs of the UK, but whom we did not expect to see in a pleasant American hostelry. We ignored his attempts to intimidate us and continued to chat between ourselves, when he suddenly stood up, shouted something unintelligible and stormed out of the bar. His girlfriend seemed stunned for a moment, then shouted, "Oh no. He's on parole," and chased him out of the door. The nearby drinkers looked at Sue and me with some sympathy and embarrassment, until I asked, "Was it something we said?" The embarrassed looks turned to friendly smiles and we chatted amicably to the men thereafter. On leaving the bar and beginning to head for the harbour, a large van full of young men pulled up unsteadily alongside and one of the men leant out of his window and shouted, "Hey you, where's the nearest liquor store?" I explained that I had no idea as I was stranger in the town, so the van pulled away with the passengers yelling abuse. Our second unpleasant incident made us wary of going any further so we decided to go into the first restaurant that we came to. We selected the Royal Indian, hoping to advance our new world experience with Native American cuisine, perhaps a buffalo or moose steak with cornbread and succotash, served by a pretty indigenous lady. It was not quite what we had anticipated, but the chicken tikka and lamb tandoori were excellent.

The following day we began our holiday proper and chose the first of our walks to reach the summit of Gorum Mountain, a modest peak of 525 feet but a good introduction the Acadia National Park. We started by driving the Park Loop Road to see Thunder Hole, a small inlet along the rocky eastern shoreline of Mount Desert Island. We read that the tide forces waves into this narrow channel and the air escapes with *a thunderous reverberation that is both deafening and thrilling*. After descending the fifty-two steep stone steps, we were overlooking this phenomenon of nature, expecting to be deafened and thrilled. We had obviously chosen the wrong time as the waves entering the cave made very little noise. Sue suggested that they rename it "Gurgle Hole," but I settled for "Fart Hole."

Not at all put off by the lack of thunder, we followed the Gorum Mountain Loop and had a fine walk, blowing away the cobwebs after two days of travelling. We climbed over bare rock and scree and followed well-trodden tracks through forested areas to the summit and stopped to survey the amazing scene over the Bar Harbor inlet to the mountains on the opposite shore. After sitting down a while to soak in the magnificent views, we descended the mountain realising that our plan for a long walk was somewhat premature as the whole route had only taken about two hours. I checked our guides and maps collected at the information centre and decided that we could manage a second summit, so set off on the Beehive Loop Trail to another peak, the 508 feet Beehive, resting half way at the unimaginatively named Halfway Mountain. We stopped for while on an overlook gazing over The Bowl, a bright blue mountain tarn or small spring-fed kettle pond, 400 feet above sea level and surrounded by verdant pine forest. Here I had the first of what Sue called, "my moments," where I can only stand and stare, incapable of speech and teary-eyed, overwhelmed with emotion by the sheer beauty of the scene. It took a few minutes to regain what I considered my usual stoic composure, but it was an experience that was to be repeated many times during our American adventures.

We descended, tired and a little footsore but proud that we had managed two (and a half) mountains in one day, until we sat on Sand beach at the foot and reviewed our achievement. We had climbed "mountains" with a total elevation of 1033 feet. Our sense of triumph was somewhat tempered when we realised that we had actually ascended considerably less than the height of Dunkery Beacon in Somerset, which we had walked many times, and perhaps one third the height of Scafell Pike. It would not be the first time that, in my enthusiasm, I had confused metric and Imperial measurements and came to understand the American penchant for hyperbole.

That evening, we again went into Bar Harbour for our evening repast, avoiding bars and Indian Restaurants and determined to find somewhere more fitting to our Maine experience. We strolled along Main Street amongst other vacationers peering in shop windows, Sue particularly enchanted by a clothes shop called *Cool as a Moose*, and enjoying the fresh evening air. We found Geddy's, *Maine's #1 Seafood Restaurant*, an obvious choice. We decided to go full Bar Harbor and ordered Maine Lobster, something we had never eaten before. The charming server, a grey-haired middle-aged lady who looked like a typical American TV mum, smiled and said to go to the counter and choose our lobster. We thought it odd, but wandered over and looked for the lobsters. We eventually found them – happily swimming around in a large tank at the side of the counter – and they were a rather dull brown colour. It came as a surprise that we were expected to pass a sentence of death on two of these beautiful creatures and had no idea what to look for in our victim. After discussing the options, we chose the two smallest, not just because the meal was priced by the weight, but because we didn't know just how much meat an executed crustacean would produce.

We sat and drank a beer for a while, then American Mum arrived carrying two plates, each with a small red lobster and a side of fries, which we now recognised as thin chips. We had no idea how to tackle the meal but on each plate was a set of nut crackers, so we guessed that these tools were for breaking into the food. We politely turned down American Mum's offer of showing us what to do, more from embarrassment than confidence. Considering that we were virgin lobster eaters, we did well, cracking, scooping, scraping, pulling and chewing liked seasoned professional lobster diners - and the meat was delicious.

Although we were given towels to clean our hands after the meal, our fingers still felt a little greasy so the first thing we did on our return to the hotel was wash our hands in hot water. Suddenly, I noticed a sharp stinging pain in my fingers which felt like they were being set on fire. Sue experienced the same discomfort and, on inspection, we found minute cuts and scratches covering our fingertips, almost certainly from the sharp shells as we cracked, scooped and scraped. Perhaps we didn't do so well after all and should have accepted American Mum's offer of tuition.

The following day, buoyed by our previous day's expedition, we selected another walk and another mountain. We again studied our provisional plan and decided to start the day with a comparatively easy three-mile hike around Jordan Pond. The day was beautifully clear and warm with cloudless blue skies as we began the day's exploration. From the starting point there is a magnificent view of The Bubbles, two more mountains which looked to me more like a rather fine pair of plump breasts that bubbles. I thought that the original pioneers had misnamed the mounds and they should be known as The Bristols. The walk was easy and relatively flat for the first part until, on reaching the northern edge, we decided that we really should climb the Bristols and find Bubble Rock, about which we had read in our travel documentation. We left the loop trail and headed up to exploring the Bristols, unsure of the exact location of our target. Sue was worried that we were lost, but I explained that I am never lost, just temporarily misplaced. We headed up and over the summit of North Bubble and stopped to wonder at the view of Eagle Lake, before dropping down then climbing up South Bubble, where we reached the stunning sight of Bubble Rock, a huge boulder perched on the edge of an overlook above the valley, seemingly defying gravity. We stared in awe. It is an enormous 100-ton chunk of white granite the size of a house and is famed as the most famous boulder in Maine, deposited on the summit of South Bubble as the last ice age receded, 10,000 plus years ago. Scientists believe the glaciers carried it from Lucerne,

AMERICANADIAN DIARIES

Maine, some forty miles away, where similar rocks can be found. We took photographs of each other pretending to push the rock over the precipice towards the valley, as thousands of other hikers must have done. We descended the mountain and returned to the trailhead, before sitting on the side of Jordan Pond for a well-earned rest and packed lunch. We were joined by a precocious brown squirrel, which sat a couple of feet away waiting to pick up any crumbs. I was surprised to see the little fellow as I had always been led to believe that all American squirrels were grey and had infiltrated British woodland at the expense of native red squirrels. Why their brown cousins had not joined them was a mystery and while I was debating the conundrum aloud, Sue was ignoring me and deliberately dropping crumbs by accident to feed the rodent.

Another day and another mountain beckoned. I checked the plan and announced to Sue that we were going to climb, or more accurately walk, St. Sauveur Mountain that day. She smiled sweetly but I thought that there was a slight look of, *not another mountain*, on her face. We wandered into Bar Harbor and stocked up on snacks for lunch before taking the quiet and rural ME-233 road to the west of Mt. Desert Island, separated from the east by the picturesque Somes Sound. We had read that this inlet of the Atlantic Ocean is the only glacial fiord is the USA, created by a glacier in the last ice age, although we weren't sure exactly what defines a glacial fiord as opposed to the other impressive inlets on the island. But to be honest, we didn't really care – it was simply magnificent. We took the St, Sauveur and Acadia Loop trail, a four-mile hike which took us through steep and challenging forest paths before opening out on a large bare rock covering the summit. Again, the views were awe-inspiring as we sat and rested at the top, naively discussing the possibility of packing up everything in England and moving to this warm, mountainous Shangri-la. We knew that it could only be a dream, but for those thirty minutes, sitting contemplatively on the rock, warmed by the Spring sunshine and overlooking Somes Sound and the surrounding hills and mountains under a big cloudless sky, the dream was reality.

On climbing down from the summit, Sue and I found a comfortable and quiet spot on the side of the sound to sit and eat our lunch. We were surprised to hear the excited shouts of youngsters nearby as they leapt from the bank, splashing and swimming happily in the waters of the inlet. I was tempted to join them, but soon came to my senses when I bent down and put my hand in the freezing water. We were also joined by an inquisitive chipmunk and, I am ashamed to say, broke the park rules again by accidentally dropping crisps for the delightful little animal to eat. When we arrived back at the hotel, I decided that I would go for a swim after all, but in the supposedly warm and inviting safety of the hotel's outdoor pool. I changed into my shorts and bravely marched across the yard with a towel under my arm and, without hesitation, dived into the pool. Within five seconds I had climbed out and walked shivering back to our room.

That evening, we again set off into town looking for a suitable restaurant and came across Freddy's Route 66, tucked away on Cottage Street. It was probably the strangest yet most interesting restaurant we had ever been to. Above the door was suspended an old yellow cab with sign advertising *Dink's Taxis* and the inside was chock full of Americana, including hundreds of photographs of American icons, kiddies' pedal cars, genuine car bonnets, old advertising signs, ancient machinery, typewriters, old toys, petrol pumps, street signs, road signs and thousands of other pieces of memorabilia – but the *piece de resistance* was a train track running round the top of the restaurant walls, with a large model train continuously circling the room. Sue and I were totally enthralled with the ambience, the atmosphere and the mood of the whole place. We took a booth and the waitress brought the menu which was yet another delight with every American offering we had ever heard of and more from bam bam shrimp, chicken quesadilla and blackened salmon to different salads, dips and fries. We were so bamboozled that we settled for the taster menu which offered small helpings of different meals, proving to be a good decision as every offering was all superb. As a bonus, each booth had its own speaker with a volume control so we were gently serenaded by Franki Valli and the Four Seasons as we dined. On the way home we agreed that it was a momentous day, but oh, what a night.

Our last day arrived all too soon and we decided that we should visit Cadillac Mountain, the highest point in the Acadia National Park and the eastern seaboard. My old legs were feeling the strain after three days of hiking and five mountain peaks, so we chose the easier north ridge trail, described as a moderate 4.4-mile hike. We started the walk from the Eagle Lake Road just south of Bar Harbor and, despite my stiffness, enjoyed a splendid 90-minute trek to the summit. As we arrived at the top, we were amazed to see that it was awash with tourists. We couldn't understand how so many people had made it there, particularly as this cross section of the American public looked anything but athletic despite their Nike, Puma and Adidas sportswear. As I stood looking at the throng in confusion, Sue tapped my shoulder and pointed to a tarmacked road leading to a large car park. I had completely missed the fact that it is possible to drive to top. Despite the magnificent far-reaching views to Frenchman Bay and the Porcupine Islands, Bar Harbor and Mount Desert Island, I felt deflated. We commented that, with one or two exceptions, we had seen no-one on our walks over the previous three days and now, at the highest point in the park, we were swamped by fat bloody tourists. Sue said I was being selfish and they had every right to be there, but I still felt somehow cheated. I began to cheer up, however, when dark, forbidding clouds began rolling in from the north and the motorists began to scramble to their cars and take off down the mountains. Although we were soaked on the return walk as the heavens opened, I felt that my displeasure was justified.

That afternoon, Sue packed for the next day's journey, while I sat looking out of the hotel window as the storm lashed down, lightning flashed and thunder echoed all around us, content that Cadillac Mountain would be freed from its plague of immobile tourists in their cars and busses. That evening we revisited Freddy's Route 66 for another fine meal, marred slightly by Sue saying I was a grumpy old man and should, "lighten up." Regretfully, I had no argument to the contrary.

Early the following morning, the car loaded, we left Arcadia and were off on the next phase of the adventure to New Hampshire's White Mountains. Now experienced in an automatic, left-hand drive car on the right-hand side of the road, we set off confidently for the four-hour drive via Bangor, on to the I-95 South and arrived at the White Mountain Hotel and Resort in North Conway in time for lunch. I avoided travelling via Hanover, New Hampshire as I was still miffed with Bill Bryson. That'll show him, I thought. The storm had followed us down from Acadia so the afternoon was spent settling into the hotel and resting after the drive, whilst planning our expeditions for the following four days of adventure.

The storm had abated in morning and we started off on our plan to conquer White Horse Ledge and Cathedral Ledge, which loomed over the hotel and North Conway. These high cliffs are a magnet for rock climbers who insanely drag themselves up almost vertical faces hanging precariously on lengths of rope. We decided to forego this experience and chose to hike the long way round, using a very basic map picked up at the hotel. We parked at Echo Lake and began the ascent via the Bryce Path, a rough track rising through a dense forest of pine trees. After an hour or so of tough walking, I realised that we were once again temporarily misplaced and I had no idea where on the track we were, if indeed we were on the right track at all. We stopped to review our situation in the middle of the forest and were interested to read on our guide sheet how to react if confronted by a bear. That did little to comfort us and, to compound our anxieties, there were crashes and flashes of thunder and lightning all around and large dollops of rain began splattering through the trees. We agreed that when in a forest with thunder echoing around us and flashes of lightning every few seconds, it's time to put discretion before valour and retreat. We turned to retrace our steps, but didn't know where our previous steps were, so made the decision to just head downhill and hope that we were going somewhere in right direction. After scrambling and sliding through the increasingly wet forest, we somewhat fortuitously arrived at the Echo Lake Road and made our way back to the car. Of course, I claimed that I had known where we were all the time and was only joking about being lost. Despite the weather, we sat beneath the cover of the trees and ate our increasingly soggy sandwiches, gazing over the lake to Cathedral Ridge and promising ourselves that we would conquer the mountains on another day. After a long rest, we went into North Conway and relieved our hiking frustration with another good old American meal at the Shalimar Indian Restaurant.

Mount Washington is the highest peak in the Presidential Range and the Northeast of America, a proper mountain at almost 6,300 feet. This was a challenge and we were determined to conquer the summit after the previous day's disappointment. Such was our determination that we browsed guides, studied maps, reviewed hiking routes, packed emergency rations, reviewed our options and decided to take the cog railway to the top. After a drive in thick fog, we arrived early at Marshfield Station and watched the odd little trains firing up ready for their day's work. We read in the station visitors' centre that The Mount Washington Cog Railway is the world's first mountain-climbing cog railway and is the second-steepest rack railway in the world, after the Pilatus Railway in Switzerland, and construction was completed in 1869. This was interesting, but not as interesting as the grey fox we spotted trotting along the track – a beautiful animal and the first grey fox we had ever seen.

As the engine puffed and strained and clanked up the steep incline, it was difficult to believe that the pines bordering the track were not growing at an angle, no matter that logic told us that trees always grow straight upwards. The engineer gave a running commentary as we progressed, most of which was lost in the noise of the engine and the loud rumble of the carriage wheels, and because all the passengers were chatting amongst themselves, possibly debating why the trees did not grow straight.

We reached the summit after about 45 minutes and we detrained (I was learning the language quite well by now and was determined to use similar terms where possible) before we set off and wandered around the summit. Although the views were spectacular, I admit to being less impressed than if we had climbed the mountain under our own steam. We read a plaque which proudly announced that on April 12, 1934, a wind gust of 231 mph was recorded at the Mount Washington Observatory, which stands as the record for the fastest surface wind measured in the Northern and Western Hemispheres. We were getting used to the American preoccupation with things being the biggest, highest, longest and now fastest. The return trip took only 30 minutes or so and again the engineer's commentary was all but lost in the general noise of the journey. As we were about to leave the train at Marshfield Station, our commentating engineer said his farewells and said that this was the first time that he had acted as guide and commentator on the journey and hoped that he had done OK. I was again surprised that this was a first for a middle-aged and obviously experienced train driver. And so again, I didn't tip him.

On the drive back to North Conway, we were looking for Arethusa Falls, the highest waterfall in the White mountains and second highest in the state, reached by a 1.5-mile, uphill hiking trail and an ideal spot for lunch. We parked in the car park alongside several other cars, and set off up the trail, following the pretty babbling Bemis Brook, fed by the falls and cascading and tumbling over bare rock forming small waterfalls and deep ponds. We stopped by a deep pool and found a comfortable rock just below the falls and were preparing to eat when I fell over on the slippery rocks. My left shin was grazed and cut and blood seeped from my injury into my sock. I, of course, made the most of my wound but my dear wife took a cursory look and said, "You won't die. Get the sandwiches out – I'm starving." And she didn't even laugh when I said that I now understood why they are called falls. When we returned to the car park there were still several cars there. Yet we never saw one other person on our walk to and from the falls. What they were doing there and where they went remains a mystery.

On returning to the White Mountain Hotel, we rested after a long day and I tried to recover from the severe damage to my leg (Sue called it a scratch) and we watched a local television station in our room. One of the advertisements promoted the Cliffside Restaurant with an all-you-can-eat buffet for just *naan-naandy-naan*. The advertisement appeared a few times and we slowly realised that we had passed the restaurant on our travels, a few minutes from the hotel. This became our regular dining experience for the remainder of our time in North Conway. The restaurant was in a large wooden building akin to an outsized Swiss chalet and the inside was fairly basic but spotlessly clean and welcoming. We selected the Cliffside Deluxe Buffet, which offered *…all you can eat of all 4 meats, roast beef, roast pork, roast turkey, baked ham, with homemade bread, homemade soups, salad bar, fresh vegetables, stuffing, real mashed potatoes, baked potatoe (sic), home baked beans, macaroni and cheese, Delmonico potatoes, gravies, etc*. Not too bad for *naan-naandy-naan*. Sue and I decided on the delicious-looking baked ham and waited in a small queue for the chef to carve our choice of meat. The meat on the baked pig's leg was ending but more than adequate for our appetites, so we ordered the succulent meat. The chef looked at us, looked at the hock and then threw it into the bin, before replacing it with another huge leg. We were amazed at the waste but I refrained from saying, "There's children starving in Africa." As Sue said when we were tucking into the feast, that first discarded joint would have adequately fed her family of two adults and five children and still have had some left for sandwiches.

The second surprise that evening was that the sides were unlimited and customers could re-visit the counter as many times and they wished to restock. Yet we saw many diners, particularly those of generous proportions, pile their plates so high that it took all their skill and balance to return to their seats carrying the mountain of food without it toppling over. Strange chap, Johnny American.

The following morning, we decided to repair the damage to my ego and try again to climb White Horse Ledge and Cathedral Ledge. This we did with no problems, dramas or traumas which made me wonder just how I had managed to become temporarily misplaced a few days before. The views were again magnificent, overlooking Echo Lake and the Presidential Range of mountains. Not for the first time, we noticed bare patches between the trees on the mountainsides and wondered why they had been cleared. I confidently told Sue that they were fire breaks to prevent forest fires spreading. She was unconvinced but I was adamant – and soon to look rather foolish.

We were back early and Sue decided on an afternoon's rest while I ventured into the hotel pool for the first time, wary after barely surviving the cold pool in Acadia. I dived in and splashed about in my clumsy imitation of swimming, and noticed that the only other bathers were middle-aged gentlemen. I nodded a greeting as I doggy-paddled past and caught some of their conversation which seemed to consist only of golf speak – seven irons, wedges, holes, flags and sand traps. I was a little upset that one of them boasted of shooting a birdie, one picked up a bogie and yet another was labelled a bandit. We were in one of the world's most beautiful areas, surrounded by mountains, lakes, rivers and wildlife, yet these chaps spent most of their time hitting a little white ball on manicured lawns into a hole, and the rest of the time talking about it. Strange chap Johnny Golfer.

We weren't finished with walking yet, despite feeling a little fatigued after the previous days' exertions, so I studied the plan and we decided one last hike. We had the choice of Mount Willard or Mount Willey. Sue stated that it must be Willard as she could not stand a day of jokes about climbing up a willy. The description Mount Willard on our guide described it as *located in the town of Hart's Location in Crawford Notch State Park*. Both names appealed to me so off we went on the half hour drive through the stunning White Mountains National Forest to Crawford Station, the start point for the climb. It was a stunning walk and fairly uneventful except for seeing some very clear and fresh bear prints in the mud which put us slightly on edge, and finding a large garter snake on the trail. Our eldest son had a garter snake as a pet, so we were not worried about the lovely animal and watched as it slowly slithered away into the undergrowth. On the return journey we met the first person we had seen that day, an elderly gentleman, who told us he was 78 years old and climbed the mountain several times a year, including during the winter when he needed snowshoes to walk. He also pointed out a dramatic rockslide on a nearby mountain which, he told us, had wiped out a cabin and killed a family of pioneers in the late 19th century. He continued telling us tales of the mountain and surrounding area, but it was hard to concentrate as there a steady trickle of pee running down his leg into his boot.

Our last day in the White Mountains came all too soon and we needed to take it easy but had not had enough of the mountains, so we decided to take a less energetic option and take the Gondola Ride up Wildcat Mountain, a 4000 feet peak near Mount Washington. In summer, the mountain chairlift is adapted and the refitted gondolas are attached to carry visitors to the mountain summit. Apparently, it was the first of its kind in the US, constructed in 1958. We drove to Pinkham Notch, located the Gondolas and took a short but pleasant and leisurely ride to the top. We *degondolised* (is that a word?) and spent a peaceful hour resting and looking at more spectacular views of the Presidential Range of mountains. I ambled across to an information board and casually started to study the illustration and description of the area. It showed a clear picture of the mountain, with many tracks running from top to bottom, each coloured red, black or green and identified as Upper Wildcat, Upper Polecat, middle catapult and other feline-related names. I called Sue over and said to look at all these hiking trails and stated how dangerous they looked, surely impossible to use. She smiled sweetly, held my hand and said, "They're ski runs, dear." I was dumbstruck. Not only had I missed the fact we had travelled up a converted chairlift for skiers, that all the tracks were ski runs, as indeed were all my "fire breaks." My low self-esteem was not improved when Sue finished her brief elucidation with an emphatic Homeresque, "Doh!"

The following morning, we set off for our fourth and last base, Captains Quarters Motel in Eastham, *...in the heart of The Cape Cod National Seashore, less than a mile from the Magnificent Nauset Light Beach*. It was an incident free drive through almost familiar territory as we passed Rochester, Dover, Portsmouth, Plymouth and Yarmouth, stopping at Barnstaple for a brief break where we were tempted to ask for Devon cream tea but settled for a coffee. This was our first experience of a motel as opposed to a hotel, but struggled to see much difference except that we could park right outside of the room. Having gorged on steak, lobster and all you can eat for naan-naandy-naan over the previous ten days we nibbled on a few crisps and a biscuit that day and still felt full.

On our first full day was inevitably a visit to the nearby Nauset Light Beach and wandered round a beautifully maintained park with three lighthouses, the three sisters, built in 1848. Unfortunately, the position chosen to build them couldn't have been too well surveyed as they were later forced to move the beacons further inland to stop them being washed away. We moved on to the Cape Cod National Seashore and the Wellfleet Bay Wildlife Sanctuary, where we saw striking red northern cardinals, American goldfinches, red-winged blackbirds and various other unidentified little brown birds. We carried on to the seashore and strolled along the beach in the sunshine, bird watching and enjoying the peace and quiet and lack of strenuous mountain trails. We met some practiced bird watchers who pointed out spotted plovers, kingfishers, oyster catchers, green-backed herons and terns. I was impressed by their knowledge and even resisted my ancient jokes about having a funny tern or nasty tern. Our new friends also warned us against greenheads, a particularly vicious little insect whose bites itch, like those of mosquitoes, but are more painful since greenheads feed by cutting a wound in the skin with scissor-like mouth parts and sucking the blood released through the cut. Whilst keeping a wary look out for greenheads, we saw voles and turtles, we poked sticks into crab holes on the beach and collected numerous shells discarded by horseshoe crabs, without knowing what to we would do with them. We ambled on the Nauset Marsh Trail boardwalks over marshland, generally soaking up the sun, sand, sea and atmosphere. We were so enchanted by the seashore that we decided the next day to visit the western shore of Cape Cod and repeat the day's activities: strolling, birdwatching, investigating and generally doing very little. On returning to the car Sue and I noticed itchy lumps on our legs, some of which had produced trickles of blood, obviously greenhead bites. We stopped on the way back and bought soothing cream and insect repellent – too little too late.

AMERICANADIAN DIARIES

To help forget our bites we went out to eat that evening to the Sandpipers Sports Pub, a bar/restaurant next to the Captains Quarters. As we entered, we were immediately struck by the fact that there were many television sets around the walls, each one showing a different sport. There was American football on one, next to baseball match and then a basketball game on another. There was even one, tucked away in a corner with soccer, but no-one was watching that. The large bar counter was square with seating on three sides and there were about eight people on each side, with several tables occupied around the bar, all occupants staring at different screens as they downed their beers. Eerily, the only sounds were the clinking of glasses and the commentors vying for attention from the televisions. We found a spare table and I squeezed through the throng to order fish and fries at the bar. The meal was soon delivered on large oval plates where the only thing visible was a massive piece of battered fish. There were fries, a very generous portion, but they were hidden beneath the fish. Having struggled our way through the repast, washed down with beer, we said our goodbyes to fellow diners and drinkers whose eyes never left the TV screens, and crossed the car park back to the motel. We walked past an outsize truck with wheels as tall as me and with the driver's door ajar. As we passed the open door of the large vehicle, we saw an equally large man, with his penis exposed and urinating over the tarmac. He looked up from the large stream of pee and said, "Hi." I managed a weak, "Good evening," as he continued to pee, before Sue whispered that it's true that everything's bigger in America.

Back in England, we had planned to go whale watching and so, as much as we were enjoying our lazy couple of days, we left our blood-stained beds and set off for Provincetown on the northern tip of the cape. It is a small town with a fascinating history which includes past times as a whaling and fishing centre and the origin of the name Cape Cod. It is also reputed be the first place that the Pilgrim Fathers set foot from the Mayflower in 1620. We stopped en-route at a small store we had discovered previously and which sold excellent sandwiches we had enjoyed for the previous couple of days. The proprietor was a friendly and helpful Cape Codder who asked us where we were off today. We told him that we off to Provincetown. He gave us a strange smile and said, "You'll find that, um, interesting." We asked what he meant by "interesting," but he just laughed and said that we would find out.

On arrival in the town, we parked in the municipal car park after entering via the way out clearly marked *No Entry*, and began our stroll via Standish Street to the harbour, ready to board the whale-watching boat. After a quiet couple of days in the mountains, the street was an exciting change, a bustling thoroughfare full of interesting shops, bars and restaurants with locals and tourists strolling, shopping and going about their daily business. The shop man was right, it was "interesting," but we could not see why he was so reserved in telling us why. We noticed a tall, very muscular man in overalls but shirtless, showing off his broad well-developed arms and shoulders, waiting on a street corner. Another chap, equally as large and well-built came across to him and they greeted each other with a prolonged kiss on the lips and wandered off holding hands. A little shocked, we looked around and realised that there were other same-sex couples, including two women who would have given the men a run for their money in the body-building stakes and were arm in arm. The more we looked, the more same-sex couples we saw, holding hands, arm in arm or cuddling and, perhaps a little slow on the uptake, we realized why the town was so "interesting."

AMERICANADIAN DIARIES

As we had an hour or so before our whale-watching boat embarked, we climbed the Pilgrim Monument, described as a *252-foot-tall campanile ... the tallest all-granite structure in the United States*. We loved yet another biggest/longest/highest description. The tower's 116 steps and 60 ramps lead to a viewing area with stunning views of Provincetown, the surrounding seashore and the harbour where the signing of the Mayflower Compact took place. After descending the tallest all-granite structure in the United States, we boarded the boat and began our hunt for whales. The guide ran through safety and emergency instructions as we left the harbour but stressed that, "We are not counting on any emergencies today." That was a relief.

The guide continued her speech, explaining that whales were, "Mammals, just like us," which seemed to surprise some of our fellow passengers. We were soon in open water and excited to see our first humpback whale leaping out of the water in a display known as breaching. It wasn't long before we saw more whales until there were around a dozen or so breaching and performing other surface displays such as flipper-slapping, tail-lobbing, and tail-breaching, all within a few feet of our boat. We were spellbound. The guide pointed out one particular whale with a calf, and said that we were very lucky to see this rare animal as she was the most studied and recorded whale in the bay. This seemed to me to be an oxymoron but we were, nonetheless, very impressed. All too soon it was time to head back to the harbour engrossed in the excited chatter of our shipmates and I have rarely seen a happier and more satisfied group. On deboarding, our excellent guide said that this was the first time that she had led a tour and hoped that she had done OK, whilst holding out her hand for a reward. I did not give her a tip.

After quick snack we spent the afternoon wandering around the Beech Forest Trail near Provincetown, woodland that is reputed to be the way that Cape Cod looked like when the Mayflower landed in the early seventeenth century. Today, the Beech Forest is one of the most densely wooded sections of Cape Cod and the trail meanders through the forested dunes, encircling the shallow waters of Blackwater Pond. It was a pleasant stroll and we managed to avoid the dreaded greenheads as we chatted about whales whilst carefully watching out for the vicious insects. We saw no-one else on the trail.

That evening, we were tempted to visit the Sandpiper to eat, but decided that the crowded bar, the non-stop television sport, the huge meals and the danger of being showered in pee was too much, so we stayed in with a pizza. It was so much safer and our feet stayed dry.

Our last day was spent visiting Chatham before packing and resting ready for the long day ahead on the morrow. I was temporarily misplaced on the way, so followed a small bus with "Dune Tours Chatham" advertised on its flanks. As we followed the bus, it did occur to me that it may have been starting a tour and could have led us away from our destination but fortune favours the brave and it led us straight into the town centre. Sue was not impressed with my navigational skills, calling it "lucky." Chatham is an old-fashioned settlement, typical of the small New England towns we had fallen in love with on our travels. Its winding Main Street is lined with historic inns, white-steepled churches, trendy eateries, chic boutiques and art galleries. We ambled through the town but soon made our way to the sea front and spent a leisurely morning doing nothing much before returning to the motel and packing ready for the trip home.

AMERICANADIAN DIARIES

It was a late afternoon flight and we had already planned to stop at the Pilgrim Memorial State Park in Boston on the way to Logan International Airport to soak up our last piece of American history before returning to Blighty. The traffic was heavy as we headed north and we inched along the four-lane highway as we approached Boston. "I suppose we should have expected this on a weekend," I pondered out loud as we inched along the road, "After all, it is Saturday."

"And tomorrow is July the fourth," Sue added. Not for the first time, I was momentarily dumbstruck. Throughout my careful and comprehensive planning, it had never occurred to me that we would be travelling on this weekend, the day before the USA's biggest holiday – in the centre of one of the USA's biggest cities. It also dawned on me that visiting such a significant memorial on the weekend of Independence Day may have been imprudent, but muttered something about knowing that but I had incorporated the possible hindrance in my schedule. I was unconvincing. We did, however, make it to the memorial park, and found it surprisingly quiet with very few visitors. We parked easily and strolled over to look at the famous Plymouth Rock, reputedly the stepping stone to the New World used by the Pilgrims from the Mayflower. This was interesting solely because of its eminence in American history but something of a disappointment. The rock was little more than a large pebble and we had seen bigger pieces of stone on Blue Anchor beach in Somerset. It was inscribed with the date, *1620*, the same year that the pilgrims landed in Provincetown and Provincetown claimed to be the first landing place, so we left a little confused.

A full-sized replica of the Mayflower is moored in Plymouth harbour and we joined a tour of the ship, immediately struck just how small the ship was. How 102 passengers and 30 crew squeezed on to a boat considerably smaller than the Isle of Wight passenger ferry, and made its way across the Atlantic Ocean was a mystery.

Our history lessons complete, we made our way back to airport and were soon flying back to Heathrow and driving back to Swindon, back to mundane normality...but already planning our next trip across the pond, for a second holiday of a lifetime.

AMERICANADIAN DIARIES

CHAPTER 5 – THE APPALATIONS

Sue and I spent many happy hours studying our new, recently purchased road atlas of the Americas, the National Geographic Adventure Edition, which included detailed profiles of all National Parks in the USA and Canada. We decided that we were now experienced American travellers and did not need Mr. Branson's help in arranging a fly-drive package and could make our own arrangements. We also agreed that we had not yet finished with the East Coast and wanted to include another national park after our infatuation with Arcadia, so began to focus our plans on the area further to the south. Our new atlas was invaluable and our studies led us towards Shenandoa National Park. How could any aspiring cowboy like the Pinehurst Kid resist the call of Shenandoa, the very name conjuring up visions of early settlers, log cabins, cattle ranchers, the American Civil War and the greatest actor ever, James Stewart. Not only that, but the park is in the northern reaches of the Blue Ridge Mountains of Virginia featured in the brilliant song by Stan Laurel and Oliver Hardy and in the words of John Denver's beautifully evocative song, *Almost Heaven, West Virginia, Blue Ridge*

Mountains, Shenandoa River. Surely no-one could resist that, so Sue agreed when I pleaded that she should take me home country roads, to the place I belong.

I was also convinced that booking accommodation ahead was unnecessary as there was an abundance of small hotels and, preferably, motels which we could select as we travelled which would offer us flexibility and add even more excitement to our adventure. Sue was sceptical, but I said, "Just trust me," at which she shook her head in an act of doubtful resignation. I conceded that we would book the first four nights and reserved our room at the Cool Harbor Motel in Front Royal, Virginia. We chose this town because it is only an hour from Washington Dulles airport and it is situated on the northern tip of the Shenandoah National Park, making it an ideal base to discover the area. And it was the end point of Mr. Bryson's attempt to walk the Appellation Trail (I had forgiven him by this time.) Our research also discovered the New River Gorge in West Virginia and Smith Mountain Lake back in Virginia, which would make an ideal round trip back to Washington DC.

The flights, again with Virgin Atlantic, the hire car and first four nights booked, we contacted Chauffeured Luxury Cars in Swindon for the trip from home to Heathrow, more convenient and somewhat cheaper than car parking at the airport. We were all ready to go and the journey went without a hitch, arriving at Washington Dulles Airport on time, picking up the car and not getting lost in the airport complex or during the drive to Front Royal. We arrived in the Cool Harbor Motel, tired but content that all was going to plan. After a rest, we found the nearest restaurant, The Golden China, for a meal. Not exactly the American dining experience we had hoped for but convenient and cheap. It was then back for a final study session of the area and early night before beginning our voyage of discovery the next day.

On waking up the next morning, we decided to forego breakfast and head straight out to the north entrance of the park after stopping at a 7/11 garage and store to fill up on gas and sandwiches and snacks. The store had a large sign over its front which proudly stated, *New Baseball Cups – What a Hit!* We had no idea what a baseball cup was until we entered the store and saw the display. We then realised that a baseball cup is a plastic protector for men's private parts, much like a cricket box, which we thought an odd item to advertise so boldly at the front of the store. Only in America.

Shenandoa National Park is traversed by Skyline Drive, a 105-mile road on the crest of the Blue Ridge Mountains from Front Royal to Waynesboro, with spectacular views of the river and Massanutten Mountains to the west and the rolling Virginia Piedmont country on the east. It also runs alongside the Appalachian trail, so we hoped that we may be able to access the trail and follow in Bill Bryson's footprints at some point. From the 7/11, we headed to the north entrance to the park, bought a weekly pass and stopped at the Dicky Ridge Information Center. The centre had just opened as we were early, usual on our first day due to our out of tune body clocks and forgoing breakfast. After the baseball cup discovery, I surmised what a Dicky Ridge may be, but was too polite or embarrassed to ask. Having absorbed more information and collected a more detailed map of our planned walk to Upper Whiteoak Falls, we started off by driving along Skyline Drive. There are many overlooks on the road accessed by laybys, which our American cousins call pull offs, and we stopped at one of the first of these after the stop at the information centre. It was called Signal Knob Overlook. With the connections between Dicky Ridge and pull offs and now knobs, I was in my sniggering, smutty element, until Sue, said firmly, "That is enough talk about Dickies, Knobs and pulling off," which made me snigger even more.

We were out of the car, standing and gazing in awe at the views of the Shenandoa valley, the fertile plains and distant mountains, enjoying the peace as the only visitors at the site, when another car arrived and parked close by. Two couples stepped out of the car and were also admiring the view, with one man speaking in a strong Geordie accent. I interrupted their conversation and said, "Better than the view over the Tyne, is it not?"

"Aye, it is," he replied, "But I don't live in Newcastle now, I live in Swindon." This was too much for my simple mind to compute. We were in a national park in America, the only people there at that moment in the early morning, talking to someone from our home town. When I had gathered my senses, I told him that we also came from Swindon and asked whereabouts he lived. He replied that his home was in Greenmeadow, an estate I lived in before marrying Sue and where I had many friends and still used the local pub regularly. In further detail, we learned that he lived in the same street as my nephew Steve and occasionally took a drink in that same pub. I think that we were both so taken aback that we just smiled and nodded as if it was the most natural encounter in the world before continuing our separate ways along Skyline Drive.

With hundreds of miles of hiking trails in the park, all of which offer fantastic views, wonderful forests, roaring rivers and spectacular waterfalls, selecting a walk was not easy but the five-mile return trek to the Upper Whiteoak Falls seemed a relatively easy and straightforward introduction. We stopped at the

Whiteoak Canyon parking area and I was pleased to see a large sign pointing to Pollocks Knob. Sue stared at me as if to say don't you dare say anything. I didn't. We were excited as we began our first walk of the holiday. It was everything we expected and more, through dense forest, over roaring, tumbling rivers and past small waterfalls cascading down bare rock faces. We made it to our destination and found the falls crashing 86 feet down over rocks into a deep pool at the bottom. We had seen no-one on the walk but there were two hardy couples swimming in the pool as we sat on a stone overlooking the pond, munching 7/11 sandwiches, as content and relaxed as we had ever been.

That evening, we resisted the lure of cheap Chinese food and drove into downtown Front Royal for dinner and discovered superb restaurant, the Grape Vine. It was everything that we had come to love about American eating places, with an excellent menu including ribs, steaks, chicken wing, clams, lobster and, of course, fries. It also had a salad bar with unlimited visits. On delivering our order of mixed fish, Sue thanked the waitress and I added, in my best BBC accent, "That looks jolly nice, thank you very much."

The waitress looked a little surprised and replied, "You're welcome...er...very much." We had forgotten the accepted American etiquette of no please or thank you. After this exchange, both waitresses were most attentive, checking that everything was satisfactory, asking where we came from, why Front Royal and why the Grapevine. We stayed long after the meal was complete chatting to our new friends. I also had a couple of beers and left a very generous tip.

The following day will live long in our memories. On gazing out of the motel window that morning we noticed a diner opposite, which we had somehow missed on our arrival, and not just any diner. It was a classic 1950s diner, the steel-clad, neon-tinged, Art Deco-style was an icon of American culture and something I never thought I would see, let alone use. We, of course, breakfasted there and the inside was like walking into a 1950's film. The décor had changed little from those days, with photos of many film stars of the post war era on the walls. I half expected to find Marlon Brando, James Cagney or James Dean sitting at the counter staring moodily into a coffee cup. Each booth had its own juke box featuring great singers like Connie Francis, Dean Martin and Patsy Cline. The fact that the individual Juke boxes did not work independently except for volume control did nothing to lesson my excitement. And the full American breakfast was perfect. I could happily have spent the day there, drinking coffee and talking to James Dean.

We decided to hike over The Pinnacles to Marys Rock, which traverses the most spectacular section of the Appalachian Trail through Shenandoah National Park. Views were described as *Expansive and frequent*. It sounded perfect. We drove to the trail start point, again following the empty Skyline drive at a leisurely pace until, after a few miles, Sue shrieked, "Bear!" I stopped the car and just over the crash barrier in the forest was a small black bear, sitting in a tree and apparently surveying the scenery. We stayed in the car for all of ten seconds before Sue got out and headed closer to our ursine sightseer. I bravely followed, warning her to be careful as the bears can be notoriously unpredictable. Sue's response that it was only a baby, whereupon I said that babies have mothers and they are very protective. As it was, we approached to within a few feet before baby bear decided that he didn't like the sight of us, or more likely, the silly cooing sounds we were making, and slowly climbed down from its perch before disappearing into the woods. We continued to our destination in joyous mood at the sighting, elatedly watching several white-tailed deer on the grass verges as we travelled.

We parked and left the remote Pinnacles Picnic Area, then crossed the road and began the steep walk towards the pinnacle of The Pinnacles. As usual, the car park was almost empty and we were typically alone on our trek through the trees. We climbed the steep forested path chatting amiably about how lucky we were and how lovely it all was, until Sue repeated her cry, "Bear!" I looked up from my map and saw, no more than 20 yards in front of us, another black bear in the foliage at the side of the trail. Only this was not a baby. It was, even by black bear standards, massive. Sitting on its haunches, I reckoned that it was about six feet tall and looked almost as wide. We stopped and looked at the bear. The bear looked at us, its nose raised as it sniffed the air. We stayed still. The bear stayed still. The standoff lasted what seemed like a long time, but was possibly no more than a couple of minutes. We had read that to run from a bear is not advisable as it then thinks that you may be prey, and you should talk to the animal quietly so that it recognises you as human. Easy. Except that talking to a 6 feet bear weighing up to 660 pounds a few feet away is not that easy. I took a deep breath and said that Sue should follow me as we walked towards the animal talking in as controlled and friendly a manner as I could manage. Quite what I said, I cannot remember but, as an Englishman, I probably asked him about the weather. We moved forwards slowly to within perhaps 20 feet when the bear gave one last sniff and turned and disappeared into the darkness of the forest. As we walked past the spot where it was previously sitting, we looked into the forest but there was no trace of the bear. I suggested to Sue that perhaps it was frightened off by the smell as I had had just shat myself. I hadn't really.

We continued the hike, looking behind us every few yards to check that weren't being followed, until we reached The Pinnacle. It was a truly impressive outcrop with an outstanding panorama across the valley to the mountains opposite. On the rocky overlook was another, younger couple and we chatted politely for a while but did not mention that we had bravely survived a bear encounter. After a short rest watching raptors circling and diving over the valley, we continued the walk with still more spectacular views to what is considered to be the best vista in the entire park, Mary's Rock, locally renowned for its 360-degree views. The climb of 450 feet was a small price to pay for such an impressive outlook. The most exciting part of the walk to me was that much of it followed the Appalachian Trail and it was not long after this that Mr. Bryson gave up his objective of completing the complete walk. Too much for you, eh Bill I smugly pondered ignoring the fact that he had already covered several hundred miles compared to my three miles.

That evening we could not resist the Grapevine again and were welcomed by our waitresses as if we were long-lost family. With additional "pleases" and "thankyous" added in to our conversation, the ladies were wonderfully attentive and seemed genuinely upset when we told them that we had only one more day in Front Royal after this, but looked forward to seeing them the next evening.

For our last day in Shenandoah, we chose to repeat our relaxed journey on Skyline Drive with a hike, after a generous breakfast at what had now become Our Diner and the usual purchase of sandwiches from the 7/11. We thought it only right that we should climb to the highest point in Shenandoah, so set off for the 4050 feet Hawksbill summit. It was an exhilarating but uneventful day: no people, no deer and, thankfully, no bears. The viewing platform at the top of Hawksbill gave another magnificent 360-degree panoramic view of the Shenandoah Valley, the Blue Ridge Mountains, and the Virginia Piedmont and we rested happy that we had achieved more than we had originally planned, yet were sad to be leaving this wonderful region.

We kept our promise and the evening was spent dining in the Grapevine where we were again warmly welcomed and spent more time chatting to our new waitress friends than we did eating. In the morning, we left Fort Royal with heavy hearts, feeling that there was more to explore, but with happy memories and feelings of excitement at a new adventure elsewhere.

Our next stop, carefully planned and documented over the previous months, was to the New River Gorge, four hours east of Front Royal. We (I) had not felt it necessary to reserve any accommodation as we (I) were sure that there would be plenty of hotels and motels available, especially as the gorge was a state park. We set off in a happy and relaxed mood, except that Sue still had a slight nagging doubt that not booking before we left may become an issue. "Nonsense, my little flower," I confidently assured her, "Have I ever let you down?" She gave me a very strange look as we crossed the border into West Virginia.

During our planning sessions, we had identified the beautifully sounding Fayetteville or nearby Oak Hill as the ideal base and looked forward to selecting our lodgings from a variety of hotels, motels and inns in the area. When we arrived in the town, we found just one motel, the Quality Inn, and despite the car park being very busy, confidently approached the desk to book a room. Our enquiry was met with a smile, a shrug and a shake of the head as we were informed that they were fully booked for the next few days. Slightly less confidently, we asked if they could recommend anywhere else. We were told that the whole area was fully booked as there was a national football tournament taking place in the town and there was no room at this or any other inn. "It's a good job our names aren't Joseph and Mary then," I quipped which confused the receptionist and Sue's anxious look turned to a glare. As we retreated, I made the excuse that Fayetteville was obviously French so what did we expect? We found the Canyon Rim Visitor Centre in the town and called in to see if they could offer any advice on possible accommodation, but were met with the same response – the area is fully booked due to the football tournament - so we grabbed a few random walking guides and left, a tad apprehensive but not yet desperate. Back in the car we headed north and saw no hotels, motels or inns on the road and, whilst panic had not exactly set in, I was becoming just a little concerned. After about forty miles of silent driving, we approached the small settlement of Summersville and, oh joy of joys, on the edge of town was a Best Western motel. We stopped and approached the reception with slight trepidation, but were welcomed with the news that yes, they had rooms available. I gave Sue a smug told you so look. And with good reason as the room was perfect: spacious, clean and comfortable and, as an added bonus, breakfast was included. I said, "That'll teach those damned Frenchies that they can't get one over on us brave English explorers."

Having travelled for about six hours it was now mid-afternoon and we had not stopped for personal refuelling so we were hungry. In the hotel car park was a restaurant called Dairy Queen and Sue suggested that we eat there. Despite my protestations that I didn't want an ice cream, in we went and, to my surprise, it was a burger joint, decked out much like any other chain diner. As Sue said, the fact that there was a prominent sign outside which read, *Chill and Grill*, should have given me a clue that other food was available. It was difficult to resist a *Bacon two cheese deluxe with fries*, but we were planning to go out to eat that evening, so settled for a small salad and a coffee, and no ice cream. It was a very wise decision as that evening, we stopped at the first restaurant we found, the Peking Chinese which offered an all-you-can-eat option. To be polite, we ate all we could. Fully replete we went to bed studying the trail guides and excited about the coming days.

The following morning after dining on our free breakfast of bagels and muffins and secreting a few more in my backpack for lunch, we decided to revisit the visitors centre in Fayetteville, where we studied the trail maps in more detail. We selected a hike alongside the New River and included the miners' trail. It is hard to imagine that this beautiful and seemingly pristine forested area was once one of the busiest and most productive coal mining areas in the country. Perhaps the most well-known of the old mines was the Kaymoor mine, now abandoned and overgrown within the forest. It seemed apt and somehow respectful that we should begin our discovery of the area by viewing the historic site, and we were able to start the exploration from the visitors' centre. The trailhead led us to a wooded track above the New River, passing the Fayette Station Rapids and Millers Folly Rapids crashing below. We wondered what had happened to Mr. Miller and what folly he had committed to have the rapids named after him, before concluding that he probably tried to navigate the dangerous stretch of water in a small boat and was drowned. We never found the real reason but were satisfied with our conjecture. We turned at a junction and followed the steep miners trail through the dense woodland, zigzagging up the gorge. Unsure that we would ever find our way out of the wilderness, we were excited when we discovered the abandoned Kaymoor mine site. Sue was particularly happy as she put on her geologist hat and joyfully pointed out a coal seam running along the hillside. Old mine buildings of both wood and stone were left to nature, gradually collapsing and being overtaken by the forest. The mine entrance, which reminded me of the entrance to a smugglers' cave, was secured by a barred metal gate through which we were able to look inside. We stood and stared into the mine for a while imagining how the miners must have felt entering this cold, black, unwelcoming hole in the hillside day after day. It sent a shiver down my spine.

Near the mine entrance was a very large notice painted clearly on a wooden panel, headed *SAFETY BOARD* with subheadings of *TIME LOST ACCIDENTS FOR YEAR* and *MONTHS WITHOUT A TIME LOST ACCIDENT*. If I understood it correctly, it seemed a bit harsh that accidents were only recorded if production time was lost, seemingly more important than if injuries were incurred or lives were lost. We stayed on the site for about half an hour, soaking up the absorbing atmosphere and talking of the hardship the miners must have endured, climbing a steep track each day before entering a hellhole and slaving in the pitch-black, digging coal. It was a very moving experience, exaggerated by another sign over the entrance to the site which read, *YOUR FAMILY WANTS YOU TO WORK SAFE*. I didn't even comment on the misuse of English.

We restarted the hike in somewhat reflective mood, using the Long Point Trail, until we reached the Arrowhead Campground site. It had developed into a very hot and muggy day so we were pleased to see that, although the site was almost empty of campers, there was small shop open on site. As we had another hour or more walking, we decided to stop for some cooling sustenance and entered the shop. It was simple wooden building, almost bare inside, with an elderly man standing behind a counter staring at us as we entered. He did not speak and continued to stare until I ordered a coke for myself and a choc ice for Sue. He moved slowly to the fridge and took out Sue's Klondike Candy Swirl and handed it over, still saying nothing. I heard the floorboards creak behind me and felt a presence at my back. I turned and was confronted by a very tall and very fat young man in faded overalls, holding out a coke can and staring at me. He smiled exposing a tongue and crooked teeth covered in what I hoped was chocolate and announced, "Cokey Cola." I took the coke and paid, leaving the shop quickly with no other words spoken. After all, I had seen the film *Deliverance*. We sat on a bench some distance from the shop, keeping an eye on the door until our treats were finished, ensuring that Abner and Cletus were safely inside. When we restarted our walk, I kept turning round to check that we were not being followed as we made our way through the woods and back to the car.

That evening, we discovered another American diner chain which was to become the regular dining experience for our stay. We drove into Summersville, very hungry after surviving on stolen muffins and a camp site treat for the entire day, and called in at Merchant Walk, a small retail park just off the highway. There we found Bob Evans Restaurant and sat in a booth very happy that we had found the perfect eating place. Outside of the window and across the highway, was a field full of bright yellow flowers which Sue identified as black-eyed susans. The evening was only slightly marred by me serenading my wife with the old Guy Mitchell hit, *Pretty Little Black Eyed Susie, cross my heart I love ya best of all.*

The following day we had chosen the Canyon Rim Trail near Anstey on the eastern side of the New River. It was a good hike yet strangely uneventful. The trail gave us wonderful views of the New River Gorge when stopping at Turkey Spur and Hawks Nest overlooks. Safe from the hillbillies inhabiting the opposite bank, everything was relaxed and gentle. The evening spent at Bob Evans meant that the peaceful, gentle day ended with a peaceful, serene meal, something that we rarely enjoyed.

After two long and stimulating but arduous hikes we decided to visit the Carnifex Ferry Battlefield State Park for our last full day in the area. The park commemorates the Battle of Carnifex Ferry in 1861, a victory for the Union troops that led to the eventual Confederate withdrawal from western Virginia. There were few other visitors as we wandered around the site and, although an enjoyable and interesting place, there was little to see of the original battle and I suggested that all the soldiers must be on leave, so we made our way down to the nearby Gauley River, a spur of the New River. We arrived at the river's edge, next to the violent, crashing Pillow Rock rapids for another purloined lunch of Best Western bagels and muffins. As we unpacked our backpacks, we heard a shout from the river and looked up to see a dinghy with six youngsters, supervised by what we hoped was an experienced guide, heading for the rapids. As they approached and hit the ferocious, churning waters, their paddles guiding them between the dangerous rocks, we literally held our breath and watched in awe as they passed. After being tossed and turned, pitching sometimes backwards through the maelstrom, the group finally reached the smooth waters beyond the rapids. Sue and I automatically broke into a round of relieved applause, not that the brave adventurers could see or hear us.

Although we had not originally planned to stay in Summersville, we found it an ideal base and were surprised to discover that the town was adjacent to the picturesque Summersville Lake, so chose an easy stroll that afternoon from the motel to the lakeside. We sat and rested, recapping on our escapades of the holiday so far and looking forward to our next stop, after another evening as guests of Bob Evans, naturally.

On our cosy planning evenings at home, we had identified an area south of Shenandoah on the southern tip of the Blue Ridge Mountains near Roanoke, which looked an ideal third stop. Hence, we set off on the four-hour drive across the Appalachians and back into Virginia to Smith Mountain Lake. We left Summersville in a thunderstorm and torrential rain followed us as we passed through towns and villages with charismatic names such as Canvas, Green Valley, White Sulphur Springs, Irongate and Flatwoods. There were also settlements which were obviously named after the pioneers who settled there: Leslie, Rupert, Dickson and Callaghan, each one fastidiously ticked off on our handwritten route plan.

It was still dark and dismal as we arrived at Smith Mountain but we were in a bright and sunny mood as we slowly followed the northeastern side of the lake looking for any likely motel. Even when we realised that this was a fairly remote area and had seen no sign of civilisation, we remained upbeat. Near the small town of Moneta, we spotted a sign on the road pointing to a campground offering cabins for hire and thought that this may be a viable option, so turned off the main road and pulled in at the campground office. The receptionist explained that they did not officially open for the season for another few days but, obviously feeling sorry for these two tired looking, simple Englanders, said that we could have a cabin for three nights, after which they were fully booked. We jumped at the chance and were soon ensconced in our rustic wooden lodge situated directly on the lakeside in a small, wooded area with a magnificent view across the lake to the opposite bank and a small harbour, in which was moored a large boat called the Virginia Dare. The room felt a little damp and had a slight stale smell which we put down to a long off season, but unpacked and settled in before starting off on a short walk in the forest. It was a quiet stroll and we had no idea where we were, but came across an ancient log hut with a small plaque explaining that this was an old tobacco growing area and the hut was where the tobacco leaves were hung to dry. I told Sue that this where the tobacco leaves were cured and further explained that I didn't even know they were ill. She was not impressed. After a pleasant meal in the nearby Pilot House restaurant that evening, we slept cosily in our not quite dry rustic cabin.

We started the next day in our usual manner by visiting the local information centre and picked up a trail map of the area. We put together our own eastern lakeside walk which included several unintentional detours (I was again temporarily misplaced) and a deliberate short diversion to Turtle Island. As we crossed the wooden walkway and explored the small islet wandering through the long grass, we were aware that we were being attacked by small insects which sneaked up on us and delighted in biting our legs. We never saw them, but felt the attacks and certainly felt the aftereffects when our legs were covered in red, swollen and very itchy lumps. We finally escaped the insect attack and returned to the mainland. Despite our spotty, itching legs we heroically made our way to the harbour we had spied from our cabin. We were intrigued by the Virginia Dare and called into the harbour office to ask if the boat was sailing soon. Indeed, the congenial young lady at the reception desk informed us, it was sailing the next day. We could not resist the temptation of a peaceful boat trip and purchased tickets for the tour. Business completed, the receptionist asked, "Where are y'all from," and seemed very excited when I replied that we were English. I immediately lapsed into my best smooth gentlemanly English accent, a cross between Terry Thomas and Leslie Phillips with a touch of west country Jethro, as we chatted. Miss Congeniality said that she had a friend in the office and could we speak to her in English. We, of course, agreed and she called out, "Mary-Lou, Mary-Lou, there's some English guys here want to talk to you."

Mary Lou emerged from the back office and I said, "Hello Ma'am. How do you do? How jolly nice to see you." She stood, mouth agape and struggled to reply, "Uh huh." As we left the office, I said, "Thanks awfully," and we both added, "Cheerio." The girls giggled and we heard Miss Congeniality say, "Did you hear that, Mary-Lou? The guys said 'Cheerio'."

Back at the campsite, we were informed that the now very red and swollen lumps on our legs were chigger bites and we should not have walked through any long grass. A bit late now, I mumbled as we returned to the cabin to apply soothing cream to our blooded chigger wounds.

We arrived at the harbour in good time for our trip on the Virginia Dare and boarded early. We were guided into the impressive and stylish dining area aboard the ship to await departure. There were only a handful of other passengers on board and we sat resting quietly, still docked for about twenty minutes after the scheduled sailing time. There was then an announcement over the speaker, telling us that departure was delayed waiting for a coach party, which had been "...held up." I suggested, perhaps too loudly, that it was probably outlaws, perhaps the James' gang that held them up. No-one laughed. The coach finally arrived and it took another twenty minutes for the ancient passengers to leave the bus and shuffle on to our vessel, obviously an outing from an old folks' home. It was then another twenty minutes as the oldies shambled around the dining room before they were seated in acceptable order. The elderly ladies were delightful, smiling amicably and chatting to us and each other as they found their seats. The old men sat silently, cutlery at the ready waiting to be fed.

After a fine luncheon cruising Smith Mountain Lake, Sue and I decided to go on deck whilst the old ladies continued chatting and the old men continued eating what the ladies had left. On the upper deck, we were treated to excellent views of the lake and surrounding hills and mountains, whilst the captain offered a running commentary on the surroundings. We sailed to the far southern tip of the lake to the edge of a massive dam. Perhaps rather naively, I had not realised that this was a man-made lake as were told that the dam was built in the early 1960s on the Roanoke River to provide hydro-electric power. I wondered at the structure and I began to mentally plan the following day's walk in the inviting hills overlooking the dam.

We travelled on and the commentary continued with the guide stating that, "On our right, we have Turtle Island." This was the very island Sue and I had walked on the previous day. The guide continued, "Before being taken over by the park authorities it was known as Chigger Island, but I guess the park people thought that Turtle Island was a little more attractive than Chigger Island." This was rubbing salt into our throbbing leg wounds, but more salt was added when, out of nowhere, a wasp attacked Sue and stung her on the hand. This wound started to swell quite alarmingly and all of our carefully chosen creams were in my backpack in the car on shore. As the pain intensified, I found a steward and asked if the boat had any first aid equipment with something to ease the pain of stings. They did not, but one crew member said that he had the solution and tobacco would ease the pain and swelling. With that, he broke open a cigarette and secured it over the sting with a plaster. Perhaps unsurprisingly, it had no effect. We later discovered that the Virginia Dare was named after the first child born from the Mayflower immigrants who settled in the Roanoke area in the sixteenth century. What became of Virginia and the other colonists remains a mystery as John White, Virginia's grandfather and the governor of the colony, returned to England to seek fresh supplies. When he returned three years later, the colonists were gone without trace. Perhaps killed by chiggers and wasps, I surmised.

The wasp sting eased and wounded but undeterred, we used our last day to hike in the hills overlooking the dam. It was a baking hot day and the walk was tough, but we made it to the top of the highest peak and sat down overlooking the dam for a well-earned rest. As we rested, we noticed about twenty or so vultures circling overhead. It was, I reasoned, either a wagon train attacked by hostiles or they thought that we were about to collapse in the heat and become their lunch. As we looked down into the lake hundreds of feet below us, we saw something very big but unidentifiable swimming just below the surface. We were unable to identify the creature but Sue disagreed with my suggestion that it may be a relative of the Loch Ness monster. What it was has remained a mystery although the camp ground reception told us that it was probably a striper which did not help.

We decided on a change of dinner venue that evening and plumped for the nearest diner to the camp, the *Hot Diggity*

Hog BBQ and Family Restaurant – Dine in – Carry Out. Whilst we ate a forgettable meal, we discussed where to spend the last two nights after being evicted from the cabin and agreed that we should call ahead and book into the Cool Harbor Motel in Front Royal again. We both felt that there was more to be explored in the Shenandoa Valley and it was within easy reach of Washington and Dulles Airport. We booked with no trouble and travelled in the morning, taking the I-81 North for a trouble-free drive. We stopped once for coffee in Bridgewater, and I was tempted to complain to the town elders that, if it was named after the Somerset town, it should be spelt Bridgwater, without the "e." However, we learnt that it was originally called Dinkletown, so anything was an improvement, with or without the "e." When we arrived in Front Royal, it was almost like coming home and, after a rest we inevitably spent a special evening in the Grape Vine, dining and enjoying the company of our special waitress friends.

We had one full day left and decided to hike Compton Peak, despite the rain which had been falling most of the night and throughout morning. Sue had read that this trail was a *hike through the forest along the Appalachian Trail to a western view and a great look at columnar jointing, an exciting geologic feature.* I had no idea what columnar jointing was, but Sue was excited at the prospect of seeing it close up, whatever it was. I was none the wiser when she read that it was formed where sets of intersecting, closely spaced fractures, referred to as joints, result in the formation of a regular array of polygonal basalt prisms, or columns. I had the distinct feeling that she had chosen the geology just to show up my ignorance, as she added that it was similar to the Devils Causeway in Ireland. This didn't help me much although I nodded sagely as we set off. Indeed, the structures were impressive and I found it difficult to imagine that these strange columns of regular shaped columns were not man-made. I refrained from expressing my views or Sue would have *womansplained* using lots of terms I wouldn't understand. And besides, I was more excited by sitting on a rock at the top of a mountain, above the rain clouds, looking down into a valley that we could not see through the mist.

That evening, we visited our favourite restaurant for the last time. The waitresses came to our table and told us that, because we had been such pleasant and friendly customers, tonight's meal was on the house. Their hospitality brought a lump to my throat and not just because I was saving money. In fact, despite our protests, they would not accept any money, although I made sure that the tip that I left was close to covering the bill.

It was a grand end to a great adventure, but we had one more interesting visit to make. The afternoon flight from Washington allowed time to visit the site of the first and perhaps the most famous of all civil war battles, the Manassas National Battlefield Park, site of the first Battle of Bull Run. We learnt that on July 21, 1861, Union and Confederate armies clashed for the first time in the Civil War on the fields overlooking the Bull Run stream. Confederate troops from the Shenandoah Valley and a brigade of Virginians under a relatively unknown Thomas J. Jackson, stood its ground, which resulted in Jackson receiving his famous nickname, Stonewall. The carnage was immense with Union losses numbering 13,824 and Confederate soldiers killed, wounded, or missing numbered 8,353 men. As we absorbed the horror of the battle, we were told that the battle was pre-planned and the gentry from Washington travelled in their horse-drawn carriages to the battlefield site to watch the slaughter from the sidelines. It was insensitive and crass of me to say that I was reminded of Leeds United and Chelsea clashes in the 1970s.

AMERICANADIAN DIARIES

We made it to the airport in good time and looked forward to our flight home, but our next trip was already beginning to form in our minds.

CHAPTER 6 - THE ROCKIES

Quite why and how we chose the next trip across the pond is clouded by memory, but I do remember that Sue has always wanted to see a glacier, despite my questioning the attraction of a mint sweet (she didn't laugh either.) For whatever reason, we decided to visit the northeast of the continent and include Canada in our itinerary, so Banff National Park in Alberta was the chosen destination before a planned crossing of the border into Montana and real cowboy country. I was confident that we had no need to book accommodation as I thought that the last trip had turned out OK, until Sue reminded me that we had travelled forty miles out of our way to find a motel in an area we had not researched, before moving on to a damp cabin that was not prepared, then returning to the one motel that we had planned before leaving. It was a convincing argument, so I conceded without a fight.

After much research we selected the town of Canmore, conveniently situated an hour's drive west of Calgary airport on the Trans-Canada Highway and close to Banff, but far enough away from the city to be very much cheaper. We looked at hotels, motels, apartments and cabins but finally selected a Bed and

Breakfast on the edge of town, with direct access to the Bow River and beneath the amazing Three Sisters, a trio of spectacular peaks which overlook the town. This was very different from our previous accommodations but we telephoned Ann and Pat at the Hidden Falls B and B and booked a room for the first week of our visit. We then planned to travel south into the USA and booked the second week in the Timbers Motel in Bigfork , Montana on the edge of Glacier National Park.

On the Thursday morning of departure, we waited excitedly to be picked up from home in the chauffer-driven car we had used the previous year, but we were not as excited as our boys who were looking forward for another two weeks freedom without interference from restrictive parents. We would rather not know what they had planned. As we approached the M4 motorway to head east towards Gatwick, a message was broadcast on the driver's radio which said that a lorry had shed its load across three lanes of the M4 near Slough and the road was closed. Our driver confidently said that these messages came through regularly and it would be clear by the time we hit Slough, so we continued our journey in optimistic mood...but not for long. As we approached Reading the traffic came to a standstill and we sat, worrying in the back seat as the traffic refused to move.

"Funny that," said our driver, "it's usually cleared by now," which did not help our growing panic. As time passed, I decided to call ahead to Gatwick to say that we would be late and ask if there was anything they could do to delay the flight. The Airport Help Desk said that they were aware of the problem and had taken appropriate action, but I was unconvinced. We arrived at Gatwick Airport at almost the exact time we should have been taking off, grabbed our cases from the car and ran to the terminal. Sweating and shaking, we read the departures board to find that our plane to Calgary had taken off on time, five minutes previously. I probably swore.

We rushed to the airline desk and explained the situation, but were told, quite unfairly in my opinion, that no, they could not turn the plane round and return to pick us up. After some pleading, arguing and stamping of feet, the desk clerk said that we could buy a ticket for the next available flight, leaving on the Saturday, two days later. With accommodation booked and the return flight still valid, we had little option but to accept. We sat down, ordered a coffee and reviewed our situation. We had another flight booked but were stuck in Gatwick airport: our chauffer had left us: we had no way of getting home: our bed and breakfast accommodation in Canmore would be waiting for us: we were tired and fretful. We had little option but to find the railway station and take the train back to Swindon. We bought a return ticket and travelled miserably back to Wiltshire, changing at Reading and then an expensive taxi from Swindon station to home. I spent what was left of the day telephoning our accommodation and changing the dates. Our boys spent the time telephoning their friends to cancel whatever it was they had arranged to take place in the house in our absence.

Saturday seemed a long time coming, but we made it to back to Gatwick by train with just one more small hiccup. The return ticket we had purchased was not valid for the weekend. Luckily, the ticket inspector was very understanding and did not charge us extra, but did warn us not to do it again. I thanked him and explained that we had no plans to repeat the exercise.

Some fourteen hours after leaving home we were happily driving the Trans-Canada highway towards Canmore in a

Pontiac Grand Am SE. The irony was not lost on us that two days previously we were stuck in static traffic on the inadequate M4 between Swindon, Reading and Slough but were now travelling easily on a magnificent Canadian Highway from Calgary to Banff passing Ghost Lake, Kananaskis and Dead Man's Flats, with views of the imposing, snow-covered Rocky Mountains in the distance. We arrived at Hidden Falls and were greeted by our host Ann and shown to our room. Whilst we had been lucky with accommodation in the past, this was extra special. The room was superb in every way, spacious and comfortable, spotlessly clean and beautifully decorated, with a balcony giving views overlooking a babbling stream and a dense forest to the snow-capped Three Sisters mountains, which looked almost close enough to touch. All our previous trials and tribulations had disappeared. After settling in we wandered downstairs to meet Ann's husband Pat, who had just returned home after work. We spent some time chatting with our hosts and discovered that Pat was a retired member of the Royal Canadian Mounted Police – a real Mountie. As if this was not exciting enough, Pat explained that he now worked for the local forestry administration, recording the wild animals in the area to ensure that they are protected and do not stray too near to the town. He described how he builds low boxes in the woods and fills them with soft earth, checking later to see what animal prints have been left. He told us that, as well as elk, other deer and small mammals, he has recorded many bears and cougars in the area. He saw the slight concern on our faces and said that we shouldn't worry as attacks are rare, which didn't really help.

He pointed out the peaks viewed from the house, explaining that, when Canmore as a mining town, the three peaks were known as the Three Nuns because the snow-capped peaks resembled nuns in white veils. They were later were renamed the

Three Sisters, individually known as Big Sister, Middle Sister, and Little Sister – or, more romantically, Faith, Hope, and Charity. Another peak he explained was known as Chinaman's Peak after a Chinese immigrant, the first man to climb it in a race the 1890's. It was, he said, now considered inappropriate to use the original name and it had recently been renamed Ha Ling Peak. Although most locals still referred to it as Chinaman's Peak. The background to the area's natural and geological history added to our mounting enthusiasm to get out and explore.

Another natural phenomenon described by Pat was the glacial lakes in the area and Sue's addiction to geology meant that visiting the small, emerald-coloured Grassi Lakes was an unmissable and ideal introduction to Banff. Despite being late June, the weather was cold, so we donned our warm hiking gear and set off from the trailhead to begin the relatively simple hike through woodland, with stunning views of the Bow River and Ha Ling Peak. We spotted squirrels, dippers and what we thought were osprey on the route before arriving at the lakes. We had read that the stunning ponds were created from a fossil reef that formed during the Late Devonian period, but that detail seemed irrelevant as we gazed across the incredibly coloured waters. We discussed whether they were blue-green, emerald or turquoise but no colour could adequately describe the loveliness of the waters as we sat and stared for perhaps an hour transfixed by their sheer beauty. We dragged ourselves away and moved on towards the top of the canyon beyond the lakes, to view famous pictographs, rock paintings on the side of the cliffs, thought to be more than 1,000 years old and painted by Kutenai, one of the indigenous peoples of Canada. To be honest, as works of art I had seen better pictures pinned on the wall at the boys' infant school, but the age and history of the splodges and stick men made the experience thrilling.

We had time left that day to take another walk, a peaceful stroll alongside the Bow River, uneventful except that we saw several large elk grazing on the opposite bank, a first sighting for us, and noticed a nest built high on a platform constructed above a telegraph pole. It was obvious that the platform was built specifically to attract a nesting bird, but whether to encourage wildlife or to prevent damage to the telephone wires was unclear. We were excited to see an osprey sitting proudly in the nest atop his high perch, confirming our previous sighting. After a well-deserved rest at the Hidden Falls, we drove into Canmore for meal at one the many restaurants in Canmore (exactly which one has gone from my memory) before returning to base and bed. As we laid in our comfortable room, the curtains left open to reveal the view, we planned the following day's excursions. This was not an easy job, as the area was full of exciting hikes and historical sites, so we tried to fit in as many as possible, centred on the resort town of Banff.

It was a cold, misty morning, making the high peaks ill-advised as a hiking destination, so replete from Ann's tasty breakfast, we began the day with a hike at Tunnel Mountain, a simple two hour walk to start our day. The indigenous people called the mountain Sleeping Buffalo because, we read unsurprisingly, it resembles a sleeping buffalo. In the 1880s, Canadian Pacific Railway surveyors had considered blasting a tunnel through the mountain for the tracks through the Bow Valley. Although the idea was abandoned, the name Tunnel Mountain stuck. Again, as this is now considered inappropriate, we were told that there were plans afoot to rename Tunnel Mountain as Sacred Buffalo Guardian Mountain, possibly because it looks like Buffalo. I am unsure whether this ever actually happened. The hike was short but enchanting with yet more wonderful views and left us time for more exploration that day.

We extended the walk to include the Hoodoos Overlook Trail. Sue explained that Hoodoos are tall, thin spires of rock formed by erosion. They consist of relatively soft rock topped by harder, less easily eroded stone that protects each column from the elements and are formed within sedimentary rock and volcanic rock formations. I thought that they were just big spikey stoney things. The overlook gave an impressive view, looking down on the hoodoos sitting beside the winding Bow River, but we vowed to make another trip to see them at ground level when the opportunity arose. As we turned to move on, we noticed many small furry animals running around on a small grassy rise, occasionally stopping and standing to attention to review the scene. We were reminded of meerkats which seemed to be on every wildlife programme on British Television, but these looked hairier and larger. We watched them for some time, chuckling at their cute antics as they scurried, sat up, argued scurried again before disappearing into their burrows. Pat told us later that they were probably hoary marmots as there were many colonies in the area.

We still had hours of daylight left, so moved on to find a suitable stop to eat our packed lunch. We started at the Spray River trailhead and walked into woods, striding through the snow and across a wooden bridge over the roaring, frothing river and headed up the trail. We eventually reached a viewpoint which looked down a deep cleft, cut out by millions of years of snow melt crashing down from the mountains and decided that this would be an ideal stop for lunch. As we returned to the trailhead, we noticed a very large and very fresh animal prints in the mud which, due to its size and lack of claw marks, could only have been made by a cougar. We hurried back to the car, hearts beating from the exercise and a little trepidation.

It was, by now, late afternoon and the clouds had cleared to expose a vivid blue sky. It was surprisingly warm, so we began another stroll alongside the Bow River. We veered into the woods and, by pure chance, we came across a wooden bridge leading to a small spring, a hole in the ground full of warm, bubbling, algae-filled water. We then noticed a small cave entrance, perhaps just large enough for a man to squeeze into, and protected by a barred metal gate. The plaque at the side of the opening explained that the springs were first discovered by three workers scouting for the transcontinental railway on August 7, 1883, and led to the development of Banff as a spa town. The men realised the potential and laid claim to the springs and surrounding lands before setting up a rudimentary hotel. We later found out that this is called the Cave and Basin Hot Springs and is the source of the warm water flowing into the Spray and Bow rivers. A wonderful history, and the reason that the spa town of Banff exists today, yet we came across it by accident and were the only ones viewing this important piece of local history. We followed the warm stream downhill reaching a pond of bubbling water and spotted a spotted a large fish with bright spots, which was swimming lazily under another bridge. After talking to Pat later, it was identified as a jewel fish or jewel cichlid and was apparently very rare.

When we ate that night in another forgotten Canmore restaurant, Sue and I agreed that three great hikes, wonderful mountain and lake views, a Sleeping Buffalo, a puma print, several elk, an osprey in its nest, hoodoos, hoary marmots, hot springs and a rare jewel cichlid wasn't a bad day out, but perhaps we deserved something less energetic and more practical for the morrow.

We decided to take the gondola ride to the top of Sulphur Mountain, just south of Banff. and eagerly boarded the small, four-seater steel and glass bubble to be lifted to the summit. We shared our ride with a young Japanese couple, soaring up above the forestry treetops before passing over the steep, rocky mountain side. As we admired the vistas of snow-covered peaks, deep valleys and the meandering Bow River, our high-flying companions stared straight ahead, holding each other tightly as if on a kamikaze mission, not looking at the stunning views or saying a word to us or each other. After eight minutes and rising 700 metres, we arrived at the top of Sulphur Mountain high above the town of Banff. The destination was a slight anticlimax. Although it offered spectacular views of six different mountain ranges stretching into the horizon from viewing platforms, it also boasted the Cosmic Ray Station described as a mountaintop discovery centre and the Castle Mountain Coffee café, the Sky Bistro restaurant, and a shop busy selling tacky souvenirs. And there were tourists everywhere, all of which rather spoilt the experience, reminding us of a motorway service station rather than a true wilderness encounter. We watched our Japanese couple as they walked to the viewing area, took copious numbers of photographs and immediately reboarded the return gondola. Their whole trip took only about half an hour, but at least they didn't stop to buy a plastic toy gondola or a fridge magnet. Sue and I took the kilometre-long boardwalk to Sanson's Peak, the highest point of the gondola station, which reduced the crowds somewhat, most visitors apparently unaware of the summit or, possibly, rejecting the thousand-metre trek as too much of a challenge.

Although the gondola station claims to reach Sulphur Mountain summit, the actual highest point is a couple of miles walk and follows the crest of the summit ridge. On returning from the easy stroll to Sansom Peak, we found the start of the trail to the true summit and off we went, leaving everyone else behind us to eat their burgers, drink diet coke and buy overpriced fridge magnets. The walk started well and we were enjoying the peace, thinking ourselves brave pioneers slipping away from the tourists and their trappings. After just half an hour or so of walking we arrived at a narrow ridge clinging to the mountainside. I started along the ridge for all of five yards when I looked down and felt strangely dizzy. I pressed myself against the sheer wall of rock and could not move. My heart was thumping and my legs refused to function as Sue asked what was wrong. "Dunno," I gasped, "I can't move. I'm stuck."

I had experienced this sensation once before, bizarrely when looking into the Devil's Cauldron on Lundy Island, but nothing like this. I was unsure whether it was vertigo, acrophobia or agoraphobia, but didn't much care what it was called. Sue reached out and held my hand as we slowly inched our way back along the ridge to safer land. We had little option but to return to the gondola station, my smugness evaporated in a cloud of shame. I excused my timidity by explaining, "You like shopping and I could do with a burger, anyway," as we rejoined the souvenir hunting and more sensible day-trippers.

After enjoying a burger and purchasing a fridge magnet and a key ring, we boarded the gondola and enjoyed the eight minute trip down the mountain. With our plans curtailed by my cowardice in the face of the altitude, we drove to the delightfully named Vermillion Lakes and wandered round the three lakes formed in the Bow River valley, at the foot of Mount Norquay between the Trans-Canada Highway and the Canadian Pacific Railway tracks. A hot spring bubbled at the third of the lakes where we rested and I began to shake off my shame. A while later, we moved on to a place that had intrigued me for some time. Lake Minnewanka. Our journey was briefly held up by a small herd of wild big-horned sheep standing in the road and refusing to move. These strange animals, led by a particularly large ram with enormous curly horns, simply stood and stared as if daring us to move, until they tired of the game and trundled slowly off the road. I giggled childishly at the name Minnewanka as we arrived at our objective and Sue shook her head, saying, "I don't know why you're laughing. The lake could have been named after you."

Another day and another walk was planned, but we were a little late that morning as we spent an interesting hour or more after breakfast talking to our hosts about the area, local wildlife and his job as a Mountie. When we finally left, we drove to Lake Louise, a few miles north of Banff and on the edge of the Yoho National Park. We made our way to the lake edge just west of the town, parked and strolled on the promenade in front of the imposing Fairmont Chateau Hotel, developed at the turn of the 20th century by the Canadian Pacific Railway as a holiday destination for wealthy travellers taking the train to cross the plains and rugged mountains. Impressive as the buildings and surrounding were, Sue and I agreed that we would much rather stay in the Hidden Falls bed and breakfast. The panorama from the walkway is probably the most photographed and most well-known view in Lake Louise and probably in the Banff National Park, with the stunning azure lake surrounded on three sides by high and commanding snow-capped mountains. At the end of the promenade, we turned onto the footpath heading east and began to follow the Lake Agnes trail leading high above the lake and into the mountains. From time to time, we heard loud roars as the snows were melting and minor avalanches of snow and ice crashed like waterfalls into the valley in the distance. After one particularly thunderous fall, a Japanese visitor appeared, running towards us in a state of fearful panic, shouting, "Avaranche, avaranche, big one, avaranche," and disappeared behind us as he ran down the mountainside, still crying, "Avaranche, big one." Sue and I shrugged our shoulders and continued the climb.

After ninety minutes of hard uphill trekking, passing the pretty tarn of mirror lake with another avaranche in the distance, we arrived at the eastern point of Lake Agnes. Our original plan was to circle the lake and climb The Beehive, a peak on the southern shore, but this was abandoned by two incidents. The first was that the climb was stiffer than we had anticipated and the Beehive ahead looked a very imposing mountain. More significantly, we found delightful wooden chalet-style log cabin high above the trail and were surprised to find that it was a cafe. I was amazed that all my meticulous planning had failed to notice that, tucked away on a forested path 400 meters above Lake Louise at an altitude of over 2000 metres, on the shores of Lake Agnes, was the Lake Agnes Tea House. Originally built in 1901, another venture by the Canadian Pacific Railway, as a refuge for hikers, and enhanced to serve tea in 1905. The log building was replaced in 1981 but still features the original windows, tables and chairs. Our original plan was abandoned as we took a table by the window and spent a relaxed hour sipping tea and watching avaranches thundering down the mountains on the opposite lake shore. As I said to Sue, it certainly beat the Robins Nest café with a view towards the County Ground in Swindon.

We had another surprise when we returned to Hidden Falls that afternoon. Pat greeted us dressed in full Mountie uniform. Sue was particularly impressed and the camera almost overheated taking snaps of Pat, Pat with Sue, Pat with Ann and Pat with Sue and Ann. After the photo session, Pat asked if we had ever seen a beaver on our expeditions. We had not, so we arranged to meet him again that evening to be taken to an area he knew that offered a good chance of seeing beavers. Just as dusk was beginning to fall, he led us across the road and through the forested area to the edge of the Bow River. From a small clearing he pointed across the river and there were two beavers going about their business on the opposite bank. Pat left us with instructions to remain still and quiet and see what happens. After a few minutes the beavers slipped silently into the water and circled round before swimming slowly towards us, passing within a couple of feet and watching us watching them with either suspicion or a well-practiced swagger. We were enchanted and Pat later explained that the beavers were very nosey animals and were simply checking us out. I wondered if they were as enchanted with us as we were with them.

The next couple of days were spent exploring areas recommended by our hosts and now good friends. We took the Johnston Canyon Trail to see spectacular waterfalls, at their peak in June snow melt. The trail ascended fairly gently along the canyon edge, through dense forest where we passed seven dramatic waterfalls crashing down the canyon sides. We walked through a cave and balanced precariously on catwalks and viewing platforms affixed to the canyon walls. This was a spectacular walk but surprisingly incident free with no temporary misplacements and no cowardly panics. Beyond the falls, a forested trail continued up reaching a lush green a meadow where water bubbled up from deep below the Earth's surface into shallow blue/green pools called the Ink Pots. On the trail we took a short break when Sue needed to pee. My job in such circumstances was to keep a lookout as she hid in the bushes at the side of the trail. On this occasion I glanced back from my guard duties just as Sue was about to squat, when I shouted, "Not there, Susan." She was about to urinate on two young garter snakes sunning themselves in the grass. Luckily, she managed to stop mid-squat and move on to leave the snakes in peace. I said to Sue when we restarted, "When those two little snakes go home later, they'll probably say to their mummy snake, 'Mum, we were just resting in the grass today when we looked up and guess what we saw.'"

It is perhaps indicative of our time in Banff that, on this hike, we saw incredible waterfalls and rapids in a beautiful canyon, magical pools of warm water, large elk grazing a few metres away, ground squirrels, chipmunks and marmots running around our feet, mountain goats clinging impossibly to the mountainside, two park rangers on horses who stopped to chat for a moment and two very lucky snakes, yet I described the day as incident free.

A visit to the abandoned ghost town of Bankhead was our next day's target. We spent a peaceful and quite emotional day wandering over the site, which began as a small coal mining community in the early twentieth century, located in the shadow of Cascade Mountain which contains high grade anthracite coal deposits. The Bankhead coal mine was operated by the Pacific Coal Company, a subsidiary (inevitably) of the Canadian Pacific Railway, and produced the coal to fuel its steam engines. The mine closed in 1922 after just seventeen years of operation as it was deemed unprofitable. From a population of around 1,000 people at its peak, there is now little left but signs placed along the trail identifying where the major buildings had once stood. It was a warm and sunny day but we knew that it would be desperately cold and snowbound in winter. As we wandered around and sat resting on the site of abandoned homes, we tried to imagine the busy town, with men literally scratching a living from the mountain and perhaps immigrant families with mothers bringing up children, setting up schools and churches in this tough mountainous environment, far from home, only for their new homes to be forsaken after just a few years.

Our final day was spent chatting to our hosts, packing and planning our route south, but we found time for one last walk. In the shadow of nearby Grotto Mountain, is the Grotto Creek Canyon trail within Stoney Nakoda territory, a landscape of cultural significance and spirituality for indigenous peoples since time immemorial. It contains tangible evidence of this history through a series of pictographs painted on the canyon walls.

We began the walk between the steep limestone walls and overhanging pines of the Grotto Creek Canyon when we saw half a dozen elderly indigenous gentlemen coming towards us. They were all dressed in the recognisable Indian cowboy style we had seen depicted in numerous westerns, with brightly patterned shirts with fringes, stetson-style hats, jeans and boots. They did not look happy and were grumbling amongst each other as we approached. I greeted then with a cheery, "Good morning," but was totally ignored as they passed, with one member of the tribe mumbling something about how he doesn't know who painted them as he'd never seen them before. I suggested to Sue that they probably thought the white man speaks with forked tongue, but was admonished for an inappropriate comment. A little further along the trail we were halted by a younger man who asked us to wait for a few minutes as the Discovery Channel was filming an interview with some elders regarding the famous pictographs. We stopped and chatted for a while and were told that the young man's name was John Snow. He explained that when settlers had first arrived in the area in the 1800s, his native ancestors were asked their names. One of his forefathers pointed to the sky in explanation, hence the name Snow after the snow-capped the mountains. He then explained that the family name was, in fact, White Cloud and the pioneers had misunderstood, but the name Snow stuck.

After several minutes, John White Cloud led us along the valley and we stopped to watch the elders and film crew discuss the next shot, before we continued. I rather hoped that they would film us but the cameraman waved us through when his camera was not recording. My chance of fame ruined, we wandered on until we reached the end of the canyon where we sat to eat lunch a few feet away from a roaring waterfall. As we looked around after our repast we noticed more pictographs on the canyon wall, clearly showing large horned animals, possibly elk, some fish and human figures. We read that the paintings were only discovered in the 1950's and, for decades since, archaeologists and academics have attempted to explain the meaning of the pictographs, who had created them and for what reasons. They have been traced, photographed, enhanced with software and compared and contrasted with rock art sites across North America. We were surprised then that such archaeological treasures were left unprotected, uncovered and unguarded within reach of the acidic fingers of any passing strangers.

We left Hidden Falls the following day with great regret but even greater memories and set out on the six-hour drive south to our next destination, Glacier National Park, Montana in the United Sates of America. The drive was easy and relaxed, staying on the BC93 all the way, passing through many intriguingly named towns on the way, we ticked off Windermere,

Skookum, Chuck, Wasa and Fort Steel before being held up by a slow police car ahead, with its blue lights flashing to slow us down. As we were waved past the car, we were amazed to find that we were in the middle of a cattle drive. Hundreds of cattle were steadily making their way along the wide roadside verge, being driven by the shouts and whistles of mounted cowboys. Real cowboys, dressed like the cowboys from a hundred western films and TV programmes I'd watched. At one time, I thought I recognised Jack Palance leading the drive, but couldn't be sure. It is impossible to explain the excitement we felt as we became part of a real cattle drive with bulls, cows and calves lowing loudly as the cowboys skilfully kept them moving and under control alongside us. After ten minutes or so we left the drive behind us and continued to the border in a state of trail-drive euphoria.

We arrived at the Roosville border crossing and left the car to report to the duty officer. We told him about our being ten-minute cowboys and he explained that, at this time of year, thousands of cattle are driven into the mountains to take advantage of the rich pastures, then rounded up and returned to the valleys before the winter snows arrive. He also checked our passports and asked whether were carrying drugs (no) or firearms (no) or fresh fruit or vegetables (no) and we were on our way. I guess that we just had honest faces as nothing was checked. We continued south on the 93 with very little other traffic, but the occasional lorry or car. It was quite noticeable that other drivers seemed very frustrated and upset with my careful driving as they passed me, often blasting their horns, but as I said to Sue, "The speed limit says eighty, and I'm doing eighty."

We found a pull-off after about an hour and stopped on a small mound for our packed lunch prepared at Hidden Falls. The lunch consisted of sandwiches containing tomato and lettuce, plus apples and bananas. We realised that we had told the customs officer that we were not importing any fruit or vegetables and were lucky not to have been locked up by the border police for carrying banned substances into the country. As we laughed and watched the traffic speed past, another realisation dawned. We had left Canada with speed limits in Kilometres per Hour and had been driving in the US where speed limits are in Miles per Hour. I had been driving at the Canadian speed of eighty KPH, or fifty MPH. No wonder that the other drivers were irritated. Sue just looked at me and shook her head.

We eventually arrived at our destination of Bigfork, advertised as the gateway to the vast Glacier National Park, with its peaks, alpine trails and grizzly bears. We found our destination, the Timbers Motel in the main street with no problems and arrived at the front desk to announce our arrival. The desk clerk studied her bookings, smiled and announced that we had arrived a day early and, unfortunately, there were no rooms available. My mind spun as I tried to absorb what she had said, referring to a copy of my plan created a week ago when we were forced to re-arrange our stay after the delay in England. I showed the receptionist my neatly printed schedule which clearly showed that we had booked Hidden falls from the 16th to the 24th of June and Timbers Motel from 25th to the 28th. She smiled sweetly and said, "Yes…but today is the twenty fourth. Your first day here is tomorrow, the twenty fifth."

I blushed deeply as I realised that my plan showed us leaving Banff on the 24th with nowhere booked that night. I tried, unsuccessfully, to appear cool and nonchalant, as we left with an embarrassed, "Thanks, see you tomorrow," and left the reception with my head held anything but high, again knowing how Joseph and Mary felt on that night in Bethlehem. Sue came to the rescue as I sat in the car in a state of uncomfortable bewilderment and she said that there was no stable, but she had noticed a motel in Kallispell a few miles north, so we should go back and try there. I did as I was told and we were soon settled into the Super 8, tired after an eight-hour drive and very hungry. We wandered out looking for somewhere to eat and the first place we came across was the King Buffet, yet another Chinese restaurant. We discussed the fact that, despite our love of all things American, it was becoming habit to settle into a new billet with an Asian meal of some kind and wondered if visiting Americans in Swindon ate at the Wing Hong in the town centre. It was a pointless discussion as Swindon was probably not on the schedule as a destination for trans-Atlantic visitors to Britain.

East of Kalispell and west of the Hungry Horse Reservoir at the north end of the Swan Mountain Range is The Jewel Basin. It is a recreation area, designated for hiking only, of 15,349 acres and includes 27 lakes and 35 miles of trails. This was an obvious place to start our adventure in Glacier National Park and we decided that the climb to the top of Mount Aeneas would make an ideal hike. I had previously noted the trail in preparation so we set off for Camp Misery Trailhead – not an ideal name for attract visitors to the remote Rocky Mountain area. At the trailhead is a ranger station perched on stilts perhaps 10 feet above the ground. We surmised that the height was either because the snow is that deep in winter or it is protection against grizzly bears and the ranger on duty had confirmed that the snow could drift that deep and there were indeed grizzlies in the area. We had encountered bears before and had recently bought bear bells, small bells which attach to backpacks and jingled irritatingly as we walked but warned bears of our approach, so we felt safe. The trail meandered through a subalpine spruce woodland before breaking into breathtaking views of the region's floral fields, mountains and lakes. Following this easy start, the track started to zigzag up steeply and the delightful Jewel Basin came into view as we approached the crest. As we trudged up the narrow, precipitous ridgeline, we met two hunters descending from the mountain, both carrying large rifles and sidearms. After exchanging pleasantries, the men asked if we were armed and seemed shocked when we said only with tinkling bells. They told us that it was dangerous on the mountain, not just because of the bears but there was a cougar who was rearing two cubs and was particularly threatening. We thanked them and continued, tinkling our bells a little more loudly. In the middle of the path at one point, we came across an extremely large lump of animal poo, still steaming in the cold mountain air. We studied the pile for a while and discussed what animal could have dropped such a load, before deciding that it could only be bear or cougar. I plumped for cougar as the dump was in the open and I assumed that there was some truth in the old rhetorical question, "Does a bear shit in the woods?" but was unsure and on we plodded. The narrow ledge leading to the summit was covered in packed snow and looked decidedly dangerous, even more so when several mountain goats blocked our way. We had seen these animals before but only from a distance and now they were within touching distance. The goats are very odd-looking creatures, with long white hair, heads which are far too big for their bodies and with many sporting rather dangerous-looking horns. As we approached, they stood their ground on the precipice and stared at us defiantly. We stopped and stared back, but they refused to be intimidated and continued to stare at us menacingly. On the scrappy piece of paper I carried with the hike directions, it clearly said, *Mountain goats are frequently sighted close to the peak, so watch out for them.* I was unsure whether this was a wildlife spotting guide or a warning but erred on the side of caution and, considering the dangerous path, we decided that reaching the summit just a few feet away was unimportant so turned back. From our retreating position, we could still see breathtaking 360-degree views of Glacier National Park, Bob Marshall Wilderness, Flathead Valley, and the glittering Hungry Horse Reservoir waters. As we turned, we gave the goats a particularly loud tinkle with our bells, at which they all scampered down the mountainside and disappeared. We laughed on the way down that we had braved two heavily armed militia, potentially lethal grizzly attacks and an irritable and protective mountain lion, only to be turned back by a few goats who were afraid of tinkling bells.

The following day, having moved into the Timbers Motel, we decided to follow the mountain road US Route 2 which ran through the National Park and is also known enticingly as Going-to-the-Sun Road. We set out early in warm and sunny weather, stopping in the small, intriguingly named town of Hungry Horse to buy lunch, and entered the park proper at West Glacier Village. We followed the road which wound its way for fifty miles amongst the snow-covered mountains with glorious views of lakes and waterfalls towards the Logan Pass visitor Centre. We stopped *en route* to gaze across the wonderful valleys and mountains of the alpine wonderland when dark clouds began to rise over the opposite peaks. Within minutes we were engulfed in thick mist which blew violently over the mountains and soon turned to snow and sleet as we scrambled back into the car. We continued, very gingerly, along the narrow mountain pass, making a mockery of the name Going-to-the-Sun Road, until we reached the Logan Pass Visitor Center. A few other hardy souls had made it to the refuge and were scurrying from their cars into the impressive chalet-style building. They were all protected by waterproof kagoules and overtrousers, hats, gloves and boots. Sue and I were in t-shirts and shorts. The sign at the entrance proudly proclaiming an altitude of 6680 feet mocked our incompetence. We were over twice as high as England's highest mountain, Scafell Pike, in a blizzard and dressed for the beach. We parked as close as possible to the Center and dashed inside, found the café and ordered a warming coffee. The whole café was hushed, staring at these two wet and windswept English idiots as we took our seats. I thought that I heard someone whisper, "British airheads," which I don't think was a compliment.

As the storm passed, we continued our journey on the mountain road to our final destination of Avalanche Lake. The narrow road was wet and slippery which was nerve-racking, but nothing compared to driving through a series of waterfalls which cascaded down the mountains and directly onto the roadside and crossed the road like a river before continuing their downward rush on the other side. The local name of Weeping Wall did not do it justice. The lake was worth the risky drive, however, and the following two-mile hike across mountain tracks in our damp clothes was magnificent. By the time we were walking, the sun had chased the clouds away and the sky was a clear deep blue, reflecting perfectly in the lake waters, against a backdrop of mountains and tumbling waterfalls highlighted in the bright afternoon light. Sue explained that lake is in a cirque basin created by a receding glacier, but I just thought it astonishingly beautiful. Perhaps the only irritation was that the local mosquito community revelled in the chance to feed on British airhead blood and seemed particularly excited about dining on our legs.

As we returned to the motel through downtown Bigfork, we spotted that the local playhouse was presenting Funny Girl, so we stopped and bought tickets for that night's show. At home. we were keen supporters of the Swindon Amateur Light Operatic

Society and felt that we should not miss this opportunity to see the Bigfork equivalent. The show was great, even the expected missed cues, out-of-step dancing and off-key singing went unnoticed, as the sheer effort and enthusiasm of the local performers made for a perfect end to a (cold, sleet and mosquitos excepted) perfect day.

The following morning, tired from our excursion exertions the previous day, we selected an easy stroll to relax and nurse our mosquito wounds which had swollen to red Smartie-sized lumps on our legs. From our Bigfork base, we wandered alongside the Swan River, an easy couple of miles on a wide gravel path, stopping to watch an osprey landing in its penthouse nest and garter snakes slowly writhing together, possibly mating in the sun. On returning to base, we took a gentle drive to the southern end of Flathead Lake and out onto Finley Point for lunch and a peaceful afternoon's rest between scratching our itching lumps. The lake is named after the Salish tribe, who were erroneously, and somewhat rudely I thought, labelled Flatheads by neighbouring tribes. It is proudly described as the largest freshwater lake east of the Mississippi.

Batteries recharged and only two days left, we decided that we should revisit the Going-to the-Sun Road and make the most of the improved weather, so we decided to visit the Logan Pass and Hidden Lake. It was again an enchanting walk, passing Bird Woman Falls. a spectacular waterfall crashing down 500 feet from the mountains. The falls are named after the Indian woman Sacajawea who led Lewis and Clark on their famous expedition to find the Pacific Ocean, although quite why they chose to trek through this inhospitable place to look for the ocean was somewhat confusing. The well-marked and mostly paved trail through Logan Pass was beautiful, surrounded by impressive peaks and home to vast wildflower meadows. It is also home to bighorn sheep, mountain goats and bears which are commonly encountered on the walk. Except that when we walked it, the trail and meadows were under several inches of packed snow and ice and the wildlife was obviously holed up somewhere more hospitable, probably surprised that these stupid humans were stumbling across their land in such inhospitable conditions. We could only follow the tracks in the snow made by other hardy souls and hope that they knew the way. The difficult trek was well worth the effort as we reached Hidden Lake. The sky and waters were a deep blue, more vivid than I thought possible and the few fluffy white clouds were matched in the lake by floating ice patches. As we stood and gazed in wonder, we noticed that the friendly little clouds were being replaced by their ominous dark cousins, a sign to return to the visitor centre as quickly as possible. We slipped and slid on the trail back and made it just before the winds began to blow hail and sleet across the car park. Luckily, we had learnt our lesson from the previous expedition and packed our cold weather gear, so donned our kagoules before going for a coffee. The storm had arrived over the mountains very quickly and other customers were already sitting there in shorts and t-shirts unaware of the change in conditions. Sue said that that I was not allowed to shout out, "American airheads," to them.

With just one day remaining, we set out for our last walk in this amazing, beautiful, mountainous wonderland and decided on a short hike in the Jewel Basin, a 15.000-acre wildlife refuge between Kalispell and Hungry Horse. With its 27 lakes and 35 miles of trails, it seemed an ideal way to end our holiday. Sue said she was feeling tired after our excursions of the previous days, so we had no specific objective, no plan, no definite trails. We said we would just stroll and enjoy being in the wilderness. We hadn't been walking long before Sue complained of feeling very tired and thought that we should make our way back as we had to pack and prepare for the long drive back to Canada and Calgary. I persuaded her to walk a little more as we crossed more snow-covered areas and lakes but, after more hints of tiredness, finally gave in and we returned to the car. We started back to Bigfork when Sue said that she had spotted a shop in Kalispell on our trips out and wanted to call in to pick up a few things for the return journey. She directed me to the shop and we pulled into the car park. Except that it wasn't just "a shop." It was a store, a superstore, a gigantic store, a mammoth store with *Wal Mart* in ten feet high letters over the door. I sank into my seat in despair, but my dear wife said I should hurry and we wouldn't be long.

To avoid any retail arguments, I abandoned her to pick up the few things she needed and agreed to see her back at the car in an hour as I wandered off around the store on my own. I was bored. I looked at the music store, the homeware, the gardening, the food hall, the clothes section and the hardware store. I looked at my watch and had been there ten minutes. I wandered off looking to see if there was somewhere to get a coffee, when I came across the sports store which I thought may have some interest. I was surprised to see that the sports section contained mainly camouflage clothing, guns, crossbows, bullets and knives. I was intrigued that this assassins' equipment was so openly on sale. After a quick look round, I approached a sales assistant behind the gun counter. "Excuse me, young man," I enquired in my best English accent, "But could I buy one of your guns." The assistant was unnerved and replied that I would need to show a driving licence first. I explained that I was English and only had a British licence, at which he looked a little confused, but said that he would go and check. I handed over my licence and he disappeared through a side door. He returned a few minutes later and said, "I have spoken to the manager, Sir, and he says that should be OK, but needs to check with Head Office first. What weapon were you thinking of, Sir?" I retrieved my licence and said that I would come back later. I did not return.

I looked at my watch. Twenty minutes gone. I walked to the car park and sat in car, looking at my watch every five minutes for what seemed like several hours. Finally, the hour was up and no sign of Susan. I went back in the store but couldn't find her. I bought a Willie Nelson CD that I didn't want. I looked round the store and thought that she may have been shot in the sports store. I returned to the car and sat listening to Willie singing *On the road again, I just can't wait to get on the road again*, and I agreed with him. After almost two hours, Susan appeared carrying several bags with a huge smile on her pretty face. "Before you start," she began, "We need all of this and they were all bargains," I groaned and drove back to hotel, in silence, realising that I had been duped. Too tired to walk, indeed.

Packing complete and ready to leave the following morning, we lay in bed that evening watching nothing in particular on television to relax before sleep and the long return drive to Calgary. As we began to drift off to sleep, a programme began about the beauty of Rocky Mountains National Park in Colorado. We both began to withdraw from our torpid state as the screen showed the wonderful mountains, lakes, rivers and waterfalls, perhaps even more spectacular than the area we had just visited. I looked at Sue, who returned my grin with a slight nod and we drifted off to sleep knowing where our next adventure would take place.

There was one more moment of euphoria as we followed the long, straight 193 road through the plains before crossing the Canadian border at Roosville. Chatting about the following year's plans, we seemed to be almost floating above the land, surrounded on all sides by nothing but pale blue sky. We now understood, for the first time, why Montana is called Big Sky Country.

CHAPTER 7 - COLORADO

A full year in the planning and we were ready for the next phase in conquering America. Our first objective was indeed The Rocky Mountains National Park but our investigations had uncovered another national park which we could visit on the visit. Hence, we planned to include Arches National Park, Utah in the itinerary. We had learnt many lessons in our previous jaunts, the most important of which was to carefully book and confirm accommodation in advance. Our carefree attitude of finding a hotel or motel randomly had caused us difficulties and belied my belief that American motels are aplenty and always have spare rooms, a confidence falsely offered by the many Hollywood films I had watched for years. We also made sure that our first stop was no more than an hour or so from the destination airport, in this case Denver, Colorado, as driving for much longer after a ten or eleven flight is not recommended. Hence, I had reserved a small motel in Georgetown, a few miles west of Denver, for three nights after arrival, followed by bookings at Moab, Utah and Grand Lake, Colorado. Nothing could possibly go wrong this year.

AMERICANADIAN DIARIES

After an uneventful but tiring eleven-hour flight, we picked up our Mitsubishi motor car and set out west towards Georgetown, passing through the city of Denver and the delightfully named towns of Village at Genesse, Soda Creek and Idaho Springs, with the Rockies in the far distance, visible all the way. An hour and a quarter later we were settling to the delightful Mountain Inn, happy that all would go smoothly this year. To unwind, we took a stroll downtown and it was empty. The town was all one would expect from a small American town, set deep in a valley in the Rockies with a wide main street lined by historic timber buildings. Yet it appeared deserted. Shops were open, restaurants were open, bars were open but we saw no-one. I half expected to see Gary Cooper waiting for the train arrive before shooting it out with a gang of desperados, but must have missed the gunfight as it was past high noon. We did, however find the Happy Cooker, a wonderful diner on 6th Street, which would become our breakfast venue for the next couple of days, and located opposite the inappropriately named Hotel de Paris. We also found the station for the Loop Railroad where we had planned to go the following day. I was very proud of my planning and organisational skills.

The next day, our plan went like clockwork: breakfast at the Happy Cooker - *Cookers Choice. Two eggs with served with with choice of bacon, sausage links or ham AND choice of a Waffle, French Toast, Toast or a Biscuit & Gravy or home-style potato's on the side 13.00 (Half order or meatless 7.50.)* It was so good that I even forgave the grammatical and spelling errors on the menu, before setting off for our pre-booked trip on the railroad. As we awaited at the terminus, we heard the ancient steam engine's whistle and watched its approach over the decidedly rickety-looking Devil's Gate Bridge, a high viaduct built across the gorge. We boarded the train and were like two excited schoolchildren as it shook and rattled back over the gorge and slowly puffed its sedate way through the mountains. At the end of the ride, we accepted the offer of an optional visit to a silver mine, donning hard hats and squeezing along narrow dark tunnels, guided by an ex-miner whose colourful description of life as a miner brought the exciting experience to life. He somewhat blotted his otherwise excellent copybook at the exit, by explaining that this was his first guided tour and he hoped we had enjoyed it, before holding out his hand for a tip. He did not get one from us.

To support the thriving silver mining community at the start of the 20th century, a large reservoir, Georgetown Lake, was created. The two-mile Bennhoff Lake Trail circumnavigates the lake and was a magnet we could not resist that afternoon. Following our train ride and walk, we were ready for a beer and some good ol' home cooking, so wandered downtown again before finding the Red Ram and settling in for a pleasant evening. The barmaid was particularly friendly and seemed genuinely surprised and flattered that an Englisher couple had chosen her town and her restaurant to visit. We, of course, played on the welcome by saying everything was, "Splendid, jolly good and terribly nice," before leaving with a happy, "Thanks awfully, cheerio."

The Happy Cooker was irresistible again in the morning - *Golden Waffles - Golden brown with your choice of strawberries, peaches, or spiced apples, and topped with whipped butter or whipped cream $10.00,* before we set off on our first proper walk of the holiday, via the Guinella Pass to Silver Dollar Lake. We followed the rough, potholed road before turning off for Naylor Lake Road, a dirt road which was even more rough and potholed, to the start of the walk. Our little Mitsubishi was possibly the most unsuitable vehicle ever for the journey, but we slowly bumped along, carefully avoiding the deep craters and crevasses until we gratefully reached the trailhead.

The full hike, to see all lakes on the Silver Dollar Lake trail is 4.1 miles long, so an eight-mile plus mountain trek may not have been the wisest selection. It wasn't too long along the trail when we were both breathing heavily, gasping for breath. What we hadn't considered was that the trail is 12,000 feet above sea level where the air is, obviously, very thin. But we were either very determined or very stupid (I thought the former, Sue thought the latter) and we continued at a reduced and more sedate pace. As we passed a smaller lake on the trail, we were welcomed by our first ever sighting of a beaver dam, something that we had only seen on television before, and we were accompanied by chattering pika, small mountain-dwelling mammals with short legs, a very round body and no tail. We commented that it is strange how these small, perhaps inconsequential sightings can be so thrilling. The exertion was worth every muscle straining, lung busting moment as we reached our target. The lake was almost a perfect circle, still frozen from the sub-zero winter temperatures and shining like a newly polished silver dollar under the bright mountain sunshine, surrounded by spectacular mountain scenery. Sue was almost speechless as she gazed over the alpine scene and could only manage a broken, "This...is...wonderful."

The Red Ram was again our choice for dinner and, as we sat enjoying our American fare and congratulating ourselves on our immaculate planning, the television above the bar was reporting something about a wildfire, a report we all but ignored. Ignored, that is, until our favourite barmaid shouted across, "Hey, were you guys planning on taking the interstate west tomorrow?"

We confirmed that that was, indeed, our plan. "Not now you aint," the barmaid said, pointing at the television, the road's closed. Half the forest's on fire and they've closed the I-70 completely. First time ever."

I believe that a mild expletive may have escaped my lips, but Americans don't understand the word, "Bollocks," so I got away with it. On returning to the hotel, we sat in bed watching television as the drama unfolded. It confirmed that the Interstate 70 west was, indeed, closed after a fire and unlikely to open for some days. We studied our USA road atlas and realised that only way to continue our holiday was to divert several miles to the south taking the I-91 and I-24 and the I-50 West, increasing our estimated journey time from five to eight hours. The only recompense was that would get to drive through other exciting-sounding towns, Leadville, Granite and Sapinero, before re-joining the I-70 at Grand Junction. After our last breakfast at the Happy Cooker - *Biscuits & Gravy - Warm, fluffy biscuits topped with creamy pepper gravy and served with sausage links $9.50,* we set off on our revised route. At various places on the way we could see thick clouds of smoke billowing from the north and at one stage, we drove through a smokescreen as the fire increased its range. I still have the front page of *USA Today* which describes the event as *The largest fire in Colorado history* and says that *as many as 40,000 residents faced evacuation.*

After a long but exhilarating drive, we arrived late, tired, but happy at our destination, The Apache Motel, Moab, Utah, gateway to Arches National Park. We chose Arches after reading an enticing description of the park in our National Parks guide. Adjacent to the Colorado River, it is a desert area consisting of red sandstone and contains more than 2,000 natural sandstone arches, including the most well-known, Delicate Arch. It also contains a variety of other unique geological formations, such as spires, balanced rocks, sandstone fins, and eroded monoliths. Due to its unique formation, the park has been used in many films over the years, including Indiana Jones, Thelma and Louise and City Slickers, but is most famous, to me anyway, for its cowboy films. It has been featured in such iconic 1960's movies as Comancheros, Cheyenne Autumn and Rio Conchos and was a favourite location for many John Wayne roles. The Apache Motel proudly claims that, whenever he was filming in the area, John Wayne preferred to stay at the motel and lodged there many times. We were told that, as a special welcome because we were English, we had been allocated John Wayne's favourite room. I slept well that night, dreaming of commanding my cavalry troop into battle, vastly outnumbered by whooping Shoshone and Navajo warriors, before leading my brave and bloodied men back to Fort Apache Motel. We felt just a little let down later that week when we were chatting to two young ladies staying in the next room to ours, who informed us that they had been allocated the very room that John Wayne stayed in when in town.

Our first task the next morning was to find somewhere to eat. We wandered along Main Street and were drawn to the Moab Diner. The moment we sat down and read the menu, we telepathically knew that this is where we would be eating for the next week. Sue and I discussed whether we were exceptionally clever at finding superb diners in America or whether all diners in America were superb. We agreed that it was probably the latter. After returning to the car following breakfast, the sky was clear and blue, and the temperature was nearly 35 degrees. I decided to stop at a nearby store to buy a cowboy hat, which I explained to Sue would be essential for the climate.

We drove out to the entrance of Arches National Park, paid our ten dollars entrance fee, and drove through the park, astounded at the amazing geological structures, to reach the trail head and begin our first walk in the desert heat of Utah. We followed the Devil's Garden Trail between towering red sandstone cliffs and worn smooth by years, possibly centuries, of feet as, long before tourism, it would have been used by native tribes, early pioneers and settlers. There were few other visitors and both Sue and I lapsed into an almost dreamlike state as we wandered past the truly amazing sandstone arches created by centuries of erosion, including Pine Tree Arch, Wall Arch, Navajo Arch, Partition Arch, Double "O" Arch and Landscape Arch, described as *The crown jewel of Devils Garden* and the longest arch in North America with a light opening of 306 feet. Between the rising walls of the canyon, we glimpsed views of distant desert and the incredible Balanced Rock, a huge monolith perched high on a slender pinnacle. It was truly spectacular and we couldn't help but compare this baking hot, arid yet beautiful landscape to that of just two days ago, when we were hiking in cold snow covered mountains.

Moab also boasts another National Park on its doorstep. Canyonlands is different but equally as spectacular as Arches and an obvious target for our next walk. The park preserves another colourful landscape eroded into numerous canyons, mesas, and buttes by the Colorado River and the Green River, divided into four areas: the Island in the Sky, the Needles, the Maze, and the Two Rivers, which carved two large canyons into the Colorado Plateau. We chose to visit the Island in the Sky, not just because it is the most romantically named of the four, but because it also contains a huge crater, Upheaval Dome, an enormous geological structure in the form of a massive crater more akin to a gigantic lunar feature. The temperature was approaching forty degrees as we set out and there was absolutely no shade on the short but steep trail. We were well prepared for the heat with a bag of nuts, plenty of water and my new cowboy hat to protect against the blazing sun. We made Upheaval Dome after about an hour's tough hiking and were in awe of the vista. A well-placed information board at the viewing area explained that the crater is six miles across. Our senses found this hard to take in and it seemed impossible that the far side of the huge depression could be that far away, yet looked almost as if we could lean over and touch it. I stood speechless and teary-eyed for a moment, while Sue ignored me knowing that I was just having one of my moments

We read that the origin of the crater remains a bone of contention with two contrasting theories. The first is the Salt Dome Theory which is a complex explanation involving inland salt seas evaporating and, under pressure, causing a salt bubble to rise to the surface and create a salt dome. I did not understand this theory at the time and still do not. The second hypothesis is the Impact Crater Theory, which suggests that the crater is the result of a huge meteorite collision. This was far easier to comprehend so Sue and I agreed that we would accept this as its true origin.

We half planned to walk around the edge of the crater, but my rudimentary calculation that a diameter of 6 miles equates to a circumference of roughly eighteen miles soon obliterated this idea, and we simply sat and admired the wonder of what we were seeing for an hour, before making our way back. We took a short diversion on the return journey to Grand View Point overlook, a viewpoint giving what we agreed was one of the best views we had ever seen. With the use of an excellent information board, we were able to identify the Colorado River

Canyon, the Monument Basin and the Needles as the vista stretched thirty-five miles across the dry desert valleys into the distance, to views of the La Sal and Abajo mountains. The description of "Grand View" seemed somewhat understated.

We returned to Moab, commenting that, strangely, we had seen some of the most spectacular scenery possible but had seen no other person at all yet, a few years previously, we were forced to join a queue of walkers to reach the modest summit of Helvellyn in England's Lake district.

We still had the afternoon to ourselves, so Sue decided to go for a haircut at a salon that she had noticed on our wanderings around town. I decided to further explore the town and we agreed to meet back at motel. As I meandered among the various shops and stores with no intention of buying anything, I was drawn to one particular building clearly emblazoned with the words *Moab Brewery*. I guessed that there was a magnetic field in there, which pulled me in despite my brain saying that entering such an establishment in the early afternoon was unwise. Inside, I found just the sort of establishment I had come to love, a long "cowboy" bar fronting several tables and decorated with all types of fascinating Americana. The fact that I was the only customer did nothing to detract from the atmosphere. The barman explained that all the beers, and there many, were brewed on site and recommended, a light ale to start. As we chatted and I drank, I found out that he was English, from Bristol, and had found the job whilst drifting across America, I had another beer. We chatted some more and I had another beer. After a couple of hours of chatting and a few more beers, I was feeling decidedly unsteady, so thanked him for his hospitality and fell off my stool. Before I left the bar, my new-found best mate insisted that I try one last beer, on the house. This, he said, was the brewery's speciality, a beer infused with chocolate. It was, I must regretfully report, the most sickly and unappetising beer that I had ever tasted, and one mouthful was enough to tell me that I would be unable to keep it down. My, by now, best ever mate insisted that it would settle after a few more swigs, so I was obliged to finish the evil concoction before waving a fond farewell and staggering out into the street. My really brilliant, best mate that I'd ever had was right and I did keep it down as I tottered unsteadily back to the motel. Luckily, Sue was in bed and taking a siesta away from the forty-degree heat, so I was able to fall into bed and a deep, snoring, alcoholic stupor. When I finally came to, she was sitting on the edge of the bed staring at me with a look of disgust mixed with anger. "It wasn't my fault..." I began, but gave up knowing that she knew that it probably was.

    The name of another park near Moab made it irresistible for a visit, and so it was that Sue and I pulled up at the Visitor Center at Dead Horse State Park in San Juan County, Utah. It again boasts a dramatic overlook of the Colorado River and Canyonlands National Park. According to legend, the park is so named because of its use as a natural corral by cowboys in the 19th century, where horses often died of exposure. It has also been a backdrop to many great films over the years, including *MacGyver* and *Mission Impossible 2*. There was limited parking at the visitor centre and, although we were the only visitors, I thought it polite to ask if we could leave the car in the car park while we walked the East Rim trail to the Dead Horse Overlook, a spectacular viewpoint above the Colorado River as it twists and turns cutting deep into the soft desert rock, hundreds of feet below. The ranger looked a little surprised and said that there was no need to walk as the road led all the way to the overlook. We thanked him, but explained that we preferred to walk. Mr

Ranger looked at us as if we were aliens and repeated, "But Sir, the road leads all the way to the lookout. You have no need to walk."

We left our car and a bemused ranger scratching his head at the visitor centre and began the easy, three-mile walk. We strolled over rock and sand amongst scrub and twisted, gnarled bushes that somehow survive in the harsh desert conditions, the sun beating down fiercely and the air still and warm. Apart from the odd lizard scuttling out of our way, we saw no other sign of life or, indeed, of dead horses, until we reached our goal. It is difficult to explain the feeling of sitting on a rock 2000 feet above a 180-degree loop of the mighty Colorado River with views of sculpted canyons, pinnacles and buttes carved by millions of years of geological activity, but I felt that we were in an almost dream-like trance. I guess that Sue was feeling it too as I had never known her sit so still for so long without a word.

We returned to Moab for the afternoon to meander round town and get some relief from the scorching sun. I avoided the Moab Brewery but we did find the Moab Museum which we had somehow missed on our previous wanderings. It was a revelation. There were fascinating exhibits describing the lives of the First People, the hardships of the pioneers, the incarceration of Japanese Americans during World War Two and the lives of trappers, traders, missionaries, government expeditions, cowboys, outlaws, homesteaders, explorers, and others. One particular exhibit intrigued me above all others. Robert LeRoy Parker, better known as Butch Cassidy, spent much of his life as an outlaw in Moab, which was used as a base for the Wild Bunch or the Hole-in the-Wall gang, and from where they planned many of their audacious train robberies. On deeper examination, the curator told me, the link to Moab is tenuous and fact may well have been overtaken by myth, but that didn't stop me imagining that we had walked the same streets as Butch and I included, somewhat unconvincingly, the Sundance Kid.

The curator, a lovely friendly lady, also confirmed the John Wayne connection to both the town and the Apache Motel (but not unfortunately, to our room.) She said that he was loved by everyone in town who treated him as another resident and not one of the world's greatest stars. She added that it was common to see him strolling down Main Street with other actors like Henry Fonda and Ward Bond and, apart from a friendly greeting, the locals took little notice of the film stars. She also told me that most visitors to Moab came from Salt Lake City, Utah, hence its nickname, Mormons On A Binge, which I rather liked.

With our time in Moab running out, we realised that we had not seen two of the most iconic sights in Arches, so we set out the next day for the long walk to Delicate Arch. This 52-foot-tall arch stands detached and isolated, dominating the skyline and is the most widely recognized landmark in Arches National Park. It is depicted on Utah car license plates and a postage-stamp commemorating Utah's centennial anniversary of admission to the Union in 1896. The Olympic torch relay for the 2002 Winter Olympics passed through the arch. Because of its distinctive shape, the arch was known as the Schoolmarm's Bloomers by local cowboys. I thought that a far better name. We located the relevant car park, signposted to Delicate Arch Road. From the parking area, we set off from the signed Delicate Arch Trailhead along the Delicate Arch Trail. For once, we had every confidence we were on the right track. And, unusually, there were many other people on the trail. This was the first time that we had had to share our wilderness experience with others and, to be perfectly honest, we did not like it. Just who were all these people in their shorts and big boots, carrying backpacks and tramping over *our* trail? As we walked, trying to avoid the interlopers, we were given a superb view of Balanced Rock, the huge boulder that appears to be delicately balanced on a slender pillar. Its iconic status cemented by its appearance in the opening of the 1989 film *Indiana Jones and the Last Crusade*. We certainly never saw anything that spectacular on our forays to the Lake District.

During our explorations in and around Moab, we noticed a small cowboy town set off the road. Closer examination showed that this was a restaurant which offered a reenactment and a country music show, so we set off to enjoy an evening of western fun. We ordered a beer at the saloon and there was a ruckus in the street outside as two cowboys settled an argument with a gunfight, one dying an awful death with several bullets slamming into his chest. Alongside other guests, we cheered and returned to our beers.

Moving on to the restaurant, we were served more beer to accompany our Desperate Dan sized steak and beans while the band played and sang songs about lonesome cowboys and cattle drives. The music was excellent, particularly surprising as the guitarist has been killed in the street only half an hour before. At one stage the singer called several people on the stage. "I'm glad I'm not going up there," Sue whispered just as the shout "From England, Susan Trueman," rang out from the microphone. Sue had little choice but to get up on stage, and was handed a lasso which she was encouraged to twirl round in a trick known the Merry-Go-Round. Her stage fright overcome, I have rarely seen her smile so much as the lasso spun wildly in time to the sound of the fiddle. At the end of the song, the band had to more-or-less push her off the stage to continue their gig.

We had just one more day left in Moab, and there was just one more walk to do before packing to leave the following morning, so boots and cowboy hat on again, we set off for Grandstaff Canyon. Until the 1960s it was called Nigger Bill Canyon, named after William Grandstaff, a mixed-race cowboy, who prospected and ran cattle in the desert canyon during the late 1870s. It was then renamed Negro Bill Canyon until 2017 when its present name was adopted. The trek was relatively simple four-mile walk through the canyon, crossing a small river beneath a waterfall to Morning Glory Bridge, an alcove arch, akin to a large cave, where we sat and munched our trail mix and happily chatted about the incredible experiences of the previous week, agreeing that the highlight was Sue's brief spell as a cowgirl stage star. We also reminded ourselves that the main reason for our visit to this part of the USA was to explore the Rocky Mountains National Park and we had just a few days left.

Before we set off on our six-hour drive to Grand Lake, we stopped for our final breakfast at the Moab Diner. On the next tables was a group of Native American men, obviously enjoying some kind of outing. I started chatting and found out that they were Navajo Indians from New Mexico, a baseball team visiting Moab to play local Navajo teams. I was thrilled to be talking to the group and they seemed as excited as I was that they were talking to folks from England. As we said our goodbyes and set off, Sue said that she was elated and we must be the only people from Swindon to ever have had breakfast in the company of a band of Navajo Indians. I replied that they are probably discussing the elation of being the only Navajo Indians to ever have breakfast in the company of people from Swindon.

135

AMERICANADIAN DIARIES

The drive east was a surreal experience. The I-70 had reopened after the wildfires but the aftermath of the disaster remained. The views of the Rockies on either side of the highway were of blackened scrub and ash with the charred remnants of shadowy trees and bushes standing sadly amongst the dark and gloomy backdrop. The smell of smoke and ash still lingered as we travelled on in a sort of perverse wonder at what we were experiencing, oddly seeing signs saying, *No Fires* and *No Fireworks* on the way. We agreed that it was a bit late for the warnings and, anyway, there was nothing left to burn.

We were about fifteen miles from our destination of Grand Lake when we passed the small town of Granby and spotted signs advertising a rodeo that evening. I was tempted to return to attend the event, but after a six-hour drive through the blackened mountains decided that it would be too much for one day.

Grand Lake was everything we had imagined and more like a Western film set than a real town. A wide, busy main street, Grand Avenue, edged with beautiful old wooden buildings housing cafes, restaurants and a variety of shops including a Trading Post, thrift shop, gift shops, clothes shops, bars and saloons. The only thing missing was horses tied up outside the saloon. We checked in to The Inn at Grand Lake, a *Rustic lodging with wraparound balcony offering lake & mountain views, plus on-site restaurant*, which was reminiscent of the hotel in the film *Last Train from Gun Hill* where Kirk Douglas played a US Marshall holding a killer in his hotel room waiting for the last train out of the town. I asked at reception and was assured neither Kirk Douglas nor his alter ego Marshall Matt Morgan had checked in. After a shower and coffee, I felt revived and said to Sue, "Shall we go then?"

She gave a knowing smile and said, "Of course. I knew we would," so off we set, back to Granby and the rodeo at the Flying Heels Arena. We parked and paid our entrance fee and headed straight for the hot dog stand, very hungry having not eaten since breakfast. We both ordered chilli dogs and coffee from the stand, served by a young lad, who said, "Say, are you guys from England?"

"We are indeed," I replied and, somewhat condescendingly, "How did you know?"

The lad looked pleased with himself and said, "Well, you talk just like Hairy Padder."

It took us a few seconds to realise who "Hairy Padder" was and I tried to think of a smart response, but knew little about the Harry Potter franchise, so just managed a simple, "Thank you very much," as we wandered away wondering how a yokel from Wiltshire could sound like a posh kid training to be a wizard.

The rodeo was superb although it was not Premiership sport. I thought it more like a Swindon Town game at the County Ground than Arsenal at the Emirates Stadium, but this added to the homely and friendly atmosphere at the occasion. We watched many different events, some of which we understood including Bareback Riding, Saddle and Ranch Bronc, Bull Riding and Steer Wrestling, but there were many we did not understand even after watching them. I still have no idea which of the events were classed as Tie Down, Ladies Breakaway Roping, Local Barrel Racing (includes eye charge) or Never Won a Buckle Chute Doggin'. One event we particularly liked was young children riding sheep, advertised as Peewee (5 and under), Mutton Bustin'. After a thoroughly enjoyable Western experience, we slowly drove the fifteen miles back to The Inn at Grand Lake and slept like babies, dreaming of Steer Wrestling and Mutton Bustin'.

Up early for our first full day back in Colorado, we took a quick stroll around town to get our bearings and, more importantly, find somewhere to eat. A few doors down from the hotel we discovered the Chuck Hole Café and our breakfast venue for that and the following days was set. Again, the perfect diner with perfect food in the perfect position.

After our stroll and a splendid breakfast, we were ready for our first walk on the last phase of our trip. Before setting off, we bought a Pocket guide to Rocky Mountain wildlife which, we hoped, would settle the few discussions (arguments) that we had when identifying various fauna on our treks. We decided to start at the Colorado River Trailhead, the obvious choice considering where we were and where we had been, and just follow the trail to see where it led. We set off from Trail Ridge Road and headed west. Again, were on our own as we followed that track through the forest, criss-crossing the Colorado River near its head waters as we progressed. At one part of the trail, we were able to stand astride the mighty Colorado and it was strange to realise that this river ran for 1450 miles across Colorada, Utah and Arizona before crossing the border to Mexico. It is responsible for creating some of the most spectacular and iconic geology in the United States, including Canyonlands and the Grand Canyon, yet here it was trickling between our legs.

It was a relatively simple walk, totally different from the mountains near Georgetown and the arid desert of Moab, and allowed us to unwind after the long drive the previous day. We spent some time just sitting and armed with our guide, managed to identify ground squirrels frolicking, grey jays, a red-winged Blackbird and a few other less conspicuous birds chattering and flitting on the woods. We had spectacular views over lake Granby and many Rocky Mountain peaks, but then we reached a junction with the Red Mountain trail through an area known as *Hells Hip Pocket*. Unable to resist the lure of the name I suggested that we "...just take a quick look up this trail." Two miles further on, we (Sue) sensibly decided that we should turn back as we were increasingly lost and unsure whether we were on the Red Mountain, in Hell's Hip Pocket or somewhere else altogether. Just as we turned, we were treated to the loudest, almost deafening, croaking noises from a trailside pond. We pushed our way through the undergrowth towards the pond and the sound immediately stopped leaving an eerie silence. We guessed that we had disturbed a frog mating orgy and the participants were shy of onlookers to their sexual antics. We also disturbed a moose, grazing next to the track. It looked up as we passed and gave a disdainful look as if slightly annoyed that we had interrupted its solitary lunch. We apologised and the animal turned its back on us and carried on with its meal, apparently satisfied with our show of regret.

Extremely happy as we were with our new quarters, a lovely town, superb lodgings and a wonderful area, we were still to identify somewhere to dine in the evenings, as the Chuck Hole closed in the afternoon. We were confident that wherever we went, the food would be fine as in all American restaurants, but we had been lucky before with the great people we had met. There was restaurant directly opposite the hotel, so that was quite obviously our first port of call. The food was fine but we found the atmosphere somewhat clinical and, although not unfriendly, it lacked the homely feel we had found before. Our search would continue.

Such was the joy of the forest trail that the next expedition was similar to the first, again starting at the same trailhead but, this time, with the objective finding Lulu City, an old mining town hidden deep in hills. Again, we strolled alongside the river until the track split and we headed north along the Kawuneeche Valley towards our goal. We encountered several moose on the walk and each one gave the same disdainful look we had seen the previous day, and a huge elk, possibly six feet tall at the shoulder, who had obviously been coached by the moose gave us a somewhat derisive look before wandering off and disappearing into the forest. We reached Lulu City, a small clearing with half a dozen or so abandoned wooden houses. The "city" was a transient mining town developed after silver was discovered in the area in 1879 by prospector Joe Shipler. By 1881, there were forty cabins and a number of business establishments, but it became apparent that the silver ore was of low grade, and that high transportation costs made mining in the area unprofitable and it was abandoned by 1885, except by Shipler, who lived there for thirty years. The Shipler cabin was the best preserved and Sue and I sat in the remains of this once proud home and tried to imagine life in the late 19th century, living in this small community scraping a living from mining. We both felt quite emotional by the experience, especially when we realised that there was just one toilet to serve the whole community. We moved on to our second objective, the Colorado River Headwater, the source of the mighty river.

Our walk was stalled several times as the local fauna came out to greet us. Moose seemed to be waiting for us on every bend on the trail and we spotted several birds unknown had it not been for our new guide. We saw American robins, which are not robins at all but members of the thrush family, a belted kingfisher, stellers jays and several small brown birds flitting across our path too quickly to identify. Next to the path, we noticed a large rodent, like a giant hamster but the size of a big overweight cat. We stopped next to the animal who ignored us completely and continued grazing on the lush greenery, occasionally glancing up at us before resuming its meal. Out came the guide again and we were able to identify our friend as a yellow-bellied marmot, which slated our natural history appetite. We stopped for our picnic lunch at the headwater and were joined by a mule deer, which stared at us for several minutes before disappearing into the thicket.

We returned to Grand Lake and, after a recuperative rest, tried the next nearest restaurant, just a couple of minutes' walk away, the Sagebrush BBQ and Grill. We immediately knew that this would the one for us. The bar had a genuine western atmosphere, the restaurant smart and spotless, the waitress, Diane, was smiling and friendly, the owner Dave was welcoming and the menu was good ol' American cooking. The only thing which threw us slightly was that there was a large bucket of roasted peanuts on each table and everyone was casting the shells onto the floor. As we nibbled a few nuts before eating, Sue was tidily wrapping the shells in her napkin ready for later disposal. As Diane delivered our meal, she took Sue's tidy, peanut-shell-filled napkin and emptied the husks onto the floor. My dear wife looked shocked until our server explained that the shells were swept up each night, but contained oils that fed the wooden floor maintaining and preserving the wood. Sue did not look convinced.

Stirred by our wildlife-spotting excursion earlier, we drove out at dusk to continue our zoological studies and were rewarded with sight of three small red fox cubs and their mother playing by the roadside, a mother elk with a days-old calf and, to great excitement, a beaver swimming in a nearby lake. The only downside to the otherwise perfect day was that I felt extremely sick after eating too many peanuts.

Our feeding stations settled for the following days, Sue and I decided to take a rest day and drive the Trail Ridge Road, a 48-mile highway heading east from Grand Lake to Estes Park. It rises to a high point of over 12,000 feet, much of the journey above the tree line and is recommended as an essential trip if visiting this part of the Rocky Mountains National Park. The drive was spectacular as we climbed up through montane forests of aspen and ponderosa pine, before entering thick subalpine forests of fir and spruce. Once above about 10,000 feet, all flora disappeared as we travelled across arctic tundra. We stopped at designated pull offs and admired the sweeping views north to Wyoming, east across the Great Plains, south and west into the heart of the snowy Rockies. We stopped at Milner Pass, part of the Continental Divide, where rivers are separated east to west, the eastern flow ending in the Atlantic and the western flow in the Pacific oceans. There wasn't actually much to see there as there were no rivers to separate, but there was a big sign explaining the divide and a welcome toilet.

A few miles on we stopped at the Tundra Communities Trailhead and the prospect of exploring a little of this arctic landscape was too much to resist. We donned our light shower jackets and set off, not realising that the temperature drops twenty degrees or more at this elevation, and it wasn't that warm back where we started. But intrepid (stupid) explorers that we are, we ignored the freezing temperature and icy wind and headed up the trail. As cold as we were, the short trek was worthwhile when we came across the rock mushrooms. These geological masterpieces are about twenty-feet high pillars, created over millennia following volcanic action where the lava pushes up from beneath the sea, creating a level of granite below a schist covering. Over time, the formations are eroded, where the granite magma erodes faster than the schist leaving the mushroom shaped columns of white granite topped by darker coloured schist crowns. Magical as the discovery was, we stayed just a few minutes before making our way back to car and another toilet, an opportune relief and necessary after the bitter cold.

As we drove on, I began to feel quite ill. My head thumped, I was dizzy and nauseous. Nurse Susan put my very serious condition down to a combination of the cold and altitude and, not realising I was at death's door told me to continue but just drive carefully. We made it to Estes Park and sat on a rock by the beautiful Lake Estes for lunch whilst I bravely recovered from my near-death experience and Sue broke all park rules be feeding inquisitive chipmunks her trail mix as they sat quietly on her lap.

Shadow Mountain Lake, a reservoir created by the Shadow Mountain Dam. forms a continuous body of water with Grand Lake, was the venue of our next visit. As the lake's altitude is "only" 8,400 feet, my newly acquired life-threatening illness of altitude sickness would not be an issue, so we strolled gently on the well-worn path on the lake edge in the warm sunshine. Our only issue was that the five-mile trail is also is also known as Echo Mountain Trail, Lookout Mountain Trail and Pine Ridge Trail, so I claimed to have walked all four trails thus completing a twenty-mile hike, but Sue said that was cheating. After the pleasant and relaxing walk where we saw beaver ponds, an osprey catch a fish and return to its lofty nest, a woodpecker which turned out to be a red-naped sapsucker and two large male elk with magnificent velvet-covered antlers, we returned to out billet and spent a pleasant afternoon sitting on the balcony watching the comings and goings in Grand Avenue below. Our relaxed observation of the mountain people going about their business was abruptly terminated when a black cloud came over the town, bringing a deluge of rain, crashing thunder and flashes of brilliant lightning. We retired to our room and watched the meteorological display in comfort.

Our last day came all too soon and we took one last walk in this mountain utopia, a short but steep slog to see Adams Falls, a spectacular cascade rushing down from the mountains and swollen by the previous day's rains. We stood and watched the torrent of water in awe before strolling back into town to prepare for our trip home. Sue decided that we had been ignoring the shops in Grand Lake so spent the afternoon visiting every retail outlet we could find. In one store, specialising in Rocky Mountain memorabilia and collectables we were chatting with the store assistant when we were joined by a lady who greeted us with, "Hey, you must be the English guys in town."

We confirmed that we were indeed the English guys, and she added, "I have always wanted to go to England. Now, what's the capital of England called again?"

I answered, "Paris," as a rather silly joke.

"That's right," she confirmed, "I have always wanted to visit Paris, England." She was not joking.

On our last evening in Grand Lake and in the Rocky Mountains, we said our farewells to our friends in the Sagebrush BBQ and Grill and I promised that we would be back. With a surfeit of beer and good food, I meant what I said and it was only as Sue steered me across the road to the hotel that I knew that

144

we would never return. America was too big and too exciting to repeat visits and that night and during the two-hour drive back to Denver International Airport in the morning, Sue and I reminisced about our experiences over the previous weeks and began planning the next year's trip.

CHAPTER 8 – THE SOUTH-EAST

It would be another five years before we visited America again. At the end of the year of visiting The Rockies, Sue and I decided that we would stop working and retire early to begin a new life abroad. This we did and moved to the small mountain village of Nigüelas in Spain. For many reasons, we were too content and too busy to contemplate long holidays but after four demanding but wonderful years of building our own house and settling in to our new life, we rather unexpectedly found that we had time on our hands. Encouraged by our successful move abroad and possibly a surfeit of San Miguel and cheap wine, we decided that we should visit the USA again, with the added objective of buying a small home there to spend holidays, perhaps for up to six months of each year. Carried away with the aspiration, we decided that we should seek a refuge in the Eastern states to reduce travel time between our existing and imaginary homes and began our search for likely areas. We researched mountain areas to cater for our love of the outdoors and hiking and, having wandered the northern Appalachians in the past, our careful research centred on the Blue Ridge and Great Smokey mountains, iconic ranges associated the early settling of the west. We were also intrigued by the comic song by Laurel and Hardy, so areas were meticulously reconnoitred and plans finalised. Flying to America from our new base near Granada in southern Spain was difficult as there were no direct flights so we arranged to fly to Heathrow, spend three days in Swindon before returning to Heathrow for our onward journey to Hartsfield–Jackson Atlanta International Airport, Georgia. We would then head north to Andrews, North Carolina stopping for a few days in Blue Ridge, Georgia to explore the mountains and because it had a steam train ride (we could never resist steam train rides), then on to Townsend, Tennessee to explore the Great Smokies. We even went as far as investigating holiday homes and identified a cabin park which sounded ideal.

All went to plan with one very slight hiccup at Atlanta. On the flight, we had befriended a young Welshman who was alone and making his first trip abroad, strangely to judge a dog show. He was very nervous on arrival, but we said that he should not worry and stick close to us as we went through customs and baggage collection – we were, after all, seasoned travellers. As we three joined the queues for passport checks, our queue seemed to be slow, so I moved to quicker moving queue, which stopped moving almost immediately and our original queue began to move forward quickly. As we waited, I spotted another fast-moving line and we moved over to join this one. It immediately stopped. By the time we had changed queues again, we were the last three passengers through passport control and the Welsh lad was starting to panic, explaining that he was being met at the airport and was now late, thank to our queue-hopping. We dashed through to the luggage collection area and could not find our conveyor as everyone else from the flight had already collected their cases and left the concourse. After much searching, we discovered our lonely luggage, travelling forlornly round and round on an unmarked conveyor. We were then directed to another area, where, after much confusion, our recently claimed luggage was taken from us and we were told that we should catch a train to the other side of the airport. Young Taffy looked bewildered, but not quite as bewildered as I felt as we travelled without our cases on what we were told was *The Plane Train, an automated people mover.* We accompanied the lad to the new luggage collection point and on to the passenger pick-up area. Fortunately, his lift was still waiting. He didn't seem too grateful for our guidance through the departure procedure as he left, obviously explaining to the impatient driver that he had been held up by these two silly old English duffers.

Having picked up our hire car, we drove the easy 102 miles north to Blue Ridge via the I-575 to our first pre-booked base, the Days Inn. The weather was cold and the accommodation was underwhelming. It was a modern motel situated next to a four-lane highway on the edge of town, packaged between the South-West Ranch diner (Cheeseburger 99c.), the Checkers Diner (Burgers half-price) and a Royal Waffle King. At least we wouldn't go hungry.

We settled in and the room was surprisingly clean and comfortable, allaying our original misgivings. We drifted into town for breakfast, not fancying a cheap burger or waffle and discovered a traditional diner labelled *The Village, Roast Beef, Chicken and more. Breakfasts*, with a car park full of trucks, always a good sign that an eating place is preferred by locals and thus more to our finicky liking. Almost inevitably, we had discovered the diner that we would use throughout our stay. I was also intrigued by a large sign across the road which announced, *Dawg Gas 267 9/10*. I never found out what Dawg Gas was and to his day I have no idea.

The weather was still cold and it had started to rain, so we wandered around the town of Blue Ridge for a couple of hours. It was yet another delightful small town with a plethora of interesting small shops and cafes. Casually making our way to the east end of Main Street, we rather fortuitously, came across the railway station where we booked a trip on the steam train for two days' time. Things were looking up and it had stopped raining so we returned to the car and drove out of town for our first walk from the trailhead beginning the five-mile Flat Creek Loop Trail.

At the Deep Gap parking lot, an excellent Information board pointed the way and we set off heading west through the woods, crossing over the numerous tributaries that flow into Flat Creek. The rain had made the trail a little boggy in places and it was cold, but Sue's careful preparation when packing back in Spain meant that we were well-equipped with boots and kagoules, despite countermanding my instructions of, "Just bung in a couple of tee shirts and shorts and my trainers. That'll do me." Buoyed by the superb scenery and tranquillity of the walk, we planned another trek near Blue Ridge the following day, again beginning the walk at the Deep Gap parking lot, but this time heading east up and over Green Mountain to Lake Blue Ridge and the Toccoa River. It was another fine hike enhanced by regular sightings of the hazy Blue Ridge mountains through the trees and encounters with white-tailed deer grazing in many of the clearings along the way. Settling into our holiday routine of eating, walking and sleeping and with both walks exceeding any expectations, we wondered why it had taken us so long to return to our spiritual home of America.

We, of course, started each morning with a trip to The Village for breakfast. In the brief time we had been there, we had become very friendly with yet another waitress, Deborah, who seemed intrigued by our English accents, perhaps confusing her when we said that we lived in Spain. One morning, as we were eating, Deborah came over to our table and asked If we had met the owner yet. We replied that we had not had that pleasure, so she pointed to the counter and said, "That's the owner over there if you want to meet him." We thanked her but could think of no reason why we should want to meet owner, so politely ignored her invitation. That same evening, Deborah was not working, but arrived at the restaurant with the owner and introduced him at our table. We chatted amiably for ten minutes or so before he said his goodbye and stressed how great it was to meet us. Deborah beamed in delight as she left and told her boss, "See, I told you so." We will never know just what she told him, but hoped that it wasn't something along the lines of, "...you must meet these strange British greenhorns who think that Spain is in England."

Our final day in Blue Ridge came all too quickly and it was time for our steam train excursion. We were excited as we caught the train at the historic depot in downtown Blue Ridge, looking forward to a four-hour, 26-mile journey along the Toccoa River through the North Georgia countryside. I was a little confused as to how a 52-mile round trip could take four hours, as an average speed of 13 mph seemed a little slow, even for an old locomotive. The first leg of the adventure took us on a one-hour trip to the quaint sister towns of McCaysville, Georgia and Copperhill, Tennessee, nestled deep in the mountains and straddling the state line. It seemed odd that one town could have two different names even though it (they) was (were) spread across two states. I commented that it was like Bristol having two names in the past, one for the part of the city in Gloucestershire and a different name for the part in Somerset. But this was America, where belonging in or to a particular state seems far more important than English towns are to their counties. We chose to sit in the open rail car, rather than an authentic indoor car, a mistake which we soon rectified as the cold mountain air soon forced us indoors. The trip was wonderful as the engine rattled and puffed through the forests alongside the river, lined with old rustic cabins nestling on the wooded banks. As we arrived in McCaysville and Copperhill, I realised that I should have read the small print when booking the trip as we now had a two-hour layover before taking the one-hour return trip through the scenic forest and back to the depot in Blue Ridge. That said, we thoroughly enjoyed wandering around the town(s) and dined on chilli dogs and fries in the Nifty 50's, an evocative and nostalgic copy of a 1950's diner, decorated with pictures of Elvis, Marilyn Monroe and many other stars of the age. I didn't like to tell the owners that a *Nifty 50* has a very different meaning in smutty schoolboy slang in England. We also crossed the bridge from one town to the other and took photographs of each other with straddling a blue line with one foot in Georgia and the other in Tennessee, as did everyone else on the trip. It was a memorable way to finish our visit to Georgia and, as we prepared to move on that evening, I sang the old Ray Charles classic "Georgia on my mind" very badly and much to Sue's irritation as I only knew the first line of the song.

It was short, one-hour drive on the I-74 to our next stop at Andrews, North Carolina, calling in to the information centre at Murphy, Cherokee County on way, where we picked up useful hiking information and another of the splendid local wildlife guides. We had pre-booked a cottage in the grounds of a large private house just south of Andrews and were truly amazed at what we found. After the basic and busy Days Inn, we discovered the complete opposite in this accommodation. Fernwood cottage was a beautiful mountain lodge in the grounds of a large house, hidden in the forests of the Nantahala Mountains. Inside, it was immaculate and spacious with natural pine floors and whitewashed pine walls, beautifully decorated and perfectly equipped with a full kitchen and bathroom. It was, without doubt, the most luxurious lodgings we had ever experienced in Europe or America. As an added bonus, there were extensive grounds with a private lake to explore. Another bonus of the accommodation was our hosts Roy and Daphne, a delightful couple who could not have been more accommodating and helpful. If this sounds like an advertisement, I apologise, but it was so remarkable that I cannot do anything but eulogise over the beautiful cottage and surroundings. Sue and I were besotted with the lodging, the grounds, the surroundings and the area. So much so that we seriously considered stocking up with provisions and not leaving the cottage for the duration of our five-night stay. This notion was augmented by the weather, which was very cold and gloomy and, as we settled in, it began to snow. We decided to take the short drive into Andrews and collect enough food and beer to last our stay but, after a peaceful day watching the snow from the cosiness of our cottage, we awoke the next day to find that the cold, inclement weather had disappeared and was replaced with blue skies and temperature hovering around 70 degrees F. or 20 degrees C., ideal for walking. From information acquired at Murphy, we chose **The Joyce Kilmer Memorial Forest** near Robbinsville, a half-hour drive away through the stunning scenery of the Nantahala National Forest and an ideal starting point for our hikes. The forest is a memorial to a local writer and poet, Joyce Kilmer, and located by Lake Santeetlah in the depths of the forest. We read that the woodland is a rare example of an old growth cove hardwood forest, an extremely diverse ecology unique to the Appalachian Mountains, with poplar, hemlock, red and white oak, basswood, beech, and sycamore trees. The loop trail was a relatively simple two miles which wound through the virgin forest in a figure eight pattern. The warning at the trailhead that wildlife encounters with large animals, such as black bears and wild boar, or poisonous snakes could be dangerous struck us as a little unnecessary.

The walk was, as expected, superb as we immersed ourselves in an historic tree wonderland, an impressive remnant of vast Eastern forests that used to stretch from the Atlantic to the Mississippi and beyond. At first, we tried to identify many of the towering trees growing alongside the trail, but our knowledge of American dendrology was somewhat limited, so we gave up and continued in tree-ignorance, simply admiring the giants rising to heights of well over 100 ft with circumferences of up to 20 ft, many estimated to be over 400 years old.

On returning to the cottage, we were invited in to the big house for coffee with Roy and Daphne. During our conversation, we commented that we had walked in the Joyce Kilmer Memorial Forest that morning and, although we had never heard of Joyce before, she must have been a very talented and popular woman to warrant having such a beautiful wilderness named after her. Daphne looked a little surprised and told us that that indeed she may have been, except that Joyce was a man.

We also expressed our fascination with America and the Appalachians in particular and our notion to buy a holiday home in the area. One of the strange coincidences that seemed to occur often on our travels was that Roy then told us that both he and Daphne were realtors and it was a couple of minutes before we realised that realtors are estate agents. They were also familiar with the cabins we that we had discovered and had planned to visit the next day. He offered to take us there to view the properties. We, of course, gratefully accepted the kind offer. Roy also kindly agreed to drive with Daphne as co-driver and we set off, but I have no idea quite where we travelled as Roy gave an unchartered tour of the area, passing through small, fragmented settlements and farms on rustic forest roads before reaching at the cabin site. Leaving the car on arrival, Sue and I stood and stared in speechless wonder. The word *Campsite* could not do justice to the sheer beauty of the stunning location. We were reminded a little of the many caravan sites we had used when holidaying in the UK, except that we had never stayed in a caravan site situated within magnificently maintained lawns and surrounded by beautiful, wooded mountains. The log cabins too were stunning, rustic masterpieces situated on generous, private plots giving a bracing feeling of light and space, yet cosy seclusion. And the weather was warm and sunny under a vivid clear blue sky, creating and almost impossibly beautiful vista. We were stunned at wonderland we had entered and Roy had to forcibly encourage us to move on to view the impressive show-cabin. Before we entered the cabin, we knew that the decision was made and we would be buying a holiday home here. The inside of the cabin confirmed our decision as the rustic charm mixed with iconic traditional western furniture, enhanced with native American adornments literally took my breath away and tears of sheer emotional joy came to my eyes. And, perhaps more to the point, it was within our budget so perhaps I was just crying with financial relief. We stopped for lunch at a local diner on the way back and enthused about the cabin over pulled pork and fries, making up our minds to buy our dream cabin and live happily ever after.

Over the next couple of days, we talked about little else and we further investigated the surrounding area. We drove to the Indian reservation town of Cherokee, the capital of the Eastern Band of Cherokee Indians and part of the traditional homelands of the Cherokee people. On the way we passed the Mountain View Baptist Church, which displayed a large sign outside saying, *Where will you spend Eternity? Heaven or Hell,* with word *Hell* aflame. We were in America's Bible Belt, but I thought this a little aggressive and alarming and was tempted to stop and tell the vicar that he should water down his threats of damnation, but I resisted temptation.

To maintain the heritage of the Cherokee, several signs for Cherokee's streets and buildings are written in both Cherokee syllabary and English, but that apart it was very much like many other little towns we had visited, except that it was very tacky, full of very cheap and garish souvenir shops selling anything that could remotely be considered Indian and made of plastic. There were no tepees, wigwams or women carrying babies in papooses, no corral housing painted ponies, no totem poles and no cowboys staked out to be eaten by ants, but then, I suppose we were naive to think that there may be. After wandering amongst the tat shops for a while, we came across a small museum which celebrated the history of the Cherokee peoples in the area, which we did find fascinating. The displays of artefacts demonstrated just what an intelligent, resourceful and creative people the Indian "Savages" were. It was also very moving, particularly as we studied the special exhibition commemorating the Trail of Tears, which recorded the forced displacement of approximately 60,000 native people in the 19th century. As part of the Indian removal, the Cherokee, Muscogee, Seminole, Chickasaw and Choctaw nations were forcibly removed from their ancestral homelands in the Southeastern United States and made to walk up to a thousand miles to newly designated Indian Territory west of the Mississippi River. We learnt that the Trail of Tears was an example of the genocide of Native Americans, often categorized as ethnic cleansing where up to 15,000 people died of disease, exposure or starvation. It was a time for reflection as we stood and quietly paid our respects to the many men, women and children who died in this brutal and evil enactment.

The hour-long drive back on the I-74 took us through Bryson City, a town that Bill Bryson visited in one of his journeys but was unimpressed, describing it as *a small, nondescript place of motels and barbecue shacks strung out along a narrow river.* We never stopped there, so cannot verify Mr. Bryson's description, but he did tend to be more critical than us about his homeland. The road ran alongside the picturesque Tuckasegee and Nantahala Rivers and sparked the desire to see more of this delightful region once we had purchased our dream cabin in the clearing. We took a break at the Nantahala Outdoor Centre, a small facility on the river specialising in white water rafting amongst other outdoor activities. Despite my reckless suggestion, Sue refused to go rafting, much to my relief. We decided instead to visit Slow Joe's Riverside Café for a coffee, which was much more to our liking. Further on we spotted a run-down wooden shack with broken down cars and piles of rubbish outside, but with a huge sign saying *Boiled Peanuts*. This I could not resist, so we stopped and I entered the less than salubrious establishment. Inside a very big man, both in height and girth, stood behind a grubby counter staring at a vast vat which was bubbling in the corner and emitting a steaming, unpleasant smell, as did the man. I asked for a bag of boiled peanuts, paid and left as quickly as possible. Now, I am a peanut aficionado. I love raw peanuts, roasted peanuts and salted peanuts, so I looked forward to enjoying the new experience of boiled peanuts with my evening Budweiser. We sat in our cabin that evening, a pack of Buds ready and opened the first of the peanut shells. This confirmed that the unpleasant smell was not just from the big man, and the taste was worse than the smell. I was able to force half a dozen down before surrendering and throwing the majority of the offending malodourous snack into the bin. It took several Budweisers to wash the taste away, so the evening wasn't wasted.

Studying our tourist information, we came across the Wilson Lick Ranger Station, a name we found intriguing as we had no idea what a Lick was, and read that the station is on the way to Wayah Bald Lookout Tower, which was even more intriguing, so that was our next exploration. The hike began from a rough National Forest Road through the Nantahala Forest and we trekked on rough paths through trees until we reached the disused ranger station. Built in 1916, the location was used by the men who kept watch over the forest below for fires. I was surprised and a little disappointed to find That Wilson Lick was simply the name of the first ranger to live there rather than an unusual Americanism for an interesting geological feature. We were overjoyed to read that the rough path here and to the nearby Wayah Tower is part of the Appalachian Trail, although I could find no record of Bill Bryson ever discovering it. Perhaps he stayed in Bryson City for too long, admiring his name on the shop and road signs. We continued to the summit where we found the impressive stone built, three storey lookout tower and information boards which told us that the tower was constructed in 1937 and contained living quarters for the watchmen for up to two months at a time, providing an uninterrupted lookout service. I casually claimed to Sue that I could do that job and two months sitting on a hill in the forest gazing over the Appalachian Mountains would suit me just fine.

This was to be our last day and last hike in the area as we had planned to move on the next day and on our way down from the tower we discussed staying in the area and spending a day exploring the area closer to our new cabin home. Fernwood Cottage was booked so we could not extend our stay there and spent our last afternoon driving closer to Andrews to search for accommodation. By this time, I was beginning to have doubts about the wisdom of our planned purchase, but Sue remained passionate about the venture, so I tried to maintain an air of enthusiasm despite my misgivings. We found nowhere suitable to stay but agreed to resume our search the following day and asked Roy and Daphne for their help in securing a billet. That evening as we sat in the cottage with a beer, Sue was unusually quiet and pensive. As we discussed what we should do next, she blurted out that she was having second thoughts about buying the cabin, which fortunately mirrored my own feelings. We decided to write a list of pros and cons to help us decide what to do. The points for the project were few, but we almost ran out of ink writing the list of points against. Looking at the facts on paper certainly focussed our minds and, after a brief discussion, we decided that it was a shortsighted and impractical idea, swelled by blind and impulsive stupidity and would be abandoned forthwith. I slept well that night but I am embarrassed to admit that we left early the next morning without facing our excellent hosts.

Much against Sue's better judgement, I had convinced her that there was no need to book the final accommodation as there would be plenty of hotels and motels in the next stop, so we headed north to Tennessee and the Great Smokey Mountains with a mixture of excitement and trepidation. Three hours later, after a couple of stops to admire views of the Smokies from the Foothills Parkway we crossed into Tennessee and arrived in the small town of Townsend, which nestles at the front door of the Great Smoky Mountains National Park in the *Peaceful Side* of the Smokies. Townsend is a ribbon development either side of the

AMERICANADIAN DIARIES

Little River Road and does not have the type of town centre or Main Street that we had come to love, but it had a lot more going for it. The history of Townsend goes back to the Cherokee Indian tribes that roamed the Smoky Mountain region and used them as hunting grounds before the first English settlers set foot here in the 1700s. The Little River Valley and the surrounding tributary streams were called Tuckaleechee or Peaceful Valley and it remained a peaceful valley after settlement, with farming as the primary livelihood of its residents, augmented by commercial lumbering.

We drove up and down the road looking for somewhere to stay until Sue lost patience with me saying, "What about that one," or, "I don't like the look of that one," or, "Where are we?" and directed me into a handsome building just off the highway with a large sign reading *Great Smokies Welcome Center*. Of course, I said that I was just about to go there anyway, even though I hadn't noticed it. We picked up leaflets, guides and various other data including a list of accommodation in the town, and soon focussed on the Bunkhouse Inn, partly for the archetypal name and partly for its location. We soon found the motel, fronted by a small café and bookstore, which seemed an odd combination. We had a coffee and established that there was a vacancy which we secured, before being directed to our cabin home for the next four days. We had hit the jackpot once again. The cabin was very clean, again spacious and well equipped and offered two bonus surprises. Each cabin on the site had been hand-decorated by the owners with murals of local wildlife and we were to spend our time there in the company of native birds including a magnificent heron, wild turkey and eagle as well as several smaller feathered friends. Our joy at the decoration was surpassed when we looked out of the patio doors at the back of the cabin and saw the Little River flowing gently past, just a few yards from the door whilst the opposite band was untamed woodland. The small garden was also furnished with a picnic table which promised peaceful al fresco dining during our stay. Hungry and tired we decided to snack before resting in our new-found paradise for the afternoon, whilst reading the plethora of information picked up at the Welcome Center. Before settling down, Sue put a few crisps the picnic table to see if it would attract any birds and, within minutes we were joined by a beautiful crimson red cardinal and a tiny chickadee. These, and some of their friends, would be regular visitors over the following days.

We strolled out that evening and arrived at *AJ's Hearth and Kettle Breakfast Buffet. Lunch and Dinner Specials. All you can eat catfish* and over-indulged on food and beer. AJ's was to become our regular choice thereafter for both dinner and breakfast.

The Abrams Falls trail was perhaps the most well-known and popular hike near Andrews and an ideal selection for our first expedition. The trailhead was easily located on the peaceful Cades Cove Loop Road and off we set, balancing across narrow rustic bridges on the clearly defined trail through woodland. As usual, we were alone throughout the walk and we took our time, strolling gently and stopping to watch squirrels and a variety of small, largely unidentified birds flitting in and out of the forest. We reached the picturesque Abrams Falls, crashing 25 feet down over a rocky cliff into a large pool. Strangely, we read later that a report named this pleasant walk in the woods as the ninth most dangerous hike in America, using casualty statistics as a result of lightning, altitude sickness, extreme weather and drowning, with 29 deaths on the trail since 1971 as a result of water related accidents. It was difficult to see how the delightful and easy trail could be dangerous, so I can only assume most of the accidents were caused by people falling or diving into pool beneath the falls. Why anyone would do that remains a mystery to me, but then, they were probably American.

On our return to the Bunkhouse, we continued our afternoon rest and bird feeding pastime, having stopped to buy a bag of wild bird seed on the way back. We were very excited by a red-tailed hawk which perched on a branch opposite and stared down menacingly at the bird table, but whether it was eyeing the small birds for lunch or fancied sharing their takeaway, we did not know. Just after the hawk had given up and departed, a large heron arrived and strode slowly and majestically upriver before spearing a small fish for its lunch. Finally, a squirrel joined the birds on the picnic table to share their repast and a Canada goose strolled over and viewed the lunch but seemed unimpressed and left without dining. It was a thoroughly entertaining, joyful and lazy afternoon.

In the evening, we booked a table at the Laurel Valley Golf Club, an unusual venture for us but it offered all you can eat catfish and a bluegrass band. As a longtime country music fan, I had always enjoyed this variation of Appalachian Mountain music and the evening was an entertaining mix of excellent food and exhilarating music. The catfish was superb and the live music by the Bluegrass Masters both familiar yet exciting, made even more enjoyable by the band's infectious enthusiasm, with the finale, a rendition of Duelling Banjos, a masterpiece of plucking and strumming. We were interrupted twice during the evening by a waitress offering us more catfish and she seemed quite surprised and hurt when we said we were replete and could eat no more. We had to explain that the meal was excellent and we really had eaten enough and simply could not manage any more, but she seemed unconvinced. Looking round at the other customers, I could understand her disbelief as every other table seemed to be occupied by rotund diners accepting several catfish refills.

We walked off the abundance of catfish the following day with an eight-mile hike on the Rich Mountain Trail leading to the Indian Grave Gap Trail. Unusually, we met other hikers on the track and they warned us that they had spotted a large black bear further up the trail, so we should beware. Thanking them we continued on our journey. We had, after all, bravely survived bear encounters before, but we still kept a careful lookout. A mile or two further on we saw a dark shadow and heard rustling on the side of the trail, just a few feet away. We stopped, hearts beating faster, and our minds racing trying to work out what we should do next. As we stood frozen to the spot, a large white-tailed deer emerged from the forest and looked at us with an amused disdain, as if to say, "Ha ha. Fooled ya!"

After lunching next to rapids which tumbled and crashed down the mountainside, we returned to the cabin for another afternoon of rest with wildlife feeding and bird spotting. Joining our usual companions at the feeding station were a tufted titmouse and a mourning dove, whilst across the river we spied a belted kingfisher in the trees and had difficulty in distinguishing another tree dweller between a sapsucker and woodpecker. So intrigued were we by the birds, that we decided to stay in that evening with a takeaway pizza and watch the wildlife. However, the birds had other ideas and, despite being tempted with a portion of a margherita, turned down our invitation to supper.

South of Townsend is Cades Cove, a scenic, one-way loop road in a valley surrounded by fertile green meadows and distant mountains. We had used parts of the road to access the walking trails, but decided to have a day's rest from hiking and take a leisurely drive around the complete loop, stopping where we fancied to enjoy the scenery and history without boots and backpacks. We left the cabin early, forwent breakfast to improve our chances of spotting exciting wildlife and began cruising the cove in the bright early spring sunlight. Our early start was soon rewarded with the first encounter of the day. Not a bear, coyote, wolf or bison crossed our path, but we were faced with an obstinate wild turkey who refused to move from the centre of the narrow road, raising its impressive tail feathers in a show of defiance, despite our warnings that Bernard Matthews was in the area. Several turkeys and white-tailed deer later, we arrived at the Dan Lawson Place, an historic log cabin. Dan Lawson was a landowner, storekeeper and postmaster in the late nineteenth century and, for a time was also Cade Cove's Justice of the Peace. It is a testament to his skills that he also built the cabin, which is still standing soundly today, although much of it looked to me as if it had been replaced or repaired.

Cades Cove Methodist church was reportedly constructed in 115 days at a cost of $115 by the carpenter and pastor John D. Campbell. Not only is it impressive that a local preacher had the skills to build the wooden place of worship, but managed to build it at a cost of exactly one dollar per day. As a cynic, it sounded a bit too coincidental to me, but made a good story. We were alone inside the church so I mounted the simple wooden pulpit and, much to Sue's annoyance, began a rather loud sermon asking, "Where will you spend Eternity? Heaven or Hell," followed by some nonsense about, "The Good Lord Jesus will send thunderbolts to destroy all sinners." Sue was making strange signs at me and, for a moment, I thought that my sermon had converted her to Christianity. It was then that she pointed to another door where two elderly people stood in apparent shock, mouths agape as if fearing their God was about to strike them down for listening to such blasphemy. We scurried away and I blamed Sue for not telling me that the church had another entrance.

Embarrassed and hungry we left Cades Cove and headed for AJ's for a late *All you can eat breakfast buffet.* We moved on to wander around Townsend and were amused to see that above the small store attached to the local filling station was a sizeable and prominent sign announcing, *TOWNSEND SHOPPING CENTER*. As we said at the time, "Not quite Brent Cross or Cribbs Causeway, is it?"

As the holiday was coming to a conclusion, our last day was spent packing and preparing for the journey, but not before one last walk, scrambling over the boulders and tumbling streams in the woods near Townsend. My five-year-old walking boots had taken a hammering over the couple of weeks and were decidedly untrailworthy, so I decided that they were not worth taking home and sought a suitable resting place for them. On the way back to the cabin, we passed the six feet high sign which said, *GREAT SMOKY MOUNTAINS NATIONAL PARK AN INTERNATIONAL BIOSPHERE RESERVE*. We decided that this would be a suitable memorial for my reliable and faithful old friends, so I climbed up and hung my boots over the sign, but was warned not to say a farewell prayer after my last *faux pas*.

CHAPTER 9 - THE NORTH WEST

It was another three years before we continued our conquest of the United States as we had then moved from Spain to central Portugal and spent the intervening time overseeing the building of a new house and settling into another new life. Age was also catching up and we decided that this would be our last expedition, so should be something really special. We spent months studying our USA Road Atlas, reading literature and asking Google about this vast country. One day, out of the blue, Sue said, "I want to go to Yellowstone," and so Yellowstone National Park it was. After focussing on the north-west, we realised that we would need more time there than our usual fortnight's holiday and, as we had no commitments, decided that we would work out where to go and what to see and not be confined by any timescales. So it was that, after much debate more study and careful planning, we had organised a four-week voyage of discovery to America's Northwest.

We spent many hours researching the trip, the most difficult part of which was the flight to Denver from Lisbon. It was a masterpiece of logistics. In order to get to Lisbon airport we accepted a lift from our home to the nearest village of Serra, a bus from Serra to Tomar, a train from Tomar to Lisbon, a taxi from the station at Lisbon to a hotel and, the following day, a taxi from the hotel to Lisbon airport, then a flight to Philadelphia, another flight from Philadelphia to Denver, before hiring a car to drive to Cheyenne, Wyoming, arriving thirty-six hours after leaving home. "Easy Peasy," I boasted. In retrospect, it wasn't easy. On the train, we sat opposite a scruffy man who stared at us throughout the journey and Sue was convinced he was a serial killer on the run. Both taxi drivers in Lisbon were stark, raving mad and we were lucky to survive their reckless driving. On the second flight, we had somehow failed to pre-book our seats and were seated three rows apart. Other families were similarly split, so I reorganised the three rows of passengers such that we and several other passengers were re-seated in family groups. On the drive to Wyoming, I almost at fell asleep at the wheel just avoiding crashing off the road. Despite that, we arrived at the Super 8 hotel in Lincoln Way, Cheyenne and were peacefully in bed by ten o'clock.

I began the next day at six-thirty with an early morning stroll and reccy into the city, before returning to wake Sue and, after breakfast in the hotel, we set off to explore the town together. Despite my best efforts to distract her, Sue spotted a Walmart where she spent a happy hour doing what she does best, before we moved on. The town was a fascinating collection of historic old buildings and we followed a route which took in the Union Pacific Depot, the Atlas Theatre, the Plains Hotel and, most importantly, The Wrangler, a store *Famous for Ranchwear Since 1943*. Dotted amongst all the attractive old red sandstone buildings were giant cowboy boot statues, unimaginatively known as the Big Boots. The eight-foot-tall boots had been magnificently decorated by talented local artists, with illustrations to show the history of Cheyenne and Wyoming. We saw boots representing the buffalo herds, the outlaws of Wyoming, memories of the old west and many more.

After a hefty sub at Jimmy-Johns, a famous Cheyenne diner, Sue and I continued our western history lesson with a tour of the town on the Cheyenne Street Railway, a ninety minute Wild West History Tour on a trolly bus. Absorbing as the tour was, I was slightly perturbed by the commentary which identified any building, landmark or monument over fifty years old as historical, which therefore made both Sue and me pre-historical.

After our history fix, we had dinner that evening at a modern roadside eatery, Shari's Café and Pies. Our amiable chat with the friendly waitress turned a little odd when she, a pie shop worker, lectured us on the obesity epidemic in America and its dangers to health. This was particularly surreal as she was very fat and smoked a cigarette between delivering each meal.

Awake early the next day, our feet were itching for a walk, so drove just 27 miles west of Cheyenne on I-80 to the Medicine Bow-Routt National Forest and the Vedauwoo Recreation Area, named by Native Americans meaning Land of the Earthborn Spirits. On our arrival, it was easy to see why they believed it was a spiritual place with massive rock structures seeming to balance, defying gravity up to 500 feet in the air. The enormous ancient Sherman ancient granite rock formations, created by ice, wind and water, are made of pink feldspar, white quartz and various other minerals giving them a surreal appearance as if designed by Salvador Dali in one of his more frenzied moments. We decided to hike the popular Turtle Rock Trail, a three-mile-long loop which, we read, was fairly flat with a few small inclines and would be easy to follow. We had no map but were confident we have no problems with the route and set off confidently from the sign indicating the start of the trail. We walked through the breathtaking rock formations as the track wound its way around the massive boulders, slabs and cliffs. We did not see any more trail markers on the way but continued to wander in awe of the geological formations, wondering how nature could produce such overwhelmingly stunning scenery. We left the track a few times, not really sure where we were but confident that the trail would eventually lead us back to the car park. We were excited to see a beaver pond and lodge amongst the spruce, fir and aspen trees but, as on our last visit to the northwest years before, we had forgotten that the area sits at a high altitude, in this case up to 8,000 feet, so we were breathing heavily in the deoxygenated air and perhaps with a little trepidation setting in. We met an American family on the way and they asked us we how far it was. As I had no idea where we were or, more to the point, where they were going, I simply said, "Not far now," and we carried on our way. Sue was annoyed, reminding me that we had been walking for two hours, not knowing where we were going or where we were at that time and I could well be sending the friendly Americans to almost certain exhaustion, exposure and death. After about three hours of walking, we suddenly came upon the car park where I pretended that I knew the way all along, but gasped a sigh of relief. Later investigations suggest that we may have actually veered onto the Valley Massif Loop, but I am still unsure.

We still had the afternoon free so, after picnicking in the shade of an overhanging rock and watching other brave hikers setting off, we returned to Cheyenne and the Nelson Museum of the West. We moseyed past exhibits of *Military, Cowboy and Native American Artifacts, Western Art and Natural History Material...* in order to be... *educated as to the history of the Old*

AMERICANADIAN DIARIES

West. The claim was fulfilled in many of the fascinating displays, but quite how a stuffed African lion, hyenas and a zebra contributed to our education of the American West passed me by.

Our last meal in Cheyenne before moving on was at a mind-boggling restaurant in the Historic quarter and walking distance from the hotel. Sandford's Grub and Pub attracted us because it had the back half of a truck sticking out of the wall above the door and encompassed the best of all the exciting American restaurants we had previously used, including a long bar with local rednecks sitting on stools sipping beer and presenting their rear cleavage to the room. Every inch of the walls was covered in American memorabilia – old advertising signs, street signs, neon signs, portraits of famous baseball and basketball players, hundreds of different beer bottles, antique kitchen equipment, old car parts, historic photographs and a plethora of other memorabilia. The menu boasted that *We specialize in the art of deep frying food,* and *...mostly known for our world-famous onion rings.* How could anyone resist world famous onion rings? After gorging on a mixture of fried food we retired to the hotel and before bed, where we watched the local news on television and there was no mention of a family dying of exposure on the Turtle Rock Trail, so we slept well that night, secure in the fact that I was not guilty of culpable homicide.

With stomachs still gurgling from a surfeit of deep-fried onion rings, we set off the following morning for the next stage of our tour, the four-hour drive on I-85 across the Great Plains to Custer, South Dakota, in the heart of the Black Hills of Dakota, made famous in the song by Doris Day in the great musical, *Calamity Jane*. I half expected to see Doris riding shotgun on a stagecoach on the road, being chased by a band of fierce Indians, but she never appeared so I guessed that it must have been her day off. We were tempted to detour to the famous settlement of Fort Laramie on the way, but reluctantly decided that we couldn't see everything the area had to offer and bypassed the old fort, a decision I still regret. We stopped for coffee in a strange town called Lusk, which consisted of a few sparse buildings on the side of the Interstate, but no houses that we could see. We did see the Outpost Café and Truck Stop however, and shared our break with several middle-aged, bearded and leather-clad bikers who eyed us with suspicion. I never told them that I was a Mod in the 1960's and clashed with their English counterparts in Brighton. We arrived in Custer without further incident and settled into our new billet, the Chief Motel, meeting Bruce, the owner. He was a bit of an oddball who couldn't stop talking, but was very friendly, interesting and helpful. A bonus that we hadn't realised when we booked the motel months before, was that he offered vouchers giving special rates for breakfast at the Wrangler Restaurant, subs at Subway and free entry into Custer State Park. We surveyed the Wrangler that evening, and enjoyed unhealthy shredded pork, jo-jo potatoes, slaw and salad. That was the dining venue settled for the duration of our stay.

Back at the Wrangler in the morning for our breakfast, we noticed a group of up to half a dozen elderly men in one corner, chatting and drinking copious amounts of coffee. We nodded politely in greeting and, after our special-rate breakfast and purchasing our special-rate take-away subs at Subway, we set off for our free-entry to Custer State Park with the hope of seeing exciting wildlife, especially American bison. We drove the eighteen-mile Wildlife Loop, stopping to look at elk, and pronghorn deer before being held up by highwaymen donkeys. These *begging burros* are not native to the Black Hills, but are descended from animals that once hauled visitors to the top of

Black Elk Peak. After the rides were discontinued years ago, the burros were released into the park. They soon adapted to their new lives by blocking the road and refusing to move until they have been fed. Fortunately, we had some apples in the car and were able to buy our freedom with a couple of granny smiths, before continuing our journey. We had seen no bison on the roadside so stopped at a small ranger station and asked where we were most likely to encounter the animals. The ranger directed us to a small gravel road and said that some had been seen there earlier that day, so we detoured onto the minor road. We soon espied a herd of bison a couple of hundred yards away in a meadow across a hedge-lined stream, and sat in the car watching the adults graze whilst young calves frolicked in the grass. We were excited by the discovery and watched with mounting anticipation as the beasts moved slowly towards us, until they were just across the stream no more than ten yards away. The excitement began to turn to mild curiosity as the herd crossed the stream and pushed through the hedgerow and wandered towards the car. We were soon surrounded by several huge animals, weighing almost a ton each when they started to move along the gravel road and, as we had bison to left and right, in front and behind, we had no choice but to join the herd as they trundled along the road. For several minutes we became part of the herd, unable to stop or move out of their path. After perhaps fifteen minutes, the lead bull decided that he had had enough of the old English couple in their hire care and veered very slowly back onto the grassland, allowing us to leave the herd and go on our way. Strangely, at no time spent being part of a buffalo migration did we feel any fear or anxiety, just a sensation of elation. On the way back to the main road we saw a sign which read, *Warning. Many visitors have been gored by buffalo. Do not approach Buffalo.* "Thank goodness that they approached us, and not the other way round, or we could have been gored," I observed.

Sue added, "And the fact that we safely protected by being in a car may have helped too." She had a point.

Following our dice with death by goring, we decided to park the car and follow the Prairie Trail Loop and Lovers Leap Trail, two connecting walks through pasture and woodland. It was a relatively gentle and very peaceful stroll and the only hazards were in crossing small brooks which Sue managed easily by ledging fallen trees across the streams and balancing over them, before laughing as I slipped from the wet logs into the water. The objective of the walk was to reach the rocky outcrop of Lovers Leap, so called after a local legend of two Native American lovers who were fleeing from the United States Cavalry and were cornered before jumping to their deaths from this point. Whilst the views were magnificent, Sue felt very sad and stood silently to pay her respects to the lovers, but I said it's only a legend and probably not true. But I still had a lump in my throat which I put down to emotion of gazing over such a stunning view.

In the state park near Custer is the Needles Highway. Named for the needle-like granite formations that rise spectacularly by the roadside, the highway is a fourteen-mile circular road passing through pine and spruce forests and verdant meadows interspersed with the impressive, rugged granite mountains. The roadway was constructed in the 1920's purely for its aesthetic beauty as it goes nowhere but back to the start and many tunnels were blasted through the mountains. It was an obvious choice for a visit ignoring Sue's trepidation about my driving and my ability to negotiate hairpin bends and narrow tunnels with just inches to spare each side of the car. Despite her concern, we managed the complete loop, stopping many times to admire the impressive views, although quite how the fourteen miles took us three hours indicates just how carefully and very slowly I manoeuvred the car through the obstacles, particularly the Needles Eye tunnel, the narrowest channel through the rocks, where I had to use a point car and hope strategy to squeeze through. After the nerve-wrangling excursion, we settled down at the side of the beautiful Sylvan Lake in the Black Elk Wilderness, name after Black Elk, a noted Lakota Sioux medicine man. The lake was a vivid blue oasis, created in 1891 when a dam was built across Sunday Gulch Creek. As we munched on our cut-price subs and admired the azure, still waters with dramatic cliffs rising to the skyline, my heart was still pounding out of pride and relief at my skills as a motorist, whilst Sue was her usual calm and relaxed self. "I don't know what you were worried about," she said, "It was an easy drive."

A trailhead next to the lake leads up to the 7,244 feet Harney Peak, the highest natural point in the U.S. state of South Dakota and the Midwestern United States and the highest summit east of the Rocky Mountains and the European Alps. It was irresistible. As we trudged up mountain paths, scrambled over bare rock, crossed small streams and forced aching legs onwards and upwards, I began to wonder if it was worth the effort, then the vista opened up and we reached the summit. I then wondered why I ever had doubts as panoramic views were afforded for miles in every direction. At the top, steps led up to a large stone-built fire tower, built in the 1930's with stone gathered from nearby French Creek. All of the stone and other building materials were hauled by men and donkeys along the three-mile trail to the summit. Little wonder that the animals are now happier holding up travellers for apples in Custer National Park. Throughout the climb, we had seen no-one. No hikers going up or coming down the trail, yet at the top there were dozens of people, relaxing and recuperating on the summit rocks. On the way back to Sylvan Lake we didn't recognise anything and we met many other hikers, which suggested that perhaps we had somehow strayed from the recommended route on our climb to the top. I tried to convince Sue that I had deliberately taken the longer, harder trail up as we needed the exercise. She was not convinced, so I blamed the poor sign posting instead. Before reaching the car, we stopped to chat to an anthropologist from Hungary who told us that he was studying the Sioux Indians on their reservation. He told us that he had reached the conclusion that they were genetically programmed to be too lazy to work, much like the Eastern Gypsies. Unusually, I could not think of anything to say and simply nodded.

As our six-mile mountain hike had been extended to at least eight miles, the next day we took an easy option and headed for Keystone and the Black Hills Central Railway. We arrived with an hour to spare before departure so wandered around the town, but were underwhelmed. The old mining community had been replaced by a tourism hotchpotch due to its proximity to Mount Rushmore and so, although the buildings maintained the pioneer appearance, they had all been revamped to cater for vacationers. There were pretend trading posts, gift shops, portrait studios, factory outlets, fast food outlets, ice cream parlours, shops selling gold and leather items, custom t-shirts, cowboy hats and every other piece of tourist tat imaginable. And there were many overweight visitors blocking the boardwalks, which made me grumble that they should not be allowed to block our way and spoil the visit. Sue said that it was ironic that I, a tourist, should criticise other tourists in a town catering for tourists. I could only reply, "Harrumph."

AMERICANADIAN DIARIES

All was forgiven when the old steam locomotive puffed its way into the station and we were able to board and start our excursion. We relaxed in comfort as the train panted, wheezed and clattered through the mountains, passing unperturbed deer, abandoned mines, Old Baldy Mountain, Indian Cliffs and Harney Peak before climbing and gasping slowly up the final hill to Hill City. The 1880 engine did well to make the last climb as all the fat tourists from town had also migrated to the train. When we had deboarded, our travelling companions headed as quickly as their chubby legs would allow to the gift shop for more tourist tat and bottles of diet coke, allowing Sue and I to sit peacefully with our cut-price subs on the station watching the engines shunting to prepare for the homeward journey. A gentle and serene return journey was only interrupted by the rhythmic snoring of a fellow passenger and, on arrival back at Keystone, we set off for the second part of our Tourism Day, an almost obligatory visit to Mount Rushmore.

We joined the throng of tubby American visitors, many of whom I was sure had been on the train, although Sue said I was being silly, and passed through the large granite entrance to come face to face with four US presidents. The sculpted heads of the presidents, George Washington, Thomas Jefferson, Theodore Roosevelt and Abraham Lincoln, are so well known that standing on the viewing platforms looking up at the monument was an almost surreal experience. I had seen this exact view so many times, in films such as North by Northwest, on television, in magazines and in many publicity notices that I felt I had been there before. We moved from viewing area to viewing area, staring at the heads from slightly different angles, as they gazed over us into space. We went to the information centre and read that the sculptor, Gutzon Borglum, oversaw its creation from 1927 to 1941: that he was assisted by his son, Lincoln Borglum:

that the heads of each president are sixty feet high: that they represent America's growth, development, and preservation: that Borglum chose Mount Rushmore because it faces southeast for maximum sun exposure: that it attracts over two million visitors each year, and so many more facts that the actual wonderment at the monument took a back seat to data and statistics. Bamboozled by a surfeit of information, we retired to the Carvers' café for a coffee, unsure whether we were excited or deflated by the experience. There were many fat people in the café too and I was beginning to think that we were under surveillance by the American Fat Tourist Society, who could remand us in custody and force feed us until we reached the minimum legal fatness. Sue just sighed and said that it was time to go.

On our way back to Custer, we stopped at Stockade Lake and a stroll around the circular lake trail, a short but tough walk which was much more to our liking. That said, we caught glimpses of another impressive monument, the Crazy Horse Memorial and decided that would be our next trip.

That evening we dined at yet another splendid venue, the Dakota Cowboy Restaurant where we enjoyed the catfish and fries from the seniors' menu, a smaller meal than the usual American feast but a welcome change. We were again surrounded by western memorabilia, including hundreds of stetsons and ten-gallon cowboy hats hanging from the ceiling and we wondered if the headgear was perhaps left in exchange for a discounted meal. We struck up a conversation with a couple who told us that they had been to the Big Thunder Gold Mine near Keystone, where they toured the mine and tried their luck in gold panning sluices. They had also visited the historic city of Deadwood City, the original home of Calamity Jane and Wild Bill

Hickock, just over an hour's drive away. I had visions of sharing a sarsaparilla with Doris Day there and showing her the gold that I had just panned with Wild Bill. This sounded exciting, but with only one day left, it would have to be consigned to another visit which we knew would never come. We had eaten quite early so finished the day with a stroll around the town and discovered that, whilst Cheyenne boasted its big boots, Custer displayed many life-sized, decorated bison. We found and photographed several of the models, viewed the Old Custer Jail and generally enjoyed a peaceful evening stroll, trying to walk off the catfish dinner.

Over another fine breakfast at the Wrangler, where we were now greeted by the old men with a friendly, "Howdy," we relaxed with a short walk on the Mickleson Trail in the town before setting off for the Crazy Horse Memorial. Crazy Horse was a Native American war leader of the Oglala Lakota. He fought U.S. Federal government against encroachments on his territories and the way of life of the Lakota people and led his people at the famous Battle of the Little Bighorn in 1876, wiping out the seventh cavalry under General George Custer. The memorial to the Oglala Lakota warrior was planned and started in 1948, a gigantic mountain monument depicting Crazy Horse riding his horse and pointing over his tribal land. Access to the statue is via the Native American Cultural Center and, as we stood there and looked at the monument, it was hard to believe that, in well over half a century, the only recognisable part of the statue is Crazy Horse's head. The rest is just, well, mountain. A scale model of the how the completed statue will look stands in the grounds of the centre and shows that the complete structure is perhaps twenty-five percent complete at best, so it could be centuries before it is complete. When we read the dimensions of the plan, it was no surprise that it is taking so long. The sculpture's planned dimensions are mind-boggling. It will be 641 feet long and 563 feet high. This compares with the heads of the four U.S. Presidents at Mount Rushmore at a mere 60 feet in height. I wondered why anyone would even plan such an unfeasible feat and why they don't just give up and leave it part finished. But then, I never imagined that man would send a rocket to Mars, invent the Internet or produce oven chips, so what do I know? We thoroughly enjoyed the Indian Museum of North America on the site, displaying historic art and artifacts of the Native American people, and the Laughing Water café served good coffee, so all was not lost.

After two days of sightseeing, we needed a walk, so spent the afternoon repeating the Stockade Lake Trail before moving on to the Gordon Stockade, originally called Fort Defiance. It was erected in 1874 by white settlers who travelled to the Black Hills during the gold rush, and was on the site of a previous encampment of Custer's Black Hills Expedition. Whether this was the exact site where Custer left to kill innocent Indian women and children and renege on the treaty that gave the Indian people the Black Hills for perpetuity was unclear. In my imagination this was where he prepared for his atrocities before his final comeuppance at the Little Big Horn. As this was our last day, Sue convinced me that we had to go shopping, so we wandered up and down Main Street looking in every shop before buying some essential supplies, that is, a pack of aspirin, at the pharmacy. She was not impressed with the Claw, Antler and Hide Co. store, which sold every non-decomposing part of dead animals killed by hunters, as the name suggested.

We stopped for beer at the Gold Pan Saloon, an authentic western bar built in 1929 with swing doors, a spittoon and sawdust on the floor, which looked as if it had not been replaced from the opening day. It was also decorated with more dead animals and animal parts, which put Sue off her drink somewhat. I was impressed with the authenticity, especially as they had two drunken young men trying to play pool and being generally loud and obnoxious. We waited for Wyatt Earp to come and arrest them and put them in the Old Jail, but he never arrived so we left after one beer and went back to the motel to prepare for the next leg of journey and Sue's dream, Yellowstone National Park.

We had our last Wrangler breakfast and said goodbye to the waitress and the group of old gentlemen who wished us well on our journey and set off northwest towards Wyoming. This was an ambitious journey of over 500 miles with an estimated time of almost eight hours without stops. My tentative suggestion of going via Deadwood was quickly and rightfully rejected, so we followed the I-90, passing through the intriguingly-names settlements of Newcastle, Gillette (Sue didn't laugh when I said, "That was a close shave,") Buffalo, Cody, Wapiti, and Pahaska Tepee. The drive across the Great Plains and the Rockies was never less than interesting and often spectacular with distant snow-capped mountains, buttes, bluffs, mesas, lakes, rivers and vast rolling prairie. Not far outside Buffalo, three hours into the trip, we spotted a settlement called Lake de Smet where we pulled off the highway for a coffee and pee break. This was a very odd place, lonely and windswept with a few prefabricated buildings seemingly dropped randomly on the prairie. We found a small service station and nervously entered the café. It was empty of life, almost apocalyptic, and we were tempted to turn and run until a thin body topped with a bald head appeared from behind the counter and stared at us.

"Are you serving coffee?" I asked the skeletal figure, as cheerfully as I could muster.

He stared more intensely and asked, "How many?" A strange question to ask two people.

"Er, Just the two," I answered, "White, please," and we sat down.

The coffee was duly delivered and I paid at the table before Skeletor disappeared. We drank up quickly, had a pee and left.

The next stage of the drive took us across the Bighorn mountains via the Powder River Pass, one of the main routes across the Rockies, created in the early days of mining in the area. As we drove higher, the weather started to change and the skies darkened. We were soon in a minor blizzard with wind rocking the car and snow swirling around us. We were unsure whether to stop or continue and decided that a short halt may be sensible, until I almost drove into the back of a lorry trundling along in front of us. This was a relief as the lorry was leaving clear tracks through the snow which we could follow with more confidence and the driver could rescue us in case of a disaster. As it was, the snow soon cleared, the wind dropped as did the road and we were able to carry on without problems, but I still felt quite heroic for braving the Arctic conditions and delivering my bride safely through the storm. On the eastern side of the pass, we stopped at a small town called Greybull for a second, well-deserved coffee at the Uptown café, before continuing the drive to Canyon Village.

After a ten-hour journey, we arrived at the entrance to Yellowstone and were surprised that, although we had booked accommodation in the park, we still had to pay the entrance fee, and the reduced rate for seniors did not apply to foreigners. Despite my tongue-in-cheek protest that we were not foreign but English, we paid up and drove on. Our excitement mounted as we entered the park and travelled through a forest of high firs before reaching Yellowstone Lake, much of which was under a blanket of ice and snow, creating a stunning winter scene, albeit in June. A few minutes later, we passed a meadow where a young grizzly bear was foraging in grass. As we stopped to admire the animal, it looked up before ambling towards us and sauntering across the road directly in front of our car, glancing at us over its shoulder as it passed. It is difficult to explain the exhilaration that we felt with our first bear encounter within minutes of arrival. The bear disappeared into the forest and we moved on to Canyon Village in the centre of the park and our holiday home. The cabin we hired was more than we could ever have anticipated. From the outside, it reminded me of the abandoned small wooden miners' cabins we had seen on our travels, and appealing to our pioneer spirit. We imagined that the inside would be very basic, but were happily surprised an interior to match any motel we had stayed in with roomy accommodation containing two large single beds, a desk and chair and a smart, modern shower and toilet. I was sure that an old-time miner could never have imagined such luxury. Having unpacked, showered and changed, we wandered around the village, surveying the bars, restaurants, shops and visitors' centre. I commented that it was like an up-market Centre Parks and Sue squeezed my hand and said, "We'll be happy here." After a quick snack from our Subway supplier, we were in bed by ten o'clock.

We had survived the previous day on coffee and subs, so looked forward to breakfast at the Soda Fountain, a restaurant on site which reminded us of the very best of American diners, and ordered the full breakfast experience, bacon, patties, eggs (over easy), home fries, pancakes with syrup (on the same plate), toast and coffee. The staff were all college students working their vacation and were all keen, helpful and polite and, intrigued by our English accents, asked odd questions like did we have electricity in Britain. I told them that some houses have now.

   For our first walk we had chosen to explore the Canyon South Rim Trail which follows the edge of a deep gorge, known as the Grand Canyon of Yellowstone. It was a predictable decision as it is the most popular in Yellowstone, according to the literature we had studied before arrival. Yet, although the café was busy, as was the village centre, it was strange but not surprising that we once we had left the resort, we saw very few people during the hike. We crossed the Chittenden Memorial Bridge, which overlooks the Upper Falls and followed an easy path along the rim to a viewpoint of the falls where the Yellowstone Rover thunders 100 feet over a lip of volcanic rock. In early June, the falls are at their most dramatic as the ice melt crashes down from the surrounding mountains. The detour down the canyon on Uncle Tom's Trail was irresistible, despite the warnings that there were more than 300 steps to negotiate both down and, of course, back up again, but the views from this viewpoint looking up at the falls were incredible. We carried on the path to the Lower Falls viewpoint and were awestruck. These falls squeeze through a narrower rim and hurtle down the narrow gap over 300 feet, nearly twice as high as Niagara Falls. Still buzzing with excitement, we continued on the South Rim Trail to Artist Point and were greeted with yet more spectacular views in both directions where the river boiled and churned as it careered down the valley 300 feet below. A little further on, we stopped for lunch at an overlook where the opposite canyon walls were composed of different coloured rocks, the pale yellows, pinks and greens like an artist's water colour palette. As I gazed over the natural beauty, I had something in my eye again.

We cut away from the canyon on the return trek and, despite warning of bear activity in the area, followed the Clear Lake Trail through placid meadows and passing pristine blue waters of Clear Lake and Lily Pad Lake, before negotiating the hydrothermal area where sulphurous gases splutter up from deep in the Earth's crust. We saw bison, a grey Jay, woodpeckers, a nesting osprey, a red-tailed kite and several yellow warblers before meeting an ill-equipped family, who again asked us the way and, again, we could only tell them to carry on the way they were going, hoping that they survived the walk. We returned to our cabin, still buzzing and wondering if we could ever match the euphoria of our first day, before relaxing in the Cafeteria at Canyon Village. The diner was packed with American families and a coachload of Japanese tourists. Not for the first time, we wondered how we could have walked one of the park's most popular trails, seeing just a handful people, yet the restaurant was crowded with overweight Americans and thin Japanese tourists. Where did our fellow visitors go during the day?

It is difficult to describe the Norris Geyser Basin, our next outing. It is a flat area of about 800 acres (perhaps 300 football pitches) surrounded by small hills and distant snow-capped mountains. We read the geological description of the areas which served to confuse my simple mind although Sue was nodding sagely as she read, so suffice it to say that it appears to be a large, mainly white plain which looks like salt (actually white sand) decorated with splashes of yellow, red, green and brown, with steaming thermal pools, erupting geysers, hot bubbling springs and bright blue acidic pools with exotic names, among them Porcelain Terrace Overlook, Black Growler Steam Vent,

Whirligig Geyser, Whale's Mouth and Crackling Lake. Threading its way through the scalding ponds is a trail consisting of raised walkways and paved paths which allow a close up look at the boiling, belching pools. Throughout the walk, we could feel the heat rising up from the magma in the Earth's crust and the strong stench of sulphur was always with us. Amazingly, dotted in this apparently toxic, hot and inhospitable terrain, valiant fir trees were clinging to life. It took us over two hours to walk the two-mile footpath, such was the mesmerizing natural spectacle and because Sue read the information boards for each and every feature. We completed the loop and found convenient seats on the first overlook, perhaps fifty yards from the car park for a well-earned rest and a sandwich. We were again pleased to see some our fat friends, though Sue assured me not the same ones as the day before, waddle up and lean over the barrier and say something like, "Is that it?" before waddling back to their cars, presumably to go and look for a MacDonalds and a well-earned burger after their exhausting hike.

In the afternoon, we drove alongside Yellowstone Lake with views of the majestic Washakie Mountains on the opposite bank, planning to stop at Bridge Bay Marina to book a lake cruise. The drive was marred slightly by the awful driving of some fellow motorists and I was forced to reprimand them on two separate occasions with a blast on the horn and some fitting Anglo-Saxon expletives. Sue accused me of road rage but I explained that I was just educating the colonists on the rules of the road. We were held up for an hour in traffic as the road and a bridge was under repair, which forced me to offer more advice to the ungentlemanly drivers. As we waited in the jam, a ranger visited each car to politely explain what was happening and why we were delayed. He was extremely courteous and I boasted that my colonist education programme was obviously working. The frustration was relieved by watching a coyote hunting in the roadside meadow. It skulked carefully, sniffing in the grass, before leaping in the air and landing headfirst then proudly standing with a small rodent in its mouth, which it showed off to the queue of cars before swallowing the victim. We finally arrived at the dock and reserved our places on the tour boat. And Sue spent a happy half hour browsing in the gift shop where she purchased a flask emblazoned with the logo *American Adventure*.

We changed our routine that evening and took Sue's new flask for a drive after dinner, stopping in the Haydon Valley at Grizzly Overlook, so called for obvious reasons. There were already eighteen cars (I counted them) in the layby which overlooked the gently rolling green valley, and there were men with big cameras stationed in front of each car. Many photographers had their equipment mounted on tripods and all had lens attachments about a foot long pointing at the valley. We squeezed our car in at the end of the row and stepped out gazing at the field, soon realising that we had gate-crashed a Boring Tourist Meeting as all the men talked about was photography and what they had managed to snap - from a car park.

"I caught a mom bear with a cub yesterday."

"Well, I got a one with two cubs on Monday."

"Yeah, but I caught a bear and a wolf together last week."

"OK, but I got a got four bears and a pack of wolves hunting a bison."

"So what? I captured a pack of wolves and a pack of bears and a cougar fight to the death over a bison carcass until only the cougar was left alive, and he sat down and cooked the bison over a campfire he built hisself before eating it with a knife and fork."

Actually, I made up some of the conversation, but that was drift. As Sue asked at the time, why do they bother? It's not really a wild animal encounter and they may as well take photos in a zoo.

Still grumbling about too many tourists the following morning, we decided to take a walk in Alum Creek, part of the Mary Mountain Trail, itself part of the Nez Perce Trail. The hike was described as one of the less-travelled routes which allowed us peace and quiet and, as Sue clearly stated, it may stop me moaning about other people and, particularly, the photographers too lazy to walk more than a yard from their cars. It was a wise decision on Sue's part as the walk was superb, following the trail through pretty meadows and woods, in hills high above the river, which was carrying large blocks of ice slowly downstream, detached from the mountains in the thaw. We found a fallen log at the turning point, ideal for a sandwich break and a cup of hot coffee from Sue's new American Adventure flask. Part of the return track took us directly through the middle of a large herd of bison, who looked at us suspiciously as we passed, although we kept our distance from the animals wherever possible. It was a little nerve-racking as we weaved through the herd, particularly as one animal, a ton of wild unpredictable muscle, crashed to ground a few yards away and rolled over taking a dust bath. I swear that ground shook and trembled. And so did I.

The boat trip was booked the next morning and we were a little uneasy as we set off for the Bridge Marina as there would be other vacationers on board, who would probably annoy me and that would annoy Sue. On the way, we saw a large grizzly sitting on the roadside and we stopped to stare at the impressive but passive beast from the safety of the car. As we stopped, a car coming the opposite was also stopped and harangued me for driving too fast (I wasn't) and said I should slow down (I had.) I am not proud of the fact that my Swindon council house upbringing surfaced and, in no uncertain terms, told him to mind his own business and called him a nosey old bugger. He immediately wound up his window and shrunk down in his seat, staring straight ahead and refused to engage in further discussion. I felt much better afterwards and began to look forward to the boat trip.

The trip was excellent and relaxing as we cruised Lake Yellowstone with an informative and entertaining commentary by Ranger Brad. At one point, he said that he would like, "...you guys to get out and hike a little bit, as only six percent of the park is visible from the road." Our plump fellow sightseers looked a little panicked about the suggestion and I guess that I looked rather smug, but said nothing. Sue wasn't really listening to Brad as the boat skipper was a tall, broad-shouldered and very handsome man and she was paying more attention to this Adonis than the Ranger.

On our return to the billet, we stopped at West Thumb on the south border of Yellowstone Lake. Here is a caldera with a number of bubbling and steaming springs, some are cauldrons where the gases force their way through pools of blue, green and turquoise water and some are mud pots where the gases throw the pink and yellow clay up to twenty feet in the air. Many of the larger pools have been named, so we watched water and mud bursting up from the deep and deep blue Abyss Poll, the steaming Dragon's Mouth Spring, the green Sour Lake and the churning

Sulphur Caldron, one of the most acidic hot springs in Yellowstone. We read that the bubbling water in the caldron has a pH of approximately 1-2, which is similar to car battery acid or stomach fluids. As I had never touched, drank or otherwise been in contact with acid from a battery or stomach fluid, this meant very little, but sounded dangerous and was very smelly. As we wandered through this alien landscape absorbed by the sights, sounds and smells of the caldera, I saw a young lad of around ten years old throwing stones into one of the cauldrons, obviously a stupid and dangerous activity. Without thinking, I shouted at him to stop and loudly explained that these are fragile geological wonders and should be treated with respect. The lad stopped and looked very confused, but not as confused as his gormless parents who quickly ushered him away, probably to throw stones into another pool where no nosey and loud Englishman would disturb his new-found hobby. Sue again admonished me for shouting at Americans, reminding me that we were guests in their country. I muttered something about not shouting at thick Americans unless they deserve it, but was silenced by one of her looks.

We were ready for a long walk the next day and chose the Lamarr Valley, part of the historic Slough Creek wagon trail into the Absaroka-Beartooth Wilderness. We set off on the hour's magical drive via the Tower Roosevelt district, through lush green valleys of the Yellowstone River and bordered by the jagged mountain peaks, stopping on the way to admire the views, particularly of the thundering waterfalls resulting from the snow melt. We came across a number of cars jammed into a layby with several men setting up their outsize camera paraphernalia, so we stopped to see what they were snapping. I the valley far below us and perhaps a quarter of a mile away was a large grizzly, asleep in the trees. We had not seen many cars on the drive, so can only assume that these photographic buffs have a method of contacting each other when a bear has been spotted, so that they can all rush to the viewpoint and talk about their cameras and lenses and lens hoods and tripods. I was pleased that the bear refused to budge as it took its nap and once again groaned that this is not the way to encounter wildlife. A few miles further on we came across another grizzly on the roadside who looked up as we stopped before ambling across the road in front of the car and climbing the opposite bank...and no-one else saw the animal except us.

We found the Slough Creek trailhead and set out on what Sue described as the best walk ever, mainly because the valley is natural and undeveloped in any way, except the rough ruts on the trail created by covered wagons of the early settlers. Sue's description may perhaps have been something of hyperbole, but it was a glorious hike through impressive woodland reaching the open meadow with the distant Bear Tooth Mountains and meandering Slough Creek River below. After two miles we had intended to fork left and follow the Buffalo Fork Trail but this track led directly into a wide bend in the flooded river, so we diverted to follow the Bliss Pass Trail. We met a lone woman hiker after another mile or two, a brave lone adventurer as there were bear warnings everywhere, and we stopped to pass the time of day. She was wearing a t-shirt emblazoned with *Rocky Mountain National Park – 1915*. I jokingly told her that we had visited the Rocky Mountains Park, but many years after her visit in 1915. She patiently explained that the date referred to when the park was founded, not when she had visited. I was glad that she had enlightened us. We stopped for our customary picnic with tea from the new flask of course and, as we rested, threatening dark storm clouds began to gather overhead so we decided to cut short the hike and return to the car. We had just crossed a hill and my mind was still on the difference in UK and USA humour, when Sue shouted, "Grizzly." I looked up and there indeed was a young grizzly bear just twenty yards away, head down nibbling at some grass. We stopped and made some noise so that the bear was not startled, and it looked up at us before wandering off into a small copse about fifty yards away. We carried on walking and talking and, as we reached the copse, the bear came out into the open, looked at us and wandered away, turning its head every now and then to check that we weren't following. As I proudly announced at the time, "Now, that's a real bear encounter."

As we approached the car park, we noticed some big, fresh bear prints on the muddy path between the trees. We then met an American family who asked if there were any bears on the trail as all the warnings had made them a little wary. Sue replied that we had seen just the one and I showed them the very clear prints, the size of dinner plates. The family looked a little nervous but decided to continue anyway and I resisted the temptation to joke about becoming a bear's lunch. As we left the car park, the storm clouds swirled overhead and it began pouring with rain. We remarked that if the bear hadn't eaten the family they would probably be washed away and drown in the river anyway.

Despite waking the next day to find that the temperature had dropped to near zero and there were flurries of snow, Mammoth Hot Springs was the planned venue of our next outing, so off we went. We were excited, looking forward to seeing more hydrothermal features, hot springs, geysers, mudpots, and fumaroles with dramatic names such as Devil's Kitchen Spring, Painted Pool, Paperpicker Spring, my personal favourites, Little Burper and the intriguingly named Hymen Terrace. As instructed, we followed the boardwalks and footpaths through the lower and upper terraces, between amazing limestone structures which reminded me of scale models of the of the Grand Canyon and canyonlands, but in yellow/white marble. Sue said that it reminded her of a giant, badly iced Christmas cake, which was probably a better description. Its construction emanated from limestone, left millions of years ago when a vast sea covered this area. Water heated deep in the Earth with dissolved carbon dioxide makes a solution of weak carbonic acid and, as the water was forced up through the limestone, it dissolved calcium carbonate, the primary compound in limestone. At the surface, the calcium carbonate was deposited in the form of travertine, the rock that forms the terraced landscape. This was interesting, but not as exciting as a giant cook badly icing a colossal cake. Perhaps suffering from the cold or perhaps because of over-exposure to hot springs, we spent less time studying the features than normal, covering the lower and upper terraces too quickly, before moving on to the nearby Beaver Springs trail where sight of beaver ponds was the promised attraction. We followed the five-mile trail through pretty meadows and woods with pleasant views of Yellowstone's scenery, but we never found any beaver ponds. Quite where we walked and how we found our way remains a mystery, but we ended up on an overlook with the park and its holiday centre, including a large and smart hotel, spread out below us. We agreed that our cosy rustic cabin was far superior to the hotel, before we somehow found our way back. About a mile from the car park, we met yet another American family who were obviously not enjoying what was probably their first ever hike, discounting the walk from a car park to their local Dunkin Donuts. They asked if they were going the right way and I explained that I had no idea as we had not found the beaver ponds, but the walk was splendid anyway. They didn't look too enthusiastic as they waddled off into the wilderness. This cheered me up after missing the ponds, but Sue said that I must stop sending tubby Americans to certain death in the wilderness. We drove back to Canyon Village with me in a jolly mood.

Back at base, we wandered around the village and realised that after several days, for some reason, we had not visited the Visitor and Education Center. There we discovered interesting exhibits about the park, but the highlight was a film describing the establishment of Yellowstone and its evolution to its present status. The film centred on the dangerous animals there, particularly bison, and showed several clips of people who got too close to the huge beasts and were tossed into the air or gored. And we had previously strolled through a herd as if they were passive cows.

After dinner that evening, we went for walk around the nearby campground and thought just how exciting and romantic it looked, sitting amongst lodgepole pines, cooking on barbeques before returning to tents or trailers for the night. I said to Sue that it must be wonderful to camp, experiencing the outdoor life in tune with nature and perhaps we should try it on our next visit. She pointed out that it was freezing and damp and, if I did follow this particular dream, I would do it without her. The following morning, we awoke to find a covering of snow everywhere looking like a Christmas card scene and this was just three days before the midsummer solstice. I decided that I didn't want to sleep in a tent. Ever.

Perhaps the most famous of all the geysers in Yellowstone is Old Faithful, so called because it blows consistently every hour or so (more accurately, between 51 and 120 minutes), every day and each eruption blasts between 3,700 and 8,400 gallons of boiling water into the air, reaching a height of between 106 and 184 feet. Quite why we had saved this visit,

I do not recall but am glad that we did. The Old Faithful area displays more prominent hydrothermal features compared to the other sites we visited, and if we had seen this area first, the impact of the other locations may have seemed less significant by comparison. It was a pleasant drive, avoiding a wandering bison on the road and viewing more coyotes as we passed the Continental Divide and arrived fifteen minutes before Old Faithful was estimated to blow. We took our bench seats, quietly waiting with perhaps a dozen other geyser-watchers for a few minutes until a busload of Japanese tourists arrived, bustling excitedly and chattering loudly around us. A friendly gentleman sat next to me and was fascinated by my camcorder, as it was similar but very much smaller than the one that he was using. After showing him how it worked, which I barely understood myself, I pointed out that it was a Canon and Japanese. He was very excited and, in fast and unintelligible language, pointed out to all his fellow trippers that I was using a Japanese camcorder. They all smiled at me and said something which sounded affable, though I have no idea what it was. They could well have been telling me to keep my hands off of their camera equipment. Soon, the old geyser (not the Japanese man) started to bubble and fart and the audience became very excited. Old Faithful then blew, shooting its steaming water high into the air for a few seconds, my new friends accompanying the eruption with loud "Oohs" and "Aahs," before both the geyser and the crowd settled down. It truly was an impressive and wondrous sight but I was still surprised when the Japanese started clapping. They actually applauded Old Faithful for the display. I was equally surprised when they then shuffled back to their tour bus and left, presumably to the next location on their whistle-stop tour.

We continued our tour of the Upper Geyser Basin on the well-marked footpaths, continually impressed by the number and variety of the bubbling, spitting and occasionally erupting fountains and the deep coloured, steaming pools. We admired Castle Geyser, Grand Geyser and Beehive Geyser, Crested Pool, Morning Glory Pool and Liberty Pool, stopping at each one and reading about the source of its name and eruption calendar. We read that there were about 150 of these hydrothermal wonders in the area and I would guess that we saw only about one tenth of them before we were geysered out and peopled out. We retired to Yellowstone Lake and discovered a long sand bar stretching into lake and running parallel to the shore, where we spent the afternoon alone, strolling along the spit, relaxing and watching goldeneye ducks on the lake. This was not as spectacular as Old Faithful but, if I am honest, I enjoyed it more.

Yellowstone is so much more than just its geysers. Rivers, lakes, waterfalls and mountains. During our visit, we had seen many wonderful sights but had ignored the park high ground. We studied our guides and maps, searching for a good mountain walk and decided on Elephant Back Mountain as tough but not too tough, short but not too short and with an overlook providing a sweeping panoramic view of Yellowstone Lake and surrounding area. The previous days' cold, snowy weather had disappeared and we set off in fine, warm and sunny weather through dense lodgepole pine forest to the summit, not put off by the bear warnings at the trailhead. We made the 800 feet climb with no problems, unusually not getting lost, and arrived at the summit where a bench was positioned offering the best views over the lake to the snowy mountains beyond. Two couples shared the bench and sat gossiping as we admired the views and waited for the bench to be vacated. We waited a long time. The couples chatted and it was obvious that they were intending to stay on the bench, so Sue and I made do with a fallen tree trunk for our well-earned tea and sandwich break. The couples were still chatting on the bench as we began the descent and Sue congratulated me for being polite and not grumpy with the bench-hoggers. The way down was uneventful except that, near the end, we met one man who stopped us and asked if we had seen his hat. I was tempted to tell him that it was on the bench at the top, but thought better of it in my new native-friendly mood and apologised that we had not.

We moved on to follow the Storm Point Trail which begins in the open meadows overlooking Indian Pond and Yellowstone Lake. We wandered alongside the pond before entering a forest until it opened out onto the scenic, wind-swept Storm Point. Our peaceful lunch was marred by a yet another fat family crashing about noisily, but I managed a smile and passed the time of day with a smile. After dining we moved on to see a large colony of yellow-bellied marmots, which lives on a rocky section of the lakeside. We were amazed and annoyed to see the fat family scrambling over the rocks, rampaging right through the middle of the marmot village, causing the delightful little rodents to scurry into their holes for safety. I bit my tongue, but could not help quietly expressing my amazement to Sue just how dim and ignorant many of our American friends are when it comes to wildlife. Soon however, the fatties tired of frightening the animals and left, allowing the colony to peek out of their hiding places before returning to their scampering games in the rocks.

The following morning, we discussed how best to spend our last full day in Yellowstone. We had seen so much yet there was still much more to see, but decided to revisit the Lamar Valley, Sue's favourite spot. On the gentle drive through the picturesque countryside, we stopped behind a ranger's truck as he was protecting a splendid young black bear moochabout and grazing on the roadside. There was one car in front of us and the female passenger immediately leapt out of the car and started to move towards the bear calling out to it and waving her camera to attract its attention. The ranger firmly told her to, "Get back in your car Ma'am." She did just that and the car drove off, without a photo. The ranger approached our car shaking his head with a look of exasperation, before saying a friendly "Hi, folks." Sue asked him, "Why do people do that?"

The ranger shook his head again and recognising Sue's English accent said, "Ma'am, you'll soon learn that American people are stupid." A man after my own heart I thought as we drove away and I smugly stated, "I told you so."

The walk was again wondrous as we watched an unidentified eagle soaring overhead and a coyote hunting alongside the river. As before, storm clouds began rolling in so we cut the walk short and returned to the car park. On the way, we met a group of elderly people just setting out and, as we acknowledged each other, I casually mentioned the storm clouds, a warning which was ignored as the oldies tottered off into the wilderness. Near the car, a bison herd was stampeding down the opposite hillside having been spooked by a wolf. Sue saw the wolf but I was too busy checking my maps and, by the time I looked up the wolf had disappeared into a thicket. Ten days in Yellowstone and this was the first wolf we had encountered and I missed it. Damn. As soon as we reached the car the heavens opened and the rain began to lash down. I expressed my doubts that the old folk could ever survive the downpour, but at least I could not be held responsible this time.

After an afternoon packing, we returned to the Canyon Village restaurant for our final meal and said a fond farewell to the waiters, who had become firm friends and invited themselves to Portugal to see us. Happily, they thought that Portugal was in

England. On the way back to the cabin, panic set in as I realised that my wallet was missing from my back pocket. As it contained all of our remaining US dollars, credit cards and driving licences, I was obviously in some distress and rushed back to the restaurant, but to no avail. After much searching, we went to the reception office to see if the wallet had been handed in. It had not. We began to work out how to manage with no cash and who we should contact, when a chubby young American walked into Reception to hand in the wallet which he had found on the floor of the restaurant. I claimed the lost property and thanked the young man, hugged him and possibly kissed him, silently vowing never to criticise fat Americans ever again. We took one last stroll around the village, sad to be leaving but happy that we had seen and experienced so much of what must be one of the most exciting places on Earth.

An early morning started with breakfast as usual in the cafeteria, where we gave away Yellowstone books and guides to Willie, our regular breakfast server. He seemed very pleased and embarrassed me by giving me a prolonged cuddle as were leaving. Sue added to my embarrassment by pointing out that I had been seen cuddling two young men on consecutive days and asked if there was there something I should tell her.

We had chosen Laramie for our final stop simply because the name conjures up pictures of cowboys and Indians, heroic cavalry, pioneers, settlers and James Stewart as Will Lockhart in The Man from Laramie. The drive to Laramie was spectacular. We headed south on the I-191 passing the northern Grand Teton mountains viewed from the road over Jackson Lake. The Tetons are a particularly impressive range, and could have come straight out of a child's painting. Several high pointed peaks zigzagged along the skyline, the brilliant white peaks standing out against the vivid blue sky. There is debate how the mountain range was named. One view is that Grand Tetons were named after the Teton Sioux Native Americans who lived in the area, but it is generally thought that they were named by French explorers as the "large breasts." Of course, I preferred the latter explanation.

Near the settlement of Moran, which seemed to exist solely as a ranger station, fire station and school, we decided to go east and travel the I-26 through the mountains because it followed part of the Wyoming Centennial Highway, included part of the famous Oregon trail and because it passed the Wind River Indian reservation. The road was all but empty as we crossed the Continental Divide at Togwotee Pass, travelled through Dubois to the end of the Centennial Byway at Diversion Dam Junction, to Riverton, Shoshoni, Casper, Glenrock, Dwyer Junction, Guernsey to Laramie. It was a beautiful but long drive of ten hours and we managed one stop at Sweetwater Station, described as *a place of scenic beauty and historic significance*. Information boards at the site informed us that the Oregon/Mormon Trail passed through here and it is called the sixth crossing of the Sweetwater River. In 1856 a group of pioneers, the Willie Handcart Company, was stranded here in a blizzard until rescued by their Mormon brethren, sent by Brigham Young from Salt Lake City. It was later part of the Rawlins to Fort Washakie Road, established as a stage and wagon freight route. We sat in the sun momentarily assuming the persona of early pioneers discovering lands unknown as we sipped coffee, courtesy of Sue's American Adventure flask, which somehow seemed very fitting.

We finally made it to the Ramada in Laramie, tired but happy and ready for two days of total relaxation before the return to our Portugal home. On our trips across the pond, we had stayed in a variety of accommodations, large and small hotels, rural motels, guesthouses and rustic cabins but this was by far the worst. Alarm bells rang before we entered the reception as the outside was littered with overflowing garbage cans and ash trays. The receptionist was surly and unfriendly. The room was spacious but smelt mouldy and everything looked worn and run down. It was late and we were tired so had little option to accept our shabby billet. The hotel did have one good point, a sports bar where we had a beer or two and a snack before retiring, trying to ignore our less than salubrious surroundings.

We awoke feeling optimistic and thinking that perhaps our tiredness after the long drive had affected our judgement of the hotel, as the musty smell seemed to have dissipated slightly overnight. At breakfast, reality returned. Bins in the restaurant area were overflowing, the grill was dirty. There was no decaffeinated coffee and no hot water. I politely pointed out the shortcomings to the cook/waitress/receptionist/cleaner who told us that they couldn't get the staff and returned to the kitchen for a cigarette. Little wonder that we were the only diners that morning. Sue and I agreed that, despite its shortcomings, it was easier to bear the hotel for another two nights and continue our exploration as planned.

We drove to Grand Avenue, the City's pleasant main street and mooched around the shops, a mixture of home town and tourist stores, but I found it difficult to concentrate as I was a little confused driving on the way there and swerved without signalling in front of a truck, then drove slowly looking for a parking space as the truck followed inches from by rear. When I finally pulled in to park, the truck driver blasted his ear-splitting horn and raised one finger at me. I took this to be a traditional Wyoming welcome greeting and I smiled back nicely. We then moved on to a large Walmart where Sue happily shopped for an hour or so while I wandered aimlessly behind her. She bought goods totalling 99 dollars, none of which we needed. I still have the receipt which shows that, amongst the twenty items purchased, she bought: *SALON BOARD 2.00, GV TEA BAGS 2.32, CRM STY HOHD 2.12, WATER GUARD 4.64 and REPL MAX BON 3.50.* I have no idea what most of these purchases were, but I do know that we bought tea bags – in America, two days before returning home.

As thanks for not moaning too much, Sue agreed to visit Wyoming Territorial Prison State Historic Site in the afternoon. As usual on our visits, there were very few visitors but we were captivated and charmed by meeting an elderly gentleman and his 10-year-old grandson, both dressed in immaculate cowboy attire. We naturally stopped and began a conversation. The man explained that the boy usually wore tee-shirts, shorts and trainers, but he thought it time he wore proper western wear and had taken him, that morning, to get kitted out. The lad looked quite embarrassed until Sue said that he looked smart, handsome and really, really cool. I quietly whispered to Grandpa, "So do you."

The Territorial Prison was fascinating. Built in 1872 and constructed of 2-foot-thick, blocks of pink sandstone, with doors and window surrounds of a deeper red sandstone, it was infamous for housing prisoners captured on The Outlaw Trail, an irregular route used by fugitive desperados, with supply stations and safe houses, that stretched for about a thousand miles, from Montana to Mexico. The jail was only open for thirty years, during which time it housed about 1,200 prisoners, including our old friend, Butch Cassidy. It was, thankfully, a self-guided tour so we did not have to follow in an uninterested group not listening to a bored guide. We spent a happy hour as we wandered around freely, stopping to view the prisoners' canteen, the guard's quarters, and other areas requisite in making the prisoners life a misery. The over-riding memory of the museum was the furnished cells, including one purported to have been used by Mr. Cassidy. There were double rows of six feet square cells housing two prisoners and two bunks, where inmates were confined for 23 hours a day. I felt almost guilty complaining because our spacious hotel was untidy and our room smelt a bit fusty.

That evening we discovered The Chuck Wagon, another typical American diner serving steaks and chicken in all their forms. The food was not only good but the portions were enormous, as were the other clientele. I felt a little conspicuous as I was the only man in the place not sporting a baseball cap and one of the few not wearing dungarees. Neither Sue nor I could finish the gargantuan platters put in front of us and I was further embarrassed when asked if we needed a doggy bag, so I thanked the waitress and said yes. We dumped the bag outside the hotel alongside the other rubbish and Sue suggested that perhaps all hotel guests had done the same, hence the build-up of detritus.

It was our final day before we were due to fly back, so we went for one final walk, exploring the Medicine Bow-Routt National Forests and Thunder Basin National Grassland. The historic land was named after the Native American pow-wows where different tribes congregated to collect mountain mahogany, an excellent wood for making bows, and to perform rituals to cure diseases and thus make good medicine. We had no map so just wandered, unsure where we were going and where we had been, but meandered through rich pasture and dense woodland before eventually finding our way back to a peaceful picnic site for coffee and subs before returning to the car park. Sue said that she had forgotten something when shopping so we returned to Laramie Grand Avenue for more shopping, then on the Walmart for more shopping. I was so enjoying myself that on leaving Walmart, I reversed into a giant truck. Luckily, no damage was done to the hire car and I angrily blamed the truck driver for his selfish driving and shouted that he should park more considerately in the future. As Sue said when we drove away, "It's a good job the driver wasn't there."

Our homeward voyage was as tiring as the outward journey. We drove back to Denver stopping just once to view the Abraham Lincoln Memorial Monument, a bust of Lincoln, 12 ½ feet high and sitting on a 30-foot-tall granite pedestal at the Summit Rest Area on Interstate 80. Impressive as the statue was, it was as nothing compared to the mountains, rivers, lakes, geysers and wildlife we were leaving behind. The whole journey took exactly 24 hours with no sleep and I carefully recorded the details:

24 June 07:30 Left Laramie	
Drive from Laramie to Denver	1.5 hours
Wait at Denver Airport	3.0 hours
Flight to Philadelphia	4.5 hours
Wait for connection	3.0 hours
Flight to Lisbon	7.5 hours
Disembark, taxi to Lisbon station	2.0 hours
Train to Tomar	2.0 hours
Bus home	0.5 hours
25 June 14:30 hrs Arrived home	

What made the trip worse was that I hadn't booked seats (again) for the first flights so Sue and I were not together, but then we had a strange slice of luck. The young lady standing in the check-in queue in front of us had been allocated the seat next to Sue, so I offered to swap her seat for mine, which gave her the advantage of an aisle seat, so she readily agreed. When we boarded, she found her new seat (my old one) filled by the fattest man in the world, so asked me for help. After studying the boarding cards, he realised that he was in the wrong seat, apologised and moved the correct seat – the one directly next to me (the lady's swapped seat). As he struggled into his proper seat, I turned to look at the young lady who was trying very hard not laugh or jump up and down in celebration. I spent 4 ½ hours squashed next to a sweating fat man who must have bathed in overpowering deodorant and aftershave to disguise his smell.

Exhausted by our journey, we rested for a day or two at home, watched the holiday videos and decided that this holiday was superb in every way and could never be equalled, so perhaps we should end our discovery of the Americas on this high note. Another couple of days later, we began planning our next trip.

CHAPTER 10 – THE GREAT LAKES

At Headlands Grammar School in Swindon, I was terrible at any subject that required study and committing facts to memory. Geography came high on my failure list. Sue's strength was physical geography and she excels at identifying bits of rock, but this did not help in selecting our next adventure. I vaguely remembered being mildly interested in learning (or not learning) about America's Great Lakes, probably because of my general fascination with anything American rather than for any topographical reasons, so we began to explore this area in some detail. I had even remembered SHMEO, the acronym which allowed us to remember the Great Lakes in order of size, Superior, Huron, Michigan, Erie and Ontario. One of the main attractions with visiting the north-east was that we could fly direct to Toronto in Canada from Lisbon, the flight taking around eight hours, a more attractive proposition than our previous trip of eighteen flying hours, including changes. Thus, the Great Lakes became our obsession for the next year's planning. We agreed that we should aim for an autumn visit to enjoy the fall colours as a bonus and again stay at the hotel in Lisbon to make the early morning flight less stressful, so early on one late August morning we were again crossing the Atlantic to the New World.

AMERICANADIAN DIARIES

We decided to stop in Toronto for four nights before moving on, which would allow us to recuperate from the flight and explore a small corner of Lake Ontario. As hotels in the city were far above our budget, we settled on a Super 8 in the small suburb of Scarborough east of the city, which was on the lake with easy access into central Toronto. The journey over the pond went without a hitch and we picked up our hired Toyota Corolla for the easy half-hour drive east from Toronto Pearson Airport on the 401 E Expressway. We found Scarborough with surprising ease but passed the motel on the opposite side of the road. We could see no way across the dual carriageway so continued to a nearby shopping mall where we hoped to be able to turn round. After several unsuccessful attempts and rejecting the temptation to call in at Popeye's for coffee, we managed the manoeuvre and finally arrived at the motel, to be greeted by the friendly Asian receptionist. After settling in to our room, we returned to the mall to buy a few essentials for our journey and withdraw some Canadian dollars. At the mall, we were somewhat surprised to find that most of the shops and shoppers were Asian, and they seemed equally surprised to see two elderly, white English shoppers amongst the sari and spice outlets. We wondered for a moment if we had landed in Delhi by mistake. Having collected a few dollars and light provisions, we decided to stretch our legs after the journey and took a gentle stroll from the motel to the Lake Ontario shoreline, our first view of a Great Lake. As the still, blue waters disappeared on the horizon, it was difficult to imagine that this was a lake, and the smallest of the five, rather than the edge of a vast ocean. It fired our imaginations and we became excited about what was to come.

After travelling for 24 hours, Popeye's was the obvious choice for a meal that evening. We didn't need to search for a restaurant, it was within walking distance and looked inexpensive. If any visitors to Canada ever find themselves in Scarborough and enjoy scruffy surroundings and surly staff serving cold, barely cooked and tasteless chicken wrapped in a soggy yellow coating with cold greasy chips, I can thoroughly recommend Popeye's.

On our first full day, we decided to take the train from Scarborough to Toronto and visit the fourth largest city on the North American continent. We drove to the Scarborough station and parked with ease in a vast, virtually empty car park, which worried us that we were parking somewhere inappropriate or even illegal, but saw no signs so abandoned the car and strolled to the station. We purchased our return tickets and made our way to the appropriate platform. As we waited for the train, I somewhat smugly reviewed our successful and problem-free trip: a perfect stop in Lisbon, the flight straightforward and on time, an easy drive to a pleasant motel and now finding the station with no apparent glitches. I was feeling rather proud of myself as the train pulled in. The doors opened and I said, "Come on Sue, jump on," before stepping into the waiting carriage. I turned to help Sue on and the doors closed with my dear wife still on the station holding her camera pointing to record me boarding the train. The train pulled away leaving a shocked Sue still standing on the platform and still pointing her camera. I have this moment in time firmly and permanently etched in my mind as we left Sue staring open-mouthed at the departing train and I vainly tried to encourage her to catch the next train by ridiculous arm waving as my fellow passengers stared at each of us in turn with a look of surprise and disgust that I had abandoned my wife.

In the minute or so to the next station, Midland, I had to decide whether to continue and hope to see her in Toronto, get off and wait at Midland or return to Scarborough. I decided to get off and wait. After two more trains had arrived and departed without Sue, I decided to return to Scarborough, but how? I was on the wrong line to go east so had to somehow cross to the other side of the station to catch the train back, without the appropriate ticket. No-one else had left the train at that point, so I made my lonely way up the stairs, not really knowing where I was going or what to do. I luckily found a ticket office where I bought a ticket to Scarborough before dashing down to catch the train back. When the train stopped at Scarborough, my heart missed several beats as Sue was not on the platform. My anxiety intensified as the train pulled away and my brain was working overtime and getting nowhere. I tried to get my panicky thoughts in order and glanced across the track to the opposite platform. It was empty except for one lonely person, sitting apparently unconcerned and waving gently at me. I had failed to realise that I had arrived on the eastbound platform, whilst Sue was patiently waiting on the westbound platform. I was overcome with a wave of relief, but still had to get back across the line. I again found my way up the stairs and across the station foyer before running downstairs to greet my long-lost love. As we met, she smiled gently and said, "I knew you'd come back for me, so I just waited."

"It was no problem, my sweet," I lied. As the next train to Toronto arrived, I gripped Sue's arm tightly and pulled her into the carriage alongside me.

My angst had subsided by the time we arrived in Toronto and we left the station to be greeted by the magnificent Old City Hall at the corner of Queen and Bay Streets. We skirted the building and came face to face with Winston Churchill, cast in bronze and standing in characteristic belligerent pose on a plinth, staring defiantly down at passers-by. I was pleased to see that directly underneath the great man was hot dog stand, of which I am sure Winston would have been grateful. This was a new experience for us as we usually avoided cities, preferring back country wilderness and small towns, so quite where walked after that, I have no real idea. We tried to follow signs that said *DISCOVERY WALK*, but soon lost the signs and, with no map, simply wandered through the city between towering office blocks housing various businesses and department stores. We quite enjoyed the stroll in the bright sunshine whilst not knowing where we were, but hoping that we were heading towards the waterfront. We finally reached the famous CN Tower and had planned to take the lift to the top, but a long undisciplined crocodile of chattering tourists put us off the idea. I was tempted to organise the rabble into a proper, disciplined English queue until my interest was taken by the adjacent Rogers Stadium, home of the Toronto Blue Jays baseball team. On a giant hoarding, I saw that the next day they were playing Tampa Bay Rays and, for a moment, I was tempted to buy tickets and return for the game, but common sense and Sue's disapproving look suggested otherwise. Besides, I may have lost her on the train station again. My disappointment was almost immediately alleviated by passing the Steam Whistle brewery and pub which was offering free beer, an offer I could not refuse. Naturally, it was only polite to buy another couple of drinks so we spent a pleasant hour in the pub before making our way across Lakeshore boulevard, the Gardner Expressway and Queens Quay to the harbour in jolly and, in my case, somewhat unsteady fashion. We enjoyed a short and gentle stroll to York Quay, where we purchased filled hot dogs from a small stand and sat overlooking the quay for an hour's relaxation.

After our rest, we used my well-trusted method of finding our way back to the station: simply head in the rough direction and hope for the best. On the way, we accidentally detoured through St. James Park, a delightful, picturesque green oasis amongst the busy streets where we took the opportunity to sit and rest again, watching black squirrels playing amongst the trees. These squirrels are morphs of eastern grey squirrels and found almost entirely in Ontario, and the U.S. state of Michigan. The reason for the genetic anomaly is uncertain, but it is thought to be an advantage in colder climates by retaining heat and/or the dark colouring helps in being less conspicuous in dark pine forests. Whatever the reason, we enjoyed their frolics before moving on, despite having little idea where to head. We eventually turned a corner and before us was station. Naturally, I told Sue that I knew where we were going all the time. We waited on the platform for the train back to Scarborough and held Sue securely to prevent any further accidental severance and, as our transport home pulled in to the platform, I grabbed her even more tightly and did not let her go until we were safely clattering east back to Scarborough.

Scarborough is only a ninety minute or so drive east of Niagara Falls and was an irresistible visit so, with little preparation, we set off assuming that if we headed east, via the nearby 401West and on to the 407West, we would be bound to reach the falls with no difficulty. Our journey did not start well. I somehow missed the 401W completely which was a little discomforting, and it soon became a nightmare as we found ourselves travelling on a busy four-lane highway which seemed to be taking us through Toronto city centre, rather than around the city as we had expected. The traffic was heavy with all four lanes packed and we had little option but to just keep going, despite reservations that we may not be going the easiest or, indeed, the correct way. It was then that we realised it was Labour Day weekend, a national holiday, and it seemed that most of the residents of Ontario were heading into Toronto and possibly Niagara. I did note that we travelled on Richmond Street and Eastern Avenue and we had then missed not only the 404W but the 407W. Somehow, we had managed to stray off the Highway and were, indeed, in the city. We carried on until we found ourselves travelling on a minor road, through small towns, but at least it was virtually traffic free as no-one else was silly enough to take this route. In a small town, I have no idea where, we stopped and went into a café for a refreshing coffee and to reassess our options. The road atlas we carried was useless as we had no idea where we had stopped, so I had little option and much against my principles, to ask the café owner the way. He looked somewhat bemused and said that, if he was going to Niagara, he wouldn't have started from here, which didn't help or ease my feeling of stupidity. He explained that we were just off the highway and if we drove two blocks north, we would be back on course. We thanked him despite his air of amusement at our predicament and followed his advice, soon meeting the Queen Elizabeth Way and the route to Niagara.

Niagara was very busy and confirmed my suspicion that most of the state was also visiting the falls as we were directed to the overflow car park. There were two roads meeting at the entrance to the car park and drivers were sensibly and courteously taking turns to enter, until it was my turn when a big 4 X 4 truck forced its way in front of us from the opposite direction. Following the directions in the parking area, I was positioned next to the big, ugly beast of a motor and its big, ugly beast of a driver. Overcoming my urge to confront big ugly man, perhaps because he was young, over six feet tall and weighed about twenty stone, we left the car park and walked towards the falls. On the grass verges next to the road leading to the falls were several families sitting and enjoying a picnic in the sun. It was strange that they were all Asian and appeared to have brought minor banquets with chapatis, naans and Tupperware boxes of spicy delights. Sue and I were hungry by this time and as the only white people joined them to enjoy our somewhat mundane Subway subs, before moving on. When we reached the overlook to the falls, I was a little disappointed. Whilst no-one could dispute the splendour of the falls themselves, I felt that I was in a theme park and theme parks are an anathema to me. From the crowds of sightseers to the skyscraper hotels, the Skylon tower, the casino, the grand helicopter adventure, the tourist boats and Guided Wine and Charcuterie Tour, the magnificence lost its magic. I half-expected to see a giant Micky Mouse giving out lollypops. Sue agreed and said that she enjoyed the far smaller but no less magical falls we had often encountered on our wilderness walks. We continued with the sightseeing however before returning to the car. The big ugly motor was still there, so I wrote note saying, *NICE CAR, SHAME ABOUT THE IGNORANT DRIVER,* and left it tucked under his windscreen wiper. I felt much better about the visit as we left the car park. And the drive back to our base in Scarborough went without a hitch via the Gardiner Expressway and Lake Shore Blvd., the roads we never found on the outbound journey.

After two hectic days of getting lost, we needed a walk so drove to Rouge Park Beach, a large wetland area on the edge of Lake Ontario and an ideal spot for wildlife watching. As we parked, we came across the first piece of exciting wildlife when we found a bulky raccoon lying in the road. It was a lovely animal with its thick shining coat, beautiful black mask and ringed tail. It was a strong, healthy animal except that it was dead. We assumed that it had been hit by a car but showed no signs of injury, so I dragged it off the road onto the grass verge so that it would not be squashed or otherwise disfigured when it went to raccoon heaven. We followed a boardwalk alongside the lake admiring elegant grey herons fishing, swans gliding on the water and great egrets posing like ghostly white statues. We followed the boardwalk to its end and stood on the strange metal bridge which spans the Rouge River, looking out over Lake Ontario. We again commented that this vast freshwater sea, reaching to the horizon and beyond, was the smallest of the Great Lakes, and yet, at nearly twenty thousand square kilometres is well over one thousand times the size of England's largest lake, Windermere in the Lake District.

We dropped down under the bridge and continued exploring the lake front from the beach, marked as the waterfront trail, although there was no trail as such. It was Sunday and Labour Day weekend, yet the beach was almost empty. We agreed that everyone else was probably at the Niagara theme park. As the beach ended and the trail moved on to a rocky lakeside, our exploration was almost cut short by a barrier across the path, with a very clear *No Entry*, notice. We stopped and considered our options. We could turn back or ignore the sign and barrier and carry on. Naturally, being good citizens and visitors to the country, we chose the latter and scrambled through the barrier to continue our walk, meeting two pleasant and friendly old ladies on the way who explained that the path was blocked as a new tarmac path was being laid but, as it was Sunday, it was safe to continue. I liked their logic. As we left the forbidden path and made our way back through the park to the car, there were several family groups settling down to a picnic lunch on the grassy areas. Again, we noticed that they were all Asian and the delightful smell of spicy treats sparked our taste buds, somewhat reducing the pleasure of our own cheese sandwiches.

AMERICANADIAN DIARIES

It was Monday the third of September and we were moving on, slightly concerned that Labour Day may be an issue in driving 250 miles to our next planned stop of Greater Sudbury. As it turned out, the drive was easy with little traffic, possibly because everyone else had gone to Niagara Disneyland again, and we drove north on the empty ON-400 road, relaxed and happy to be away from city life in the clear and sunny weather. We cruised past Horseshoe Valley, Moonstone and Otter Lake, before switching to the 69 at Parry Sound. The empty roads, exotic place names and wonderful weather made this one of the most pleasant drives imaginable and it was only at Sue's insistence that we stopped after a couple of hours for a break and coffee, calling in at the Moose Lake Trading Post. From the outside it looked an ideal stopping point, a rustic wooden lodge with a full-sized statue of a moose guarding the entrance and run by native Canadians. Inside, I was not so keen as it included a large shop selling a variety of tourist tat and, of course, I lost my wife for an hour while she spent my hard-earned beer money. At least this gave me the opportunity to snooze in the car for a while, protected by Bruce the Moose. Our journey continued through Britt Station, across the Key River and past Wanikewin (I upset Sue by mispronouncing the name again) before pulling in to our next lodgings, the Moonlight Inn and Suites, Sudbury.

Of the many motels on our trips, this was certainly one of the best. Friendly and helpful hosts offered spacious and spotless rooms with pleasant views over woodland from the rear windows. It had the bonus of a large and agreeable dining room on site providing an inclusive breakfast. We were not the only ones to be impressed by the accommodation as we were to find out a couple of days later. After unwinding from the long drive, we strolled down to the nearby Ramsey Lake and spent a relaxed hour on the rocky Moonlight Beach before driving into town for a stroll around Sudbury. We meandered through the streets of the old town, which was reminiscent of a small English market town, and came across the Town Hall which incorporated a Tourist Information Centre. It was little more than a small desk in a small office off the entrance hall, but we approached the clerk sitting behind the desk and asked if there was any tourist information we could take away. Oddly, she seemed somewhat surprised by our enquiry, as if tourists were a rarity in a tourist office, but after explaining that they had little literature, she disappeared into an adjacent office (or it could have been a cupboard) and returned with several little gifts, two imitation Sudbury coins, a small flag, two badges dated from three years previously and other odd pieces of memorabilia. We left somewhat underwhelmed and found a small restaurant called Respect is Burning Kitchen and Bar. We ate and sipped a beer or two, as a report came on the television about wildfires causing destruction in Central Portugal. We lived in Central Portugal and we were very interested in the report, but we did not recognise any of the areas shown in the film, although the coincidence that we were in a restaurant called Respect is Burning amused us somewhat. When we returned to our motel later, we checked our emails and there was a mail from a friend in Portugal which simply said, "Don't worry – we have checked and your house is OK," which worried us.

      We had chosen Sudbury as a destination solely because the town was about halfway between Toronto and our next chosen stop at Brimley near the Canadian/American border. After booking the motel months before, we had conducted some basic research of the area and were intrigued that the town claimed to have the World's tallest chimney at 381 feet high and by Dynamic Earth, a nickel mine in the town offering tours. With little more than this basic information we set off the next day to the mine, without really realising what we were about to experience. At the entrance to the complex was Sudbury's iconic attraction, the Big Nickel, a thirty feet high silver coin erected on tall legs and an exact replica of the 1951 Canadian nickel. It was constructed in 1964 to symbolise the wealth that Sudbury has contributed to the Canadian economy through its nickel production. We thought it an odd, but somehow intriguing monument and a fitting introduction to what we were about to see.

After paying the admission fee, we were supplied with hard hats as the guide introduced our tour with a potted history of the mine. As is the norm in such circumstances, the guide's efforts were in vain as Sue and I, and the half dozen other tourists, ignored her lecture and took photographs of each other with silly expressions under our hard hats. We were then shuffled through the miners' changing room, decorated with more hard hats and various items of mining apparel, to an open, rather rickety-looking lift, into which we squeezed. As the lift dropped into the bowels of the earth, a dramatic voice told us that the area was hit by a ten-kilometre-wide meteor some two billion years ago, driving thirty kilometres deep into the ground, and thus creating various rare and valuable minerals. "So much for God creating the Earth and everything in it," I whispered to Sue, perhaps too loudly.

We were then guided through a dark, narrow mine shaft, littered with more mining artefacts and again the visitors ignoring the guide's valiant efforts to educate us. The major relic that took my attention was the toilet, a simple wooden seat with three bum-sized holes and no privacy. Obviously, I sat on one of the toilets for a photograph but wondered how anyone could defecate in the open, sitting next to work colleagues and in the presence of other workers. It was my worst nightmare. After squeezing and ducking through the tight underground passages, we returned to the lift and were rapidly elevated back to the surface, relieved that I had not needed to poo. In the reception Sue was intrigued by a display of the various minerals and spent half an hour with another guide, diligently studying the various bits of coloured rock while I chatted to another guide about the living and working conditions of miners, particularly what they felt about pooing with no privacy.

Just northwest of Sudbury, through Chelmsford and Larchwood are the Onaping falls, reached by a relatively easy two-and-a-half-kilometre trail, and an ideal way to leave other tourists and guided tours and retreat into the wilderness for the afternoon. We followed the A Y Jackson trail and enjoyed a joyful walk before reaching the beautiful falls from the A Y Jackson lookout. We scrambled down a steep, stony path to the river at the foot of the falls, where I sat on a rock looking over the tumbling waters as they crashed at our feet. The falls were by no means the spectacular size or power of Niagara, but there were no hotels, casinos or helicopter rides, just peace and tranquillity. And there was no chance of Micky Mouse appearing. As I sat peacefully, I pondered on who A Y Jackson was and why the trail and falls were named after him while Sue spent a happy half an hour explaining the geology of the valley and identifying odd rock formations, formed, we guessed, by the meteor impact and sculpted by centuries of tumbling water. Returning to the motel, I researched the name A.Y. Jackson and discovered that he was a prominent Canadian artist, a member of the Group of Seven, a collective of landscape painters. His most famous work was the painting *Spring on the Onaping River*, which was displayed at Sudbury Secondary School until it was stolen in 1974. I felt somehow very excited as we had been to the Onaping river and viewed almost the exact scene depicted in the artwork that afternoon. I wondered if the painting was ever recovered, but further investigation showed that it had not, which saddened me.

We dined well that evening in the adjacent Chateau Quay tavern, the only slight fly in the ointment was that the lady proprietor appeared a little confused, which we put down to the fact that we had heard her speaking only in French and my attempts at conversation were thwarted by mixing schoolboy French with stuttering Spanish and Portuguese. It was a bonus that we managed to order anything to eat. We found out later that she spoke perfect English and was confused by my Frenportspanglish language.

As we settled back into the motel, it was a little odd that we seemed to be the only residents, but we put it down to being out of season and our good luck. We awoke the following morning to a noisy mix of chattering voices and clattering activity below our room. Looking out from the balcony, we saw what looked like an invasion, as if the Moonlight Inn had been annexed by a battalion of yuppies which, in a way, it had. Young people in baseball caps worn backwards and baggy shorts were shifting roll cages, boxes and luggage across the car park, so we wandered down amongst the chaotic throng and approached the reception desk to find out what was going on. We were told that the gang were a movie crew, there to film scenes for a movie called Cas and Dylan, starring Richard Dreyfuss and directed by Jason Priestley, an apparently famous actor who starred in something called Beverley Hills 90210. Since the days of Jaws and Close Encounters, Sue's favourite actor had been Mr. Dreyfuss so she was almost speechless with excitement. We had no idea who Jason Priestly was, but the name seemed vaguely familiar. After breakfast surrounded by the apparently manic hubbub, we returned to our room and I immediately grabbed my movie camera and began filming the scene below. A young lady, who obviously considered herself very important, shouted up to me that filming was not allowed and to stop immediately. I was tempted to shout back that I thought Canada was a free country so she should bugger off, but I simply stopped filming as I had already captured the scene for posterity. And she was a bit scary.

We were tempted to hang around the motel and wait for an introduction to Richard Dreyfuss, but I decided that the young lady may shout at me again, so we decided to go walking and set off for the Bell Park Trail around Lake Ramsey. The trail took us over wooden walkways and clear paths, through park and woodland and beautiful lake beaches. We then made our way via a forest track to the adjacent Laurention Lake and continued the walk, after first noting that a warning sign stated that bears were prevalent in the area. As we had seen many such signs before, we naturally ignored the warning and carried hiking. The walk was a joy, flat and relatively easy and we spotted a beaver dam, herons, chipmunks, squirrels and woodpeckers, before cooling our feet in the cold lake waters and making our way back. A few minutes from the car, we heard a rustling on the side of the path and a large black shadow moved away into the thick woodland. We stopped and, hearts beating, and caught a glimpse of a black bear's bottom as it disappeared into the trees.

Back at the motel, there were yet more young people in baseball caps moving things about and shouting, and we were directed to park away from the main accommodation. As we walked back through the noisy throng, a small chubby, grey-haired man was walking towards us. As we passed, we nodded a brief "Afternoon" and he said, "Hi," before we went our separate ways. We then stopped and looked at each other. "Was that

Richard Drefuss?" Sue asked with a strange, awe-stricken look. I looked back at the small, chubby man and answered, "I think so. He hasn't aged too well, has he."

Before we could say more, we were crossing through the film apparatus in the car park and almost bumped into a tall, handsome chap who smiled and said, "Hi. How are you?"

"Fine thanks, and you," I mumbled, as the man smiled and carried on his way. Searching the internet that evening we realised that in the space of a few seconds, we had met, and conversed with Richard Dreyfuss and Jason Priestly, although "conversed" may be just a tad exaggerated.

After dining in the Chateaux Quay with the confused madame that evening, we took a stroll around the motel and noticed a huge Winnebago parked at the back of the lot. We agreed that this must be Mr. Dreyfuss's accommodation for the duration of filming and, though tempted, decided it would be imprudent to knock on his door to continue our conversation, so resisted the temptation.

We were enjoying our last splendid breakfast in the motel the next morning, taking our usual seats by the window, when Richard (I felt that by now we were on first name terms) strolled past, looked in and waved at us like the old friend we now considered him. Sue and I discussed staying another day or two to spend time with our new pals, but agreed that they could manage without us and continued with our plan to move on.

As the trigger for this visit was to visit the Great Lakes, our next stop was arranged to see the greatest of the great, Lake Superior. We drove through Sudbury, passing the chimney which we had now learnt was only the World's second tallest, and on to the 17W, the famous Trans-Canadian Highway. With such a grand-sounding name I had expected to follow a major motorway, bustling with at least three lanes, but was pleasantly surprised to find a single lane rural road for much of the journey. We pottered peacefully along with almost no traffic, passing more evocatively named towns like Blind River, Iron Bridge and Echo Lake but perhaps the two most intriguing were the small settlements of Espanola and Spanish, particularly as this area was first settled by the French. We later learnt that the towns were so named when a Spanish explorer married a local Anishinaabe woman and taught her and their children to speak Spanish. When the French *voyageurs* heard Spanish being spoken by the local natives, they remarked, "Espagnole," and the river was named the Spanish River, another little snippet of local history that had always intrigued us on our travels. We stopped for a break at the Serpent River First Nation Gas and Convenience Trading Post, where Sue took advantage of my good nature and spent time in the gift shop, before moving on and reaching our destination, the border of Canada and the USA at Sault St. Marie. On the way, we were intrigued to pass a horse-drawn buggy, trotting along the hard shoulder of the road with a family of folk in very old-fashioned dress whom we thought were probably Amish and we were to meet more of their community later.

Sault St, Marie is split over both sides of the border with half of the town in Ontario and half in Michigan's Upper Peninsula, connected by the impressive International Bridge over the St. Marys River. The border post is on the American side and we were welcomed by the Stars and Stripes fluttering gently over an austere building where we stopped to show our passports. After answering a few basic questions, "Why are you here? Do you have any drugs? Do you have a police record?" (I was tempted to answer the last question by saying that I had once owned an LP by Sting, but thought better of it) the customs officer waved us through with a cheery, "Have a nice day." We drove on to the nearby small town of Brimley and Willabee's Motel, home for the next four nights. The motel was, again, an excellent choice, with an added bonus that it had an attached building with a roadside sign that read *Willabee's Restaurant and Lounge,* but a smaller sign on the side much more to my liking, *Cosy Inn Bar.* Happily, we could walk back to the motel from the next door bar after a beer or several. It was an obvious venue for our evening repast after a recovery snooze, so that evening, we entered the Cosy Inn for what was to become a regular outing. After a perhaps one too many beers whilst chatting to identical twin brothers at the bar, we had what I described at the time as "The best meal ever," delicious whitefish, cooked to perfection with fresh crispy fries and home-made slaw. Despite being replete from the meal and, possibly, an excess of beer we took a stroll to Waiska Bay, an inlet where the St. Marys River enters the eastern reaches on Lake Superior. The sunset over the bay was a cornucopia of reds and yellows shimmering through thin clouds and reflected in the still waters. It was truly awe-inspiring and we returned to the motel as happy as we had ever been. I had noticed that the motel reception had a coffee machine, so early the next morning before Sue was awake, I called in to grab a quick fix of caffeine to find that there were five or six other man sipping coffee there. The receptionist introduced me as the *English Guy* and I spent ten minutes explaining why I was in this small community, all the way from England. I enjoyed being the centre of attention and repeated the visit the following mornings but had, by then, ceased to be an alien curiosity and simply listened to their chats, usually about the weather which suggested their English heredity.

AMERICANADIAN DIARIES

The Soo Locks in Sault St. Marie are a set of parallel locks built in 1855 to enable large cargo ships to travel between Lake Superior and Lake Huron. This was our exciting destination for the first full day in Michigan. On arrival, we strolled around excitedly around the dock area for a while before making our way to a viewing platform over the locks and watched a massive freighter, the Indiana Harbor, negotiate its way through the locks on its way from Huron to Superior. At over 1,000 feet long and 105 feet wide, this was no mean feat and Sue said that she was glad I wasn't the driver or it would never have made it. Next to us on the viewing area was another family of Amish dressed in their eighteenth century style clothes, the bearded men in their typical mutza suits and the women in Mennonite Cape Dresses. The church members are known for their Christian values and simple living, but not for their personal hygiene if the smell of this particular group was anything to go by.

After lunch we took a Soo Locks boat trip on La Voyageur, a small pleasure boat which travelled on the river, through a smaller lock than that used by the freighters, passing massive stone-built warehouses on the shore and under the International Bridge before stopping in the shadow of one of huge freighters, the strangely named Tim S Dool, before returning to base. Sue and I were pleased that the other passengers were made up of two outings of American pensioners, who told us that they were *snowbirds,* who migrate from colder northern regions to the warmer south during winter. This trip was part of their northern, summer migration. I rather liked this idea and suggested we became snowbirds in England, and idea scotched when we realised that the is nowhere warm in winter in England.

In the evening, I left Sue making herself beautiful and retired to the bar early, "To ensure that we get a good table, dear," and again joined the company of the twins, this time accompanied by their nephew. It was strange that they did not drink in rounds, but each man had a small pile of dollar bills in front on him on the bar. When they ordered another beer, the barmaid simply helped herself to a dollar bill as payment until, I assumed, their pile was gone when it signified time to go. We chatted amiably and I found out that the twins were both widowers called Ron and Don and their nephew was John. Their surname was Carrick although the family name was Ho, passed down by their great grandfather, a member of the indigenous Ojibwe/Chippewa Indians. They always called the bar, "The office," where they were known as the Ho-Row and the Cosy Crew. Following our introductions, they seemed amused when I sang an out-of-tune rendition of the old Crystals' hit, *Da Doo Ron Don John, Da Doo Ron Don*. They were intrigued by the fact that we were staying in their small community and actually apologised telling me there was, "Nothing to see here." By the time Sue arrived, I was admonished for being somewhat merry, but had made three great friends. And I continued to go to bar early to ensure that we had a good table for the next three evenings. Our hosts in Willabee's told us later that, to their knowledge, we were the first English visitors to stay there and hence the interest shown by my breakfast and bar-room buddies.

Brimley is a small town of just 500 people, situated in Chippewa County in Michigan's Upper Peninsula. Despite the local view that there was nothing to see there, we set out next day to explore the immediate area, starting with a gentle walk around Monocle Lake on the shores of Lake Superior in the Hiawatha National Forest. Simply repeating those location names gave me goose pimples. The short loop trail took us along the lake shore and through forest paths with views across Superior, the perfect anecdote to the busy previous days' travelling, sightseeing and boat trip. On the shoreline we came across Point Iroquois Lighthouse, also known as Light Station, built to guide freighters traveling through Whitefish Bay, but happily now a museum open to the public. We climbed the 72 spiral steps to the top of the tower and gazed over of Lake Superior, before entering the museum displaying the stories, photographs, antiques, and artifacts of lightkeepers and their families, the room restored to the way it looked in the early 1950s. On the drive back to Brimley, we stopped to study an accurate scale model of the lighthouse and a freighter set on the side of the road near the Bay Mills Indian Reservation, but sadly with no description of who made it or why.

The following day was to be our last in Brimley and we crossed the border into Canada, again stopping at the customs post, to take the Agawa Canyon Tour Train, a 114-mile, ten-hour excursion north of Sault St. Marie, Ontario. In the town, we quickly found the train station but could not find our way into the depot, nor could we find anywhere to park until we realised that we had driven past the car park three times in our search. After much grumbling about poor signposting, we safely parked in plenty of time for our excursion. The huge train, The Mongoose Lake, arrived rumbling and spitting as it towered over us and came to halt. We boarded by climbing steep steps into the carriage and were soon rumbling through the awesome granite rock formations and mixed forests of the Canadian Shield, travelling over towering trestle bridges, alongside pristine northern lakes and rivers, including the impressive Montreal River. The spectacular journey was enhanced when we were called to the dining car and presented with the best of American dining – a full breakfast of sausage patties, crispy bacon, two eggs over easy, hash browns and pancakes with maple syrup. After such a feast, we needed something to burn off the calories and were greeted with the perfect opportunity at the turning point of the train ride when we stopped at Agawa Canyon station, where there was a 300 stair climb to a viewing platform. Sue and I were determined to be first to climb the tower and set off at a gallop, overtaking struggling, mainly elderly passengers on the climb, but half a dozen younger and fitter travellers were also in the unofficial race and easily beat us to the top, smugly greeting us at the zenith. No-one, including us, admitted that they were racing. The view from the top was impressive but we were surprised to see that the majority of fellow passengers had not bothered with the climb and just sat resting at the track side, with many of them eating picnic lunches. After the enormous breakfast aboard, we could only wonder at their constitutions. We still had an hour or so before the return journey and we took the opportunity to explore the deep canyon following the trails to the wonderfully named Black Beaver Falls, Bridal Veil Falls and Otter Creek Falls where the waters tumbled into the canyon, happy that our over-indulgence with breakfast had been avenged. Tired from the journey, the climb and hike, I slept like a baby on the way back and was told that I snored loudly, eliciting looks of disapproval from some fellow passengers on arrival. I apologised and explained that I was English, which seemed to placate the antagonism.

As we entered the Cosy Inn on our last evening, I was touched to hear a great cheer from the Ho boys as I arrived. Sue and I ate our last superb whitefish dinner and I then stayed in the bar with the *Ho-Row* while she returned to the room to pack. During our conversation, I learnt that residents of Michigan's Upper Peninsula are called Yoopers and my drinking colleagues declared that they would make Sue and me Honorary Yoopers. I was very proud and broke Ho Row convention by buying a couple of rounds. After genuinely touching goodbyes, I made my way unsteadily back to our room glowing with bonhomie and Budweiser.

During our survey of the area in the months before our trip, we stumbled across the Pictured Rocks National Lakeshore, an area of Lake Superior which derives its name from a thirteen mile stretch of colourful sandstone cliffs, rising up 200 feet above lake level. Over millennia, wind rain and changes in the lake levels have been sculptured the rock faces into shallow caves, arches, and statuesque formations resembling castle turrets, whilst rain and weathering have coloured the sandstone into an amazing natural artwork. Just a couple of hours away from our current base, this was a geological feature that Sue could not, and would not, miss. We left Brimley with some regret, but happy memories and exciting anticipation of what was to come. The destination was Munising, a small town located on the southern edge of Munising Bay, also known as the South Bay of Grand Island Harbor. As we set off, Sue reminded me that I was 65 years old that day, and I could think of no better way to spend my birthday than a steady drive to a new adventure in the USA.

Sue's planning again paid dividends and we eagerly booked into the Terrace Motel, a small family-owned lodging with large, spotless rooms in a quiet situation yet close to the town centre. Having checked in and unpacked, we strolled around the town and, again, found the type of small town that we had come to admire, with the downtown area's wide streets, bordered by a variety of shops, bars and restaurants. We soon identified the venue for that evening's meal, the Dogpatch Restaurant, offering *Soups, Greens 'n' fixins*, including char-broiled steaks, fresh whitefish and *awsum* sandwiches. Who could resist?

AMERICANADIAN DIARIES

The following day, we needed exercise so called in at the town Tourist Office to gather information on any recommended hikes in the area. Around the town, we had noticed several outlets advertising pasties for sale which, being west country folk, struck us as rather odd and intriguing. At the tourism centre, we were told that Yooper pasties originated from Cornish miners who migrated to the Western Upper Peninsula to work in the copper mines and are, "Real Cornish, but better." We wanted to try these better pasties and found a small shop on the edge of town, Muldoon's, which sold their *Award-winning traditional Cornish pasty*. The kitchen where the treats were prepared was open, so we were able to watch the cooks preparing the food. We were most impressed with the speed and skill of the operators and even more impressed with the cleanliness of the kitchen. We immediately bought two *Muldoons' Pasties - Fresh Daily*, as sustenance on our hike.

We selected a ten-mile trek just north of Munising, the Chapel Falls Loop, which promised a vigorous forest hike, before ending up on the lakeshore. It included a number of interesting sights, all labelled with the prefix *Chapel*. A short drive through the Hiawatha National Forest took us to the trail head and we set out, pasties securely packed, for our first objective, Chapel Falls. We were not long into the walk along a clear track through the maple woods, when we almost trod in something large and brown on the path. A quick study immediately answered the age-old rhetorical question about what a bear does in the woods. After an hour's relaxing walk, stopping at a viewing platform and gazing over the scenic Chapel Basin, we came across the falls which drop 60 feet as they cascade towards Chapel Lake. After a brief coffee stop, we continued through the forest to Chapel Beach, a beautiful stretch of white sand on the shore of Chapel Lake and one of the highlights of the area, Chapel Rock. This iconic landmark stands like a thirty-feet high natural statue on the lakeshore at the mouth of the Chapel River, created by 4000 years of continual erosion. The rock is crowned by a 250-year-old single white pine tree and quite how a tree had grown and survived on top of the sandstone edifice was a mystery to us, but we stayed and wondered at the beauty of the structure – and enjoyed our pasties.

We followed the picturesque lakeside trail back to Mosquito Beach, thankfully free of the biting insects, before cutting back through the forest to the trailhead. A long and satisfying trek except that we never find out the origin of the *Chapel* designation.

After our exertions the previous day, we chose an easy boat trip on Lake Superior to view the picturesque cliffs from the lake. It was a warm and sunny morning as we boarded the small boat and cruised the Pictured Rocks National Lakeshore. The name Pictured Rocks comes from the many colours, stained by minerals when groundwater seeps through the cracks and trickles down the 200 feet cliffs. The rock faces are coloured red and orange from iron, copper blue and green from copper, brown and black from manganese and white from limonite with an almost infinite variation of colours in between. From the boat, we managed to identify much of the area we had walked previously, particularly chapel rock and beach, but were also introduced to many other quaintly named rock formations such as Miners' Castle, Indian Drum, Battleship Rock, Indian Head, Rainbow Cave and Painted Coves. As the boat headed back to port, the weather abruptly changed and rain lashed down and the vessel rocked and rolled in the face of the strong accompanying wind. We made back it to the departure point, cold and windswept, just as the sun burst from behind the cloud, the wind stopped and the warmth returned.

With the upturn in the weather and feeling the need for more exercise and wildlife spotting, we spent the afternoon at the Seney Wildlife Refuge, just 45 minutes east of Munising and offering the perfect environment to unwind from our boat trip. We were not disappointed. As Sue investigated the visitors' Centre, probably studying rock formations, I stayed outside and was accompanied by a grey squirrel who performed at my feet, posing, digging and scratching in the loose earth of the garden. I was chatting amicably to the playful little rodent, unaware that Sue had left her geology studies and was watching me, wondering with whom I was holding a conversation. I was I little embarrassed when she realised that I was debating the techniques and merits of dirt-scraping with a squirrel. We set out on the Northern Hardwoods Ski Trail, one of the many trails designed for the snowy Michigan winters. Just as we were getting into our stride, we were halted by a large turtle about the size of deflated basketball as it trundled slowly across the path in front of us. We watched as the delightful animal very slowly turned its head, stared at us and left the path to continue its leisurely journey towards the nearby lake. We followed the Turtle's lead and continued our walk in a similarly sluggish manner. As we meandered over the trail, veering on to the Otter Run Trail and wandering around the pretty lakes, we spotted herons, sandhill cranes, frogs, toads, swans, more squirrels and a couple of large poo piles which we could not identify. Overall, it was a splendid afternoon, marred only by the map in the Visitor Center which showed a designated hunting areas. So much for a wildlife refuge, but that's America.

The unpredictable weather continued the following day so we decided to visit the small community of Grand Marais, a pleasant hour's drive northeast on a quiet country road. We broke the journey with a visit to Grand Sable where we climbed down impressive 300 feet high dunes to the lakeshore and wandered along the sandy beach. The path down is, or was, a sandy log slide where foresters slid huge tree trunks from a sawmill down to the lake to be loaded onto ships and transported around the Upper Peninsula. Whilst I gazed out over the crashing waves on a grey and uninviting Lake Superior, Sue spent a happy hour collecting small pieces of agate from the beach. We walked on to Grand Sabel Falls, another series of imposing waterfalls cascading down the cliffside, and decided to climb the steep path by the side of the falls. We were rewarded for our efforts by stunning views from viewing platforms built on the route. Our lust for the open air and hiking more than satisfied and being cold and windswept, we moved on to Grand Marais and were delighted to find Archie's West Bay Diner, a retro rail dining car converted to an iconic 1950's café. Our server was a cheerful and welcoming host and we joined in the American theme by ordering chilli dogs and fries, but declined the almost mandatory Coco Cola, settling for water. Replete, we strolled out to the large grassy area at the lakeside and were greeted by a sign announcing a farmers' market. We stared at the large empty space and noticed one man beside a small table with a hand painted sign saying *Pasties*. Feeling sorry for the lonesome vendor we strolled across and began to chat with him. I asked, "Why are you only stall at a Farmers Market?"

He looked around him at the empty space and seemed genuinely surprised, before shrugging and answering, "The weather, I guess."

Sue felt sorry for the vendor and kindly bought four pasties before he looked around again, folded up his table and moved away. We wandered round the small village and were surprised to come across the Pickle Barrel House, a two-story cabin built in the shape of a large barrel with a smaller barrel extension. The house was built by a children's author William Donahey, who created the Teenie Weenies, cartoon characters who lived under a rose bush in a pickle barrel. The strange residence was used as a holiday home by Mr. Donahey and his wife for ten years and we were fascinated, if somewhat bemused by the strange holiday home.

Our next expedition was planned. The Beaver Lake and Little Beaver Lake via Lake Superior Trail Loop, part of the North Country Trail, a few miles from Munising was our objective, but was almost voided by the weather. It was grey and cold with sleet assaulting the car as we cruised gently out of town and on to the country road towards the trailhead. The road was covered in slushy snow and ice and the way ahead was shrouded in an eerie mist. Our pioneering spirit came to the fore as we drove on carefully through the deep slush and thick mist, feeling like valiant explorers, despite following a truck advertising Muldoons Pasties. The truck turned off, but we carried on and managed to find the trailhead and began the walk, ignoring the cold and threatening black clouds which had appeared overhead. The walk was a repeat of so many we had taken before, but never ceased to fill us with joy and excitement. The weather remained wintry but dry as we followed the North Country Trail alongside Lake Superior before cutting inland to the Beaver Basin and crossing rustic wooden bridges over sparkling streams through rich dense forests. We followed paths alongside the clear pristine waters of Big and Little Beaver Lakes, listening to songbirds singing and woodpeckers pecking, stopping only to enjoy a home-made pasty purchased from Mr. Lonely. We returned to the trailhead just as the black cloud decided to empty its considerable payload and we sat in the dry confines of our car relaxed and thankful that the weather gods had been kind to us.

AMERICANADIAN DIARIES

Grand Island sits a mile or so from the southern shore of Lake Superior, settled in the early 1800's as a fur trading post to trade with the Ojibway Indians. The following morning, we drove to the small ferry dock just west of Munising and bought tickets from a rustic wooden cabin on the lake side before boarding the small boat. It was a pleasant if brief crossing to the island where we disembarked at Williams Landing, named after Abraham Williams and his wife who were some of the first settlers to brave life on the Lake Superior frontier. We ambled up the wooden walkway from the landing stage, passing a frontier cabin originally built in 1845 and a designated historical monument. Sue and I commented how, in the mid nineteenth century, our home town of Swindon was building a huge railway factory with many streets of terraced houses nearby providing "modern" housing for its workers, yet this was still a virtually unexplored land with pioneers building primitive log cabins and living almost as hunter-gatherers. With this rather abstract thought, we continued our own pioneering and hiked alongside the inlet to the small Duck Lake before reaching our planned objective of Trout Bay, where we sat for an unusually long time, resting and gazing over the lake to the mainland, identifying the places we had visited on previous expeditions. And we enjoyed lunch, another Yooper pasty. We detoured on the walk back and came across the island cemetery where we spent a happy hour reading headstone inscriptions of island inhabitants, ranging from the mid-19th century through to those lost in two world wars to more recent times, an interesting if slightly macabre diversion.

With only a couple of days left in Munising we travelled a few miles west to visit territory we had not yet explored and, once again in the Hiawatha National Forest, headed for the Au Train Songbird Trail. Au Train is another of the many townships in the area which, although covering 158 square miles has barely one thousand residents. All we saw of the town was the odd house set some distance off the road and was a reminder how vast and thinly populated much of the US is. The trail itself left the road leading to a campsite which was uninhabited when we visited and, from this trailhead, wound through forest and fields. It was a pleasant, quiet stroll and again were on our own with just unseen chattering birds for company. We reached an observation platform on Au Train Lake's Buck Bay and stopped to rest, blanketed in an aura of peace and serenity. I was gazing over the bay through my binoculars hoping to catch sight of the waterbirds or, perhaps an osprey, when I caught sight of a large bird in the distance. Excitedly I focussed in on the bird and, much to my joy, saw that it was clearly a bald eagle. The bird flew gracefully towards us until it was directly overhead where it circled, looked down at us, and flew slowly away into the forest. This was our first definite sighting of the national emblem of the United States and one that perhaps gave me as much pleasure as any wildlife we had seen on our travels.

Still buzzing from our bald eagle sighting we finished the walk and headed back towards Munising. On the way, we had passed through the small community of Christmas. It consisted of one or two houses and a store displaying a sign saying *Santa's Workshop*, decorated in full Christmas fashion with 30 feet high Santa Claus welcoming visitors and another sign saying, *North Pole*. It was irresistible, so we stopped and browsed inside the store where every item was Christmas themed, from Christmas trees and baubles to snowmen of all sizes, reindeer and sleighs and a plethora of Christmas themed gifts. We began to chat to the shop assistant who told us that the town of Christmas was established by one Julius Thorson, who built a factory for holiday-themed products here in the 1930s and the small community took on the festive name in the following decade. We also heard much of the shop assistant's life story as she explained how she moved north from her southern home to see more of the country and ended up working here. She said and that she was thinking leaving the area and returning to her native Florida as chilly weather was depressing. She seemed very lonely so Sue bought some unwanted baubles just to cheer her up.

We wandered out of the store and began a short exploration of Christmas, which didn't take long as there was little to explore, but we did find a fascinating old, abandoned house behind the shop. It was a large and rustic, two-storey wooden building and evocative of an impressive frontier cabin, perhaps built by a leading town citizen such as the local mine-owner, cattle rancher or judge, as seen in many a western. In retrospect, we guessed that it the home of Mr. Thorson, but did not return to the store to find out as we did not fancy another episode of the assistant's life story.

Our final day in Munising was spent preparing for the next journey and pottering around Munising Lake shore, but we treated ourselves to a slap-up meal at the Brownstone Inn that evening. The stone-built inn reminded us of a typical country English pub and we dined extravagantly on broiled whitefish again, although both admitting that we missed our pasties.

We headed northwest through the rain on the I-41 to the Keweenaw Peninsula on the horn of the Upper Peninsula, passing many small communities including Ishpeming, Imperial Heights and Bovine before reaching our destination, the Super 8 at Houghton, Michigan. We have always found Super 8 motels to be excellent, but this one exceeded even Sue's high expectations. It was a new building, spotless in every way with the customary large rooms and an added bonus of magnificent views across the Houghton Canal, also named the Portage Canal, part of the

Keweenaw Waterway which separates the northern Copper Island from the Upper Peninsula mainland. On the opposite bank we could see the handsome buildings nestling amongst deep woods on the shore of Houghton's twin town of Hancock. To our left we had a perfect view of the Portage Bridge, an impressive iron structure which joins the two towns and which has a middle section which rises to allow large transporter ships to pass underneath. The motel also had small a garden with picnic tables directly on the canal side and directly outside of our room. Sue's detailed research beforehand had really come up trumps again.

The inclement weather remained, limiting our reconnaissance of the town so we drove across bridge to Hancock for no other reason than to drive across the bridge. As we reached the opposite shore, the rain eased and the sun forced its way through the clouds, persuading us to return to the hotel and take a walking tour of the immediate area. We strolled alongside the canal in well maintained gardens before diverting into the downtown area and Sheldon Avenue, an equally well-maintained street with a variety of shops, diners, motels and small businesses housed in two and three storey red brick buildings, another perfect representation of small American towns. We veered into the Douglas House Saloon, a historic drinking and eating establishment built in 1860 to satisfy the thirst of early Copper Country workers. There was just one other customer sipping beer at bar, an older gentleman with whom we struck up a friendly and informative conversation. He told is that the saloon was nicknamed *The Dog* or *The Doghouse* and had seen little changes over the years as the hub of Houghton nightlife in Copper Country, so called because the area was a copper mining community from the mid-1800s until the late 1960s. We bought the old boy a couple of beers and it would have been rude to allow him to drink alone so, by the time we left, both he and I were cheerfully unsteady as we went our separate ways.

Intrigued by our new friend's stories we set out on our first trip to the far north of the peninsula to Copper Harbour, a port town built to export the ores mined in the area via Lake Superior. We headed east of downtown Copper Harbor to Fort Wilkins Historic State Park, an early restored frontier United States Army base, originally built in 1844 to protect the vital port of Copper Harbor from the Ojibwe during the early years of the copper mining boom. The park has been restored as a 19th century army outpost and, as there were few visitors on this bitterly cold day, Sue and I could feel the isolation yet homely camaraderie of the troops stationed in the most northerly part of Upper Michigan. We visited the barrack rooms surrounding a large, grassed square, entered the recreated camp store, crammed with 19th century artifacts and wandered around the old bakehouse and blacksmith's workshop exhibiting the tools of their respective trades and inspected the original canons and fortified defences. We strolled for a while on the shores of the adjacent small lake, delightfully named Fanny Hooe, before setting off for an afternoon's exploration of the Brockway Mountain Drive, a nine-mile scenic roadway which runs from Copper Harbor to Eagle Harbor, along the ridge of Brockway Mountain and rising to 1,320 feet above Lake Superior. The drive was spectacular and, had it not been bleak, wintry and windy, would have offered good walks from the road, but we made do with views over the surrounding lake, Eagle River and forests, too cold to leave the comfort of a warm car. We moved on to the town of Copper Harbour and risked the weather by stopping and leaving the car to wander along 6th Street Docks, but the whole area seemed abandoned. No one else was in sight and the nearby bakery, café and ferry service were deserted. And I was dying for a pee. Unable to find anywhere open, I was forced to stand and urinate in the open, aiming rather expertly into the dock, which felt somewhat liberating, but Sue said was rude and embarrassing.

Returning to base, Sue pointed out that the car's petrol gauge was on red, but I allayed her apprehension by mansplaining that we had enough fuel to reach Houghton where we would fill up. I was confident in my plan, until we reached a barrier blocking the highway with a prominent sign saying, *Road Closed*, with no further explanation. We had to turn around and travel back several miles to find an alternative route home. We eventually navigated our way, stopping at an old-fashioned and somewhat run down garage to fill up, much to our relief, although I claimed that this was always in my contingency plan. On our return to Houghton, we warmed up with a visit to Joey's Seafood and Grill a plate of *Joey's Famous Fish'n'chips*. All was well with the World.

The sun had finally agreed to make an appearance which allowed us to take advantage of the canal side picnic tables to enjoy a coffee and the impressive views across to Hancock. As we relaxed a ship cruised slowly past approaching the Portage bridge. We watched as the whole central section of the bridge slowly raised allowing the vessel to pass underneath before gently lowering into place. I was surprised because I had mistakenly thought that the bridge would raise two drawbridges like London's Tower Bridge, and to see the whole middle section rise and fall was truly amazing. Sadly, this was the only time we saw the bridge raised in the five days we stayed, despite spending hours peering out over the waterway.

Despite the changeable weather, we were determined to resume walking after a couple of sightseeing days, so set out for

Sturgeon River Sloughs State Wildlife Area. A slough, pronounced "sloo," in this case is a wetland, marshy area with slow moving rivers winding through the long, lush grasses and verdant trees and bushes. Our hopes of spotting wildlife were high and we were hoping to see deer, bears, otters, beavers and mink with the chance of osprey or bald eagles overhead, particularly from the viewing tower built for the purpose. We braved the strong, cold winds and the stronger, colder rain and set out on the Sturgeon Marsh nature trail off US-41 in Chassell. On the side of the river, we found marks where a beaver had started to fell a tree by chewing through the trunk, but had apparently given up before completing the job. We carefully climbed a high observation tower but the increasingly strong wind made this a precarious act and there was nothing to observe, the local wildlife obviously ensconced safely somewhere out of the weather. Although the trail was beautiful, our early optimism was misplaced as the weather deteriorated further and we were finally beaten back, returning to the car to seek shelter having spotted no wildlife anywhere on the trek. The animals obviously had more sense than Sue and me.

Undeterred we moved on and the weather improved slightly, encouraging us to start another hike, this time on the Chassell Classic Ski Trail, designed as the name suggests for cross-country skiing, but with no skis and no snow, we were walking. The trail took us on a narrow grassy path through dense woodland where the trees were tinted red and yellow as they began to adopt their fall colours. We circled a small tarn before the return walk and were suddenly halted as an unsuspecting skunk waddled out onto the path just two yards in front of us. We stared at the skunk as it stopped and stared at us. We did not move, knowing the reputation that the animal has for spraying a noxious, oily liquid from a gland under its tail, leaving a smell which is all but impossible to remove. After a few seconds, which seemed longer, of Mexican stand-off, the skunk must have considered us unworthy of spraying and turned, raising its thick bushy tail, presumably as a warning, before returning to the undergrowth. Breathing sighs of relief, we carried on, carefully watching out for further attacks, and made it back to the start with no more skunk ambushes. As we prepared to drive home, we noticed a prominent sign at the trailhead that said, NO DOGS NO WALKING NO SKATING. There was no ice to skate on and we didn't have a dog so admitted guilt on just one count.

That evening, we returned to the Douglass Saloon for a few beers and a Yooper curry, but not before stopping at Roy's Pasties to stock up on the treats for our journey tomorrow. Outside Roy's was a board which read, *The best pasties in the Universe*. We wondered what the bakers of Bude or Bodmin would say about that claim.

Saying a fond farewell to Houghton and Hancock, we began the five-hour drive to our next venue, the town of St. Ignace on the northernmost shore of Lake Michigan. The rain had stopped and the sun was again illuminating the stunning forest landscape bordering the slightly longer rural route along the US-35 and US-2, the fall colours noticeably deepening as we headed south. We stopped twice, once at a sign marking the northern most point of Lake Michigan and again in the lakeside town of Manistique to enjoy the best pasties in the universe, which were not as good as Muldoon's.

Replete with pastie, we pottered on alongside the lake until the famous (in Michigan) Mackinac Bridge came into view, signalling the imminent arrival at our next temporary home in St Agnace. The suspension bridge connects the Upper and Lower Peninsulas of Michigan, spanning the Straits of Mackinac which joins Lakes Michigan and Huron. We found the Sunset Motel, unusually without getting lost, and settled in quickly. It was a simple no-frills lodging and perfect for us, offering a distant view of the bridge. In the evening, we set out looking for somewhere to eat and came across ten feet high, fibreglass statue of a fat lad dressed in red and white checkered dungarees and carrying a tray of burgers above his head. This was irresistible, not only because it was ultra-American, but because it offered a unique photo opportunity for me to stand next to the model, mimicking its pose and looking silly. This was our introduction to the Big Boy diner and we never wavered in our loyalty to the restaurant over the rest of our stay. It was not exactly refined fine dining, but never has a thick, juicy unhealthy burger with fries tasted better.

More unhealthy but tasty dining at the Big Boy the following morning set us up for our first hike on the Maple Hill Trail near Rudyard, once again in the Hiawatha National Forest. The rain was heavy as we approached the trailhead but we bravely ignored the weather and set off on the trail, although Sue soon tired of my hilarious jokes about it being *ruddy 'ard* walking hence the name of the town. We were rewarded for our bravery with a stimulating walk as the rain stopped and the sun filtered through the green, yellow, orange and red foliage, but the return of the rain cut our walk short so we retreated to the motel for a well-earned afternoon nap before our big night out in Big Boy.

Refreshed after the long drive and short walk of the previous day, Sue and I needed a good hike so set out on the Horseshoe Bay trail on Lake Huron, variously described as six, eight or ten miles. After a short walk through woods from the trailhead we reached the dunes then the long, curved beach of the bay and headed north on the sands, with Mackinac Island on the horizon. The stroll started in bright sunshine until fierce winds and a brief but heavy storm engulfed us, before the black clouds were blown back out to sea. We managed only the six-mile walk, not through the weather or lack of energy but because there were interesting rocks and shells on the shoreline which Sue could not resist studying. I lounged on a large piece of driftwood and offered her encouragement, happy to sit and rest. As my backpack was covertly filled with interesting pebbles, we again commented that we were alone as the two-mile long sandy bay was deserted. We again commented that the only times that we met others on this holiday were in places where food was served. We gazed across the sparkling waters of the lake to the island, we decided that it would be our destination on the following day, our last in St. Ignace.

I carefully emptied my backpack outside of the motel room in the morning, hoping Sue wouldn't notice that her collection of pebbles was missing and we set off for the Arnold Transit Co. ferry to Mackinac Island, via Big Boy of course. The crossing was a little rough as the unpredictable weather continued, until we pulled in to the peaceful and impressive harbour of the main town, confusingly called Mackinaw. The port is surrounded by large colonial houses and beautifully maintained colourful gardens, which reminded us of the Victorian seaside town of Lyme Regis in Devon. The main Street also had that same Victorian feel but with an American slant, with its clapperboard houses and boardwalks lining the street. No motor vehicles are allowed on the island, so the street was a lively hub of visitors on bicycles or in horse drawn carriages, stopping to visit the various cafes, diners and tourist tat shops creating a busy but welcoming and relaxing atmosphere. We watched a man with a horse-drawn truck shovelling up the poo deposited by the many horses in town. I said that I could do that job. We also wandered round the grounds of the Grand Hotel with rooms advertised at $450 per night, ten times what we were paying at the Sunset Motel.

We (I) soon tired of the shops and decided to hike to Mackinac's two most well-known geological features, Arch Rock and Sugar Loaf. We headed east from the town before the well-marked paved path took us north above the shoreline through delightful woodland with glimpses of the sparkling lake through the trees. The wind was picking up as we reached Arch Rock and mounted the viewing platform to view the rocky archway carved by water and wind erosion, with the bright blue waters of Huron shimmering through the natural frame. As the wind increased, we cut inland and followed another track, Sugar Loaf Road, through more forested land as the wind increased and dropping autumn leaves were swirling round us. We reached the Sugar Loaf, a 75-foot-high limestone stack created by erosion after the last ice-age and a truly impressive and beautiful geological sculpture. We wanted to move on further into the island's interior, but the wind seemed, by now, hurricane strength and trees were beginning to bend under its power so we turned south and followed the quickest route back to safety. We stopped briefly at the site of an old defence stronghold, Fort Holmes, but were happy to make it back to Mackinaw without being crushed by falling trees. The lake was now a boiling, swirling maelstrom as waves crashed on the shore and boats tossed in the harbour, so we settled into a bar for a beer, waiting for our return boat to the mainland. We were happy and relieved to see that our ferry was the only one running, the waters too rough for smaller craft, and I didn't fancy staying on the island at $450. As we boarded, the captain told us that Mackinac bridge was closed due to the high winds and jokingly added, "Hold on tight, Sir," which I did not find funny. The boat pitched and tossed as we crossed Mackinac Straits towards St, Ignace and the closed bridge seemed to be swaying in the misty distance, but Sue said that was probably the effect of the beers or the thought of spending money to stay on the island. After a turbulent journey, we made it back safely, thanks to the skill of the ferry crew. I thanked the captain for getting us back to port in one piece and for his invaluable advice, as I had certainly held on tight all the way.

We had become very friendly with our waitress at Big Boy and on our last evening, she stopped at our table for a chat, wishing us well on our journey. She proudly pointed a lad working at the pay desk and said that he was her son and announced that he was training as a supervisor in the restaurant. He was a huge, obese lad and I had to hold my tongue and not ask if the diner was named after him.

We were up at six o'clock for the last leg of our adventure, a 300-mile, six-hour drive back across Canada to Manatoulin Island and a car ferry to Tobermory. The drive meant retracing much of our journey to St. Ignace, travelling back on the I-75 to cross the border at Saulte Ste. Marie again and then heading east and south on Highway 17 and 6 to Manatoulin Island, before catching a ferry at South Baymouth to our destination. Although long, the drive was almost magical, travelling through places we had previously passed on the outward journey before heading over empty roads and bridges across virtually uninhabited islands of Lake Huron to our destination. We stopped just twice, first at Espanola where we had a coffee break at Tim Hortons, a well-known chain of Canadian diners. We loved the ambiance of the café, particularly as we shared the stop with a coachload of ancient pensioners who made us feel like youngsters. The coffee was served in smart mugs emblazoned with the name *Tim Hortons* and Sue was very taken with them, asking me to ask the server if we could buy two mugs. I was told that, "No, Sir, we don't sell the mugs." I took this to mean that they were free, so we left the store suitably refreshed and smuggling two of Tim Horton's coffee mugs.

We stopped again for a quick break overlooking Georgian Bay and were treated to a display by a large group of sandhill cranes producing a chorus of loud, rattling bugle calls, which kept us entertained for a while before continuing our journey to the ferry port of South Baymouth. We were early for our scheduled departure so took advantage of the spare time to sit on rocks next to the historic, wooden, 115-year-old South Baymouth Range Front Lighthouse and lunch on takeaway subs from Tim Hortons. We sat in the sun for an hour talking about our adventures until the ferry came into view and docked silently in the small harbour. I was somewhat surprised how big the boat, the Che-Cheeman, was and felt more than a little nervous about driving aboard. We drove around to the port and I was even more nervous as I had no-one to follow on board, so I held back in the car park until two other cars headed the queue. Maintaining the bronze medal position I slowly and carefully managed to manoeuvre the car aboard safely with a profound sense of relief. The fact that the car in front zipped quickly and confidently into position and was driven by a small octogenarian lady with thick spectacles and a tremor did nothing to diminish the sense of pride at my achievement.

A pleasant two hours cruising later, we negotiated the tricky deboarding and drove the three minutes to our new billet, the Harbourside Motel, Tobermory on the north of the Bruce Peninsula, another excellent piece of homework by my wife. As the name suggests, the motel faced directly on to the pretty Little Tub Harbour, over a small boardwalk which circled the marina. It was easy to see why the small, picturesque town of Tobermory was named after the capital of the Isle of Mull in the Scottish Inner Hebrides, although I unsuccessfully tried to convince Sue that it was named after a ginger cat. We spent the late afternoon wandering around the harbour in the fading sunlight, looking over the tiny inlet and selecting which house and boat we should buy to spend our dotage in this beautiful location.

We awoke the following morning to the bluest of blue and cloudless Canadian sky, a complete change from the storms we had experienced on previous days in Michigan. We strolled alongside the harbour to Craigies, a small diner on the harbourside which looked exactly like the type of eating house we had come to admire. The full American/Canadian breakfast was excellent, but the service was atrocious and the staff sullen and unhelpful, so this was crossed off our list for dining in future.

The Cypress Lake trail was our objective for our first trek and we were not disappointed. It was a beautiful loop trail around the lake, through some open, paved tracks and several detours into the woods. It was a stunning way to explore the lake and waterways of the area with several creeks, rivers, and a few small waterfalls. We also discovered a few wooden walkways with stunning views opening out onto the smooth, azure lake. We did make one slight error by following a group of nattering women who were ignoring the incredible surroundings, chatting noisily as they walked, so we diverted away from them into the woods, getting lost for a while. When we finally found our way back on track, they had disappeared and we resumed our usual solitary exploration. Although the walk was accompanied by constant bird song, our wildlife spotting was restricted one pileated woodpecker and a dead porcupine.

That evening we bypassed Craigies in our search for a suitable restaurant and noticed a small but smart hotel on the opposite side of the harbour, displaying a prominent sign simply saying, *Fish and Chips*. We immediately entered and the Tobermory Princess Hotel and Restaurant became our dining venue for all future meals in the town.

Our discovery walks continued with a cliff top trek to the Grotto and Indian Head Cove, the final leg of the Bruce Trail, a hiking route in southern Ontario running from the Niagara River to the tip of Tobermory. The walk was one of the most spectacular we had undertaken as the trail followed the cliffs across stunning sheer limestone cliffs plunging 60 feet down to Georgian Bay. The path led across many bare outcrops overlooking the bay, before reaching the Grotto and Grotto Arch. The two geological features, the objective of our mission, were a little disappointing. The Grotto was a cave which was impossible to enter and the arch was relatively unimpressive. I checked my maps and guide to ensure that were at the right location, but to this day wonder if we had somehow missed something at the site or even missed the site completely. Undeterred we continued, scrambling over the unimaginatively, if accurately named Boulder Beach, before climbing the cliffs to Overhang Point where the rock has been eroded leaving the surface shelves perched out into the bay with nothing beneath them. We stood on the overhangs, taking many photographs to record our bravery before setting out inland on stoney paths for the return journey through the woods. Narrowly avoiding stepping on a sunbathing adder on the way back, we stopped at the Bruce Peninsula National Park and Fathom Five National Marine Park Visitor Centre. Despite its impressive title the centre was closed, but we managed to climb the 113 steps up the observation tower for a wonderful view over the woods to the Tobermory and the bay.

AMERICANADIAN DIARIES

With just two days left in the Bruce Peninsula, we decided to do something different so, instead of carefully planning and executing walks on documented trails, we simply went out exploring. This was against everything I normally insisted on, but with no plans, no maps and no ideas, we became like Happy Wanderers who *loved to go a-wandering ... my knapsack on my back.* We a-wandered around the harbour, through woods, on shorelines and across marshes. We saw wild turkeys, pitcher plants, a leopard frog, a beaver swimming, lots of rocks (including some, Sue informed me, that were 400 million years old and found in only three places on Earth.) We drove around the northern peninsula, stopping wherever the fancy took us. We passed small farms. We poked about in ponds. We sat and picnicked by the side of Lake Huron and Georgian Bay. We somehow found ourselves strolling on Singing Sands and leaping across crevasses on remote tracks. We did not meet another human being on the explorations. Sue was euphorically happy to just aimlessly potter and stroll, but without my maps I felt lost, which indeed we often were.

The journey back to Toronto went without a hitch although, in retrospect, our plan to stay overnight in Scarborough was not wise. It meant driving past the airport and through the frenzied traffic of Toronto to reach the motel on the other side of the city, before returning through the same madness to the airport. We spent the afternoon repeating our meandering in Scarborough Bluffs, next to Lake Ontario and again noticed many families picnicking in the park, all of them Asian. We mentioned this to our friend in the Super Eight and he explained that the district is a popular destination for new immigrants to Canada and it is one of the most diverse and multicultural areas in the country. This settled my curiosity and he recommended that we take advantage of the diversity by eating than night in the

Charminar Indian Cuisine, serving possibly the best curries in the Universe. We did and they were.

AMERICANADIAN DIARIES

CHAPTER 11 – NEW YORK NEW YORK

Almost two years had passed before we embarked on our next road trip, and Sue and I spent many happy hours in our Portuguese home studying, investigating and planning where we should visit. Although I have never understood the desire to complete lists of places to visit, every European country, every US state, every Disney theme park, every pub in Swindon or any other pointless ambition, I felt that we should visit all of the five Great Lakes and should complete the set with Lake Erie. Since I was a young boy, I had been interested in the noble art of boxing and was intrigued by the number of top fighters who trained in the Catskill Mountains. World Champions Rocky Marciano, Jake LaMotta, Sonny Liston, Ingemar Johansson, Muhammad Ali and Larry Holmes had all set up camp in the mountains to prepare for title fights, so my fascination lasted decades. Apart from a brief walk around Toronto, we had not experienced any great North American cities, so agreed that perhaps we should resolve this omission. We were ageing quickly and found long flights debilitating so agreed that the destination must be reached by a direct flight from Lisbon. These considerations were part of the planning process and we finally managed to create an itinerary which would satisfy all criteria. Fly to New York, drive to the Catskill mountains, on to Lake Erie, back to the Adirondack mountains and Rhode Island before returning via New York. My planning complete, it was again over to Sue to complete the minor details like deciding exactly where to stay, defining how long in each place and selecting accommodation. Simple.

Everything finally arranged, we stayed in our usual hotel in Lisbon overnight before the early morning flight to the Big Apple. This year, the hotel room had an added bonus. On the bedside cabinet was an *Intimacy Kit*, consisting of condoms in *pepper colours*, lubricants including anal cream, vibrating rings, love dice and, strangely, mint drops. Sue took one look at the pack and simply said, "No."

Because the flight landed at Newark Liberty Airport in New Jersey and due to the ridiculously expensive hotels in New York, we had chosen to stay a few days in a Super 8 in North Bergen, New Jersey across the Hudson River from New York City. The motel offered a regular shuttle service to the city via the Lincoln Tunnel, so visiting would be no problem. Picking up the car from Newark, we headed north and somehow found ourselves on the I-95, arriving in North Bergen with little trouble fifteen minutes later. Our luck ran out when we spotted the motel on the opposite side of the freeway and had to negotiate several flyovers, some bridges, the freeway and a few smaller roads to reach our destination. We toured North Bergen three times, catching several glimpses of the Super 8 signs but unable to find a way in. Our fifteen-minute journey had now lasted an hour. We finally managed to get close to the motel and pulled in to an iHop restaurant car park to check our maps and see if there was an easy way of crossing the ten lanes of the I95 to our destination. As we sat in the car trying to work out where to go a car pulled up and the driver asked, "You guys need help?"

I explained our situation and the good Samaritan said, "Just follow me," before driving off. Exactly where he led us, I know not, but we ended up a few minutes later in the Super 8 car park. Our guide gave us a cheery wave and drove away, without even stopping to be thanked. Sue pointed out that we two naive old Brits were lost in the middle of the most heavily populated urban area of the USA with its associated crime rate, and had just trusted a complete stranger to lead us through unknown neighbourhood streets, simply because he said to follow him. I replied that I was not worried as I had always been a good judge of character. Sue was unconvinced.

Having settled in to the motel, we were hungry after a long day. We needed to eat and the only restaurant we knew amongst the jumble of busy roads was the iHop, so we set off on foot to sample the first American dining delight of our visit. Walking alongside the busy highway, and across an even busier flyover was not the most relaxing journey we had ever taken, but we made it to the iHop and found it clean and comfortable with good service, tasty food and, best of all, a seniors' menu at a reduced price. Of course, I tried to convince Sue that I had planned the original detour to this restaurant as reconnaissance all along, but again she was unconvinced and told me that I must stop telling fibs.

It was Saturday morning and, after a bunfight for the complementary breakfast in the hotel reception area, we caught the earliest shuttle from the Super 8 to New City with some eagerness. Our enthusiasm was amplified by a mad Mexican driver who seemed to break every rule of the road on purpose and by sitting next to a man wearing a backpack which contained a dog. The dog was wearing sunglasses. After driving at breakneck speed, possibly on the wrong of the road and listening to all other motorists being harangued in Spanish, we were dropped off at 7th and 47th, although I had no idea what that meant. We left the small underground bus station and arrived in Duffy square, a modest plaza where we found a street market selling bric-a-brac and food of all kinds and, whilst Sue browsed amongst the stalls, I was trying to work out where we were on my map. I finally clicked that 7th Avenue is the main thoroughfare through the city and the crossing streets are named in order from 1st Street to somewhere in the hundreds. I felt a bit silly as the layout is obvious and simple, but I pretended that I had known all along as we made our way along 7th Avenue, which I thought was also called Broadway but was unsure, before turning left on 34th Street and arriving, as if by magic, at the Empire State Building. We showed our tickets, purchased online in Portugal, and took the lift to the 86th floor. The day was bright and perfectly clear and it is impossible to describe the view stretching for miles in all directions, over the surrounding city, the Hudson and East Rivers and beyond, so I won't try, but it was a truly exhilarating experience. We took too many photographs, some just of the view and some with each of us posing and grinning like Cheshire cats. A helpful tourist offered to take photographs of the two of us together and I repaid the kindness before noticing that several visitors were chatting and swapping camera to do the same thing. The relaxed joy and affability were everywhere which, being something of a curmudgeon, I found unnerving. As we returned to the lift, we studied the wall with photographs of famous visitors, many we recognised and many we did not, but a little apart from the main gallery was a picture of Mark Labbett, *The Beast* from the TV quiz show, *The Chase*. An American family were discussing who he was before the father pronounced that he was definitely, "That big English guy who plays Shrek."

We moved on, taking time to soak up the atmosphere of Broadway and Times Square, buzzing with thousands of people. Every available space on buildings was taken up with huge, garish screens advertising everything imaginable - beer and coke, retail stores, restaurants, cars, films and things I didn't understand, but mainly promoting Broadway shows. Amongst the throng, there were hustlers everywhere selling tickets for the city's attractions, several moving statues, people in fancy dress selling something and there was Mickey and Minnie Mouse, also selling something, and all the time the advertising flashed and flickered around us. At one end of the square tiered seating had been erected, so we were able to climb to the top tier and survey the hectic scene below, thankful to be temporarily out of the hubbub. On a building next to grandstand a big screen was advertising *Jersey Boys,* showing many clips from the musical which we had already purchased tickets to see. I complained to Sue that we could have saved money by sitting there for two hours and looking at the screen rather than buying tickets, but she just shook her head. It was soon time to move on again but not before stopping to watch two attractive, scantily clad young ladies playing guitars strapped beneath their large and partially unfettered bosoms on a traffic island and advertising something called Naked Cowgirls, which may have been a themed restaurant, a film or a show, but Sue said I could not go and ask them what and where it was.

We had long decided that when in New York we would go to pay our respects at the 9/11 or Ground Zero Memorial, built to pay tribute to the 2977 innocent people who lost their lives in the 2001 suicide attacks on the Twin Towers. From Times Square, we found our way to the magnificent Grand Central Station and, after some confusion, a seven feet tall security guard pointed us to the correct subway train to Battery Park on the southern tip of Manhattan. We caught the train and arrived without incident, resting in the park with a coffee before taking the short stroll to the 9/11 memorial. It was a truly moving experience with the name of everyone whose life was lost in the attack inscribed on bronze parapets surrounding the twin reflecting pools, which are located in the footprints of the former Twin Towers. Perhaps the most poignant were those victims that had a small posy or a single rose left against their name, presumably placed there in remembrance by a relative. Sue and I walked round in complete silence, both teary-eyed.

We decided to walk back to the bus drop-off point, perhaps not realising that it was four miles and would take almost two hours following 7th Avenue, with a detour to see Wall Street, which wasn't worth it. It was an odd feeling knowing that we were walking through one of the greatest and most famous cities in the World but much of it, away from the busy tourist areas, felt like any other rather lacklustre town outskirts. To our surprise, we found the bus station easily and returned to the motel without further incident. By the time that we had reached the Super 8, we were both shattered after our busy and, generally, exciting day, but not too shattered to take advantage of the iHop's seniors' menu at reduced price again.

It was Sunday and we thought that there could be no better way to spend the day of rest than strolling around Central Park before attending the pre-booked show, *Jersey Boys*. The visit was a memorable experience, not just because it is a well maintained urban green area but, because just repeating the name of location made us tingle with excitement: *Central Park, between Upper West Side and Upper East Side, Manhattan, New*

AMERICANADIAN DIARIES

York City. I am not sure if we saw the park's main attractions, the Ramble and Lake, Hallett Nature Sanctuary, the Jacqueline Kennedy Onassis Reservoir or Sheep Meadow as, for once, we did not feel the need to plan or follow a map in order to see famous landmarks. Just being there, with the skyscrapers of the city towering above the immaculate lawns and imposing trees was enough. That said, we did make one definite detour to visit Strawberry Fields, the memorial to John Lennon, where we sat and rested for a while, watching New Yorkers jogging, skating and cycling over the memorial plaque, which I found a little disrespectful until Sue pointed out that the Beatle would probably have approved. On leaving the park, we were accosted by a young man dishing out fliers for a Subway, I started to wave him away when Sue said that the leaflets were offering a 10% discount and sent me back to sheepishly ask for the discount voucher.

After our discounted lunch, we set out for the August Wilson Theatre on Broadway to see Jersey Boys. I was confused because it was a Broadway show but the theatre wasn't on Broadway. It was on West 52nd Street, which is off Broadway, but it was not an Off Broadway show. My confusion did not last long as we took our seats in the theatre with the usual pre-curtain hubbub of the audience. Next to us were two couples who sounded northern European, perhaps Scandinavian or German, and were conversing in English. I heard one man say, "Is there a story? I don't like shows without a story," to which the other replied, "I have no idea what it's about."

"Probably Germans, then," I whispered to Sue.

We had chosen the musical Jersey Boys as we were, after all, staying in New Jersey and the show is about the musical quartet, the Four Seasons who were formed in Newark, New Jersey. Going to watch Les Misérables or The Phantom of the

Opera would not have had the same appeal. We were not disappointed. The show was superb as we listened, and sang along (quietly) to *Sherry, Rag Doll* and *My Eyes Adored You*. I was so into the story and the music that by the time Frankie Valli sang *Fallen Angel*, I was finding it difficult to stop tears rolling down my face.

We awoke the next day with the four seasons still buzzing in my head and looked out of the motel window to see a misty and rainy day with heavy traffic crawling on the 495, the road we had to take to catch the ferry for our next visit, the Statue of Liberty and Ellis Island. I was nervous about driving in the busy commute but, by the time we had managed to grab a bagel or two amongst the breakfast throng, the traffic had reduced and we set out with more confidence. The drive turned out to be easy, cruising through The Heights, Newark Avenue and Jersey City to the ferry departure point and we were soon cruising through the gloom in a boat across the Hudson.

The first stop was at Ellis Island, the arrival point for all immigrants in the late 19th and early 20th centuries, when there was a huge influx of mainly European settlers seeking a new life and the American Dream. More than 12 million people were processed on the island and it is now The National Immigration Museum. Sue and I spent a stimulating couple of hours at the museum, passing through the vast immigration hall and marvelling at the photographs, documents and memorabilia of those times. One hall held our attention for a long time, where there were a number of microfiche machines holding the names of all immigrants to pass through the Island and Sue and I spent a fascinating if frustrating time searching to see if any of our ancestors had passed through. There were hundreds of Truemans and Henleys and the sheer number was mind-blowing, but none that we could tie down to originating in our home towns. There was, however, one Keeping, my mother's maiden name, who came from Bath where her father was born and raised. Is too coincidental that this man, Ernest Keeping, moved from Bath to the USA and is not related?

The Four Seasons songs were now replaced in our brains by immigrant names and the optimism, bravery or desperation that led them to cross the Atlantic to seek a new life in the west as we returned to the ferry and disembarked at Liberty Island. We wandered around the World's most famous statue and took far too many photographs, both of the statue and across the Hudson to New York City, shrouded in mist. After exhausting our photographic views, we moved on to climb inside the statue to ascend to the statue's crown. There was some confusion at the entrance desk when several people were asking to be admitted to the crown, only to be told that they must have pre-booked tickets. We, rather smugly, moved to the front of the queue and showed our tickets which Sue had had the foresight to purchase online before we left Portugal, and much to the chagrin of the disappointed visitors. We climbed the 162 metal stairs in a tight helix to reach the compact confines inside the crown before gazing out of the small windows at the hazy city and river vistas. We descended the stairs and left the building expressing our wonder, perhaps too loudly, of the views, before catching the ferry back to New Jersey.

I took a deliberate detour on the way back to North Bergen to pass through Hoboken in search of 415 Monrow Street, the birthplace of one of my musical heroes, Frank Sinatra. After several failed attempts, we found the address but I was disappointed to find that the apartments had been pulled down and replaced by a new office block with a large star embedded into the wall to identify it as the singer's birthplace. Many of the surrounding buildings, had remained intact, however, so it was easy to imagine young Francis Albert Sinatra playing in these streets between the apartment blocks before leaving to become a music legend.

Much as we had enjoyed New York City, we were excited to be moving on to the mountains inland and once again braved the heavy morning traffic to head north to the Catskill Mountains. Once we had left the urban conurbation and were heading north on the I-87, it was a pleasant and relaxing cruise with long, straight and almost traffic-free roads taking us through the New York state forests in the sunshine. We were again enthralled by the names of the towns we passed through, Hackensack, Ho-Ho-Kus, Tuxedo, Poughkeepsie and, perhaps the most iconic, Woodstock. Quite surprisingly considering my navigation history, we easily found our way to Phoenicia and the cabin we had rented. Simpler Times Cabins is a small campsite about half a mile from the small town of Phoenicia and was, and probably still is, the most peaceful and relaxing paradise. From first sight, we fell in love with the small redwood cabin we had hired. The inside was beautifully and rustically decorated, superbly maintained with a surprisingly spacious bedroom, bathroom and a kitchen area, but the key delight was outside where a porch overlooked a large grassy area surrounded by trees. My first thought was *Cabin in the Clearing*, my favourite childhood TV western or it could have been where the Clampett family lived before becoming *The Beverly Hillbillies*. Sue decided to take a snooze after the busy time in NYC and I sat on the porch in the sunshine, studying my maps and guides. I immediately I felt relaxed and at home as I planned the following days' explorations.

AMERICANADIAN DIARIES

That evening, we strolled into Phoenicia and were greeted by another piece of heaven as the town was like travelling back in time to a pioneer settlement, unchanged since the last century. The main street was lined with attractive colonial houses, a strangely bleak-looking but well stocked supermarket, several other stores, a small theatre, and, most exciting, an appealing diner, Brio's. One house, partially hidden by bushes and trees had a sign which read:

POSTED

No Poachin' No Trespassin' No Nuthin'
This applies to friends, relatives
Enemies and YOU
~~VIOLATORS~~ SURVIVORS WILL BE PROSECUTED

On top of the sign was an animal skull, which we found somewhat intriguing.

We had a few drinks in Brio's and an excellent dinner before strolling back to our cabin where we both slept the sleep of the saved and thankful.

Simpler Times offered a free breakfast in the office and reception area of the owners' home and we took advantage of the kind offer, enjoying good coffee with bagels and English muffins, which were neither English nor muffins but tasty, nonetheless. We chatted with the proprietors, Ethan and Shane, and learnt that this had been a family business for three generations and they had lived in the Catskills all their lives enjoying hiking, hunting, and fishing. Their tips and advice on the area were invaluable as we began our own exploration.

AMERICANADIAN DIARIES

For our first walk we chose a well-known and fairly challenging route to West Kill Mountain via Diamond Notch and West Kill falls. It was a grey, wet and wintry morning but we heroic Brits were undeterred by what was, after all, typical British Summer weather. We found the trailhead easily, next to the deserted Devil's Tombstone campground and found a register to be signed by everyone entering the wilderness area. We assumed that this was checked daily to ensure that we had made it back from the hike but were unconvinced whether this was encouraging or not. We set off past the pretty little Notch Lake on a well-worn track through the forest to our first objective of Diamond Notch Falls. The rain continued as we trekked on and this added to our sense of adventure as we arrived at the falls. The twin cascades were in full flow after the rains and crashed down into a pond before tumbling over a series of rocks and smaller falls where thousands of years of erosion had created a beautiful rocky sculpture of polished whirls, swirls and curls. At the side of the falls there was an open fronted log shelter, a lean-to designed we assumed for overnight shelter for *thru hikers* – we were still learning American lingo as we went. After a cup of flask coffee at the lean-to, we set off over a rustic wooden bridge towards our next objective, West Kill Mountain summit. It was a long hard flog through the trees but we finally made the summit, clearly marked by a rustic sign nailed to a tree. We gazed out over what was described as one of the most spectacular outlooks in the Catskills, but the misty rain restricted the view, although it created a ghostly and surreal scene which we both found exhilarating. We dropped down and followed the trail back to the car agreeing that the rain had added to the thrill but one such experience was enough and we hoped for better weather in future.

AMERICANADIAN DIARIES

The rain gods ignored our request and the next day was wet and miserable although we weren't either as we started out south to visit the Shawangunk Mountains, known as *The Gunks* and selected purely because we liked the name. We arrived at the Mohonk Preserve, a nature reserve of cliffs, forests, fields, ponds and streams, with 40 miles of hiking trails. At the entrance was a sign (they seemed to like signs in this part of the US), which said that day visitors should pay twelve dollars to enter the reserve and, although we decided that it should not apply to English visitors and it was raining, we reluctantly paid anyway. From the visitor centre, we decided to take the easy route and started out on the Undercliff-Overcliff Loop. We walked on a wide gravelled track between imposing, sheer cliffs rising each side before climbing a rocky cliff to the East Trapps Connector Trail and returning on the Overcliff Road. The hike promised ... *sweeping vistas of the Wallkill Valley (from Undercliff) and the Catskills and Clove Valley (from Overcliff)*, but due to the rain and mist, we could see very little but returned to the car park tired, wet and happy.

We ate at Brio's again that evening, over-indulging in comforting pizza and chatting with the serving staff, a pretty girl and her handsome boyfriend, before strolling home as the rains finally stopped which augured well for the next day.

We awoke to heavy rain. Undeterred we decided to explore the area just south of Phoenicia, but each time we stopped the precipitation became heavier, so we drove on to the next stop on our itinerary which was also too wet to visit. The rain eased as we drove past the Ashoken reservoir and we left the car to walk over the bridge across the man-made lake but, almost immediately, the heavens opened again and we were forced back to the car soaking wet. We carried on and diverted to the famous town of Woodstock, host to numerous Hudson River School painters in the late 1800s during the Arts and Crafts Movement, but more well-known for the 1969 music festival, often still shown on television documentaries about the hippy and free love era. I'm not sure what I expected to see there, perhaps long-haired, moustachioed men and thin, topless women, now in their seventies but still dancing oddly under the influence of LSD, but all we found was a pleasant small town. There were a couple of odd sightings. A large "statue," perhaps ten feet tall composed of various toys including dolls, plastic animals, teddy bears and Disney characters, was built in a front garden. On the roadside was an official-looking sign (I said they liked signs) which read:

> ON THIS SITE STOOD
> A LOCAL MARKET BANKRUPTED
> BY THE MONOPOLISTIC, MAKE-IT-
> CHEAPER-IN-INDIA, ANTI-UNION
> BIG BOX STORE WHERE YOU SHOP
> EDUCATION
> DEPARTMENT 2007

We imagined that the sign was created by old hippy festival goers who never went home. We later found out that, although the town is famous for lending its name to the Woodstock Festival, the site of the event was actually almost 60 miles away in Bethel.

On our travels, we had noticed the Phoenicia Diner, a retro restaurant which we wanted to visit but it did not open in the evenings when we preferred to eat. As our day was cut short by the inclement weather, we decided that this was the ideal opportunity to eat there. It was a memorable meal served in a memorable diner, which could have come straight out of the

1950's. A long counter with a line of fifteen metal and red-padded stools, several cosy booths and a menu offering great food. Sue opted for a bowl of Braised Pinto Beans & Kale soup while I chose the Tortilla Soup with free range chicken, avocado and tortilla chips. Just to be sociable, we shared a large bowl of fries. We tried to walk off the effects of the feast with a stroll alongside Esopus Creek at the rear of the diner, and finished the day with another stroll along Phoenicia's Main Street. The small theatre was advertising a forthcoming musical, *The Robber Bridegroom*. As I have explained, when we lived in England, Sue and I had been regular supporters of SALOS, the Swindon Amateur Light Operatic Society and enjoyed locally produced shows, so we purchased tickets for the opening night in two days' time. The one lady pottering in the theatre seemed surprised that we wanted to see the show, perhaps confused by our English accents, but sold us tickets anyway.

We could not leave the Catskills without a ride on the Delaware and Ulster Heritage Railroad, from Arkville just twenty miles from our base in Phoenicia, to Roxbury. It had the added bonus of giving access the Catskill Scenic Trail which started just north of Roxbury and we had a two hour wait there which gave us time to hike a little of the trail. We arrived at the station early and, after purchasing tickets for the trip, strolled around the yards admiring the old steam and diesel engines. I climbed into the driver's cab in an old steam locomotive and an engineer sitting in a sleek blue and silver cab shouted something unintelligible at me. I climbed down, head bowed, and sheepishly approached the engineer expecting a dressing down.

He leaned out of the cab window and said, "Cumonup," so I did. I climbed up into the cab and spent a few minutes pretending to drive the train and explained to Casey Jones that I came from Swindon, one of the biggest and certainly the best railway engineering town in Great Britain, if not Europe. He nodded sagely, but it was obvious he had never heard of Swindon and was doubtful about Great Britain and Europe. It was soon time to board as our train pulled into the station. I was pleasantly surprised and excited to see that the sleek silver carriages we being pulled by the train that I had previously driven, the Rip Van Winkle Flyer. And Casey waved at me as the train stopped.

We gently rolled along, through the lush meadows of verdant Catskill countryside alongside the East Delaware River, past attractive farmhouses with the tree-covered hills in the distance. Arriving at Roxbury, we deboarded and I asked one of the staff, an elderly man with a long grey beard and woolly hat, where we could find the start of the Catskill Scenic Trail. He explained where the trail began and told us that if we looked left from the trail after two miles or so, we would see his house, the only one visible from the trail, where he was now going for lunch. We walked through the town and noticed most of our fellow passengers crammed into a café enjoying a coffee while we strode past. They looked a little surprised to see someone walking further than the nearest coffee shop. We found the trail which was created from an old railway line and continued to run alongside the East Delaware River, so the route was flat and easy walking. We had to keep an eye on the time but spotted a beaver dam and the blooded head of a deer with nothing more of the animal anywhere to be seen. As we walked, Sue suddenly bent over and groaned in pain. She had agonising stomach cramps which almost brought her to tears. I panicked. We had little choice but to turn round and head back to the town, so I supported her as we staggered back along the trail before reaching the main road, making a shorter return journey to town. At one point, she bent double and I thought that she was about to die, faint or have baby, so I panicked again. As she bent over, grunting in pain and I just stood there like a useless idiot, a car stopped and our bearded friend leaned out of the window and asked if we were OK. Seeing Sue's distress, he offered us a lift back to the station, an offer we gratefully accepted. On arrival back at the station, the gentleman asked if he could get Sue anything. "Just a toilet," was her flustered response, so beardy directed her to the ladies, where she disappeared for what seemed like hours but was probably five minutes. When she finally reappeared, she said she felt better and I didn't like to go into any more details. We sat in one of the open wooden carriages on the return journey and Sue was fine although she didn't join in my out-of-tune rendition of *The Cannonball Express*.

That evening we arrived at the Phoenicia Playhouse and settled in to enjoy the Robber Bridegroom. We were not disappointed as, much like SALOS, the dancing wasn't perfect and some singing was a bit off-key, but the joyful enthusiasm of the performers more than made up for the minor shortcomings. The story, based on a Brothers Grimm fairy tale, takes place in 18th century Mississippi and follows the Robin Hood-like Jamie Lockhart, a legendary character in Mississippi folklore, who rescues Clemment Musgrove, the wealthiest plantation owner in Natchez Trace, from the Harp gang, and attempts to woo and win his daughter Rosamond. We had never heard of Natchez Trace before and little did we know that we were to get to know it well within a couple of years. The leading lady, Rosamond, was played by a pretty girl who had obviously had professional training at some time and her leading man, the handsome Jaimie, was the perfect partner. Whilst Rosamond was the more accomplished performer, the real star of the show was the leading man, Jaimie. Both seemed vaguely familiar, but we put this down to the fact that we had seen many musicals and had possibly confused them with the leads in other shows.

The weather had finally broken the following day and we awoke to blue skies and sunshine. We immediately donned our walking boots and looked forward to a trek in the hills to take advantage of the sunshine. North–South Lake is an 1,100-acre leisure area in the Catskill Forest Preserve near Palenville, overlooking the Hudson River valley. The twin lakes nestle in an escarpment 2,250 feet above sea level and 1,700 feet above the valley floor, claiming a view of five states. The walk from here to North Point gains a further 1000 feet and offers several rocky ledges offering even wider views. The area is rich in history, the first part of the Catskills recognised as a recreational area and known as America's First Wilderness. This was irresistible.

We parked next to North Lake near a small beach and set out in in a mood of cheerful optimism. The climb through the forest on a rocky path between high cliff faces and was fairly tough, but worth every step. When we reached the first viewpoint at Artist's Rock (there was sign identifying the point), a smooth cliff top outlook gave amazing, far-reaching vistas over the Hudson Valley. After a short viewing stop, we set off again, climbing above the precipice to the next point, Sunset Rock, which offered a different but equally stunning view back to the lakes. We moved on following a stoney, sun-dappled forest path to Newman's Ledge before a steep climb to our destination of North Point. We sat there on a large rock and just stared at the view that had unfolded beneath the vivid blue sky, which more than compensated for the rain-soaked hikes of previous days. We dropped down on a different path, stopping just once to admire the beautiful Ashley Falls before reaching Mary's glen and back to North Lake where we sat for an hour just looking and resting our weary limbs.

Although feeling the effects of the seven mile walk and climb, we felt obliged to take advantage of the improved weather and planned another hike the next day, this time to Giant Ledge on Panther Mountain. It was selected because of its name as much as the scenery, another seven-mile mountain trek. It was a long flog to the ledge, on a well-walked forest path, again rewarded with magnificent views from the rock outcrop. Unusually, there were other walkers on the trail and we passed the time of day with a group of young hikers who overtook us. At the ledge, we again chatted to the group and one young lady told us that this was the first time that she had ever been hiking. "...and I bet it won't be the last," I responded.

Her eyes opened wide and her jaw dropped as she answered, "Er...I'm not so sure."

As we trudged down the mountain, my thighs, calves and feet ached to the extent that I felt as if my short legs would give way any moment, but managed to continue to the trailhead without complaint. We had, after all, hiked 15 miles over steep, rough terrain including climbing the equivalent of Scafell Pike, over two days. As I pulled myself into the car, body barely able to move, Sue said, "Strange about that girl not enjoying the hike."

"Shame," I agreed, thinking that I too may never hike again.

In Brio's for our last meal in Phoenicia, the serving staff came to take our order and we suddenly realised that we were being served by *Rosamond* and *Jaimie* from the theatre production. We chatted about how much we had enjoyed the show and ascertained that *Rosamond* had, indeed, attended stage school but *Jaimie*, her real-life boyfriend, had never been on stage before and it had taken much persuasion and cajoling to get him to appear. We didn't say that we thought he was the real star of the show. The couple seemed genuinely impressed and delighted that we had travelled over from Europe to see them act, dance and sing on stage.

I was also pleasantly surprised to see that there was a special offer of a jug of beer at half price, so thought it rude to reject the offer. The jug of Catskill Brewery Devils Path IPA arrived at our table and was somewhat larger than I had imagined, but I manfully finished the ale which gave Sue time to complete her meal with a massive slice of home-made cake. After having another chat and photographs taken with our theatrical heroes, we decided that Sue needed to walk off her extra-large slice of cake and I needed to stagger off my extra-large jug of beer, so we took the longer walk home via High Street, a small semi-residential area on the opposite bank of the Esopus Creek. As we strolled unsteadily along the dark road, our way was suddenly lit up by thousands, perhaps millions of tiny bright lights dancing around us. The fireflies had emerged and performed their frantic but elegant lightshow to accompany us. A fitting end to our stay in the Catskill Mountains.

The 436-mile, seven-hour drive to Geneva-on-the-lake, Ohio is somehow wiped from my memory. I know that we travelled the I-86 West, through northern Pennsylvania, but remember almost nothing of the journey, what we saw on the way or exactly where we stopped. I do remember that we did stop once at a roadside diner which appeared in the middle of nowhere. Our second stop was made somewhere near the city of Erie, on the shores of Lake Erie, our first view of the most southerly of the five Great Lakes, but I remember nothing more than a short walk on the lake shore.

Arriving at the resort was a surreal experience, like time-travelling back to the 1950s and I checked to make sure that the hire car was not a disguised DeLorean. We passed under a large metal arch with the name *Geneva-on-the-Lake* built into the wrought iron structure and an equally large sign announcing, *Thunder on the Strip Sep 4-7*, which bemused us. We continued along Lake Road, known as The Strip, which was lined with one and two storey wooden rustic cabins, small motels, bars and restaurants, all of which looked as if they had been unchanged for over half a century, except for the large, garish signs advertising each business. There were also several vintage American cars parked at the roadside, immaculately restored and maintained. Sue and I were immediately enthralled. We turned into a side street, S Spenser Drive, without getting lost and checked in with our hosts at Beachstone Cottages. We were directed to our cabin which, from the outside, looked a little well-worn and small, but our time-travel adventure continued when we entered and found that it had Tardis-like qualities, large, comfortable and well furnished. As Sue unpacked and snoozed, I sat in the enclosed porch reading guides and maps in preparation for this leg of our travels and again felt relaxed and content. Well done wife, coming up trumps again.

After a rest following the long drive, we went out and wandered along The Strip, soaking up the happy holiday atmosphere and selecting which of the many eating places would be graced with our presence. As the light faded, the bar, restaurant and advertising signs illuminated the street into a bright, brash American adult fairyland. We sauntered up and down, surveying the eating places and were drawn to Eddie's Grill, a typical old-style diner advertising steakburgers, hot dogs, French fries and root beer. In we went and were pleased with the choice as the 1950's ambience continued with its furnishings, even having an old juke box with music from greats like Elvis, Connie Francis, Johnny Tillotson and Bobby Rydell (after whom Rydell High School In *Grease* was named.) Above the counter was a prominent sign with the order, *ENJOY YOUR VACATION*. Sue and I didn't need telling as we sat under a giant cheeseburger fixed to the wall and tucked into *Eddie's famous wings* with a side of *tater tots* and a few bottles of Corona Extra with *Heartaches by the Number* playing in the background.

We walked a similar route the following morning looking for somewhere for breakfast and The Strip had changed. The day was overcast and grey, the neon lights were off and most businesses were closed. Just a few people were out, scurrying to work, heads down or cleaning up after the night's revelries. If streets could have hangovers, then The Strip had a stinker. We headed towards Lake Erie on a side street and came across Mary's Kitchen, a small restaurant which looked just perfect, and indeed it was. It was old-fashioned in terms of décor and, especially, in terms of the service where the waitress was friendly, polite and charming. We sat in the porch area beneath a sign which stated:

BREAKFAST
S.E.R.V.E.D
MON. – FRI, 7:00 A.M.
SAT., SUN. & HOLIDAYS
7:00 A.M.

AMERICANADIAN DIARIES

I whispered, "Just as well that it's Wednesday."

We had decided to spend the day pottering around the area, so explored more of Geneva-on-the-lake than just the strip as it shook off its hangover and came back to life. We stopped at its famous Ferris wheel, sat in an old fire engine and wandered the side streets. We moved on for a walk around Geneva State Park, a quiet oasis after the bustle of the town with acres of beautiful woodland and several areas of freshwater marsh, including Cowles Creek, No Name Creek, and Wheeler Creek, criss-crossed by miles of hiking trails. With no specific route, we just rambled through the wetland, past the small peaceful lakes, spotting a grey heron relaxing in a tree and listening to a bittern booming. We left the park and settled on Breakwater Beach where, uncharacteristically we sat for most of the afternoon gazing over the shimmering waters of Lake Erie.

During my relaxing research on the porch, we discovered yet another train trip which was irresistible, so set off the next day to ride the Cuyahoga Valley Scenic Railroad. We drove south for an hour, passing Cleveland, Ohio to Independence and the station of Rockside, before boarding. The train, which was pulled by a huge diesel engine, took us through the Cuyahoga Valley alongside the rushing Cuyahoga River and several stops on the way with fascinating names including Peninsula, Indigo Lake and Botzum. Arriving at the final stop of Akrom, we had three hours before the return journey and so we set out to walk as much of the Ohio & Erie Canal as time allowed. We found the Towpath Trail with (for us) surprising ease and meandered alongside the historic canal through the Cuyahoga National Park. Our original plan was to follow the well-maintained towpath north to Botzum and catch the return train there but, after over an hour's walk, we realised that we had no idea where we were and may never reach the next station, so returned on the same path back to Akrom. We turned at the site of South Park Village which according to an historic marker was the site of a native American village, excavated in the 19th century and was a centre of Whittlesey culture, an archaeological designation for a Native American people who lived in northeastern Ohio from A.D. 1000 to 1640 A.D. It was an agricultural society growing maize, beans, and squash but, after contact with early European settlers, the population decreased due to disease, malnutrition, and warfare. About 1640, the Whittlesey villages were abandoned and it is not known where or how the inhabitants relocated. This was another sad story of the native peoples which put us in reflective mood for the return trek. We were cheered however, by watching a young deer and a large turkey vulture on a field standing a few feet apart and staring at each other. The stand-off lasted several minutes before the deer backed down and trotted away and the turkey raised its tail feathers in triumph.

Cleveland Ohio is famous as an industrial powerhouse due its position on Lake Erie giving access to Lakes Superior and Huron via the Soo canal. After completion of the Ohio & Erie Canal, the city grew to become Lake Erie's transshipment point for lumber, copper and iron ore, and rail shipments of coal and farm produce. But the most exciting thing for Sue and me was that it is home to the National Rock and Roll Hall of Fame. This was an opportunity we could not miss. Our research also showed that there was a Major League Baseball game arranged, Cleveland Indians versus Detroit Tigers, and we decided to kill two birds with one stone and see both attractions on the same day. We drove the main lake road knowing that we were bound to arrive at the Hall of Fame at North Coast Harbour, and pulled in to the car park with no hitches. We were surprised that the venue closed at 5 o'clock, but calculated that we had plenty of time to take in the Hall of Fame before a half-hour walk to Progressive Field for the baseball's ceremonial first pitch at one o'clock and, assuming a three-hour game, finish at four o'clock, giving plenty of time to get back to the car before five. I was quite proud of my plan.

At the Hall of Fame, we watched the introductory film in the small cinema before beginning our tour of the exhibits of memorabilia from all types of rock culture including gospel, blues, rhythm & blues and folk, country, and bluegrass. Although I was a fan of American music, particularly country, we concentrated on the British bands first with exhibitions covering the Beatles, The Rolling Stones and The Who amongst others. But I'm afraid that I soon tired. There are only so many old guitars and stage outfits in glass cases that an elderly gentleman can look at before preferring a cup of coffee in the café. After a coffee break and mooching around more increasingly monotonous exhibits, it was happily time to leave for the baseball game. It was an easy stroll following East 9th Street all the way until we made it to Progressive Field. As we cut across the car park to the stadium, we passed a rowdy bar, The Thirsty Parrot, an apt name for the noisy, squawking pandemonium of drinkers around the watering hole.

The venue was a most impressive, modern stadium, very different from where had spent much of my sporting life spectating from Stratton Bank at Swindon's County Ground. We had time to spare, so strolled down Rally Alley, a pedestrian street alongside the stadium, busy with the throng of spectators. We and stopped to photograph Sue with two men dressed in old-style baseball kit under a sign reading *Cleveland Blues*, although we didn't understand the connection with the Indians. Inside the stadium we grabbed a hot dog at the *Ballpark Classics* food stall and mooched around the club shop before taking our seats. There was a buzz of expectation inside the arena and we were particularly fascinated by a huge screen at one end under the massive *INDIANS* sign and a banner reading *THIS IS TRIBE TOWN*. Political correctness had thankfully not reached Cleveland.

As the game started, we noticed that the stadium was barely half full. The supporter in the next seat explained that many spectators don't bother with the first couple of innings, preferring to arrive late when the action has warmed up. When it did start, the atmosphere was exhilarating as the pitcher wound himself up, both figuratively and literally, before releasing a 100-mph hard ball at the batter. The batter swung his bat and, if he connected, we heard a loud click a second later as he scampered away and slide tackled a little cushion. I was a little confused who was batting and who was bowling and how many runs were scored, but kept a keen eye on the big screen which told me that the Tigers were winning two nil after the first innings. Despite lots of pitching, batting and cushion tackling, it was still two nil after the third innings when it started to rain very heavily and the game stopped. As many spectators made for the cover of the food hall area, I confidently told Sue it was only a shower and would soon pass. I was wrong. We were soaked and were soon squeezing into the covered stand with our fellow spectators. By the time that the rain stopped and the game restarted, we realised that we could not stay to the end or our car may be locked in the car park at the R and R Hall of Fame. And we were dripping wet, so decided that we should reluctantly leave the ball game unfinished. It was shame, but we had thoroughly enjoyed the visit anyway and, to be honest, did not care who won.

In need of exercise after four days of relative inactivity, we made the short drive to Ashtabula for a brisk walk on the 42-mile Western Reserve Greenway Trail. We chose this walk, not only because it promised an interesting route, but because it was a section of the Underground Railroad, a network of secret routes and safe houses used by escaping African enslaved people seeking refuge in Canada. The route was uncomplicated, following a level, paved road through attractive woodland and we maintained a brisk but steady pace, which helped to alleviate the fatigue that had started to set in. We walked for about two miles, stopping to read several interpretive notices on the way, before turning and making the return journey. It didn't match our Catskill Mountain hikes for effort or scenery, but was an ideal way of burning off a little of Eddie's grills and Mary's breakfasts.

We still had most of the afternoon, so moved on to Indian Trails Park, a wildlife area surrounding the Ashtabula River. We dropped down a steep incline in the river valley and played ducks and drakes, skimming stones across the water. We held the World Skimming Championship which Sue won with a stone making nine skims or bounces, although I tried unsuccessfully to disqualify her for an illegal skim action but had to withdraw my objection and settle for the silver medal. We clambered up on to the road and strolled through the Smolen–Gulf bridge over the river, at 613 feet the longest covered bridge in America. We followed this visit by moving on to Liberty Street and the shortest Covered Bridge in America. I boasted that not many British people can boast that they have achieved the feat of visiting both the longest and shortest covered bridges in America. Whilst at the bridge we met a couple who asked that I take their photograph standing in front of Liberty Bridge. During the subsequent conversation, the couple explained that there are 125 covered bridges in Ohio and they are visiting and photographing each one. Neither Sue nor I could think of anything to say.

During our wanders along The Strip, we had seen many bikers and had learnt that it was favourite destination for motorcyclists, most of whom seemed fifty years old with unkempt beards, pot bellies and bad dress sense, dressed in old leather waistcoats and greasy jeans. We had also learnt the Thunder on the Strip was an annual event when bikers from all over the country gather there to compare bikes and beards and drink too much beer. We were not prepared for the Sunday however, when we returned from a gentle walk in the sunshine at the State Park and along the beaches of Lake Erie to see the whole Strip crowded with leather-clad mid-lifers with shining motorcycles in every parking bay. Every bar was full of bikers, particularly The Pavillion Restaurant which had a long balcony packed with bikers, its downstairs bar and patio area were also packed with bikers and, from the balcony, a banner was displayed announcing *We love Bikers*, which was just as well. As we passed one open air bar, we stopped to look at the array of shining motorcycles, when one big, bearded, bald, leather-clad motorcyclist shouted something we did not understand and the whole pack burst into laughter. I smiled and waved which caused more hilarity but I never discovered the source of their amusement.

The weather took a turn for the worse and we had constant showers, so our outings were restricted by staying close to home, but we had interesting walks on the lakeside and surrounding wildlife areas. Oddly, the weather always cleared in the evenings and our itinerary included visiting a bar overlooking the lake and watching the sun set over the water. The one exception to our customary evening was when England played Costa Rica in a World Cup game. Sue stayed in our cabin while I sat in a large outdoor sports bar, completely alone except for the bored bartender, watching the game and sipping a few Budweisers. The rain was drumming on the gazebo roof, it was cold and the game was an awful no score draw. It was little wonder that the few Americans who passed by looked at me as if I was an insane alien, which I suppose I was.

We spent our last day in Ohio wandering around the small city of Geneva (not on the lake) which was much like any other small American community with some exceptions. On a wall there was a display labelled, *History of the American Flag*, which displayed twenty-seven Old Glories, the Stars and Stripes, at first glance identical. On closer examination, the number of stars changed with the inclusion of each new state, but it was still a very odd exhibition. Another wall displayed eight plaques under the heading Preserving History, commemorating conflicts from the Revolutionary War of 1776 through to the Spanish American War of 1898, but stopped there for some reason ignoring both World Wars and the Korean War, which we thought odd.

Even stranger was that we read that, on April 12, 1966, the city claimed ownership of the moon. The Declaration of Lunar Ownership was announced simultaneously with the city's 100th anniversary and claimed that … "the physical property of the moon shall belong exclusively to the citizens of Geneva, Ohio." Geneva also held an annual Grape Jamboree but it was unclear if the two things were connected.

AMERICANADIAN DIARIES

As we left the Geneva-on -the Lake and the 1950's to continue our journey, the banner under the town sign now read, *RIBS ON THE STRIP*, and we never did find out what that was about.

North of the Catskills is another mountain range, the Adirondacks, the largest national park in the USA and the same size as Yellowstone, Yosemite, Grand Canyon, Glacier and Great Smoky Mountains national parks combined. It is perhaps most well-known as the home of Lake Placid, host to the 1980 Winter Olympics and our next destination. We drove north on the I-90, following the eastern shore of Lake Erie, then east at Buffalo, past Rochester and north on the I-81 at Syracuse before the final leg turning east on State Route 3 to Saranac Lake. It was a long, eight-hour, 500-mile drive but quite relaxing on the excellent American Roads with little traffic. We stopped just once for coffee, at Herrings in the Black River Recreational Area, before arriving at Amanda's Village Motel, Saranac Lake, tired but happily looking forward to more mountain adventures. The motel was perfect, a typical *Mom and Pop* establishment, family run and friendly, with small but tidy wooden cabins and views across a small park to Lake Flower. We were welcomed by the motel's owners, Joe and Edie, who were great hosts and spent some time with us, offering advice on where to go what to see and, most importantly, where to eat. Edie also proudly explained that Joe made the best coffee in America and we were welcome to cups of the nectar every morning from reception.

Hungry after the drive, we walked into the town and found the recommended restaurant, the Downhill Grill. It looked as good, or better, than our hosts had described, a smart diner offering the best that American dining can offer – tidy and spacious with comfortable private booths and a menu which had dishes we had never heard of. It made it difficult to choose between Classic Reuben, Chipotle Chicken or Chimichanga when we had no idea what they were. The only drawback was that the food was geared towards gargantuan American appetites and tasted too good to leave, so left us waddling home like pregnant ducks. In the morning, I drifted into the motel reception while Sue was getting dressed and accepted the offer of two cups of the best coffee in America. Joe modestly delivered the beverages and chatted amicably about other English guests they had had and told us more about the area. By the time I escaped, the coffee had cooled and Sue was unimpressed. Not only was it lukewarm but far too strong and very bitter, probably the worst coffee in America. Strangely, because Joe was so nice I repeated the process for the following three mornings, collecting the coffee from reception and chatting to Joe, taking the drinks back to our room and pouring them down the sink. On that first morning, we also used another of our hosts' recommendations for breakfast, but were very disappointed. We had to wait to be seated for far too long, the service was poor, the serving staff surly and, most unusually, the food was less than perfect, so this was immediately crossed off our list of repeat visits

Still recovering from the long drive the day before, we decided not to drive but explore the immediate area around Saranac Lake so set out for a walk around Lake Flower and its big sister, Oseetah Lake. It was easy walking, but we broke one of my golden rules and set out without a map, so had little idea where we were, although I was confident that we were close enough to our base not to be completely lost. Starting at the pristine park and boat launch area at lakeside we were soon in the wilderness area around the lakes. The ground was boggy in places and some paths ended up in marshland meaning that we had to retrace our steps several times, and it rained. But getting wet with muddy boots and soggy, cold clothing was a small price to pay for the peace and tranquillity, the views over the lakes and general feelings of contentment that the hike brought. The one small fly in the ointment was that Sue had spotted a shopping mall the previous day and insisted that we needed provisions for the stay, so we had to make our way to the stores afterwards. I satisfied myself with looking at an old Cadillac in the car park whilst Sue shopped, and I never asked what, if anything, she bought.

During our exploration we had noticed a large restaurant on the edge of town, the A-1 Buffet and Sushi, not exactly American Home Cooking, but probably more suited to our limited appetites, so we settled there for the evening. In the centre of the restaurant was a 20-foot-long wooden boat with a massive figurehead of a swan or possibly a goose, it was hard to tell, inside of which were hot plates containing every Oriental dish imaginable. In another area was a selection of western meals from steaks to chicken to pork, burgers and chips. It was a stunning collection of culinary delights but the most delightful thing was that it was another all you can eat offering. For a reasonable charge, customers could take any amount of any food or mixtures of food until they exploded. Some of the other diners looked as if they were just about to do so. The following morning our breakfast disappointment was soon repaired when we found a small diner on the edge of town. It was on the ground floor of a red brick, three story building which had no name, just a sign that read *Home Cooking and Breakfast*. As soon as we entered the café, we were smitten. It was a basic, homely dining room which held just half a dozen small wooden tables, seated at two of which were elderly, rough looking mountain men in dungarees who smiled a welcoming greeting as we arrived. We sat at a spare table, and the lone server gave a broad smile and said, "Hi. What can I get you guys?" The full American breakfast was irresistible and superb, the people friendly and it just felt right. That was our dining venues resolved for our stay: the unnamed café for a friendly atmosphere with a tasty, unhealthy breakfast and all we could eat for dinner...and pray that we didn't explode.

A stay in the area would be incomplete without visiting Lake Placid, so we set off on the NY-86 East to the famous ski area. The actual ski runs were some miles north of the city at the whiteface mountain ski resort, which did not hold much interest to us. We had lived near the ski resorts in Granada, Spain and had visited them many times so we guessed that the village was likely to be dead at that time of year, but we wanted to see the ski jump area just outside of the city. On the way, we noticed an historic marker directing us to John Brown's Farm and swerved off the main road to see what was there. As we travelled down the narrow road to the small settlement of North Elba and the farm, I was loudly singing, "Glory Glory Hallelujah," hoping that this John Brown was the famous abolitionist who campaigned against slavery prior to the American Civil War. It was a chance find, but one that had a remarkable and profound effect on us both. The park was, indeed, that John Browns's home, beautifully maintained with manicured lawns, a pristine sparkling blue lake and his superbly renovated home, the entire site giving wonderful views of the surrounding woodland and mountains. We were excited that we found his actual grave and, as we approached, I was still merrily singing, "John Brown's body lies a mouldering in the grave and his soul goes marching on." We read the inscription on his grave. It explained that he was so much more than just an abolitionist. He had led an anti-slavery group and, "*...took an active part in the contest against the pro-slavery* *party. He gained in August 1856 a victory at Osawatomie over a superior number of Missourians who had invaded Kansas (whence his surname "Osawatomie") He conceived the idea of becoming a liberator of the negro slaves in the south and on the night of October 16, 1859 at the head of a devoted band of 22 followers he seized the United States Arsenal at Harper's Ferry, Virginia with the view of arming the negroes who might come to his fortified camp. In the fight with United States troops and civilians which followed he was overpowered and taken prisoner October 18, 1859, was tried by the commonwealth of Virginia at Charlestown, Virginia and executed December 2, 1859."*

He was then buried here with twelve of his followers, after his body was moved by his family from Charlestown, eight hundred miles to his home for interment. I stopped my silly singing as the words caught in my throat, and felt both embarrassed and irreverent. Sue held my hand and gave it a gentle squeeze as we stood, heads bowed in deference to a truly great man.

We continued our visit, passing a statue of John Brown with his hand on the shoulder of young black boy, representing the slaves that he had given his life to free, and on to a tour of his home. It was a simple two-storey, wooden home with wood floors and walls and simple wooden furniture. Whenever possible, Sue and I avoid conducted tours, but sometimes they are unavoidable and here I was glad that we listened to John Browns' story in more detail, sympathetically elucidated by an excellent guide. As we left the site and moved on, we drove in silence, each deep in our own thoughts of what we had just experienced. And I didn't sing again.

AMERICANADIAN DIARIES

Just 200 yards along John Brown Road, we found the clearly signposted turning to the Olympic Ski Jump Complex. We followed the signs, passing a kiosk with the entry fees posted outside. The kiosk was empty, so we ignored the ticket machines, assuming that it was free entry that day for English visitors and entered the centre. We climbed to the top of the ski jump and stood on the viewing platform looking down at the almost vertical jumping ramp which the contestants ski down before throwing themselves into the air for some 200 yards, hopefully landing safely after dropping almost 400 feet. It was incomprehensible madness to us mere mortals. As we looked down, we could see several youngsters sliding down the landing slope on plastic trays, another feat of madness in my eyes. We took the short, 45-second gondola ride down the hill and back up again, wary in case we had to show our non-existent entry ticket, and stood on the Olympic winner's rostrum, Sue selecting the gold medal position of course as she had, after all, won gold at the World Skimming Championship. We also studied a ten feet high poster, showing how the jump suits had evolved over the years, with one suit modelled by the unmistakeable figure of Eddie the Eagle Edwards. We thought it strange that Eddie had evolved from being possibly the worst Olympic ski jumper ever to being a poster boy for the event. It made us proud to be British.

We spent most of the afternoon mooching around the city of Lake Placid, which was a typical holiday town akin to Weymouth, with a mix of local and tourist shops, a pleasant interlude but fairly unremarkable except for a trio of scruffy, grubby, bearded young men busking on the sidewalk, playing excellent Bluegrass music. They were enthusiastic and talented, so good that I uncharacteristically gave them five dollars, which surprised Sue and me. I hoped that they spent the money on soap.

We were ready for a long walk in the Adirondacks and chose St. Regis Mountain, a four-mile hike located in the St. Regis Canoe Area. We arrived at the trailhead early on a bright sunny day and, after first signing the book to alert people of our presence, set off crossing a wooden bridge over the St. Regis River and through mature pine forests passing many towering boulders and huge, mossy cliffs, which, Sue informed me, were glacial erratics, and weaving our way through a hardwood forest of large white pine, hemlock, and maple trees. It was a gentle, easy climb until we crossed a bridge over a small, rocky stream, when the trail became very steep including a short stone staircase. Our legs ached as we pushed on to the summit squeezing between huge rock walls until we reached a scenic overlook and the main trail to the summit. It was an open, rocky area where we sat and rested gazing over views of Loon Lake Mountain to the north and Matumbla and Mt. Arab to the south. There was also an old iron fire tower and we wanted to climb 100 feet to its top, but the steps started halfway up and there was no way that we could see to reach it. To be honest, I found this a relief. We took our time on the descent, spotting several garter snakes on the track, a big, mottled toad hiding in the rocks and impressively huge bracket fungus on the trees, small incidents which added to our joyful, if tiring, day.

Our legs still suffering a little, we decided that we would ignore mountains and settle for exploring the McKenzie Mountain Wilderness the following day, mainly because it is my sister's married name, which I accept was an odd reason. We found the trailhead for the area and again signed in before beginning our leisurely walk. But the stroll soon turned into another mountain hike as we could not resist the challenge of climbing McKenzie Mountain. Again, we hiked through wonderful forests, over boulder-strewn brooks and up rocky pathways until we reached the McKenzie Mountain Summit sign nailed to a tree. The peak led to large open cliffs and outcrops, providing stunning views of Saranac Lake, Baker Mountain and Lake Flower, nestled among the forests in the distance. On the descent, with our old legs complaining, we vowed that we would stay on lower ground the next day.

Studying my maps as I sat on the porch at Amanda's, drinking a beer and smoking a well-earned cigarillo, I noticed the Sentinel Range Wildlife Area, a lower lying park with five small lakes and an ideal location for a more comfortable stroll. Map at the ready, off we set and soon found the trail head to begin our walk to Owen Pond. It was a perfect stroll after the previous days' exertions, on muddy paths and boardwalks, highlighted by meeting hundreds of beautiful white admiral butterflies on the path at one point. We stopped and looked in amazement as the handsome creatures carpeted the track, their wings moving gently as they opened and closed. We walked slowly and carefully through the kaleidoscope of lepidoptera as they fluttered all around us, creating a magical moment. A little further on, we were greeted by a chorus of frogs, croaking and belching in a synchronised chorus, which stopped immediately as came into view. We failed in our mission to circumnavigate the pretty lake as, after clambering over fallen trees and passing under sheer cliffs of Kilburn Mountain, we met a marshy bog, impossible to traverse on foot. We were not at all disappointed as we retreated and retraced our steps on the same track, as the hike was the idyllic antidote to recover from our mountain adventures.

AMERICANADIAN DIARIES

Whiteface Mountain, home of the 1980 Olympic skiing competitions is almost 5000 feet and known as one of the High Peaks of the Adirondack Mountains. We read that the summit offers a 360-degree view of the Adirondacks and, on a clear-day, glimpses of Vermont and Canada. That was a narrative that we could not miss and was our target for out last day in the area. The choice was also helped by the fact that there was the Cloudsplitter gondola ride to the summit. Although there are many eight-seater gondolas travelling continuously up the mountain, we shared one with just two other passengers, remarkably another young Japanese couple who again sat stock still, holding on the sides of the cabin and staring straight ahead. Despite my attempts to engage in conversation, they did not react and looked terrified. The gondola rose for fifteen minutes and did, indeed, seem to split the cloud as we left a clear base and travelled through one cloud layer before the vistas reopened. Then we hit another cloud layer, so thick that when we left the car at the top of the mountain, we could barely see each other, let alone the far-reaching views. We stumbled about at the summit for a while before admitting that we were unlikely to see New York State and certainly not Vermont through the thick encompassing cloud, so decided to descend. Our Japanese friends didn't join us on the descent and we presumed that they were lost somewhere in the clouds looking for Canada. We had travelled for perhaps two or three minutes when the Gondola stopped, leaving us swinging in the air for several minutes. Of course, I was very brave in telling Sue not to worry as everything was alright, whilst simultaneously almost peeing myself with fear, before there was a loud clunk and we continued our smooth journey down.

AMERICANADIAN DIARIES

On the road back to Saranac Lake we noticed a recreation area with a prominent sign on the building which read, *High Falls Gorge*. I had missed this during my research of the area, but pulled into the parking lot anyway. It turned out to be a worthwhile stop where we could *Witness History at The Ancient Valley of Foaming Water*. The gorge is an impressive, deep crevice carved by the Ausable River over many thousands of years. Native Americans gave High Falls Gorge the name The Ancient Valley of Foaming Water, due to the natural foam that develops from the waterfalls tumbling through the narrow ravine. On the gorge side were steel walkways, giving access to the plummeting waters, fed from the main falls, past Mini and Rainbow Falls to Climax Falls. I liked the idea of visiting Climax Falls. The walkway had viewing platforms with glass floors which offered an exciting perspective over the crashing waters. An added attraction was the one-mile nature trail through Climax Forest, one of the few remaining virgin forests in the Adirondacks, and one we could not resist. It was such a splendid stop that I pretended that I had planned it all along but saved it for Sue as surprise as we should reach Climax together. Why do women always know when a man is lying?

That evening, our last in Saranac Lake, we decided to return to the Downhill Grill, and were ruminating over our visit, specifically, why on two lovely lake walks and two stiff but exciting mountain hikes, we had not seen another person. Yet this was a vacation resort, so again wondered what the American holidaymakers do with their time. We then looked around the packed restaurant at many stout diners, ploughing through plates loaded with stacked, six-inch high burgers supplemented with enormous sides of fries and onion rings and our question was answered.

AMERICANADIAN DIARIES

Rhode Island is famed as the smallest of the fifty American states and is not an island, but is close enough to New Jersey to make it a convenient last stop on this exploration. The five-hour drive was a delight, a bright sunny day and virtually no other traffic as we headed south on the I-90 following the Hudson River, passing Fort William Henry (featured in the Last of the Mohicans,) through Saratoga Springs (famous for horse racing,) past Albany (capital city of New York State) and into Massachusetts, through Springfield, where we called in for lunch at the Fifties Diner, which was unsurprisingly decorated just like a typical fifties diner and where we hoped to see The Simpsons but they weren't there. We turned onto the I-95, into Rhode Island, past Providence to the Super 8 in West Greenwich. The actual location of the motel is a suburb of West Greenwich called Nooseneck, which I found quite appealing, although I was later told that this was not named after the infamous lynching that I had invented.

On the way to our new billet, we had passed a Denny's, a restaurant chain I had used in Texas when working, but was surprised when Sue said that we had never visited a Denny's as a couple. What sort of husband was I who had never treated his wife to the Denny's experience? I vowed to correct this oversight. The diner was just as I had remembered and Sue was not disappointed as we perused the menu of typical American fare with *Country-Fried Steak, Fried Fish Platter* and my favourite, *Plate Lickin' Chicken Fried Chicken*. Dinner was sorted for the next few days.

We spent the next day in relaxed explorer mode, travelling the few miles to the historic town of East Greenwich, where we meandered alongside Greenwich Cove, an inlet of Greenwich Bay, itself an extension of Narragansett Bay, stopping to gaze over the water from a boat launch, before wandering into the town. Main Street was almost like a film set for a typical small town, with any number of cafes, antique shops, galleries, convenience stores, bag shops, shoe shops, jewellery shops, nicknack shops and flower shops. Sue's shop craving satisfied and getting overheated (perhaps at the thought of spending money in my case), we stopped in a small café for a drink and, unusually, ordered a glass of lemonade and a Coca Cola. We sat outside in the sun, refreshed with the sugary mixtures but, as we got up to leave, the waitress approached us and asked, "Don't you want a refill?"

We replied that we had had enough thank you, when our server pointed at a sign that said *Free Refills* and exclaimed, "But it's free refills."

"No thanks," we affirmed, "we're fine."

She looked astonished and repeated, "But refills are free," again pointing at the sign that said *Free Refills*.

We shook our heads and repeated that we were full, thank you, and wandered off, with the waitress left standing looking first at us, then our empty glasses, then the sign and shaking her head in apparent disbelief.

We spent the afternoon at Narraganset beach. We strolled along the boardwalk, paddled in the warm waters and watched the locals queuing at the burger van. Following the lemonade/Coca Cola incident, we thought it better to avoid embarrassment and ignore the van which advertised *New England Frozen Lemonade – All Natural Slush*, for fear of upsetting the vendor and which did not sound too appealing anyway. We remarked that the town and adjacent beaches were reminiscent of the smaller, timeless seaside resorts of North

Devon or the Gower Peninsula in South Wales and we felt relaxed and almost content, but aching for a long walk.

Block island is a small island, a little smaller than the Isle of Wight, situated twelve miles off the southern end of Rhode Island and close to New York's Long Island. It promised excellent hiking trails on The Greenway, rolling hills, stunning vistas and amazing wildlife. And it was a short boat trip to get there, so we rushed to the ferry port at Point Judith, Narragansett, just in time to catch the boat across Block Island Sound to New Shoreham, Block Island. The day was warm, the skies were blue and the sea was calm as we relaxed on the hour-long cruise, enjoying a coffee on board as Rhode Island slipped from view. We disembarked at New Shoreham and set out along High Street passing interesting, and occasionally grand, colonial houses before turning off onto a small dusty lane through the countryside. We turned again onto a smaller, dustier road before reaching The Greenway, a series of linked footpaths and trails across the island. The countryside was very green with gentle rolling hills and meadows of wild flowers separated by lush hedgerows. We could almost have been walking on the Wiltshire Downs. We soon reached our main objective, the smooth and tranquil Fresh Pond, a small blue oasis nestling amongst the lush, undulating fields. We came across a historic marker explaining that this was one of the very early European settlements, with the settlers living in caves and rustic shelters before they claimed land and began building permanent homes and their first church in 1772. We strolled along the trail around the lake, stopping for a picnic and watching thousands of tadpoles swarming at the water's edge, before moving on to Rodman's hollow, a glacial outwash basin and the first conservation area on Block Island, although to me it looked like just another field, pretty but unremarkable. On our return to the harbour at New Shoreham, we were relaxed and happy, tired and thirsty so we debated whether to slake our thirst at one of the many ice cream parlours or relax at the Water Street Inn. Unsurprisingly, beer beats ice cream every time, so the inn it was.

In Denny's that evening, we were planning the next day, July fourth, Independence Day, and wanted to find a small town to join in with the celebrations. Our waitress suggested two options, the main parade in the island capital, Providence, or a smaller party in a nearby village. We were also informed that the village was a hotbed for supporters of independence during the Revolutionary War. This augured well and we decided that we would prefer the modest, home-spun, revolutionary attraction, so set out in the morning for Chapechet, Glocester. We arrived in the village to find nothing apart from a few flags decorating the main street and wondered if we had made the right choice, but carried on. As we exited the village, we noticed a hive of activity in a field just off the road and pulled in to see what was happening. Here was a chaotic scene with many trucks and trailers being decorated, people milling about in 18th century dress, soldiers smoking and drinking beer and children running around in fancy dress, all to a cacophony of trumpets and drums. We met a gentleman at the entrance who explained that the townsfolk were preparing for the parade here and it was due to leave the area in about half an hour to parade through the town, so we beat a retreat and returned to Main Street. We found a car park just off Main Street, behind the Glocester Town Hall, strangely empty, where we parked in readiness for the festivities. It rained. Not just a shower, but a tropical storm as rain crashed down, flooding the car park and reducing visibility to a few feet. After about half an hour of sitting marooned in the car, the rain eased and we could hear the sound of distant drums, so we abandoned our vehicle and splashed across the car park to the street, finding refuge under the forecourt of a nearby petrol station, opposite the Chepachet Volunteer Fire Station.

The rain was now slight and the sidewalk began to fill with local residents taking up their places to view the carnival, some settling down with picnic tables and chairs and an air of excited expectation. Next to the petrol station, a group of men had set up a beer tent, which immediately grabbed my attention. Soon, the parade came into view and began its march past. It was an enthralling spectacle, led by a small squad of soldiers in combat gear, followed by a group dressed as revolutionary soldiers with rifles shouldered, a pipe band of ladies in 18th century costume and a Scottish pipe band, the Fife and Drums Corps, in full Scottish regalia and with bagpipes wailing. There were old and new trucks decorated with stars and stripes, a lone plump cheerleader tossing her big stick as she marched, a brass band, various groups dancing along in fancy dress, many floats, one decorated as settler homesteads by the Chepachet Union Church and towing a sinking ship. One float carried prisoners in gaol with a banner reading ~~MAYOR~~ *PRINCE OF PROVIDENCE*, which we didn't understand. The parade was concluded by several fire engines with their sirens blaring, at which time we slowly concluded our visit by wandering over the route of the parade as the locals stayed put with their picnics. I approached the men in the beer tent and wished them a good day. One asked me where I was from and, on my reply of, "England," said, "You got some balls coming here today," and gave me a beer. The men also explained that this was known as the Ancients and Horribles Parade, but none could explain the reason for the sobriquet.

Our decision to visit Chepachet was vindicated and a wonderful way to conclude our tour of the New York area, although we had one last visit the following day to the seaside at Newport. We took the two-mile cliff walk along Memorial Boulevard, before we set out for the Newark Liberty International Airport and our flight home, wondering if we could ever match such a wonderful road trip in the United States of America.

AMERICANADIAN DIARIES

CHAPTER 12 – DIXIE

It didn't take Sue and me long to make up our minds that we would make one more road trip in our beloved USA. We set out simple rules for the trip. Again, it had to be a direct flight from Lisbon and somewhere we had not explored before, which left us with just one realistic option. We would fly to Miami, Florida and plan our route from there. We studied road maps, interrogated the Internet, argued and debated the options, but I was adamant that we should see the Mississippi River, something I had wanted since reading the Adventures of Tom Sawyer as a lad, and include New Orleans because it sounded so exciting, before agreeing and sketching out a rough plan. We would take a couple of days to recuperate in Miami before driving across Florida to the state's west coast, move on to Alabama, Mississippi and Louisiana, returning to Miami by a circuitous route. The plan agreed, I then left Sue to do the easy job again and focus on each proposed stop and identify the most suitable location, review that location and select a specific area, study that area and decide how long to stay there, find suitable accommodation within our limited budget, determine suitable dates to travel accounting for weather and avoiding peak holiday seasons. And arrange the flights and car hire. I continued to support her with words of encouragement.

We followed our previous routine of staying overnight in Lisbon before flying to Miami, feeling fresh and enthusiastic on arrival after a trouble-free journey. The trouble would come later. After picking up the hire car we set out for Homestead, a Miami suburb and agricultural area situated between Biscayne National Park to the east and Everglades National Park to the west. And the name sounded like a gentle rural retreat. And there was a Super 8 motel. Perfect.

It was also a simple thirty-mile drive south from the airport on the Florida Turnpike, so we set out in buoyant mood. As we entered Homestead we turned right and soon spotted the Super 8 across the dual carriageway to our left and turned off on to the feeder road, where we again spotted the motel, still on our left, so we turned left again, and again as we circled our destination four times without finding the access road. We finally stopped at a Krispy Kreme for a coffee and asked the way. The young serving lady looked bemused and pointed out the café window and said, "It's just there, look," before we explained that we knew where it was but couldn't find it. She stared at us, stared out of the window and repeated that it was, "Just there, look," finally pointing out the adjacent road which led to the motel's entrance. She walked away shaking her head. We left the Krispy Kreme and somehow managed to follow her direction of "Over there" and arrived at the Super 8, somewhat embarrassed at our (my) lack of navigation skills. The motel was fine and we had spotted an Applebee's restaurant next to the Krispy Kreme, so our evening meal venue was set.

AMERICANADIAN DIARIES

We settled in to our Super 8 room and it was a fine autumnal evening so we decided to walk to the restaurant, which meant that I could not embarrass myself again by touring the neighbourhood by car in search of the hotel on our return. Applebee's is a chain of typical American diners, so typical that we could equally have been in a Denny's, iHop or Bob Evans and not noticed the difference. Even the food offering was largely similar with handcrafted burgers, huge steaks, double-glazed ribs and chicken tenders appearing large and, of course, fries with everything. We loved it. Replete from an excess of meat and, in my case, Budweiser we set out on the ten-minute stroll back to our billet in the dark. As we turned the corner a few yards from the motel entrance, a big four-by-four motor pulled up alongside and an Asian lady leaned out of the vehicle's window and screamed, "What are you doing walking here? This place is dangerous. Someone was stabbed to death just yesterday on this corner. Run back to your hotel straight away and make sure you lock the door." With that, she closed the window and put her foot down hard on the accelerator and roared away. We were naturally a little shocked and hurried the last few yards back to the motel. The motel reception was open so we called in and related the experience to the receptionist, who listened patiently and added, "That was good advice." It was later that we found out that Homestead, despite its pleasant and appealing name, has the highest crime rate in Florida and one of the highest in the USA. And our dice with death did not end that night.

In the morning, we strolled across the motel parking lot to the dining room, keeping a careful look out for homicidal criminals on the way, and settled on a table near the door ready to make a quick exit should we be held up by marauding bandits. Everyone inside appeared friendly as we took our seats and nodded greetings to our fellow diners. I went to the coffee machine and began pouring two drinks and said good morning to a large young man of mixed race. He replied, "Are you guys English?"

I answered that I was and he immediately went into a bizarre speech about the evils of our home country, specifically ranting, "Did you know that your queen kills babies and eats their brains?"

I tried to laugh this off saying that it was complete nonsense, but he became more animated, loudly telling me, "It is true! It's on the Internet. And Pastor Elijah told us so and he talks directly to God hisself."

I nervously replied that I did not believe in any of this religious nonsense and hurriedly made my way back to our table with the coffees and bagels. As Sue and I began our meal, the young man was talking to his companions and pointing in our direction. A woman from the group then stood up and shouted loudly, "We have non-believers amongst us," and pointed at us across the room. She continued the haranguing as the other diners stared in our direction, most with looks of embarrassed uneasiness. I grabbed the coffees and Sue and we made for the door, escaping back to our room and eating breakfast with the blinds down and the door securely locked.

Our nerves settled after eating, we were relieved to see a small bus emblazoned with *Christ is The Way* and *Jesus Saves* pulling out of the car park and hopefully leaving us in safety, so we cautiously left the motel and took the short drive to the Everglades national Park, a few miles to the west. We were excited about exploring the vast subtropical wetland ecosystem with its River of Grass formed by sawgrass marshes and mangroves. It also offered the opportunity to see exotic wildlife being home to the Florida panther, bobcats, and black bears as well as a vast array of birds including herons, egrets, bald eagles and osprey, but the real thrill of the area is the abundance of alligators and crocodiles.

At the park entrance we stopped at the Ernest Coe Visitor Center, named after a local naturalist and environmentalist, who spent his later years working to promote the Everglades to National Park status. We spent a happy hour watching wildlife films, studying maps, reading leaflets and listening to plump Americans asking park rangers if there was a Wendy's in the park. After absorbing as much information as our brain storage could cope with, we moved on into the park and Royal Palm Visitor Center. This centre was smaller and less well-equipped, but offered the gateway to the wildlife areas with trails leading into the wilderness. We eased ourselves in to the area with the half mile Anhinga Trail, a boardwalk over Taylor Slough, a freshwater sawgrass marsh. We had read that the anhinga, after which trail was named, is a cormorant-like bird, also called the snakebird, darter or water turkey and is abundant in the area. As we stepped onto the boardwalk, an anhinga was perched, balanced on its huge, webbed feet on the wooden railing no more than a foot or two away from us, its head cocked to one side and completely unperturbed by our presence. What a start to our short stroll. As we moved on through the mangrove swamp, we the spotted a grey heron, an ibis and our first alligator, bathing motionless under the water with just its eyes and snout above in the air. This was a magic moment, which would be oft repeated in the following days.

AMERICANADIAN DIARIES

Returning to the visitor centre, we followed a second path, the Gumbo Limbo Trail, a paved path which meanders through a shaded, jungle-like forest of gumbo limbo trees, royal palms, ferns, and air plants. It was an easy stroll and we were fascinated by the odd-looking gumbo limbo tree, with its thick branches spreading in all directions like a manic red octopus. It was amusing to read that that the red, peeling bark resembles the skin of a sunburned visitor, hence its nickname, the tourist tree. Sue was even more fascinated by the air plants, looking like straggly green beards which attach themselves to the trees and feed solely by absorbing water and nutrients from the air, rain, and dew. Happily, we never found a Wendy's.

In the afternoon, we took the short drive through the Everglades, along the Main Park Road to Flamingo Bay, where we wandered along the coastline and took a short and peaceful boat trip in Florida Bay. It seemed the perfect end to the almost perfect day, all thoughts of being murdered by religious nutcases a distant memory. Except that we made sure that we drove to Applebee's for dinner that night.

Since reading *A Farewell to Arms*, written by Ernest Hemingway, I had long been fascinated by Key West on the Florida Keys where the author lived and drank heavily with his group of writers and artists. I convinced Sue that it was worth the three-hour drive along the Florida Keys to soak up the artistic atmosphere of the town, and she reluctantly agreed. After almost an hour's driving on the Overseas Highway, crossing the sea between several islands via impressive bridges, we reached Key Largo, almost unknown pre-Trump, and saw a sign for Coral reef State Park. Sue suggested that we pull off for a short break and visit the park. We arrived at a visitor centre and car park where we were greeted by eight beautiful white ibis nonchalantly pecking around a small grassy area, their long, curved beaks stabbing into the well-watered ground, presumably feasting on some small unsuspecting creatures living there. This was an exciting start but there was more to come. As we moved on, we were treated to the sight of a large iguana, the size of a well-built bulldog, which crossed our path and waddled into nearby trees. Animated by the animals, we meandered on and found three walks signposted, The Wild Tamarind Trail, the Grove Trail and the Mangrove Trail. Not being particularly interested in fruit trees, we set out on the Mangrove trail, which led us deep into the swamp, finding our way along boardwalks and narrow paths through a tunnel of mangrove roots and the occasional gumbo limbo tree. It was short but fascinating hike and, as Sue happily picked her way through the dense mangroves, I had the distinct feeling that I had been conned, a notion confirmed when Sue suggested that we take our picnic lunch to the nearby Far Beech and rest awhile. The "awhile" took the rest of the afternoon as we sat on the almost deserted beach and explored the surrounding coastline, scrambling over the pebbly shore and watching more ibis stabbing small creatures amongst the rocks. It became obvious that we would not have time to reach Key West and Mr. Hemingway's home town would have to wait until another day, which never came.

We were so enamoured with the state park that we drove north the following day for the Shark Valley Visitor Center. Why it was called Shark Valley was mystery as it is as far from sea as it is possible to be in southern Florida, but we later learnt that it was because of its proximity to the Shark River Slough, which flows into the Shark River, which derives its name from the fact that sharks give birth to their young in the river. We immediately took the Bobcat Boardwalk Trail, an easy stroll through sawgrass slough and tropical hardwood forests, which promised great views of local wildlife, and we were not disappointed as an alligator swam towards us before deciding that we were not worth eating, turned and swam back to the shade of a tree. Just as exciting was finding a massive spider with very long black and yellow legs, resting in its web in the sun. We later identified the arachnid as a golden silk orb weaver, also known as a banana spider in Florida, and a venomous beast. Perhaps I should not have stroked it to make it move.

Returning to the visitor centre, we debated whether to try another hike or catch the Shark Valley Tram tour. The debate lasted about five seconds and we boarded the tram for the two-hour trip. It was a wise decision as the open sided electric vehicle cruised through the flat watery Everglades with a knowledgeable ranger explaining the unique ecosystem as we travelled. We saw more alligators swimming amongst the sawgrass and stopped to view an alligator nest. I was amazed that the nest looked just like a large bird's nest floating on the water. The outward journey stopped at an observation tower, where we were given time to get out and explore. The tower is the highest point that visitors can reach by foot in the entire Everglades Park, with a seventy feet elevation offering panoramic views of up to twenty miles in all directions. The only issue was that all the other tram tourists also climbed the tower, gabbling and taking photos. But when I muttered a complaint under my breath, Sue glared at me and explained that we could not be on our own all time. I continued to mutter. On the return journey, I was more relaxed and with the hum of the electric engine and drone of the ranger, I fell asleep. When I awoke, Sue said that I slept deliberately to ignore the other passengers. I muttered again.

AMERICANADIAN DIARIES

We left the tourist trail behind us in the afternoon and drove a small loop road away from the main highway, through the Big Cypress National Preserve, stopping several times to see alligators swimming or resting in the waters at the roadside. This was much more to my liking as we met no-one, even stopping for a short, secluded walk on Pace's Dike Trail through the cypress swamp, simply because we liked the name.

We spent our last day in Homestead exploring the local area, wandering around Dane Fascell Park, a verdant oasis of lawns and trees perched on the edge of Biscayne Bay. We followed the boardwalk over the bay and meandered along Convoy Point Jetty, a long, thin spit reaching out to the east. We scrambled over the rocky shoreline, watching pelicans cooling their feet in the vivid blue waters and unsuccessfully tried to catch Florida lizards as they sunbathed on great fossil-decorated rocks. We sat on the rocks in the sun and just gazed across the bay in silence. Sue said that it was like being on holiday, which was odd as we were, but I knew what she meant.

We left the area and found a small store where we purchased lunch and followed signs to Homestead Bayfront Park, hoping to find a peaceful place for our picnic. It was a superb little park with a white sandy beach surrounding a stunning man-made lagoon. There were picnic tables under the shade of coconut palm trees, a small play area for children and views across Biscayne Bay. And the best thing about the find was that, apart from four pensioners, joints creaking as they exercised in a group, it was quiet and deserted. We sat at a picnic table and dined regally on trail-mix and Old Fashioned Cherry Orchard Pie. After yet more sitting doing nothing in particular, we set out to stroll around the lagoon, for once without my backpack which felt quite odd. We passed notices of beach rules warning parents to ensure that their children don't drown, not to leave litter and the usual common-sense directives which are posted to avoid legal culpability if there are accidents. We reached the far side of the lagoon and smiled as we looked back across the pool and agreed that it was odd that the warning signs about drowning never mentioned alligators, allied to the fact that a large alligator was resting in water just below us. We drove back to the motel, relaxed and happy, but there was one more treat in store as we stopped to watch a very, very big crocodile on the side of the road, the first croc we had seen on our trip. The perfect end to a perfect day with fish and chips at Applebee's still to come.

When we were planning and organising our trip, we had difficulty booking the next stop online so I telephoned the Beach Front Motel in Cedar Keys on the north west coast of the Florida peninsula to confirm the booking. On hearing that I lived in Portugal, the helpful receptionist told me that she had friends who were Portuguese and she had always wanted to visit the country. She also said how much she enjoyed Portuguese sausages. I was tempted to take her a Chouriço as a goodwill gesture, but thought that the US customs may not approve. After a six-hour drive on the Florida Turnpike via Miami, Palm Beach, Orlando and Dunkin Donuts somewhere on the way, we arrived at the motel tired but eager for our next adventure. I went the reception area and introduced myself. The receptionist remembered my call and said, "Yes Sir, that's one place I really want to visit, Portugal. Some folks round here want to visit New York or even Europe, but not me. I just want to get in my car one day and head south, not stopping until I reach Portugal."

I was a little surprised but resisted the opportunity to say that if she did that, she would fall off of America at Key West and drown. To this day, I cannot imagine where she thought Portugal was situated. I never mentioned the sausage to her.

We still had time to wander around the town and found Cedar Key enthralling, the embodiment of an American seaside town a bit like *Jaws* meets *The Perfect Storm.* There were streets of immaculate, colonial houses with small cafes and homely shops. Dock Street was the main tourist area with bars and restaurants with memorable names, The Rusty Hook, Steamers Clam Bar, the Big Deck Bar (which I deliberately misread) and The Tipsy Cow, all rustic wooden diners perched on the seafront in buildings that looked as if they had been roughly assembled by ancient sailors using driftwood. We were particularly enamoured by a street sign where directions to various attractions and facilities were illustrations, produced, I would guess, by the local school. The pointer to the fire station was a picture of a fire engine, the docks by a boat, the police station by a police car, a café by a coffee cup and so on with each illustration carefully and beautifully crafted by a child's hand. Many shops had eccentric displays, my favourite of which was outside of Sally Needle Quilt shop where a full-sized skeleton was sitting on a chair holding a sign saying *Waiting for My Wife*. I knew just how he felt. I was mesmerised by the town as the sky was lit up by a glorious sunset and I was lit up by a few beers at the Big Deck Bar. Sue and I agreed that this was yet another excellent choice as a place to stay.

As we studied the area to select our first expedition, we came across the Suwannee Wildlife Refuge, a few miles north of Cedar Key, and an ideal place to begin our exploration of this part of Florida. We were finalising our plans and it suddenly dawned on us, perhaps belatedly, that the Suwannee is the very same river featured in the opening line of the song *Old Folks at Home*,

AMERICANADIAN DIARIES

"Way down upon the Swanee River" and in the great Al Jolson's recording of the Irving Berlin classic, *Swanee (how I love you.)* This link to my love of old American music underlined the essentiality of the trip. The pleasant drive took us through flat, tree-lined grassland, passing small settlements hidden behind the trees, the only way of knowing they existed was by small clusters of mailboxes near rural sideroads. We parked in the small lot next to the visitor centre and immediately set off to see the iconic river via the Shell Mound Trail, strolling through more mangrove swamps on narrow paths and boardwalks, passing many small ponds and again watching alligators bathing, nonchalantly ignoring our presence. The wildlife on our walk was spectacularly exciting and we found small unidentified crabs wandering around the paths and, at one time a looming of black vultures circled overhead. Separately, a squadron of pelicans unswervingly passed over as if on a mission. We nearly stepped on a giant eastern lubber grasshopper and saw juvenile white ibis and cormorants at the water's edge. We also passed the mound of shells after which the trail is named, an archaeological site with a large bank of shells created by Native Americans, primarily composed of oyster shells, and believed to be up to 7,000 years old. When we reached the Suwannee, we stood on the viewing platform with superb views of the river and, once again, I had a moment where I was speechless, overwhelmed that I was there, the Swannee River. My speechlessness lasted just a few seconds before I broke into a very bad and out-of-tune rendition of, "Way down upon de Swanee River."

We were so enamoured by the flora and fauna discoveries of the area that the next day we decided to visit Cedar Key Scrub State Reserve, another wilderness area renowned for its wildlife. We pulled in to the parking lot and parked our small car next to the only other vehicle there, a large four-by-four truck. As we were leaving the car, the owners of the big truck returned to their motor and we passed the time of day with them, two big men with two big rifles slung over their shoulders. During our conversation, they told us that they had shot a cottonmouth dead, but that was all they had managed to kill that day. They did say that they had seen a bobcat and, "...coulda killed him, but he was too pretty." This did nothing to calm our slight nervousness about entering the area, particularly after seeing a sign on the entrance gate stating, *Hunting Season – In Progress*, but we set out anyway. The scrub simply means an area of stunted vegetation and we made our way along the paths between the undergrowth, hoping to catch site of some of the native animals. We were soon rewarded with sight of an eastern ribbon snake in a small pond, swimming quietly with just its head above water. At that time, we didn't know if this attractive reptile is venomous (it isn't) so left it alone, quietly enjoying its aquatic hunt for frogs for its lunch. We then came across the cottonmouth, also called the water moccasin, a beautiful four-feet long snake with striking brown camouflage. Except that this one had half of its body blown away, presumably by our friends' rifles. How anyone could kill such a beautiful creature for pleasure was beyond both Sue and me. It was very sad and put a damper on the walk, not helped by the fact that a vulture was sitting on the branch of a tree nearby, no doubt anticipating a tasty snake dinner.

That afternoon, we mooched around Cedar Key, uncharacteristically without a plan, which I found unnerving but Sue told me to live dangerously for once and become a free spirit. I grumbled but accepted her command, and was very glad that I did. As we wandered along Bay Street, we came across Cedar Key

Aquaculture, a building dedicated to raising and farming clams for which the area is famous. As I looked in to the workshop, I noticed several displays and posters explaining the work, so wandered in to see what was happening. I met a very helpful man who seemed surprised to see a stranger wander into his place of work, but took time to explain everything about the breeding and raising clams for food. Sue and I spent a fascinating half-hour with the clam man, although I was unconvinced that we should have been there without an appointment. Our tour of the town ended on a sombre note at the town's war memorial where the names of all those who had taken part in both World Wars were proudly displayed, including three with Sue's family name, Henley. That evening, our last in Florida for a while, it was only fitting that we dined on Cedar Key clams at the Steamer.

Before leaving for our next destination, I was up early and, whilst Sue was packing, I took a last farewell stroll along Dock Street and again marvelled at the almost shanty-town look of the wooden buildings. Little did I know that a few years later Hurricane Helene would almost destroy the town, as described in the local news, "*Hurricane Helene brought severe impacts to Cedar Key, Florida, with reports of an 8-foot storm surge that submerged much of the coastal town. The storm's nearly 100 mph winds and 12-foot storm surge resulted in extensive damage, particularly to residential properties and local businesses...The storm has left Cedar Key struggling to recover, with iconic local businesses such as the Faraway Inn and the Beachfront Motel suffering heavy damage or destruction.*" I hoped that the friends we made there were safe and the Beachfront motel receptionist made it to Portugal, even though she had no idea where it was.

We drove north on Florida's US-19, passing Chiefland and Fanning Springs, before turning west on the I-10 through

Tallahassee and crossing the state border at a large roadside sign reading *Sweet Home Alabama*. We arrived at the town of Opp after the pleasant six-hour journey and settled in to the Executive Inn. The motel was not as grand as it sounded, but was slightly above the basic motels we were used to. Opp was not a usual holiday destination and the owners, a delightful family from India, told us we were the first English visitors that they had had stay there and seemed surprised that we had chosen their hotel. We found it difficult to explain that the reason was simply that it was a convenient stop on the way from Florida to our next destination of Natchez, Mississippi. We were too embarrassed to tell them that the other reasons for staying in Opp were that the town was home to a rattlesnake rodeo and we had read that there was an exhibition of scarecrows in the local state park.

We had time after the long drive to wander round downtown Opp, which was like another ghost town. It was typical small town America with a wide street lined with local retailers, but there were no customers. The shopkeepers stood as if in a daze, staring out of the shop windows and doors, waiting to pounce on any potential purchasers. We felt that we were taking part in the start of an apocalyptic film, where the only survivors apart from ourselves were zombies disguised as shopkeepers. We did, however, find the offices of the local newspaper, the Opp News and, happy that the lady in the office was not a zombie, we bought a copy of the paper. Back at the motel, I scanned through the usual stories of school fetes, traffic issues and minor infringements and came across an advertisement for *AWF – Alabama Wildlife Federation Cook-off,* taking place the next evening at the Covington Center Arena, just seventeen miles east of the motel. Being keen amateur naturalists, it was an event that we could not miss and was immediately added to our schedule.

Opposite the hotel was a small retail park with a Chinese Restaurant, an easy and perhaps lazy choice for dinner after the long drive. We took our seats in the restaurant and the owner came to take our order accompanied by his daughter, a pretty little girl, around eighteen months old. I played with the child, pulling silly faces and making silly noises as we ordered, which seemed to please her as she responded with jolly smiles and chuckles, but was not prepared for what happened next. As the owner left to prepare our order, he sat the little girl on my lap and left her there...for about twenty minutes. I kept making silly noises, and like most children, she never got bored, though I started to wonder if we'd adopted her for good and were expected to take her home. The man finally returned with our food and, almost reluctantly, gathered up his daughter and retreated whilst we ate.

A good walk was in order for the day, so we chose the South Loop Trail in the Conecuh National Forest south west of Opp. We found the trailhead easily near Wing, Alabama and set out on the eight-mile forest walk with confidence which, in retrospect was misplaced. The trail took us through a beautiful forest full of pine trees, swamps, and ponds as expected, but we came across an abandoned cabin, possibly an overnight stop for long distance hikers, which was not mentioned on any guides. Whether we were on the right trail or not, we never knew but we eventually found the ponds which were on the route, so were happy. We stopped at Open Pond for some time watching a huge southern toad taking an ungainly stroll through the long grass and moved on to Buck Pond where a notice warned us not to feed or molest alligators. We both agreed that no one should need telling not to interfere with a gator.

Back at the Executive Inn, we were excitedly getting ready for our evening out to support local wildlife and discussed what sort of event it would be. Obviously as it was a *Cook Off,* there would be food and, we guessed, demonstrate numerous ways that the fauna of the area could be supported and preserved. We found our way to the arena with surprising ease and parked amongst the large 4X4 trucks before entering the arena. There was a twenty-dollar entrance fee, but all food and drink would be free thereafter and, of course, the money would help the local wildlife. The stadium was a large open arena surrounded by a spectator gallery and used, we were told, as a rodeo venue. Around the edge of the arena were perhaps thirty tables with barbeques, the crackling sounds and meaty smells of delicious cooking filling the air. Each stall had a notice describing the food on offer and we began a tour of the delights on offer. We looked at each other as it simultaneously dawned that the participants were cooking wild animals that they had killed. I re-read the notice at the entrance and it clearly stated, *Wild Game Cook Off.* I had missed the significance of the *Wild Game* part. So, we were there not to support local wildlife but to eat it. I shrugged and we decided to enjoy the occasion, and eat our twenty dollars' worth. There were stalls selling every type of wild animal imaginable, including wild boar (hog), deer, turkey, quail, snake, alligators and small game of dove, rabbits, squirrels, raccoons, opossums, and waterfowl. We toured the hall, chatting with the stallholders who, as usual, were intrigued that British people were there. The offerings were given enticing names such as Goose Gumbo and Swine and Dine and we took several small snacks, choosing those dishes we had never eaten before and probably never would again. As the band blasted out *Sweet Home Alabama,* we dined on barbequed alligator, snake, raccoon and opossum, each snack delicious. Every so often placed between stalls was a large tub filled with cans of Budweiser which was the perfect accompaniment.

On the way in, we had invested in a couple of raffle tickets. The band stopped playing and the host announced that it was time to draw the raffle. He displayed and described the two prizes...a Stoeger 12 gauge 3 ½ inch Automatic Rifle and a Browning 308 Lever Action Rifle. I was relieved that my number did not come up. After the draw, I approached the raffle organisers and asked if I could hold the guns, to be told, "Why sure, why not?" giving Sue the opportunity to take a memorable photo of me holding two deadly rifles, hopefully not loaded.

When I went upstairs to the washroom, I entered into conversation with a short, stout and bearded young man with a baseball cap worn the wrong way round. After finding out that I was English, he insisted that I met his family and, after collecting Sue, we made our way to his stall, the Swine and Dine. On the side of his exhibit was a big Boar's head, wearing a battered cowboy hat, which allowed me to return the favour and photograph Sue under the head. My new pal explained that this was the head of an enormous hog and it took three dogs to bring him down. He then proudly showed us a video of three American pit bulls savagely attacking this same poor animal. We never ate pork for while after that.

We left the arena after an entertaining evening and chatted whilst driving back to Opp about the glimpse into Alabama life. The fact that hunters could and would kill and eat almost anything living seemed almost surreal except that we were assured that a licence is required for all wildlife and it is deemed necessary to control overpopulation of pests whilst maintaining a natural environment. Most of the chow was prepared by elderly grandmothers, mothers and young girls. Seeing sweet pre-teen girls happily dissecting animals for cooking was unusual from a squeamish British viewpoint. At the same time, nearly all the men and boys stood around chatting while the food was prepared, yet all were relaxed and happy with this arrangement and women's liberation had not quite reached Alabama. Perhaps my biggest surprise was that, although the beer was effectively free, no-one abused the provision and not one person was drunk. I could only imagine what would happen in similar circumstances in Britain where there would be a race to consume as much beer as possible before being sick in the emptied bins. Sue also noticed that, although over 25% of the population in Alabama is black, we did not see one black or even brown face at the event.

Just forty-five miles north of Opp via the small towns of Andalusia, River Falls and McKenzie is the modest settlement of Georgiana, fairly insignificant except that it was the boyhood home of the great country music star, Hank Williams. His home is now a museum and an irresistible attraction to a country fan like me, so off we went. We soon found the place of homage at 127 Rose Street. It was a modest home although not the basic wooden shack that one may imagine being home to a poor southern boy. A wide set of stairs led up to a porch covering the whole width of the house, almost like entering a miniature colonial mansion set in attractive, well-maintained gardens. We paid a small entrance fee to a charming southern lady at the door and began our unguided tour of the house. We were the only visitors except for a big American gentleman who was shouting something unintelligible to the lady about his friend Johnny Horton, another country star of the 1950's. We wandered around the home looking at photographs, memorabilia, posters and personal items of the great man including some of his spectacular stage suits. It was an interesting and memorable half hour, but I was a mite disappointed as little of the furnishings of original house remained and I would have preferred to see the house as it was when Hank lived there. Johnny Horton's loud friend departed, we thanked the door lady and I casually remarked what a pretty town Georgiana was. She replied that it was "perty" before the blacks moved in, as they were given government aid to buy places and the white people couldn't afford to live there now.

I was slightly taken aback as she added, "D'you know, we even got a black president now, so no wonder?"

I jokingly warned her to be careful what she said or they may give a black person her job. She looked aghast and firmly told me that, "No black is ever gonna work in here."

To Kill a Mockingbird, Harper Lee's novel exposing racial intolerance in the Southern States, is generally regarded as one of the greatest American books of all time. It is one of the few novels that I have read twice, once as a teenager and again in the weeks before this trip. I was excited to find that the story's setting of Maycombe is based on the small town of Monroeville, just a few miles away from Opp and Georgiana. Monroeville was also Harper Lee's home and it has a museum dedicated to her life and the novel. There was no option but to make the pilgrimage. The museum is situated in the old courthouse where much of the novel takes place and, in the film of the book, the courthouse scenes are actually a recreation of the Old Monroe County Courthouse in a studio, meticulously designed to match the original.

We entered the courthouse and stood in the dock where the accused Tom Robinson stood: we sat behind the bench where lawyer Atticus Finch sat and we paced the floor where he paced: we viewed the scene from the balcony where Scout Finch viewed the proceedings: we sat in the chair where Mayella Ewell gave her dubious evidence: we sat in the jury seats where the all-white jurors gave their verdict. Except of course we didn't because it was fiction. However, for an hour or more, in my head I really was at the trial and lived the part of the main characters, especially the hero played by Gregory Peck. We finished the visit sitting in the courthouse grounds with our sandwiches and watching the small southern town world go by. I think that Sue became just a little irritated that I continued to act the part of Atticus Finch whilst picnicking and for the drive back, so I had to regain her respect by allowing her to walk amongst the deserted shops in Opp ghost town once again.

It was our last day in Alabama and we were yet to visit one of the main attractions, *Scarecrows in the Park* or the *Rattlesnake Rodeo*. The rodeo was not on during our visit, so that was out, but we made our way to the Frank Jackson State Park to see the scarecrows. We strolled along footpaths in the wooded park viewing the scarecrows created by various organisations and families from the local community. We saw scarecrows in a covered wagon by Sue and Billy Hudson, scarecrows constructed in the shape of crosses from the local church, a scarecrow pony and rider by the Two by Two Petting Zoo, scarecrow sailors, soldiers and airmen by the American Veterans, a scarecrow bluegrass band, a scarecrow in jail with a notice saying *Don't drink and drive,* and many more representing schools, a dentist, a car repair company, churches and various associations. There were even two scarecrows in a motorboat on the Jackson Lake, but perhaps the strangest was the Opp Gun Shop display of three scarecrows holding rifles, situated next to scarecrows from the Adellum Baptist Church under a sign that stated, *Blessed be the Nation Whose God is Lord.*

We continued our tour of the park by crossing the 150-yard bridge to a small island in the middle of the lake, made a little wary by a sign warning us to beware of alligators and snakes. We stopped to chat to four young lads whose sulky and sullen teenage behaviour gradually changed to friendly, if slightly arrogant conversation when they found out we were English. They were boasting of the wonderful and exciting Opp lifestyle, although they had never been outside the state of Alabama. They confidently told us that we should visit the state coastline, stating that it had, "The best beaches in world...by far." We never mentioned Cornwall, the Gower Peninsula, Portugal's Algarve or any of the other wonderful coastlines we had visited and knew well.

It was time to move on. We were finally going to see Tom Sawyer and Huckleberry Finn country, Riverboats, Old Man River, the Big Muddy, the great Mississippi River. After watching The Robber Bridegroom in Phoenicia on our previous road trip, we had been fascinated by the town of Natchez and had read much about the town's history, uncovering early American racism and corruption and its role as a major depot for early trade on the Mississippi.

We headed west on the US-85 for the seven-hour journey via more descriptive small American towns, Monroeville, Coffeeville, Waynesboro and Monticello. We passed one town where the pristine grassed roadside verge featured many American flags, under each of which was a simple white cross inscribed with the name of a local service veteran. It was quite moving and I said to Sue that the UK could learn a lot from the Americans about respect and pride for their service personnel. At one point, we passed fields on either side of the road, which were a sea of white stretching for many miles. These were some of the famous southern cotton fields, historically one of the main sources of labour for the enslaved black peoples of the area and, again, we found ourselves moved by a mix of sadness and elation as we drove in silence. We stopped just once on the long trip, at a remote roadside eatery, Bimbo's Family Restaurant near Silas, Alabama. As we entered the diner, we were immediately fascinated by the atmospheric décor, a museum of local life. A table at the entrance displayed an alligator head, a buffalo skull, Indian arrowheads and a variety of other memorabilia. Huge, stuffed freshwater fish adorned the walls alongside relics of Native American life. The menu was the archetypal diner fare but, sadly, we were not hungry after a big breakfast and long drive so settled for a shared Po Boy sandwich and coffee. As we finished and were discussing the trip, we were joined at the table by a large man in dungarees, who introduced himself as Bimbo. We chatted about the objects on display and I was particularly interested in all the Indian arrowheads, asking where he found them. "On the ground," he replied, "Just on the ground." As we were leaving, Bimbo told us to wait a minute and disappeared into a back room. He returned a minute later with two arrowheads, which he presented to me, refusing any payment. I suggested that we delayed our trip, and looked for accommodation in Silas, just to return to Bimbo's to eat and search for arrowheads. Sue gave me one of her looks, so I shut up and carried on driving.

AMERICANADIAN DIARIES

We soon passed the border from Alabama greeted by a large sign which read *Welcome to Mississippi – Birthplace of America's music,* before reaching Natchez and the Days Inn on the edge of town. It was late afternoon and we had been travelling for eight hours, but we couldn't wait to see the town and river so after a quick coffee in our room, we left the motel and took the short drive into town. We parked easily, strolled over a small grassy knoll and had our first sight of the Big Muddy below us. On our left was the Vidalia Bridge, which crossed the river to Louisiana on the opposite bank. I just stopped and looked at the scene as if in a dream, surprising myself at how emotional I was about simply looking at a river. Sue broke my dream by saying, "Look at that," and pointing upstream where a boat was pushing ten barges downriver. We surmised that it could be a cotton shipment heading towards New Orleans, which was fanciful but completed the scene and made us happy.

We overlooked the docking area where a riverboat was in port, tastelessly emblazoned with the name *Isle of Capri Casino Hotel Natchez.* We were unsure whether this was an hotel operating on the riverboat or an advertising hoarding for a casino hotel in the town. Whichever way, it was an ugly, vulgar sign which rather spoilt the atmosphere so we chose to ignore it.

That evening, we walked from the motel, searching for somewhere to eat and, ignoring MacDonalds, Taco Bell and KFC, came across Shoney's, a restaurant we had never tried before, so in we went. It was another chain selling the usual fare of fried fish, burgers, ribs, steak and wings but had the added attraction of an extensive all-you-can-eat buffet at a reasonable set price, consisting mainly of fried fish, burgers, ribs, steak and wings. It was impossible to eat a sensibly sized meal as the mains and sides were all irresistible - and we were hungry. The return walk to the motel seemed much longer that the outward stroll, possibly because we were both carrying a belly full of unhealthy, fattening but delicious food.

Natchez is historically divided into two distinct districts. The port area at the bottom of the bluff on the riverside is known as Under-the-hill and the main town is On-top-of-the-hill. Under-the-hill served as a bustling river port in the nineteenth century where steamboats, keelboats, and flatboats would dock and the area was notorious for its slave-trading, lawlessness, gambling, prostitution and violence. On-top-of-the-hill is the main residential and commercial districts, overlooking the river. It was home to the plantation owners and cotton merchants in magnificent mansions. The Historic Downtown Trail is a three-mile trek through the celebrated city, taking in both districts and our first choice for a discovery walk. We began from the historic Spanish Esplanade, where we had viewed the Mississippi the day before, a narrow strip of green that fronts the town and skirts the edge of the Natchez Bluff. We began the exploration Under-the-hill and wandered the dock area, paying special attention to the old tavern, reputedly a favourite drinking hole of Mark Twain, although we could see no evidence that he had supped pints there. After absorbing ourselves in antebellum history and culture, we followed the clearly marked trail to On-top-of-the hill and continued our wanderings through the 19th century commercial district, marvelling at Greek Revival mansions and elaborate Victorian houses, immaculately maintained residences fronted by impeccable front gardens. We did pass one home that stood out from its picture-perfect neighbours. It was a little shabby and covered with every type of garden ornament possible including angel statues to flower pots, teapots, flags, notices, plastic animals, old toys and much, much more. It was very odd, much like the display we saw in Woodstock earlier on our travels. We passed the Kings Tavern, dating from 1789 and the oldest building in the town, now owned by the local historic society but, unfortunately, it wasn't open so my growing thirst could not be slaked. We viewed a very old timber shack which was just about still standing but had no description when it was constructed and why. We met a gardener called Dave who chatted for half an hour about the history of the town and, more specifically, some of the gardens he maintained. We entered the first Presbyterian Church which had a "Natchez in Historic Photographs" exhibition. We stopped at a memorial to the Confederate Army in the Civil War although we understood that, in Natchez, Johnny Reb had surrendered without firing a shot.

I was historied-out after three hours and ready for a reviving coffee, when we returned to the esplanade, but I was revitalised to see a group of prisoners from the local jail working there. They were dressed in baggy, bold green and white hooped trousers and white t-shirts marked *MDOC CONVICT*, MDOC being the Mississippi Department of Corrections. They were peacefully assembling a nativity scene in the park, meticulously cleaning up the area as they worked. Sue remarked that it was an excellent use of free labour and a sensible first step to rehabilitation. I had to agree, but thought having to wear the silly trousers was enough to stop them offending again.

It was back to the all-you-can-eat buffet at Shoney's that evening, where we met four visiting New Yorkers, who introduced themselves as Pearl, Nancy, Ruby and Wendell and were fascinating company. We compared trips across America, although they were more interested in hearing about life in England and Portugal. It was an ideal opportunity for me to tell some (tall) stories and we separated after swapping addresses and promising to keep in touch, which we all knew would not happen.

The Natchez Trace is an historic trail which runs from Nashville, Tennessee, to Natchez, approximately 440 miles. The trail was created and used by Native Americans over 10,000 years ago and used by nomadic and itinerant tribes before the early European explorers, traders and immigrants made use of the pathway. We were fascinated to learn that the merchant flatboats travelling from the north to Natchez depended on the flow of the river to propel them southwards, but the boats were unable to return against the river's flow so the sailors walked back north, using the trace for part of their trek. The boats were dismantled in Natchez and the wood used, often for buildings in the growing town. Along the route, early entrepreneurs built inns, also known as stands, to provide board and lodging to the returning travellers. In the 1930's the trace was developed as a scenic road, the Natchez Trace Parkway, which generally followed the old walking trail, although parts of the original trace still exist. The history made the parkway an irresistible draw. As we drove along the two-lane highway we stopped at a sign which marked a part of the original trail with a sign that outlined that its history and added that it was travelled by *American Indians, traders, soldiers, "Kaintucks", postriders, settlers, slaves, circuit-riding preachers, outlaws, and adventurers*. Perhaps it would be now amended to include naïve English pensioners. The old trace remains as a deep cleft worn by thousands of years of travellers and we abandoned the car to follow it a mile or two before it became impassible. I found the atmosphere very poignant as I tried to imagine all those who had travelled this way before while I tried to work out what a *Kaintuck* was.

We returned to the car and moved on before stopping at another path which led to Emerald Mound, a 35-foot-high grassy hill, constructed by native Americans between 1200 and 1730. It was reminiscent of Wiltshire's Silbury Hill, except that it was open for access. Again, we were the only people there and spent a peaceful and reflective half an hour wandering over the historic monument, trying to imagine native life a thousand years ago.

Our next stop on the trace was Mount Locust Inn, one of the stands built for travellers. The site was settled by Native Americans for a thousand years before the inn was constructed in the late eighteenth century. It then served the men from the flatboats making their way back north and, we learnt, were called Kaintucks after Kentucky frontiersmen who used the trace. A mystery solved. The inn, not much more than a simple rustic log cabin, was now a museum with much of it maintained just as it was a century and more ago. It displayed the simple wooden furniture and basic cooking and eating implements and the very basic sleeping arrangements, where five men would share a small bedroom or simply sleep in the open on the wooden veranda floor. It was a fascinating look into the past, but paled into insignificance when we found the slave cemetery next to the building. The cemetery holds the remains of 43 enslaved people but there are no headstones, no crosses, no indication of who is interred where, just a small clearing amongst the trees. There is a notice which lists the people known to be buried there, displaying just ten names.

We were warned that a storm was due that evening so ate at the motel. It was a wise decision as the thunder grumbled and lightning flashed around us. The rain was torrential, flooding the car park as we stayed in and enjoyed the spectacle from the comfort of our room. We commented how we seemed particularly adept at attracting storms on our visits to America.

Across the Mississippi river is the state of Louisiana and home to the Bayou Cocodrie Wildlife Refuge, established to conserve some of the last remaining, least disturbed and largest stands of bottomland hardwoods in the Lower Mississippi Valley. The refuge offers a variety of ecological habitats for wildlife, with more than 150 species of birds and other wildlife, notably a thriving population of Louisiana black bears. We could not resist the opportunity to visit, so we crossed the Vidalia Bridge from Natchez, looking forward to a day of bird and bear spotting. After our encounter with the Alabama Wildlife Federation, we did wonder whether the refuge conserved the animals to kill and eat, but were assured that this was not so. We headed west and left the main highway on Poole Road, a minor lane through deep forest towards the refuge but were stopped when the road was flooded after the previous night's storm. The muddy water was blocking the road and we pulled to a sudden halt to discuss whether to continue. Discretion being the better part of valour, we had little choice to save our souls and turn back. With no other plan in place, I began to panic when Sue said something designed to increase my trepidation, "Let's not worry about a plan, we'll just wing it." I rarely did anything without a plan, but this was becoming a regular occurrence and my dear wife was adamant, so wing it we did. We returned to Natchez and parked in our familiar spot overlooking the bluff, Sue smiling contentedly, while I tried to control my anxiety. As we gazed over the river, now a deeper brown that usual with debris from the storm floating gently downstream, we noticed that an impressive paddle steamer had arrived at the dock below us. We wandered down the hill to see the imposing boat, the American Queen. The riverboat tourists were leaving the boat and wandering aimlessly, wondering what to do with no-one giving them orders. I admit to feeling a tad superior as they were just aimless day trippers, whilst we were temporary residents and knew our way around the wonderful city. I was half expecting Bart and Bret Maverick to disembark, immaculately dressed and counting the money from their poker winnings, but they never showed. Waiting patiently by a small table on the grass was a charming lady selling *Caroline's creamy home-made pecan pralines*. We chatted to Caroline and learnt that she met every tour boat with her sweet treats to help boost her pension and, although I had no idea what a praline was, I bought some. I have to say that they were truly delicious to anyone who likes the sweetest of sickly sweets, which we do not, so they were surreptitiously dumped in the nearest bin.

With no plan, this was Sue's day so, unsurprisingly, she chose to visit downtown Natchez, an area that I had previously ignored as I guessed that it would consist mainly of my innate aversion – shops. It was fascinating. We stopped for a coffee in the Cotton Alley café and chatted at length with the waitress about nothing in particular, we passed the Black Cat club where Jerry Lee Lewis made his stage debut aged thirteen, wandered between the beautiful old buildings and studied a variety of goods on offer displayed in shop windows. We made a disappointing visit to the Museum of African American History and Culture which started well, viewing exhibits explaining the history of slavery in the town. There was one particularly poignant exhibit covering the Rhythm Nightclub fire, where over 200 African American Natchez citizens were either burned or trampled to death. This also answered a question I had pondered for a few days, the origin of the old song Natchez Burnin,' by

Howlin' Wolf, which I had listened to as a young man during my brief blues period. Our visit was marred by an interfering old (white) man who insisted on guiding us through the exhibits and explaining what we could have read on the detailed descriptions on each display. He was so pushy and we were so irritated by his interference that we left before completing the visit. We did have time, however, to read about the Forks of the Road in Natchez, one of the largest slave markets in the South. We immediately headed for the site on our self-guided tour. We found a simple and peaceful triangle of parkland with notices explaining its significance in the deplorable history of slave trading and stopped for a while in quiet contemplation, trying to imagine the horrors of its past.

On our way back to the Days Inn, we stopped at the Grand Village of the Natchez Indians, a 128-acre grassy park containing three prehistoric Native American mounds, much like Emerald Mound but far larger. Two of the mounds, the Great Sun's Mound and the Temple Mound, have been excavated and then rebuilt to their original sizes and shapes. We read that atop the Temple Mound, the bones of previous chiefs were found and a sacred, perpetual fire was kept in the Temple's inner sanctum, representing the sun from which the dead chiefs had descended. Abandoned Mound is not excavated and will be preserved intact. We strolled around the serene site, lost in peaceful contemplation, our meditation was abruptly interrupted by a visiting group of energetic schoolchildren. Whilst the young teacher was explaining the significance of the mounds, the girls ignored her and chatted amongst themselves and the boys ran up the mounds before rolling down, shouting loudly and generally having a wonderful time. We watched them for some time happily enjoying their antics and Sue smiled and said, "Kids are all the same wherever you go," and I said, "No wonder the Native Americans abandoned the site with all this mayhem going on."

We were still intrigued by Natchez Trace and discovered that there was one undeveloped sunken track nearby, the Potkopinu section, a three-mile National Scenic Trail, Potkopinu being the Natchez Indian word meaning Little Valley. The trail has some embankments over twenty feet high, the path worn down by centuries of foot travel by Indians, Kaintucks and, reputedly, by bison migrating from north to south. As we drove along the parkway to the trailhead, we were surprised to see a large barred owl sitting quietly on the roadside, so we slowed gently and stopped. The great bird, the size of an eagle, gently flapped its huge wings, rose upwards and settled ten feet up in a tree watching us with as much interest as we watched it. We tired of the staring contest with the giant bird and continued the drive. A little further on, we saw four coyote pups playing on the opposite roadside verge and another stop was essential as watched the cute canines play-fighting on the bank. We could not have wished for a better start to the day, and our contentment continued when we parked to begin the walk. The trail was beautiful in the balmy Autumn conditions with the sun's rays sparkling as they filtered through the trees lining the path. We followed the trace for its full three miles imagining that we were Kaintucks heading home after sailing down the Mississippi and unloading our cargo in Natchez. As usual, we saw no-one on our journey, which added to our joyous sense of serenity.

We still had the afternoon to relax and decided to take a pleasure drive around the area with no specific objective. I was almost converted to Sue's wing-it philosophy. We passed through the delightful small town of Port Gibson, with its beautiful tree-lined avenues and impressive homes spaced generously along the avenue. It looked like the epitome of ideal southern country living. A little further on we espied some strange pillars just off the road, marked *Windsor Ruins*, so stopped to take a look. There were around twenty impressive stone columns where once there had been a magnificent mansion, but with little information on its history or how it became abandoned. We moved on, stopping at what looked an abandoned set of buildings blanketed in dark green foliage, as if it had been taken over by a strange alien lifeforce. As we stood on the bank at the roadside, gazing over the bizarre site, I was aware of sharp stinging sensation on my legs and looked down to see my legs covered in small black ants, by which time Sue was dancing away with her legs similarly covered. We were forced to remove our shoes and socks as the stinging became more severe and wash our feet down with drinking water, but our legs were still stinging as we drove back to base.

While Sue snoozed, I went to the motel reception and used their public PC to research where we had visited. I discovered that Port Gibson was the third oldest town in Mississippi and, during the Civil War, it was spared from destruction following the Battle of Port Gibson since, legend has it, General Ulysses S. Grant said that it was, "Too beautiful to burn." I read that Many of Port Gibson's antebellum buildings remain today, and much of the downtown area has been listed in the National Register of Historic Places. The nearby Windsor Ruins are noted as one of Mississippi's most iconic places, a historic site of the Windsor plantation. It was once the home of wealthy planter Smith Coffee Daniell II, who owned thousands of acres of land in the Mississippi Delta and also owned hundreds of slaves. In its glory days, the four-story structure witnessed many historical events before being destroyed by a fire in 1890. Now, there are just twenty-three full columns and five partial columns remaining at the site. The strange vegetation-covered buildings were part of Rodney, a ghost town and popular place to visit, but apparently difficult to find, which gave me smug pleasure. The invasive plant covering the buildings is kudzu, a native plant from Asia and known as *the vine that ate the South*. When I returned to our room, I woke Sue and I explained what I had discovered and pointed out that, had we known all this beforehand, our visit would have been so much more informative and interesting, hence no more winging it. She said, "What about the ants?" and went back to sleep. I sneaked back to the Reception and found out that our attackers were fire ants, a species accidentally introduced from South America, but thought it better to save that piece of information for another day.

It was sadly our last day in Natchez and we decided on a lazy day wandering around the town for which we had gained a great affection. We headed to the Natchez City Cemetery which seemed a fitting way to say goodbye. Established in 1822 on the bluffs high above the Mississippi River, it offered an insight into the region's personal histories and revealed stories of the inhabitants over its two hundred years of occupation. It was a moving and humbling experience. It was noticeable that the occupants of the cemetery were all white European and the enslaved people had a separate area known as the Pauper's Field. Here, there were many unmarked graves, although there is a token monument dedicated to the memory of the enslaved people buried there. In direct contrast, one section of the graveyard is dedicated as a military cemetery where row upon row of identical, beautifully maintained headstones sit amongst manicured lawns. We discovered one grave with the name of

Clarence Henley who served in the US navy in World War Two and we wondered if it could have been one of Sue's distant relatives, an intriguing and fitting way to end our visit.

Much as we loved Natchez, we could not help but be excited about our next journey to the celebrated city of New Orleans, Louisiana, the Big Easy. We headed south on the US-61, known as the Blues Highway, towards the state capital of Baton Rouge, passing Wilkinson, Woodville and Wakefield, commenting that the road should be renamed the *W Highway*. The weather was dreadful for the whole drive with torrential rain limiting our speed and vision. As we neared New Orleans, we were unnerved to pass many signs saying *Evacuation Route,* and hoped that we were not on the edge of another Hurricane Katrina which devastated the city a few years before. By the time that we reached our motel, another Super 8, the rain had eased and we had survived. The motel was a few miles away from the city centre, but was up to the excellent standard we had come to expect and we settled in for a well-earned rest after the tiring drive. Too weary to go out that evening, we opted to eat in our room and were fortunate that next door to the motel was the *Food Plus Grocery Store – Cigarettes, Beer, Liquor, Sandwiches, Snacks,* so we wandered over to purchase a simple snack for the evening. The store appeared closed except for a barred window, behind which sat a bored looking gentleman. I ordered a local newspaper, sandwiches and crisps and asked why the window was so securely barred. He looked somewhat surprised at my innocent question and replied, "Son, this is New Orleans," before returning with the requested fare. I hurried back to base.

Tucked away in the newspaper was an advertisement for the Oak Street Po Boy Festival. We had eaten po boys many times before, but had not realised that these rolls, baps or cobs in

England are a New Orleans speciality with the *po* being a phonetic interpretation of the word *poor*, hence *poor boy sandwiches*. It seemed like the perfect way to begin our exploration of the city, so we worked out how to get to Oak Street without using the car. In the morning, breakfasted, dressed and a plan in place, we crossed the road and waited for a bus into the city centre. After ten minutes, the bus arrived and we boarded and spent fifteen minutes surrounded by a strange cross section of New Orleans wildlife. A scruffy man who may have been under the influence of alcohol or drugs, talked loudly to everyone and no-one in particular, pointing out landmarks on the route, while two large black ladies spent the journey telling him to shut up. At each stop the driver also told the man to shut up, but to no avail. Another gentleman spent the whole journey telling a disinterested fellow passenger that his wife had been unfaithful, some of the details of which were X rated, and at least three passengers slept and snored loudly.

We left the bus and its menagerie of locals at Canal Street in the city centre and strolled along the busy shopping thoroughfare until we found the depot for the Saint Charles Streetcar, where we boarded a tram and took our seats for the ride to the festival. It was a fascinating forty-minute journey through the city, although I have no idea where we were or where we went. It just felt exhilarating to be on a Streetcar travelling through this iconic conurbation. Somehow, we alighted at the right place and a very busy Oak Street was immediately in front of us. I was quite proud that we had made the ten mile journey across New Orleans and found our objective, albeit taking almost two hours. Oak street is a normal suburban high street with a variety of shops, cafes and businesses but is closed to traffic and turned into a hectic food market during the Po Boy

Festival. The street was lined with stalls, selling the classic snack, a crisp crust, baguette-style bread with a mind-boggling selection of fillings. We were tempted with their standard fillings of shrimp, catfish, roast beef or oyster and more adventurous creations such as shanghai shrimp, okra, Caribbean catfish or smothered rabbit. We made our way down the street marvelling at the stalls and watching the crowds milling around as locals placed chairs on the pavement and watched the event unfold. At the end of the street was a stage on which a band was playing traditional blues music as youngsters danced at the front of the platform. Although we had dined on a Super 8 breakfast that morning, the delights on offer were tempting and we broke our tour by refuelling with a turducken sausage po boy prepared by Knights of Columbus, a local Catholic charity. Despite its unsavoury-sounding name, the server explained that turducken is a popular Louisiana dish, consisting of a deboned chicken stuffed into a deboned duck, stuffed into a deboned turkey - and it was delicious. We spent the afternoon at the festival, wandering, watching and chatting until we started our return journey by streetcar, by foot and by bus to the Super 8.

We were up very early the next morning excited about the day ahead. We considered ourselves lucky to find the po boy festival and our good luck continued the following day. We had planned to visit New Orleans' famous French Quarter and start by visiting the Welcome Center at Basin Street Station. I studied my maps overnight, but was nervous about negotiating the apparently complex driving conditions in a busy American city. We were, as usual, also concerned about parking, but headed off hoping to find a cheap, or free, car park somewhere convenient. After passing over the Highrise Bridge spanning the Inner Harbour Canal, we aimed the car south-west on the I-10 until we reached Orleans Avenue where we turned and began slowing down, driving towards Basin Street, looking for the Welcome Center. Sue suddenly shouted, "In there," so I immediately swerved right into a large, and largely empty, car park. We parked and left the car to see where we were and before us was a magnificent red brick building with a sign above the arched entrance saying *Basin St. Station*, now the Information Center. Not only had we found our objective but the parking was free. I raised my right hand to give Sue a high five, but she glared at me and said, "Don't be silly. You spent two hours last night looking at maps, so knew where we were and it was easy." I mumbled that it was only one hour and wasn't easy.

As we entered the building, I began to quietly sing the Ella Fitzgerald classic *Basin Street Blues*, but couldn't remember the tune or the words except the bit that goes "...they call it Basin Street..." which warranted another stern glare. Inside, the historic building was beautifully maintained with a huge light and airy room displaying many exhibits ...*capturing and featuring the culture and history that makes New Orleans one of the most unique cities in North America,* yet it still maintained the look and feel of a busy nineteenth century train station. We were enthralled and spent a long time looking at the exhibits and chatting to the knowledgeable and helpful staff. Again, the information desk lady seemed as interested in us as we were with the city, asking about life in England and Portugal as we researched about life in what we now knew as NOLA (New Orleans Louisiana.)

Leaving the station, we walked south along St. Louis Steet, passing interesting, mainly residential buildings until we arrived at the junction with the famous Bourbon Street, the cultural and historic centre of the French Quarter. This is also the centre of nightlife in the city and quiet at that time day with just a few sightseers and local going about their business, cleaning up after the previous night and preparing for that night's revelries. The architecture was particularly fascinating with its blend of French, Spanish, and Caribbean influences creating Creole Townhouses, many dating back to the late 18th and early 19th centuries, decorated in vibrant colours and first floor wrought-iron balconies. Yet there was a contradiction where the ground floors of the historic buildings were a brash mix of bars, restaurants, souvenir shops and strip clubs. We loved it, and spent a happy hour roaming the street, looking at and in the now quiet but gaudy hospitality venues, only stopping to watch a television crew filming a scene from *NCIS New Orleans* which, we were told, was a popular crime drama in the USA, although we had never heard of it.

We then headed south on St, Louis Street to the riverside area where we were thrilled to see two paddlewheel riverboats docked, both offering evening dinner trips on the Mississippi. We had to decide between the Natchez and the Creole Queen, but decided that the Creole Queen was more alluring and booked cruise tickets for two days' time. Moving on, we found the French market with open air stalls selling mainly food and local crafts, much like an English farmers' market. We needed sustenance after the busy morning and settled in an eatery in the heart of the market ordering jambalaya, a delicious rice dish, and gumbo, a rich spicy stew. I remember sitting there deep in thought after eating before saying to Sue, "Who would have thought that an ageing couple from Swindon would ever be sitting in the French Quarter market, New Orleans, dining on jambalaya and gumbo?" I had never seen her look so happy and content as her face broke into a wide smile, but that may well have been wind from the effects of the gumbo.

We moved on to Jackson Square, a small, but beautifully maintained historic park (everything here was historic) where we ordered a coffee at an open-air stall and sat on a park bench, resting while watching and listening to a small jazz trio playing. Yet another magic moment in a magic day before we retraced our steps back to the car and motel.

I have had an interest in Second World War history since learning at a very early age that my father had defeated Rommel and his panzers almost single handedly in North Africa. New Orleans is home to America's National WWII Museum and was our objective on the following day. We again took advantage of the easy, and free, parking at Basin Street Station and walked the mile and a half to the museum. On the way we admired the elegant buildings on Canal Street including the magnificent Saint and Carllton Ritz Hotels, before turning onto Camp Street, originally named in Spanish, Campo de Negros. We passed a number of original shotgun houses, narrow, single-story homes which, we were informed, allow a bullet to pass straight through if fired from the front door. Why anyone would build a house for such an odd reason was a mystery, but interesting, nonetheless.

The museum was excellent, with fascinating photographs, exhibits descriptions of the war. We were moved by an exhibit with films and photographs telling the stories of some of men and women who fought in the jungles of the South Pacific, the deserts of North Africa, and across the devastation of Western Europe. Over 16 million Americans military personnel participated in fighting on foreign soil and more than 414,000 of them did not return. The sombre mood continued with exhibits detailing the rise of Nazi terror and persecution of Europe's Jewish population leading to the Holocaust, and the effect of the conflict on the servicemen and their families after the war. There were first hand reports and interviews with those whose lives were changed forever by the war and, as we passed through the halls dedicated to the heroes and victims, I found it both heart-breaking and yet uplifting. We were glad to leave the personal histories behind us and concentrate on the exhibits of fighter planes and bombers suspended from the ceiling as if in flight, replicas of the army barrack rooms and a model of the D-day landings with an accurate copy of all the boats and planes involved, which really hit home the magnitude of the operation. There was a great exhibit showing the North Africa campaign with genuine tanks and armoured vehicles, but that had somehow missed the fact that my dad had been the main reason for the success. They also seemed to think that the war started in 1941, ignoring the two years that the British Empire stood alone against the Axis powers. We had mixed feelings of sadness at the personal losses and pride in the success of good over evil as we left the museum, physically and emotionally drained.

On our travels around the city, we had spotted the Nirvana Indian Restaurant in Magazine Street and decided that a warming curry would revive us, so caught the tram outside the museum and trundled through town, somehow alighting at the right stop, the thought of a garam chicken soup followed by lamb rogan josh would soon put us back on our feet. The restaurant was closed. A little deflated we made our way back towards the French Quarter and found an iHop in Canal Street, settling for chicken strips and fries (seniors' portion.)

Slavery loomed large in New Orleans, from the names of some streets to historic landmarks and we decided that we should learn more of its history, so drove to Vacherie, Louisiana on the west bank of the Mississippi River to visit the Laura Plantation, a historic Louisiana sugar plantation which used slave labour. It is open to the public and known for its impressive Creole-style manor house, slave quarters, and sugar fields. Unfortunately, the entrance fee includes a guided tour so we had little choice but to join other visitors as we were led around the *Big House,* a beautiful Creole mansion and home to the plantation owners' family. The tour seemed a trifle rushed, the guide repeating a well-rehearsed but uninspiring homily, largely ignored by the following group and making it impossible to concentrate on the beautiful rooms and furnishings. We were moved outside to the preserved slave quarters, simple, wooden, one-room shacks tucked away out of sight of the Big House. Again, the guide was efficient but lacklustre, except when she talked about the abolishment of slavery in the late 19th century when the enslaved people stayed on as workers but had to be paid. I asked what I thought a relevant question, "Were the workers paid a decent, living wage?" The (white) guide's response is something I will never forget, when she replied that the workers, "... had somewhere to live and could grow their own food, so what more did they want. They didn't need money?" The whole group of (white) visitors were visibly shocked and the guide hurried on to the next shack. It seemed that racism was still alive and thriving in Louisiana.

We were excited that evening as we were off to travel the Mississippi on the Creole Queen, and arrived at the dock early, waiting for our orders to board. We were the first on board at six fifteen to ensure that we soaked up the atmosphere every available minute, and made a lone tour of the paddle steamer. We were immediately struck by the impressive, elegant dining room, laid out for our evening meal and certainly different from our normal basic diner surroundings. We toured the promenade decks and stopped overlooking the port watching our fellow guests arrive with a feeling of joyous anticipation. With a loud blast of its hooter, the paddle steamer pulled out and left the mainland, travelling upstream under the Crescent City Connection twin bridges and, as the sun set over the city, we tried to identify the places we had previously visited. We were soon called into dinner and settled in a window seat before investigating the expansive buffet, as a jazz band played in the corner. We agonised over red beans and rice, jambalaya, Cajun seafood pasta, Cajun braised beef brisket, chicken and sausage gumbo and more, before carefully taking a sample of each delicious offering. The dining experience was completed with a white chocolate bread pudding with whiskey sauce. By the time the meal was finished, it was dark and, replete from an excess of everything, we returned to the promenade deck and watched our sister ship, the Natchez, sailing past, lit up in the night like a Christmas tree, its lights reflected in the river as it glided past. Whilst most of the other passengers stayed in the ballroom listening to the jazz and dancing, we stayed on the deck watching the lights from New Orleans on the riverside. The return to port was truly awe inspiring as we approached the city, ablaze with lights reflecting in the still waters of the river. We stood on deck and romantically held hands, transfixed by the glittering sight, one that we will never forget.

It was still early in New Orleans terms so we continued the evening with a stroll along Bourbon Street. I have revelled on Blackpool's Golden Mile, I have wandered London's West End and partied on Benidorm's strip, I have fallen out of a nightclub in Deep Ellum, Dallas and I have staggered around Lisbon's nightspots in the Bairro Alto, but I have never seen anything like Bourbon Street at night. It seemed that every building housed a brightly lit shop, a bar, nightclub or strip joint with dazzling lights and brilliant neon signs advertising venues such as The Swamp, *Prohibition, Hustler Club (Home of the Hustler Honeys,) Rick's Bar* and my favourite, *Huge Ass Beers*. Most bars were open to the street and had jazz or blues bands playing, the sounds echoing up and down the boulevard. The streets were crowded with people promenading and, like us, soaking up the electrifying atmosphere. The one drawback was that I had to drive back to the motel so was unable to take advantage of the Huge Ass Beer, but was compensated by the intoxicating atmosphere.

The following day was Thursday 26th November, Thanksgiving Day. We had read that there was to be a Bayou Classic Thanksgiving Parade along Canal Street so set out again for the city and headed for the parade route via Bourbon Street. The revelry of the previous evening had subsided and the street was almost empty except for people cleaning up after the previous night's partying and preparing for that night's repeat performance. A few inquisitive tourists strolled around as we did, and we stopped to watch two young lads, perhaps eight or nine years old dancing on the sidewalk. They had beer bottle tops affixed to their shoes and tap danced with amazing skill and vigour, collecting a few dollars from the captivated passers-by. When we reached Canal Street, spectators were taking up their positions and we managed to find a spot at the front of the growing crowd and could hear the sound of distant drums as the parade was under way. We could feel the excitement in the onlookers as the sound grew closer and the start of the parade came into view. It was led by five motorcycle policemen with lights flashing and sirens blaring to clear anyone from the road and followed by a junior marines' band, the musicians immaculately dressed in their smart dress uniforms. They were the forerunners to an eclectic mix of other groups, bands, dancers and floats, playing music and marching and dancing as they passed. We saw troops of scantily clad girls sashaying in perfect time, brass bands, drum bands and marching bands each consisting of perhaps one hundred young people, parading proudly as they played, all dressed in their flamboyant military style dress. There were squads of cheerleaders in colourful, glitzy outfits twirling batons, waving pom-poms and flags as they marched and danced, the parade interspersed with tractors pulling intricately decorated trailers representing the city's heritage. We did not count, could not count their numbers, but estimated that there were over fifty troupes of performers, each with up to one hundred or more members, so the parade must have numbered around five thousand cheerful and dedicated young people. Notably, nearly all, at least 95% of participants, were African Americans although only around 60% of the New Orleans population is black.

Following the parade, we strolled on to the Mississippi waterfront to say goodbye to the Big Muddy and watched the parade bands disbanding. It was then late afternoon and we suddenly realised that we were hungry and went to find somewhere for a meal. We wandered about for a while looking for somewhere other than a chain diner to make our last meal in NOLA memorable, rejecting iHop and burger joints. We were spoilt for choice but settled on a small restaurant called Country Flame in Iberville Street, a small thoroughfare away from the main tourist area, attracted by a board outside offering a Thanksgiving Special. It was a fortunate and yet superb find. Inside it had the atmosphere of a homely, slightly upmarket restaurant with classic southern states feel and décor. And it had tablecloths and linen napkins. We were shown to a small table in a corner, which was quiet but allowed us to satisfy our nosiness by having an expansive view of the rest of the restaurant. Of course, we ordered the Thanksgiving Special and were rewarded with a magnificent feast of roast turkey, stuffing, mashed potato with gravy, macaroni cheese, sweetcorn and carrots and, strangely, a side of nachos with a chilli sauce. The only issue was that they served American-sized portion and, although we were hungry and gave it our best shot, we were unable to finish the feast. Sue even left some of her favourite macaroni cheese and turned down the seasonal sweet of pumpkin pie.

In attempting to walk off the dinner, we set out once again for a last stroll along Bourbon Street. If the previous evening was electrifying, I'm not sure how to describe this evening. The street was packed with happy revellers such that it was difficult to negotiate through the throng. Every crowded bar, strip joint and brothel was competing with its neighbours with jazz and blues music blasting and neon lights flashing, while street musicians performed for people dancing in the street. There were street artists dressed as assorted monsters and illuminated ghosts and ghouls dancing for dollars and our young friends with the bottle-tops tapping on the sidewalk. An attractive lady walked past with "Photos $5" written across her naked breasts. Sue looked at her, looked at me and just said an emphatic, "No." A flashing mobile disco emblazoned with *God Gave his Only Son* attracted a large crowd of dancers as tourists stopped to watch or join in, which seemed most odd in such an ungodly atmosphere. Everyone was in joyous mood as they strolled amongst the mayhem or sat in the open-fronted bars watching the musicians or, more often, watching the partying crowd outside. There was no disorder, no loud troublemakers and no aggression and no fighting as everyone seemed to have absorbed the Bourbon Street happy air. Regretfully, we finally left the merriment behind and strolled up a virtually deserted Toulouse Street back to the car and our motel. It was a fitting end to our time in the wonderful and exciting city of New Orleans.

We were up early the next morning prepared for the six-hour drive on the I-10 East to our next stop of Tallahassee, the capital of Florida. It was an easy and pleasant run via Biloxi Louisiana and Mobile, Alabama into northern Florida before arriving in the Suburban Extended Stay Hotel in the delightfully named Silver Slipper Lane. Unlike the standard motels we were used to, the hotel consisted of apartment-style accommodation with a mini-fridge, microwave, coffee maker and a kitchenette. After the excitement of NOLA and a long drive, we had an early night, waking refreshed the following morning, a Saturday and Sue's sixtieth birthday. I had given our two boys and the in-laws the hotel address and they had sent birthday cards, which had thankfully arrived at the hotel. I was up before Sue and collected the post from the hotel reception. I casually left the envelopes on the breakfast table and they greeted her when she surfaced, along with freshly made coffee and toast with boiled eggs for breakfast. She was delighted with the romantic gesture and had a tear in her eye until I somewhat ruined the moment by singing an out-of-tune version of "My Tallahassee Lassie," an old Rolling Stones song. As I explained, the thought was there even if the execution was less than perfect.

Our research discovered that the city is home to Mission San Luis, an Apalachee-Spanish Living History Museum which celebrates the settlers of the early 1700s with living history interpreters in period dress, reconstructed period buildings, exhibits, and archaeological research. That morning there was a demonstration of culinary traditions at the annual Giving Thanks celebration. It promised that guests would learn how people and foods from the New and Old Worlds came together at San Luis. It sounded like a splendid way to discover more about the area and may even have offered free food, so off we drove across town to the event. The mission itself was a strange construction, a huge wood and thatch dome like a giant mushroom, built as a mission to convert Apalachee Indians to Christianity. On this day, it housed exhibits of local crops of corn, pulses and squashes presented by folk in period dress but not an Apalachee to be seen. After reviewing the exhibits, we moved outside into the mission grounds where we watched demonstrations of woodworking, food preparation, cooking over a fire pit and smoking meat and fish on a barbacoa. We attended presentations about hunting, sowing, growing, harvesting, and preserving food in the early days of the pioneers and settlers. We also visited the historic church and replicas of early homes, all of which gave a fascinating glimpse into the past. We met many people in period dress, but nowhere did we see an Indian, so could only assume that the attempts to force a European religion on the native population had failed. And we were never offered any food, so left and drove downtown, getting totally lost before hunger and desperation forced us to stop at a MacDonald's for a burger. Not knowing where we were, we became lost again trying to get back to the hotel and finally arrived late afternoon after an unconducted tour of Tallahassee. Later, we tried to trace our route on a small city map we had acquired, but were still none the wiser, so settled for the fact we had enjoyed a pleasant drive around the city and spotted Kacey's Home Cooking buffet near the motel on our way back. Dinner was sorted.

AMERICANADIAN DIARIES

We hadn't ventured on a long rural walk for several days and were itching to explore more widely, so we set out to the Edward Ball Wakulla Springs State Park, a wildlife sanctuary just a few miles south of Tallahassee. We were pleased to find an excellent visitor centre at the park entrance and spent a happy hour learning about the springs, one of the world's largest and deepest freshwater springs with an average flow of about 400,000 US gallons per minute. The opening of the spring is 180 feet (55 m) down, and its many miles of its underwater tunnels have been explored by cave divers, a fact that confirmed that there must be mad people in Florida. We learnt that Paleo Indians camped at the spring 12,000 years ago, where they hunted mastodons, bison, and other ancient animals. The bottom of the spring bowl is littered with bones of their prey alongside those of giant sloths, giant armadillos, and camels. We were surprised and pleased to learn that there were boat trips on the water, an unexpected bonus that we booked for the afternoon, in the hope of seeing a mastodon or camel. This left us plenty of time for a walk and we set out on the Wakulla Springs Trail, starting on a boardwalk before leading us deep into the forest alongside the dark, mysterious waters of the spring. The trail meandered through thick woodland, densely populated with trees that we could not identify, although our guide map told us that somewhere along the way, amongst others we must have passed baldcypress, pignut hickory, sweetgum and my favourite, loblolly pine. I complained to Sue that we never saw a mastodon or a camel and did not identify a loblolly, a comment that received no more than a look of pity and a shake of her head.

We made it back to the visitor centre in time for a coffee and sandwich before boarding the small boat for a trip around the lake. The skipper gave a first-rate commentary as we glided along and he pointed out anhingas, gallinules, egrets and black vultures perched threateningly in the trees of the surrounding forest. We also passed close to several large alligators resting in the long grass on the shore, unperturbed by our passing as they waited patiently for some unsuspecting turtle or snake to cross its path to provide lunch. As the boat cruised further along the waters, the guide pointed out where the 1954 film *Creature from the Black Lagoon* was filmed and the very tree from where Johnny Weissmuller balanced on a branch and made his famous cry in early Tarzan films. After the fascinating boat outing, we returned to the centre for another coffee and were saddened to see a massive, eleven feet long, 650 pound stuffed alligator displayed amongst the tourist information. The description accompanying the poor animal explained that he was known as Old Joe and was an attraction in the waters of the spring for many years until the day that a ranger found him dead, shot between the eyes. Despite a number of confessions, the murderer was never identified and Old Joe now lies in state with the inscription that reads, *This is Old Joe's first and only cage. He had never harmed man, woman, child or pet.* It was strange that a dead alligator could arouse such moving emotions.

We returned to Kacey's Home Cooking that evening. The restaurant offered an all-you-can-eat buffet which always made us feel somewhat inadequate. We always took a small helping of salad or soup, followed by one meat offering and vegetables, before returning to the buffet to try another small sample or perhaps a sweet, eating small English-style portions. Our American cousins on the other hand tended to pile their plates as high as possible with an assortment of, to us, incompatible food, perhaps chicken and pork chops with fries and spaghetti and cheesecake. The bonus of competing with the American appetite is that Sue and I have no competition at the salad bar. We were pleased that the main course menu changed each day and, as this was Sunday, were expecting roast of some kind. Unfortunately, the idea of Sunday roast does not seem to have crossed the Atlantic but we dined royally on salad followed by meat loaf and mashed potatoes with a selection of vegetables, the repast completed by banana pudding, and all at a reduced seniors' price.

Half an hour's drive south from Tallahassee is the shoreline of the Gulf of Mexico and St. Mark's National Wildlife Refuge, established as a wintering ground for migratory birds in 1931. It consists of different coastal habitats including saltwater marshes, tidal creeks, and river estuaries and an enticing destination for brave explorers. We read that the refuge is home to various mammals including black bear, bobcat and coyotes, in addition to the now customary alligators and snakes.

The refuge centre offered an interesting and informative information centre, where we spent half an hour or so scanning the displays and collecting hiking maps before setting out on a walk. As we left the centre, a fluttering in the bushes caught our attention and Sue immediately recognised monarch butterflies: hundreds of them. These beautiful and fragile creatures were on the migration path from northern America and southern Canada to their overwintering sites in central Mexico. This journey of 2000 miles is the longest migration of any insect and many of them regularly stop at sites in Florida their way, using it as a service station to recuperate before its onward journey. It was strange that, of all the wildlife we had encountered on our trip, these small, delicate orange and black butterflies were in some ways the most exciting.

AMERICANADIAN DIARIES

There were several recommended walks and we were undecided which one to follow so set out from the visitor centre to explore the nearest trail to the centre, the Plum Orchard Trail. It started at an observation deck overlooking the small lake and was a short hike through the lush, shaded forest with views across Plum Orchard Pond from another observation deck. We moved on into the forest and passed several alligators, lazily resting and the water's edge and ignoring us trespassing on their home ground. In the trees we heard a short, sharp sound and looked up to see two female grackles (we looked it up later) screeching at us as we passed – a grackle cackle. After the visitor centre visit, the lepidoptery study and the short walk, it was lunchtime and we settled down on a seat overlooking the park for our usual sub meal, discussing what to do next. We decided that we would drive to the coast and just relax there for the afternoon, but we both knew that we would not resist another walk. It was short but fascinating drive through far reaching swampland, passing several ponds before we reached the car park at St. Marks light boat ramp and followed the Lighthouse levee Trail to the shore. As we reached the beach, there were hundreds, perhaps thousands, of small, red fiddler crabs carpeting the grassy sands and, as we carefully moved forward, they scuttled to one side leaving a clear pathway to the ocean, reminding us of the parting of the Red Sea. I, naturally, claimed to be Moses and Sue said that it was quite possible as he was supposed to be 120 years old. I'm not sure that it was a compliment.

As we looked out to sea, we noticed a large black shape moving slowly towards us. It was not clear but we thought that this could only be an American saltwater crocodile, so we quickly skurried away along the beach, safely out of reach of the croc.

AMERICANADIAN DIARIES

We settled on a wooden bench conveniently placed near the lighthouse for some time gazing out to sea and happily were not threatened by more crocs before making our way back.

We returned to Kacey's in the evening for our all-you-can-eat buffet (seniors' price) and began chatting to a couple, Ron and Helen, who were taking a road trip around the south from their home in Arkansas. We chatted for some time about their lives in *The Natural State* and about our lives in Europe. They also insisted on buying a bottle of wine to share and I didn't need too much persuasion to accept the kind invitation. They were very keen to meet again and suggested that we get together the following evening but we had to refuse the offer, explaining that this was our last night in Tallassee before moving on. They seemed genuinely upset, so we ordered another bottle wine which helped us all to overcome the disappointment.

Another day, another town as we were back on the I-10 heading south to Melbourne, Florida. Quite why we chose Melbourne, I do not remember. It is an unremarkable mid-sized town on Florida's east coast, separated from the sea by the wide Indian River. Its only claim as a holiday destination is its proximity to the Kennedy Space Centre on Cape Canaveral but it is also a popular centre for retirees, which is hardly a recommendation for lively vacationers. I guess that we selected it because it was conveniently located for access to Miami Airport and because it has a Super 8 Motel. Despite this unappealing summary, we grew to love the town.

After an incident free drive through Florida and settling in to the Super 8 in the late afternoon, we wandered into the downtown area and came across a prominent sign on a gantry over the street proclaiming *Melbourne Historic District*. After a quick survey of the main street, it was obvious that *Historic* meant the buildings were from the 1950s and 60s. Our brief visit over, we set off to return to the motel, when we spotted a bar called Chumley's on Depot Drive, near the railroad track. We struck lucky as the watering hole was the nearest thing to a proper pub that we had ever found in the USA. It was a long bar with plain but comfortable tables and chairs, the room decorated with old advertisements and memorabilia reminding us of a small English country inn. It even had two dartboards. We looked at the menu and here the similarity ended as the food was all-American fare, mainly hot dogs, sandwiches and burgers, served with curly fries, seasoned fries, cheesy fries, disco fries, depot fries and tater tots. We ordered drinks and a sandwich and spent a happy couple of hours eating and chatting. I think that I may have had a small beer too many as I walked somewhat unsteadily back to the motel.

I tried to convince Sue that my lethargy the next morning was due to tiredness after the long drive from Tallahassee, but she made a point of being extra cheerful and noisy as my punishment for my over-indulgence and then trying to deceive her. She did, however, agree that we should spend a quiet day to recover and we headed off for the coast at Sebastian Inlet State Park a few miles south on the narrow strip of land, an isthmus between Indian River and the Atlantic Ocean. We strolled along the deserted beach looking for shells and sea turtle nests and continuing our new hobby of sitting and staring out to sea. We reached Barrier Island Sanctuary and followed an easy half-mile interpretive nature trail, through the trees away from the beach and, for once, ignoring the visitor centre. We ambled back to beach and discovered a long fishing pier stretching out to sea, with twenty or more fishermen lining the rails. We watched in amazement as almost ever cast from almost every fisherman caught a large fish. I have never fished and never wanted to since spending five hours being sick in a boat on a fishing trip from Littlehampton. I have watched sea fishermen many times in the UK and never seen anything caught except seaweed, but here it seemed impossible not to end up with a large flapping fish on the end of a line. Sue immediately identified the fish as a type of mackerel, her identification verified by a cool black man who sang as he fished, and who said to us, "Just watch this," before dropping his line into the sea and pulling out yet another Atlantic Mackerel a minute later. No wonder he was singing a happy spiritual song. We also saw a few large unidentified fish which our new angling expert said were snook. It was, he explained, more prized than the mackerel because it, "Tastes real good." As we left the pier, we could see several pelicans squabbling on the rocks below and soon the reason for their bickering became clear. Tables and sinks had been installed on the path above the rocks, allowing the fishers' catches to be beheaded, gutted and cleaned, with the scraps thrown to the plump and well-fed birds.

We left the fisherman and pelicans to their fishing and headed towards a small nearby beach for our usual picnic lunch, evading several big, ugly wood storks that stood their ground and glared menacingly at us as we passed, annoyed that we had disturbed their peaceful day out at the seaside. We settled on the lone picnic table on the beach, amongst the strangest birds that we had ever seen. They were tern-like in appearance with a black crown, nape, wings and upper body and the forehead and underparts were white. The strange feature was the long beaks which were orange and black with the lower mandible extending inches longer than the upper beak. They were ungainly as they busied themselves on the sand but once in flights that were very graceful, barely beating their wings as they glided low over the sea and dropped their lower beak into the water as they flew, obviously to collect any unsuspecting creatures near the surface. We later discovered that were black skimmers. Our birding experience was not yet complete as we watched an osprey circling overhead looking for prey before it gave up and moved on. Our wildlife spotting did not stop there. As we made our way back to the car, two gopher tortoises, the size of footballs, plodded across our path, one stopping and stretching its neck to stare at us with what looked like a bemused smile. When I was a child, almost every home owned a tortoise and it had never occurred to me that they could be found wandering around freely in the wild in America.

In the motel reception there was the usual collection of advertising leaflets and guides which I always perused and I collected those of interest to read in the room. As Sue snoozed late in the afternoon, I was scanning the fliers and came across one for the Taste of India restaurant and immediately began to dribble. Having missed out on the Nirvana in New Orleans, I was getting withdrawal symptoms caused by a lack of curry, so left the leaflet on Sue's pillow for when she awoke. This was not a very subtle hint, but it worked and that evening was spent dining royally on delicious spicy mixed starters and lamb rogan gosh with basmati rice and onion bhajis. I even broke my golden drink and drive rule and indulged in Taj Mahal premium lager. A storm had broken as I drove home fully satiated and perhaps a little jolly, getting soaked as we crossed the car park to our motel room. We sat and watched the heavy rains lashing down before retiring for a comatose night's sleep.

The Kennedy Space Center on Cape Canaveral is just thirty-five miles north of Melbourne and we discussed whether a visit was worthwhile. We agreed that perhaps it was a unique opportunity that we should not miss, so drove north on the I-1 to visit the iconic space station, the base for the most famous of all space exploration launches. From here, the Apollo, Skylab and Space Shuttle programs were conducted, including the first manned lunar landing, although we admitted that this meant little to us. After an easy and pleasant drive, we parked, paid and entered the huge complex having our photographs taken next to the famous NASA globe, wondering just how many thousands of similar snapshots had been taken over the years. We took the obligatory guided coach tour of the vast site, stopping at the vehicle assembly building, the launch complex, and other nondescript buildings. With the exception of a close-up look at the launch site, it was a pretty dull tour although the guide tried his best to make looking at an office block or factory interesting. At the end of the tour, we visited the original control centre where we sat in cinema seats overlooking banks of computer screens above which were three massive screens showing close up films of a rocket taking off, while an over-dramatic voiceover explained that it was a rocket taking off. We moved on to the rocket garden an exhibition of giant rockets to be used on flights but, although authentic, these rockets had never been anywhere. We moved on to an exhibition of other pieces of equipment including moon modules and lots of metal things that had something to do with space travel, but looked as if someone had made them from giant baked bean tins in their sheds. We saw another film of a moon landing with even more dramatic commentary saying it was a moon landing. I was bored, but Sue seemed to be enjoying it, so I feigned interest. We moved on to look at more metal things and see more dramatic films, but by then I had switched off completely, while trying to maintain an enthusiastic air. After a long and tiring day, it was time to leave.

On the way home, we talked about the visit and Sue admitted that she had been quite bored at times, but carried on as I had been enthusiastic. We agreed that we were glad we went but it was more akin to a Disney theme park than a discovery visit and we would have been far happier wandering along a beach or getting lost in a mangrove forest.

We went out that night and found Shells Sea Food restaurant, a splendid diner specialising in *Today's Catch* which included fish we had never tasted, like grouper, monkfish and mahi mahi. We found a quiet booth and, confused by the offerings, had a plate of mixed fish and had no idea what we were eating except that it was all delicious. Although full of the sea food delights, we returned to Chumleys for a nightcap of several beers which washed away the disappointing day. I felt really well, although Sue insists that I had adopted a strange gait on the stroll back to the motel and almost fell over several times. She did not laugh when I said that it was the fish that had made me flounder.

It was our last day of the holiday, so I stayed in bed later than usual which was nothing to do with the previous night's over indulgence in the bar. At least that's what I told Sue as my head pounded and my tongue felt like a well-used doormat. When I finally felt able, we wandered downtown and spent some time browsing along the historic centre. We looked in antique shops, art shops and junk shops. We perused shops selling jewellery and strange scented objects. We inspected shops selling clothes, Cuban cigars, gourmet food and wine and useless gifts. Whilst Sue was happy as she dragged me from store to store, I tried to maintain a positive attitude but, deep down, I knew that this was my penance for over-supporting the country's beer industry on the previous evening. I insisted that a late hair of the dog was the cure for my illness, so we returned to Chumley's in the evening for more beer and our last evening meal. We chose the most American meal we could, two quarter pound hot dogs and depot fries with nothing green. As we chatted to the barmaid and two young lady customers, we mentioned that we were walking back to the Super 8. They looked aghast and said that we should never walk in this area at night as it was too dangerous and we could be robbed, assaulted, mugged, raped, murdered or worse. Our walk to the motel back was much brisker than usual.

We were ready to leave in the morning and had noticed an appealing restaurant on our previous wanderings, so stopped at the Apollo Diner before leaving Melbourne. The diner was full of elderly patrons, relaxing in pairs or foursomes over a leisurely meal or simply a morning coffee. We guessed that many of our fellow customers were snowbirds, who had migrated south from other parts of the country for winter. We were in a veritable snowbird roost. We went full hog and ordered the Country Skillet breakfast, eggs, onions, sausage, home fries and sausage gravy. With coffee, it was the perfect way to end our visit before we returned to Miami airport and the flight back to Lisbon.

Throughout the meal, the drive, the wait at the airport and the flight home, neither Sue nor I mentioned where we would like to go for our next trip to the USA. We telepathically understood that this was the last time we would travel across the pond, happy that we had done and seen everything we had dreamed of sixteen years before.

AMERICANADIAN DIARIES

BRIEF EPILOGUE

We never returned to the Americas after the visit to the Deep South. There was much that we would like to have seen and places we would like to have visited, but ageing limbs, joints and brains can no longer stand the long flights and drives. I shall never see the Grand Ol' Opry, visit Elvis Presley's Gracelands or John Steinbeck's Salinas in California. I will never visit Truemanville, Nova Scotia, but Sue and I have great memories of our time in America and Canada that will last forever.

My final and everlasting view of the Americas is this. They are young countries, the children of European nations, procreated by brave explorers and settlers, but yet to fully mature. Whilst European countries have developed for two thousand years and more, our stateside offspring are just a few hundred years old. The young countries have passed the questioning and obstinate childhood days and are just over the rebellious teenage years. They have now matured and are successfully making their own way in the world, whilst keeping a close and respectful relationship with their old countries. Let us hope that the love and respect between us continues. With the current state of the world, we sure need their support.

Printed in Dunstable, United Kingdom